James Inglis

Sport and Work on the Nepaul Frontier

Or, Twelve Years sporting Reminiscences of an Indigo Planter

James Inglis

Sport and Work on the Nepaul Frontier
Or, Twelve Years sporting Reminiscences of an Indigo Planter

ISBN/EAN: 9783337148942

Printed in Europe, USA, Canada, Australia, Japan

Cover: Foto ©ninafisch / pixelio.de

More available books at **www.hansebooks.com**

SPORT AND WORK

ON THE

NEPAUL FRONTIER

OR

TWELVE YEARS SPORTING REMINISCENCES

OF AN INDIGO PLANTER

BY

"MAORI"

London

MACMILLAN AND CO.

1878

[The Right of Translation is reserved]

PREFACE.

I WENT home in 1875 for a few months, after some twelve years' residence in India. What first suggested the writing of such a book as this, was the amazing ignorance of ordinary Indian life betrayed by people at home. The questions asked me about India, and our daily life there, showed in many cases such an utter want of knowledge, that I thought, surely there is room here for a chatty, familiar, unpretentious book for friends at home, giving an account of our every-day life in India, our labours and amusements, our toils and relaxations, and a few pictures of our ordinary daily surroundings in the far, far East.

Such then is the design of my book. I want to picture to my readers Planter Life in the Mofussil, or country districts of India; to tell them of our hunting, shooting, fishing, and other amusements; to describe our work, our play, and matter-of-fact incidents in our daily life; to describe the natives as they appear to us in our intimate every-day dealings with them; to illustrate their manners, customs, dispositions, observances and sayings, so far as these bear on our own social life.

I am no politician, no learned ethnologist, no sage theorist. I simply try to describe what I have seen, and hope to enlist the attention and interest of my readers, in my reminiscences of sport and labour, in the villages and jungles on the far off frontier of Nepaul.

I have tried to express my meaning as far as possible without Anglo-Indian and Hindustani words; where these have been used, as at times they could not but be, I have given a synonymous word or phrase in English, so that all my friends at home may know my meaning.

I know that my friends will be lenient to my faults, and even the sternest critic, if he look for it, may find some pleasure and profit in my pages.

JAS. INGLIS.

CONTENTS.

CHAPTER I.

Province of Behar.—Boundaries.—General description.—District of Chumparun.—Mooteeharree.—The town and lake.—Native houses. The Planters' Club.—Legoulie 1

CHAPTER II.

My first charge.—How we get our lands.—Our home farm.—System of farming.—Collection of rents.—The planter's duties . . 7

CHAPTER III.

How to get our crop.—The 'Dangurs.'—Farm servants and their duties.—Kassee Rai.—Hoeing.—Ploughing.—'Oustennie.'—Coolies at work.—Sowing.—Difficulties the plant has to contend with. —Weeding 14

CHAPTER IV.

Manufacture of Indigo.—Loading the vats.—Beating.—Boiling, straining, and pressing.—Scene in the Factory.—Fluctuation of produce.—Chemistry of Indigo 27

CHAPTER V.

Parewah factory.—A 'Bobbery Pack.'—Hunt through a village after a cat.—The pariah dog of India.—Fate of 'Pincher.'—Rampore hound.—Persian greyhound.—Caboolee dogs.—A jackal hunt.— Incidents of the chase 39

CHAPTER VI.

Fishing in India.—Hereditary trades.—The boatmen and fishermen of India.—Their villages.—Nets.—Modes of fishing.—Curiosities relating thereto.—Catching an alligator with a hook.—Exciting capture.—Crocodiles.—Shooting an alligator.—Death of the man-eater 48

CHAPTER VII.

Native superstitions.—Charming a bewitched woman.—Exorcising ghosts from a field.—Witchcraft.—The witchfinder or 'Ojah.'—Influence of fear.—Snake bites.—How to cure them.—How to discover a thief.—Ghosts and their habits.—The 'Haddick' or native bone-setter.—Cruelty to animals by natives 63

CHAPTER VIII.

Our annual race meet.—The arrivals.—The camps.—The 'ordinary.'—The course.—'They're off.'—The race.—The steeple-chase.—Incidents of the meet.—The ball 75

CHAPTER IX.

Pig-sticking in India.—Varieties of boar.—Their size and height.—Ingenious mode of capture by the natives.—The 'Batan' or buffalo herd.—Pigs charging.—Their courage and ferocity.—Destruction of game.—A close season for game 84

CHAPTER X.

Kuderent jungle.—Charged by a pig.—The biter bit.—'Mac' after the big boar.—The horse for pig-sticking.—The line of beaters.—The boar breaks.—'Away! Away!'—First spear.—Pig-sticking at Peeprah.—The old 'lungra' or cripple.—A boar at bay.—Hurrah for pig-sticking! 93

CHAPTER XI.

The sal forests.—The jungle goddess.—The trees in the jungle.—Appearance of the forests.—Birds.—Varieties of parrots.—A 'beat' in the forest.—The 'shekarry.'—Mehrman Singh and his gun.—The Banturs, a jungle tribe of wood-cutters.—Their habits.—A village feast.—We beat for deer.—Habits of the spotted deer.—Waiting for the game.—Mehrman Singh gets drunk.—Our bag.—Pea-fowl and their habits.—How to shoot them.—Curious custom of the Nepaulese.—How Juggroo was tricked, and his revenge . . 104

CHAPTER XII.

The leopard.—How to shoot him.—Gallant encounter with a wounded one.—Encounter with a leopard in a Dak bungalow.—Pat shoots two leopards.—Effects of the Express bullet.—The 'Sirwah Purrul,' or annual festival of huntsmen.—The Hindoo ryot.—Rice-planting and harvest.—Poverty of the ryot.—His apathy.—Village fires.—Want of sanitation 125

CHAPTER XIII.

Description of a native village.—Village functionaries.—The barber.—Bathing habits.—The village well.—The school.—The children.—The village bazaar. — The landowner and his dwelling. — The 'Putwarrie' or village accountant.—The blacksmith.—The 'Punchayiet' or village jury system.—Our legal system in India.—Remarks on the administration of justice 139

CHAPTER XIV.

A native village continued.—The watchman or 'chowkeydar.'—The temple.—Brahmins.—Idols.—Religion.—Humility of the poorer classes.—Their low condition.—Their apathy.—The police.—Their extortions and knavery.—An instance of police rascality.—Corruption of native officials.—The Hindoo unfit for self-government 156

CHAPTER XV.

Jungle wild fruits.—Curious method of catching quail.—Quail nets.—Quail caught in a blacksmith's shop.—Native wrestling.—The trainer.—How they train for a match.—Rules of wrestling.—Grips.

—A wrestling match.—Incidents of the struggle.—Description of a match between a Brahmin and a blacksmith.—Sparring for the grip.—The blacksmith has it.—The struggle.—The Brahmin getting the worst of it.—Two to one on the little 'un !—The Brahmin plays the waiting game, turns the tables *and* the blacksmith.—Remarks on wrestling 171

CHAPTER XVI.

Indigo seed growing.—Seed buying and buyers.—Tricks of sellers.—Tests for good seed.—The threshing-floor.—Seed cleaning and packing.—Staff of servants.—Despatching the bags by boat.—The 'Pooneah' or rent day.—Purneah planters—their hospitality.—The rent day a great festival.—Preparation.—Collection of rents.—Feast to retainers.—The reception in the evening.—Tribute.—Old customs.—Improvisatores and bards.—Nautches.—Dancing and music.—The dance of the Dangurs.—Jugglers and itinerary showmen.—'Bara Roopes,' or actors and mimics.—Their different styles of acting 187

CHAPTER XVII.

The Koosee jungles.—Ferries.—Jungle roads.—The rhinoceros.—We go to visit a neighbour.—We lose our way and get belated.—We fall into a quicksand.—No ferry boat.—Camping out on the sand.—Two tigers close by.—We light a fire.—The boat at last arrives.—Crossing the stream.—Set fire to the boatman's hut.—Swim the horses.—They are nearly drowned.—We again lose our way in the jungle.—The towing path, and how boats are towed up the river.—We at last reach the factory.—News of rhinoceros in the morning.—Off we start, but arrive too late.—Death of the rhinoceros.—His dimensions.—Description.—Habits.—Rhinoceros in Nepaul.—The old 'Major Captān.'—Description of Nepaulese scenery.—Immigration of Nepaulese.—Their fondness for fish.—They eat it putrid.—Exclusion of Europeans from Nepaul.—Resources of the country.—Must sooner or later be opened up.—Influences at work to elevate the people.—Planters and factories chief of these.—Character of the planter.—His claims to consideration from government 203

CHAPTER XVIII.

The tiger.—His habitat.—Shooting on foot.—Modes of shooting.—A tiger hunt on foot.—The scene of the hunt.—The beat.—Incidents of the hunt.—Fireworks.—The tiger charges.—The elephant bolts.—The tigress will not break.—We kill a half-grown cub.—Try again for the tigress.—Unsuccessful.—Exaggerations in tiger stories.—My authorities.—The brothers S.—Ferocity and structure of the tiger.—His devastations.—His frame-work, teeth, &c.—A tiger at bay.—His unsociable habits.—Fight between tiger and tigress.—Young tigers.—Power and strength of the tiger.—Examples.—His cowardice.—Charge of a wounded tiger.—Incidents connected with wounded tigers.—A spined tiger.—Boldness of young tigers.—Cruelty.—Cunning.—Night scenes in the jungle.—Tiger killed by a wild boar.—His cautious habits.—General remarks . 227

CHAPTER XIX.

The tiger's mode of attack.—The food he prefers.—Varieties of prey.—Examples.—What he eats first.—How to tell the kill of a tiger.—Appetite fierce.—Tiger choked by a bone.—Two varieties of tiger.—The royal Bengal.—Description.—The hill tiger.—His description.—The two compared.—Length of the tiger.—How to measure tigers.—Measurements.—Comparison between male and female.—Number of young at a birth.—The young cubs.—Mother teaching cubs to kill.—Education and progress of the young tiger.—Wariness and cunning of the tiger.—Hunting incidents shewing their powers of concealment.—Tigers taking to water.—Examples.—Swimming powers.—Caught by floods.—Story of the Soonderbund tigers 247

CHAPTER XX.

No regular breeding season.—Beliefs and prejudices of the natives about tigers.—Bravery of the 'gwalla,' or cowherd caste.—Claw-marks on trees.—Fondness for particular localities.—Tiger in Mr. F.'s howdah.—Springing powers of tigers.—Lying close in cover.—Incident.—Tiger shot with No. 4 shot.—Man clawed by a tiger.—Knocked its eye out with a sickle.—Same tiger subsequently shot in same place.—Tigers easily killed.—Instances.—Effect of shells on tiger and buffalo.—Best weapon and bullets for tiger.—Poisoning tigers denounced.—Natives prone to exaggerate in giving news of tiger.—Anecdote.—Beating for tiger.—Line of elephants.—Padding dead game.—Line of seventy-six elephants.—Captain of the hunt.—Flags for signals in the line.—'Naka,' or scout ahead.—Usual time for tiger shooting on the Koosee.—Firing the jungle.—The line of fire at night.—Foolish to shoot at moving jungle.—Never shoot down the line.—Motions of different animals in the grass . . 266

CHAPTER XXI.

Howdahs and howdah-ropes.—Mussulman custom.—Killing animals for food.—Mysterious appearance of natives when an animal is killed.—Fastening dead tigers to the pad.—Present mode wants improving.—Incident illustrative of this.—Dangerous to go close to wounded tigers.—Examples.—Footprints of tigers.—Call of the tiger.—Natives and their powers of description.—How to beat successfully for tiger.—Description of a beat.—Disputes among the shooters.—Awarding tigers.—Cutting open the tiger.—Native idea about the liver of the tiger.—Signs of a tiger's presence in the jungle.—Vultures.—Do they scent their quarry or view it?—A vulture carrion feast 282

CHAPTER XXII.

We start for a tiger hunt on the Nepaul frontier.—Indian scenery near the border.—Lose our way.—Cold night.—The river by night.—Our boat and boatmen.—Tigers calling on the bank.—An anxious moment.—Fire at and wound the tigress.—Reach camp.—The Nepaulee's adventure with a tiger.—The old Major.—His appearance and manners.—The pompous Jemadar.—Nepaulese proverb.—Firing the jungle.—Start a tiger and shoot him.—Another in front.—Appearance of the fires by night.—The tiger escapes.—Too dark to follow up.—Coolie shot by mistake during a former hunt 295

CHAPTER XXIII.

We resume the beat.—The hog-deer.—Nepaulese villages.—Village granaries.—Tiger in front.—A hit! a hit!—Following up the wounded tiger.—Find him dead.—Tiffin in the village.—The

Patair jungle. — Search for tiger. — Gone away! — An elephant steeplechase in pursuit.—Exciting chase.—The Morung jungle.—Magnificent scenery. — Skinning the tiger. — Incidents of tiger hunting 312

CHAPTER XXIV.

Camp of the Nepaulee chief.—Quicksands.—Elephants crossing rivers.—Tiffin at the Nepaulee camp.—We beat the forest for tiger.—Shoot a young tiger.—Red ants in the forest.—Bhowras or ground bees.—The *ursus labialis* or long-lipped bear.—Recross the stream.—Florican.—Stag running the gauntlet of flame.—Our bag.—Start for factory.—Remarks on elephants.—Precautions useful for protection from the sun in tiger shooting.—The *puggree*.—Cattle breeding in India, and wholesale deaths of cattle from disease.—Nathpore.—Ravages of the river.—Mrs. Gray, an old resident in the jungles.—Description of her surroundings 325

CHAPTER XXV.

Exciting jungle scene.—The camp.—All quiet.—Advent of the cowherds.—A tiger close by.—Proceed to the spot.—Encounter between tigress and buffaloes.—Strange behaviour of the elephant.—Discovery and capture of four cubs.—Joyful return to camp.—Death of the tigress.—Night encounter with a leopard.—The haunts of the tiger and our shooting grounds 344

CHAPTER XXVI.

Remarks on guns.—How to cure skins.—Different Recipes.—Conclusion 357

LIST OF ILLUSTRATIONS.

Tiger Hunting—Return to the Camp	*Frontispiece*
Coolie's Hut . .	*Page* 22
Indigo Beating Vats .	27
Indigo Beaters at work in the Vat .	30
Indian Factory Peon .	38
Indigo Planter's House	39
Pig Stickers	103
Carpenters and Blacksmiths at work	150
Hindoo Village Temples . .	157

SPORT AND WORK

ON

THE NEPAUL FRONTIER.

CHAPTER I.

Province of Behar.—Boundaries.—General description.—District of Chumparun.—Mooteeharree.—The town and lake.—Native houses. The Planters' Club.—Legoulie.

AMONG the many beautiful and fertile provinces of India, none can, I think, much excel that of Behar for richness of soil, diversity of race, beauty of scenery, and the energy and intelligence of its inhabitants. Stretching from the Nepaul hills to the far distant plains of Gya, with the Gunduch, Bogmuttee and other noble streams watering its rich bosom, and swelling with their tribute the stately Ganges, it includes every variety of soil and climate; and its various races, with their strange costumes, creeds, and customs, might afford material to fill volumes.

The northern part of this splendid province follows the Nepaulese boundary from the district of Goruchpore on the north, to that of Purneah on the south. In the forests and jungles along this boundary line live many strange tribes, whose customs, and even their names and language, are all but unknown to the English public. Strange wild animals dispute with these aborigines the possession of the gloomy jungle solitudes. Great trees of wondrous dimensions and strange foliage rear their stately heads to heaven, and are matted and entwined together by creepers of huge size and tenacious hold.

To the south and east vast billows of golden grain roll in successive undulations to the mighty Ganges, the sacred stream of the Hindoos. Innumerable villages, nestling amid groves of plantains and feathery rustling bamboos, send up their wreaths of pale grey smoke into the still warm air. At frequent intervals the steely blue of some lovely lake, where thousands of water-fowl disport themselves, reflects from its polished surface the sheen of the noonday sun. Great masses of mango wood shew a sombre outline at intervals, and here and there the towering chimney of an indigo factory pierces the sky. Government roads and embankments intersect the face of the country in all directions, and vast sheets of the indigo plant refresh the eye with their plains of living green, forming a grateful contrast to the hard, dried, sun-baked surface of the stubble fields, where the rice crop has rustled in the breezes of the past season. In one of the loveliest and most fertile districts of this vast province, namely, Chumparun, I began my experiences as an indigo planter.

Chumparun with its subdistrict of Bettiah, lies to the north of Tirhoot, and is bounded all along its northern extent by the Nepaul hills and forests. When I joined my appointment as assistant on one of the large indigo concerns there, there were not more than about thirty European residents altogether in the district. The chief town, Mooteeharree, consisted of a long *bazaar*, or market street, beautifully situated on the bank of a lovely lake, some two miles in length. From the main street, with its quaint little shops sheltered from the sun by makeshift verandahs of tattered sacking, weather-stained shingles, or rotting bamboo mats, various little lanes and alleys diverged, leading one into a collection of tumble-down and ruinous huts, set up apparently by chance, and presenting the most incongruous appearance that could possibly be conceived. One or two *pucca* houses, that is, houses of brick and masonry, shewed where some wealthy Bunneah (trader) or usurious banker lived, but the majority of the houses were of the usual mud and bamboo order. There is a small thatched hut where the meals were cooked, and where the owner and his family could sleep during the rains. Another smaller hut at right angles to this, gives shelter to the family goat, or, if they are rich enough to keep one, the cow. All round the villages in India there are generally large patches of common, where the village cows have free rights of pasture; and all who can, keep either a cow or a couple of goats, the milk from which forms a welcome addition to their usual scanty fare. In this second hut also is stored as much fuel, consisting of dried cow-dung, straw, maize-stalks, leaves, etc., as can be collected; and a ragged fence of bamboo or *rahur*[1] stalks encloses the two unprotected sides, thus forming inside a small court, quadrangle, or square. This court is the native's *sanctum sanctorum*. It is kept scrupulously clean, being swept and garnished religiously every day. In this the women prepare the rice for the day's consumption; here they cut up and clean

[1] The *rahur* is a kind of pea, growing not unlike our English broom in appearance; it is sown with the maize crop during the rains, and garnered in the cold weather. It produces a small pea, which is largely used by the natives, and forms the nutritive article of diet known as *dhall*.

their vegetables, or their fish, when the adjacent lake has been dragged by the village fishermen. Here the produce of their little garden, capsicums, Indian corn, onions or potatoes—perchance turmeric, ginger, or other roots or spices—are dried and made ready for storing in the earthen sun-baked repository for the reception of such produce appertaining to each household. Here the children play, and are washed and tended. Here the maiden combs out her long black hair, or decorates her bronzed visage with streaks of red paint down the nose, and a little antimony on the eyelids, or myrtle juice on the finger and toe nails. Here, too, the matron, or the withered old crone of a grandmother, spins her cotton thread; or, in the old scriptural hand-mill, grinds the corn for the family flour and meal; and the father and the young men (when the sun is high and hot in the heavens) take their noonday *siesta*, or, the day's labours over, cower round the smoking dung fire of a cold winter night, and discuss the prices ruling in the bazaar, the rise of rents, or the last village scandal.

In the middle of the town, and surrounded by a spacious fenced-in compound, which sloped gently to the lake, stood the Planters' Club, a large low roofed bungalow, with a roomy wide verandah in front. Here we met, when business or pleasure brought us to 'the Station.' Here were held our annual balls, or an occasional public dinner party. To the north of the Club stood a long range of barrack-looking buildings, which were the opium godowns, where the opium was collected and stored during the season. Facing this again, and at the extremity of the lake, was the district jail, where all the rascals of the surrounding country were confined; its high walls tipped at intervals by a red puggree and flashing bayonet wherever a jail sepoy kept his 'lonely watch.' Near it, sheltered in a grove of shady trees, were the court houses, where the collector and magistrate daily dispensed justice, or where the native *moonsiff* disentangled knotty points of law. Here, too, came the sessions judge once a month or so, to try criminal cases and mete out justice to the law-breakers.

We had thus a small European element in our 'Station,' consisting of our magistrate and collector, whose large and handsome house was built on the banks of another and yet lovelier lake, which joined the town lake by a narrow stream or strait at its southern end, an opium agent, a district superintendent of police, and last but not least, a doctor. These formed the official population of our little 'Station.' There was also a nice little church, but no resident pastor, and behind the town lay a quiet churchyard, rich in the dust of many a pioneer, who, far from home and friends, had here been gathered to his silent rest.

About twelve miles to the north, and near the Nepaul boundary, was the small military station of Legoulie. Here there was always a native cavalry regiment, the officers of which were frequent and welcome guests at the factories in the district, and were always glad to see their indigo friends at their mess in cantonments. At Rettiah, still further to the north, was a rich rajah's palace, where a resident European manager dwelt, and had for his sole society an assistant magistrate who transacted the executive and judicial work of the subdistrict. These, with some twenty-five or thirty indigo managers and assistants, composed the whole European population of Chumparun.

Never was there a more united community. We were all like brothers. Each knew all the rest. The assistants frequently visited each other, and the managers were kind and considerate to their subordinates. Hunting parties were common, cricket and hockey matches were frequent, and in the cold weather, which is our slackest season, fun, frolic, and sport was the order of the day. We had an annual race meet, when all the crack horses of the district met in keen rivalry to test their pace and endurance. During this high carnival, we lived for the most part under canvass, and had friends from far and near to share our hospitality. In a future chapter I must describe our racing meet.

CHAPTER II.

My first charge.—How we get our lands.—Our home farm.—System of farming.—Collection of rents.—The planter's duties.

My first charge was a small outwork of the large factory Seeraha. It was called Puttihee. There was no bungalow; that is, there was no regular house for the assistant, but a little one-roomed hut, built on the top of the indigo vats, served me for a residence. It had neither doors nor windows, and the rain used to beat through the room, while the eaves were inhabited by countless swarms of bats, who, in the evening flashed backwards and forwards in ghostly rapid flight, and were a most intolerable nuisance. To give some idea of the duties of an indigo assistant, I must explain the system on which we get our lands, and how we grow our crop.

Water of course being a *sine qua non*, the first object in selecting a site for a factory is, to have water in plenty contiguous to the proposed buildings. Consequently Puttihee was built on the banks of a very pretty lake, shaped like a horseshoe, and covered with water lilies and broad-leaved green aquatic plants. The lake was kept by the native proprietor as a fish preserve, and literally teemed with fish of all sorts, shapes, and sizes. I had not been long at Puttihee before I had erected a staging, leading out into deep water, and many a happy hour I have spent there with my three or four rods out, pulling in the finny inhabitants.

Having got water and a site, the next thing is to get land on which to grow your crop. By purchase, by getting a long lease, or otherwise, you become possessed of several hundred acres of the land immediately surrounding the factory. Of course some factories will have more and some less as circumstances happen. This land, however, is peculiarly factory property. It is in fact a sort of home farm, and goes by the name of *Zeraat*. It is ploughed by factory bullocks, worked by factory coolies, and is altogether apart and separate from the ordinary lands held by the ryots and worked by them. (A ryot means a cultivator.) In most factories the Zeraats are farmed in the most thorough manner. Many now use the light Howard's plough, and apply quantities of manure.

The fields extend in vast unbroken plains all round the factory. The land is worked and pulverised, and reploughed, and harrowed, and cleaned, till not a lump the size of a pigeon's egg is to be seen. If necessary, it is carefully weeded several times before the crop is sown, and in fact, a fine clean stretch of Zeraat in Tirhoot or Chumparun, will compare most favourably with any field in the highest farming districts of England or Scotland. The ploughing and other farm labour is done by bullocks. A staff of these, varying of course with the amount of land under cultivation, is kept at each factory. For their support a certain amount of sugar-cane is planted, and in the cold weather carrots are sown, and *gennara*, a kind of millet, and maize.

Both maize and gennara have broad green leaves, and long juicy succulent stalks. They grow to a good height, and when cut up and mixed with chopped straw and carrots, form a most excellent feed for cattle. Besides the bullocks, each factory keeps up a staff of generally excellent horses, for the use of the assistant or manager, on which he rides over his cultivation, and looks generally after the farm. Some of the native subordinates also have ponies, or Cabool horses, or country-breds; and for the feed of these animals some few acres of oats are sown every cold season. In most factories too, when any particular bit of the Zeraats gets exhausted by the constant repetition of indigo cropping, a rest is given it, by taking a crop of oil seeds or oats off the land. The oil seeds usually sown are mustard or rape. The oil is useful in the factory for oiling the screws or the machinery, and for other purposes.

The factory roads through the Zeraats are kept in most perfect order; many of them are metalled. The ditches are cleaned once a year. All thistles and weeds by the sides of the roads and ditches, are ruthlessly cut down. The edges of all the fields are neatly trimmed and cut. Useless trees and clumps of jungle are cut down; and in fact the Zeraats round a factory shew a perfect picture of orderly thrift, careful management, and neat, scientific, and elaborate farming.

Having got the Zeraats, the next thing is to extend the cultivation outside.

The land in India is not, as with us at home, parcelled out into large farms. There are wealthy proprietors, rajahs, baboos, and so on, who hold vast tracts of land, either by grant, or purchase, or hereditary succession; but the tenants are literally the children of the soil. Wherever a village nestles among its plantain or mango groves, the land is parcelled out among the villagers. A large proprietor does not reckon up his farms as a landlord at home would do, but he counts his villages. In a village with a thousand acres belonging to it, there might be 100 or even 200 tenants farming the land. Each petty villager would have his acre or half acre, or four, or five, or ten, or twenty acres, as the case might be. He holds this by a 'tenant right,' and cannot be dispossessed as long as he pays his rent regularly. He can sell his tenant right, and the purchaser on paying the rent, becomes the *bona fide* possessor of the land to all intents and purposes.

If the average rent of the village lands was, let me say, one rupee eight annas an acre, the rent roll of the 1000 acres would be 1500 rupees. Out of this the government land revenue comes. Certain deductions have to be made—some ryots may be defaulters. The village temple, or the village Brahmin, may have to get something, the road-cess has to be paid, and so on. Taking everything into account, you arrive at a pretty fair view of what the rental is. If the proprietor of the village wants a loan of money, or if you offer to pay him the rent by half-yearly or quarterly instalments, you taking all the risk of collecting in turn from each ryot individually, he is often only too glad to accept your offer, and giving you a lease of the village for whatever term may be agreed on, you step in as virtually the landlord, and the ryots have to pay their rents to you.

In many cases by careful management, by remeasuring lands, settling doubtful boundaries, and generally working up the estate, you can much increase the rental, and actually make a profit on your bargain with the landlord. This department of indigo work is called Zemindaree. Having, then, got the village in lease, you summon in all your tenants; shew them their rent accounts, arrange with them for the punctual payment of them, and get them to agree to cultivate a certain percentage of their land in indigo for you.

This percentage varies very considerably. In some places it is one acre in five, in some one in twenty. It all depends on local circumstances. You select the land, you give the seed, but the ryot has to prepare the field for sowing, he has to plough, weed, and reap the crop, and deliver it at the factory. For the indigo he gets so much per acre, the price being as near as possible the average price of an acre of ordinary produce : taking the average out-turn and prices of, say, ten years. It used formerly to be much less, but the ryot nowadays gets nearly double for his indigo what he got some ten or fifteen years ago, and this, although prices have not risen for the manufactured article, and the prices of labour, stores, machinery, live stock, etc., have more than doubled. In some parts the ryot gets paid so much per bundle of plants delivered at the vats, but generally in Behar, at least in north Behar, he is paid so much per acre or *Beegah*. I use the word acre as being more easily understood by people at home than Beegah. The Beegah varies in different districts, but is generally about two-thirds of an acre.

When his rent account, then, comes to be made out, the ryot gets credit for the price of his indigo grown and delivered; and this very often suffices, not only to clear his entire rent, but to leave a margin in hard cash for him to take home. Before the beginning of the indigo season, however, he comes into the factory and takes a cash advance on account of the indigo to be grown. This is often a great help to him, enabling him to get his seeds for his other lands, perhaps ploughs, or to buy a cart, or clothes for the family, or to replace a bullock that may have died; or to help to give a marriage portion to a son or daughter that he wants to get married.

You will thus see that we have cultivation to look after in all the villages round about the factory which we can get in lease. The ryot, in return for his cash advance, agrees to cultivate so much indigo at a certain price, for which he gets credit in his rent. Such, shortly, is our indigo system. In some villages the ryot will estimate for us without our having the lease at all, and without taking advances. He grows the indigo as he would grow any other crop, as a pure speculation. If he has a good crop, he can get the price in hard cash from the factory, and a great deal is grown in this way in both Purneah and Bhaugulpore. This is called *Kooskee*, as against the system of advances, which is called *Tuccaree*.

The planter, then, has to be constantly over his villages, looking out for good lands, giving up bad fields, and taking in new ones. He must watch what crops grow best in certain places. He must see that he does not take lands where water may lodge, and, on the other hand, avoid those that do not retain their moisture. He must attend also to the state of the other crops generally all over his cultivation, as the punctual payment of rents depends largely on the state of the crops. He must have his eyes open to everything going on, be able to tell the probable rent-roll of every village for miles around, know whether the ryots are lazy and discontented, or are industrious and hard-working. Up in the early morning, before the hot blazing sun has climbed on high, he is off on his trusty nag, through his Zeraats, with his greyhounds and terriers panting behind him. As he nears a village, the farm-servant in charge of that particular bit of cultivation, comes out with a low salaam, to report progress, or complain that so-and-so is not working up his field as he ought to do.

Over all the lands he goes, seeing where re-ploughing is necessary, ordering harrowing here, weeding there, or rolling somewhere else. He sees where the ditches need deepening, where the roads want levelling or widening, where a new bridge will be necessary, where lands must be thrown up and new ones taken in. He knows nearly all his ryots, and has a kind word for every one he passes; asks after their crops, their bullocks, or their land; rouses up the indolent; gives a cheerful nod to the industrious; orders this one to be brought in to settle his account, or that one to make greater haste with the preparation of his land, that he may not lose his moisture. In fact, he has his hands full till the mounting sun warns him to go back to breakfast. And so, with a rattling burst after a jackal or fox, he gets back to his bungalow to bathe, dress, and break his fast with fowl cutlets, and curry and rice, washed down with a wholesome tumbler of Bass.

CHAPTER III.

How to get our crop.—The 'Dangurs.'—Farm servants and their duties.—Kassee Rai.—Hoeing.—Ploughing.—'Oustennie.'—Coolies at work.—Sowing.—Difficulties the plant has to contend with.—Weeding.

HAVING now got our land, water, and buildings—which latter I will describe further on—the next thing is to set to work to get our crop. Manufacture being finished, and the crop all cut by the beginning or middle of October, when the annual rains are over, it is of importance to have the lands dug up as early as possible, that the rich moisture, on which the successful cultivation of the crop mainly depends, may be secured before the hot west winds and strong sun of early spring lick it up.

Attached to every factory is a small settlement of labourers, belonging to a tribe of aborigines called *Dangurs*. These originally, I believe, came from Chota Nagpore, which seems to have been their primal home. They are a cheerful industrious race, have a distinct language of their own, and only intermarry with each other. Long ago, when there were no post carriages to the hills, and but few roads, the Dangurs were largely employed as dale runners, or postmen. Some few of them settled with their families on lands near the foot of the hills in Purneah, and gradually others made their way northwards, until now there is scarcely a factory in Behar that has not its Dangur tola, or village.

The men are tractable, merry-hearted, and faithful. The women betray none of the exaggerated modesty which is characteristic of Hindoo women generally. They never turn aside and hide their faces as you pass, but look up to you with a merry smile on their countenances, and exchange greetings with the utmost frankness. In a future chapter I may speak at greater length of the Dangurs; at present it suffices to say, that they form a sort of appanage to the factory, and are in fact treated as part of the permanent staff.

Each Dangur when he marries, gets some grass and bamboos from the factory to build a house, and a small plot of ground to serve as a garden, for which he pays a very small rent, or in many instances nothing at all. In return, he is always on the spot ready for any factory work that may be going on, for which he has his daily wage. Some factories pay by the month, but the general custom is to charge for hoeing by piece-work, and during manufacture, when the work is constant, there is paid a monthly wage.

In the close foggy mornings of October and November, long before the sun is up, the Dangurs are hard at work in the Zeraats, turning up the soil with their *kodalies*, (a kind of cutting hoe,) and you can often hear their merry voices rising through the mist, as they crack jokes with each other to enliven their work, or troll one of their quaint native ditties.

They are presided over by a 'mate,' generally one of the oldest men and first settlers in the village. If he has had a large family, his sons look up to him, and his sons-in-law obey his orders with the utmost fealty. The 'mate' settles all disputes, presents all grievances to the *sahib*, and all orders are given through him.

The indigo stubble which has been left in the ground is perhaps about a foot high, and as they cut it out, their wives and children come to gather up the sticks for fuel, and this of course also helps to clean the land. By eleven o'clock, when the sluggish mist has been dissipated by the rays of the scorching sun, the day's labour is nearly concluded. You will then see the swarthy Dangur, with his favourite child on his shoulder, wending his way back to his hut, followed by his comely wife carrying his hoe, and a tribe of little ones bringing up the rear, each carrying bundles of the indigo stubble which the industrious father has dug up during the early hours of morning.

In the afternoon out comes the *hengha*, which is simply a heavy flat log of wood, with a V shaped cut or groove all along under its flat surface. To each end of the hengha a pair of bullocks are yoked, and two men standing on the log, and holding on by the bullocks' tails, it is slowly dragged over the field wherever the hoeing has been going on. The lumps and clods are caught in the groove on the under surface, and dragged along and broken up and pulverized, and the whole surface of the field thus gets harrowed down, and forms a homogeneous mass of light friable soil, covering the weeds and dirt to let them rot, exposing the least surface for the wind and heat to act on, and thus keeping the moisture in the soil.

Now is a busy time for the planter. Up early in the cold raw fog, he is over his Zeraats long before dawn, and round by his outlying villages to see the ryots at work in their fields. To each eighty or a hundred acres a man is attached called a *Tokedar*. His duty is to rouse out the ryots, see the hoes and ploughs at work, get the weeding done, and be responsible for the state of the cultivation generally. He will probably have two villages under him. If the village with its lands be very extensive, of course there will be a Tokedar for it alone, but frequently a Tokedar may have two or more villages under his charge. In the village, the head man—generally the most influential man in the community—also acts with the Tokedar, helping him to get ploughs, bullocks, and coolies when these are wanted; and under him, the village *chowkeydar*, or watchman, sees that stray cattle do not get into the fields, that the roads, bridges and fences are not damaged, and so on. Over the Tokedars, again, are Zillahdars. A 'zillah' is a small district. There may be eight or ten villages and three or four Tokedars under a Zillahdar. The Zillahdar looks out for good lands to change for bad ones, where this is necessary, and where no objection is made by the farmer; sees that the Tokedars do their work properly; reports rain, blight, locusts, and other visitations that might injure the crop; watches all that goes on in his zillah, and makes his report to the planter whenever anything of importance happens in his particular part of the cultivation. Over all again comes the JEMADAR — the head man over the whole cultivation — the planter's right-hand man.

He is generally an old, experienced, and trusted servant. He knows all the lands for miles round, and the peculiar soils and products of all the villages far and near. He can tell what lands grow the best tobacco, what lands are free from inundation, what free from drought; the temper of the inhabitants of each village, and the history of each farm; where are the best ploughs, the best bullocks, and the best farming; in what villages you get most coolies for weeding;

where you can get the best carts, the best straw, and the best of everything at the most favourable rates. He comes up each night when the day's work is done, and gets his orders for the morrow. You are often glad to take his advice on sowing, reaping, and other operations of the farm. He knows where the plant will ripen earliest, and where the leaf will be thickest, and to him you look for satisfaction if any screw gets loose in the outside farm-work.

He generally accompanies you in your morning ride, shows you your new lands, consults with you about throwing up exhausted fields, and is generally a sort of farm-bailiff or confidential land-steward. Where he is an honest, intelligent, and loyal man, he takes half the care and work off your shoulders. Such men are however rare, and if not very closely looked after, they are apt to abuse their position, and often harass the ryots needlessly, looking more to the feathering of their own nests than the advancement of your interests.

The only Jemadar I felt I could thoroughly trust, was my first one at Parewak, an old Rajpoot, called Kassee Rai. He was a fine, ruddy-faced, white-haired old man, as independent and straightforward an old farmer as you could meet anywhere, and I never had reason to regret taking his advice on any matter. I never found him out in a lie, or in a dishonest or underhand action. Though over seventy years of age he was upright as a dart. He could not keep up with me when we went out riding over the fields, but he would be out the whole day over the lands, and was always the first at his work in the morning and the last to leave off at night. The ryots all loved him, and would do anything for him; and when poor old Kassee died, the third year he had been under me,

I felt as if an old friend had gone. I never spoke an angry word to him, and I never had a fault to find with him.

When the hoeing has been finished in zeraat and zillah, and all the upturned soil battened down by the *hengha*, the next thing is to commence the ploughing. Your ploughmen are mostly low caste men—Doosadhs, Churnars, Moosahurs, Gwallahs, *et hoc genus omne*. The Indian plough, so like a big misshapen wooden pickaxe, has often been described. It however turns up the light soft soil very well considering its pretensions, and those made in the factory workshops are generally heavier and sharper than the ordinary village plough. Our bullocks too, being strong and well fed, the ploughing in the zeraats is generally good.

The ploughing is immediately followed up by the *hengha*, which again triturates and breaks up the clods, rolls the sticks, leaves, and grass roots together, brings the refuse and dirt to the surface, and again levels the soil, and prevents the wind from taking away the moisture. The land now looks fine and fresh and level, but very dirty. A host of coolies are put on the fields with small sticks in their hands. All the Dangur women and children are there, with men, women, and children of all the poorest classes from the villages round, whom the attractions of wages or the exertions of headmen Tokedars and Zillahdars have brought together to earn their daily bread. With the sticks they beat and break up every clod, leaving not one behind the size of a walnut. They collect all the refuse, weeds, and dirt, which are heaped up and burnt on the field, and so they go on till the zeraats look as clean as a nobleman's garden, and you would think that surely this must satisfy the fastidious eye of the planter. But no, our work is not half begun yet.

It is rather a strange sight to see some four or five hundred coolies squatted in a long irregular line, chattering, laughing, shouting, or squabbling. A dense cloud of dust rises over them, and through the dim obscurity one hears the ceaseless sound of the thwack! thwack! as their sticks rattle on the ground. White dust lies thick on each swarthy skin; their faces are like faces in a pantomime. There are the flashing eyes and the grinning rows of white teeth; all else is clouded in thick layers of dust, with black spots and stencillings showing here and there like a picture in sepia and chalk. As they near the end of the field they redouble their thwacking, shuffle along like land-crabs, and while the Mates, Peons, and Tokedars shout at them to encourage them, they raise a roar loud enough to wake the dead. The dust rises in denser clouds, the noise is deafening, a regular mad hurry-scurry, a wild boisterous scramble ensues, and amid much chaffing, noise, and laughter, they scramble off again to begin another length of land; and so the day's work goes on.

The planter has to count his coolies several times a-day, or they would cheat him. Some come in the morning, get counted, and their names put on the roll, and then go off till paytime comes round. Some come for an hour or two, and send a relative in the evening when the pice are being paid out, to get the wage of work they have not done. All are paid in pice—little copper bits of coin, averaging about sixty-four to the rupee. However, you soon come to know the coolies by sight, and after some experience are rarely 'taken in,' but many young beginners get 'done' most thoroughly till they become accustomed to the tricks of the artless and unsophisticated coolie.

The type of feature along a line of coolies is as a rule a very forbidding and degraded one. They are mostly of the very poorest class. Many of them are plainly half silly, or wholly idiotic; not a few are deaf and dumb; others are crippled or deformed, and numbers are leprous and scrofulous. Numbers of them are afflicted in some districts with goitre, caused probably by bad drinking water; all have a pinched, withered, wan look, that tells of hard work and insufficient fare. It is a pleasure to turn to the end of the line, where the Dangur women and boys and girls generally take their place. Here are the loudest laughter, and the sauciest faces. The children are merry, chubby, fat things, with well-distended stomachs and pleasant looks; a merry smile rippling over their broad fat cheeks as they slyly glance up at you. The women—with huge earrings in their ears, and a perfect load of heavy brass rings on their arms—chatter away, make believe to be shy, and show off a thousand coquettish airs. Their very toes are bedizened with brass rings; and long festoons of red, white, and blue beads hang pendent round their necks.

In the evening the line is re-formed before the bungalow. A huge bag of copper coin is produced. The old Lallah, or writer, with spectacles on nose, squats down in the middle of the assembled coolies, and as each name is called, the mates count out the pice, and make it over to the coolie, who forthwith hurries off to get his little purchases made at the village Bunneah's shop; and so, on a poor supper of parched peas, or boiled rice, with no other relish but a pinch of salt, the poor coolie crawls to bed, only to dream of more hard work and scanty fare on the morrow. Poor thing! a village coolie has a hard time of it! During the hot months, if rice be cheap and plentiful, he can jog along pretty comfortably, but when the cold nights come on, and he cowers in his wretched hut, hungry, half naked, cold, and wearied, he is of all objects most

Coolie's Hut.

pitiable. It is, however, a fact little creditable to his more prosperous fellow-countrymen, that he gets better paid for his labour in connection with factory work, than he does in many cases for tasks forced on him by the leading ryots of the village in connection with their own fields.

This first cleaning of the fields—or, as it is called, *Oustennie*—being finished, the lands are all again re-ploughed, re-harrowed, and then once more re-cleaned by the coolies, till not a weed or spot of dirt remains; and till the whole surface is uniformly soft, friable, moist, and clean. We have now some breathing time; and as this is the most enjoyable season of the year, when the days are cool, and roaring wood fires at night remind us of home, we hunt, visit, race, dance, and generally enjoy ourselves. Should heavy rain fall, as it sometimes does about Christmas and early in February, the whole cultivation gets beaten down and caked over. In such a case amusements must for a time be thrown aside, till all the lands have been again re-ploughed. Of course we are never wholly idle. There are always rents to collect, matters to adjust in connexion with our villages and tenantry, law-suits to recover bad debts, to enforce contracts, or protect manorial or other rights,—but generally speaking, when the lands have been prepared, we have a slack season or breathing time for a month or so.

Arrangements having been made for the supply of seed, which generally comes from about the neighbourhood of Cawnpore, as February draws near we make preparations for beginning our sowings. February is the usual month, but it depends on the moisture, and sometimes sowings may go on up till May and June. In Purneah and Bhaugulpore, where the cultivation is much rougher than in Tirhoot, the sowing is done broadcast. And in Bengal the sowing is often done upon the soft mud which is left on the banks of the rivers at the retiring of the annual floods. In Tirhoot, however, where the high farming I have been trying to describe is practised, the sowing is done by means of drills. Drills are got out, overhauled, and put in thorough repair. Bags of seed are sent out to the villages, advances for bullocks are given to the ryots, and on a certain day when all seems favourable—no sign of rain or high winds—the drills are set at work, and day and night the work goes on, till all the cultivation has been sown. As the drills go along, the hengha follows close behind, covering the seed in the furrows; and once again it is put over, till the fields are all level, shining, and clean, waiting for the first appearance of the young soft shoots.

These, after some seven, nine, or perhaps fifteen days, according to the weather, begin to appear in long lines of delicate pale yellowish green. This is a most anxious time. Should rain fall, the whole surface of the earth gets caked and hard, and the delicate plant burns out, or being chafed against the hard surface crust, it withers and dies. If the wind gets into the east, it brings a peculiar blight which settles round the leaf and collar of the stem of the young plant, chokes it, and sweeps off miles and miles of it. If hot west winds blow, the plant gets black, discoloured, burnt up, and dead. A south wind often brings caterpillars—at least this pest often makes its appearance when the wind is southerly; but as often as not caterpillars find their way to the young plant in the most mysterious manner,—no one knowing whence they come. Daily, nay almost hourly, reports come in from all parts of the zillah: now you hear of 'Lahee,' blight on some field; now it is 'Ihirka,' scorching, or 'Pilooa,' caterpillars. In some places the seed may have been bad or covered with too much earth, and the plant comes up straggling and thin. If there is abundant moisture, this must be re-sown. In fact, there is never-ending anxiety and work at this season, but when the plant has got into ten or fifteen leaf, and is an inch or two high, the most critical time is over, and one begins to think about the next operation, namely WEEDING.

The coolies are again in requisition. Each comes armed

with a *coorpee*,—this is a small metal spatula, broad-pointed, with which they dig out the weeds with amazing deftness. Sometimes they may inadvertently take out a single stem of indigo with the weeds: the eye of the mate or Tokedar espies this at once, and the careless coolie is treated to a volley of Hindoo Billingsgate, in which all his relations are abused to the seventh generation. By the time the first weeding is finished, the plant will be over a foot high, and if necessary a second weeding is then given. After the second weeding, and if any rain has fallen in the interim, the plant will be fully two feet high.

It is now a noble-looking expanse of beautiful green waving foliage. As the wind ruffles its myriads of leaves, the sparkle of the sunbeams on the undulating mass produces the most wonderful combinations of light and shade; feathery sprays of a delicate pale green curl gracefully all over the field. It is like an ocean of vegetation, with billows of rich colour chasing each other, and blending in harmonious hues; the whole field looking a perfect oasis of beauty amid the surrounding dull brown tints of the season.

It is now time to give the plant a light touch of the plough. This eases the soil about the roots, lets in air and light, tends to clean the undergrowth of weeds, and gives it a great impetus. The operation is called *Bedaheunee*. By the beginning of June the tiny red flower is peeping from its leafy sheath, the lower leaves are turning yellowish and crisp, and it is almost time to begin the grandest and most important operation of the season, the manufacture of the dye from the plant.

To this you have been looking forward during the cold raw foggy days of November, when the ploughs were hard at work,—during the hot fierce winds of

March, and the still, sultry, breathless early days of June, when the air was so still and oppressive that you could scarcely breathe. These sultry days are the lull before the storm—the pause before the moisture-laden clouds of the monsoon roll over the land 'rugged and brown,' and the wild rattle of thunder and the lurid glare of quivering never-ceasing lightning herald in the annual rains. The manufacture however deserves a chapter to itself.

CHAPTER IV.

Manufacture of Indigo.—Loading the vats.—Beating.—Boiling, straining, and pressing.—Scene in the Factory.—Fluctuation of produce.—Chemistry of Indigo.

INDIGO is manufactured solely from the leaf. When arrangements have been made for cutting and carting the plant from the fields, the vats and machinery are all made ready, and a day is appointed to begin 'Mahye' or manufacture. The apparatus consists of, first, a strong serviceable pump for pumping up water into the vats: this is now mostly done by machinery, but many small factories still use the old Persian wheel, which may be shortly described as simply an endless chain of buckets, working on a revolving wheel or drum. The machine is worked by bullocks, and as the buckets ascend full from the well, they are emptied during their revolution into a small trough at the top, and the water is conveyed into a huge masonry reservoir or tank, situated high up above the vats, which forms a splendid open air bath for the planter when he feels inclined for a swim. Many of these tanks, called *Kajhana*, are capable of containing 40,000 cubic feet of water or more.

Below, and in a line with this reservoir, are the steeping vats, each capable of containing about 2000 cubic feet of water when full. Of course the vats vary in size, but what is called a *pucca* vat is of the above capacity. When the fresh green plant is brought in, the carts with their loads are ranged in line, opposite

these loading vats. The loading coolies, 'Bojhunneas'—
so called from '*Bojh*,' a bundle—jump into the vats, and
receive the plant from the cart-men, stacking it up in
perpendicular layers, till the vat is full: a horizontal
layer is put on top to make the surface look even.
Bamboo battens are then placed over the plant, and
these are pressed down, and held in their place by horizontal beams, working in upright posts. The uprights
have holes at intervals of six inches. An iron pin is
put in one of the holes; a lever is put under this pin,
and the beam pressed down, till the next hole is reached
and a fresh pin inserted, which keeps the beam down in
its place. When sufficient pressure has been applied,
the sluice in the reservoir is opened, and the water runs
by a channel into the vat till it is full. Vat after vat
is thus filled till all are finished, and the plant is allowed
to steep from ten to thirteen or fourteen hours, according to the state of the weather, the temperature of the
water, and other conditions and circumstances which
have all to be carefully noted.

At first a greenish yellow tinge appears in the water,
gradually deepening to an intense blue. As the fermentation goes on, froth forms on the surface of the
vat, the water swells up, bubbles of gas arise to the
surface, and the whole range of vats presents a frothing,
bubbling, sweltering appearance, indicative of the chemical action going on in the interior. If a torch be applied
to the surface of a vat, the accumulated gas ignites with
a loud report, and a blue lambent flame travels with
amazing rapidity over the effervescent liquid. In very
hot weather I have seen the water swell up over the
mid walls of the vats, till the whole range would be
one uniform surface of frothing liquid, and on applying
a light, the report has been as loud as that of a small

cannon, and the flame has leapt from vat to vat like the flitting will-o'-the-wisp on the surface of some miasmatic marsh.

When fermentation has proceeded sufficiently, the temperature of the vat lowers somewhat, and the water, which has been globular and convex on the surface and at the sides, now becomes distinctly convex and recedes a very little. This is a sign that the plant has been steeped long enough, and that it is now time to open the vat. A pin is knocked out from the bottom, and the pent-up liquor rushes out in a golden yellow stream tinted with blue and green into the beating vat, which lies parallel to, but at a lower level than the loading vat.

Of course as the vats are loaded at different hours, and the steeping varies with circumstances, they must be ready to open also at different intervals. There are two men specially engaged to look after the opening. The time of loading each one is carefully noted; the time it will take to steep is guessed at, and an hour for opening written down. When this hour arrives, the *Gunta parree*, or time-keeper, looks at the vat, and if it appears ready he gets the pinmen to knock out the pin and let the steeped liquor run into the beating vat.

Where there are many vats, this goes on all night, and by the morning the beating vats are all full of steeped liquor, and ready to be beaten.

The beating now is mostly done by machinery; but the old style was very different. A gang of coolies (generally Dangurs) were put into the vats, having long sticks with a disc at the end, with which, standing in two rows, they threw up the liquor into the air. The quantity forced up by the one coolie encounters in mid air that sent up by the man standing immediately opposite to him, and the two jets meeting and mixing confusedly together, tumble down in broken frothy masses into the vat. Beginning with a slow steady stroke the coolies gradually increase the pace, shouting out a hoarse wild song at intervals; till, what with the swish and splash of the falling water, the measured beat of the *furrovahs* or beating rods, and the yells and cries with which they excite each other, the noise is almost deafening. The water, which at first is of a yellowish green, is now beginning to assume an intense blue tint; this is the result of the oxygenation going on. As the blue deepens, the exertions of the coolie increase, till with every muscle straining, head thrown back, chest expanded, his long black hair dripping with white foam, and his bronzed naked body glistening with blue liquor, he yells and shouts and twists and contorts his body till he looks like a true 'blue devil.' To see eight or ten vats full of yelling howling blue creatures, the water splashing high in mid air, the foam flecking the walls, and the measured beat of the *furrovahs* rising weird-like into the morning air, is almost enough to shake the nerve of a stranger, but it is music in the planter's ear, and he can scarce refrain from yelling out in sympathy with his coolies, and sharing in their frantic excitement. Indeed it is often necessary to encourage them if a vat proves obstinate, and the colour refuses to come—an event which occasionally does happen. It is very hard work beating, and when this constant violent exercise is kept up for about three hours (which is the time generally taken), the coolies are pretty well exhausted, and require a rest.

During the beating, two processes are going on simultaneously. One is chemical—oxygenation—turning the yellowish green dye into a deep intense blue;

INDIGO BEATERS AT WORK IN THE VATS.

To face page 30.

the other is mechanical—a separation of the particles of dye from the water in which it is held in solution. The beating seems to do this, causing the dye to granulate in larger particles.

When the vat has been beaten, the coolies remove the froth and scum from the surface of the water, and then leave the contents to settle. The fecula or dye, or *mall*, as it is technically called, now settles at the bottom of the vat in a soft pulpy sediment, and the waste liquor left on the top is let off through graduated holes in the front. Pin after pin is gradually removed, and the clear sherry-coloured waste allowed to run out till the last hole in the series is reached, and nothing but dye remains in the vat. By this time the coolies have had a rest and food, and now they return to the works, and either lift up the *mall* in earthen jars and take it to the mall tank, or—as is now more commonly done—they run it along a channel to the tank, and then wash out and clean the vat to be ready for the renewed beating on the morrow. When all the *mall* has been collected in the mall tank, it is next pumped up into the straining room. It is here strained through successive layers of wire gauze and cloth, till, free from dirt, sand and impurity, it is run into the large iron boilers, to be subjected to the next process. This is the boiling. This operation usually takes two or three hours, after which it is run off along narrow channels, till it reaches the straining-table. It is a very important part of the manufacture, and has to be carefully done. The straining-table is an oblong shallow wooden frame, in the shape of a trough, but all composed of open woodwork. It is covered by a large straining-sheet, on which the mall settles; while the waste water trickles through and is carried away by a drain. When the mall has stood on the table all night, it is next morning lifted up by scoops and buckets and put into the presses. These are square boxes of iron or wood, with perforated sides and bottom and a removeable perforated lid. The insides of the boxes are lined with press cloths, and when filled these cloths are carefully folded over the *mall*, which is now of the consistence of starch; and a heavy beam, worked on two upright three-inch screws, is let down on the lid of the press. A long lever is now put on the screws, and the nut worked slowly round. The pressure is enormous, and all the water remaining in the *mall* is pressed through the cloth and perforations in the press-box till nothing but the pure indigo remains behind.

The presses are now opened, and a square slab of dark moist indigo, about three or three and a half inches thick, is carried off on the bottom of the press (the top and sides having been removed), and carefully placed on the cutting frame. This frame corresponds in size to the bottom of the press, and is grooved in lines somewhat after the manner of a chess-board. A stiff iron rod with a brass wire attached is put through the groove under the slab, the wire is brought over the slab, and the rod being pulled smartly through brings the wire with it, cutting the indigo much in the same way as you would cut a bar of soap. When all the slab has been cut into bars, the wire and rod are next put into the grooves at right angles to the bars and again pulled through, thus dividing the bars into cubical cakes. Each cake is then stamped with the factory mark and number, and all are noted down in the books. They are then taken to the drying house; this is a large airy building, with strong shelves of bamboo reaching to the roof, and having narrow passages between the tiers of shelves. On these shelves or *mychans*, as they are called, the cakes are ranged to dry. The drying takes two or three months, and the cakes are turned and moved at frequent intervals, till thoroughly ready for packing. All the little pieces and corners and chips are carefully put by on separate shelves, and packed separately. Even the sweepings and refuse from the sheets and floor are all carefully collected, mixed with water, boiled separately, and made into cakes, which are called 'washings.'

During the drying a thick mould forms on the cakes. This is carefully brushed off before packing, and, mixed with sweepings and tiny chips is all ground up in a hand-mill, packed in separate chests, and sold as dust. In October, when *mahye* is over, and the preparation of the land going on again, the packing begins. The cakes, each of separate date, are carefully scrutinised, and placed in order of quality. The finest qualities are packed first, in layers, in mango-wood boxes; the boxes are first weighed empty, re-weighed when full, and the difference gives the nett weight of the indigo. The tare, gross, and nett weights are printed legibly on the chests, along with the factory mark and number of the chest, and when all are ready, they are sent down to the brokers in Calcutta for sale. Such shortly is the system of manufacture.

During *mahye* the factory is a busy scene. Long before break of day the ryots and coolies are busy cutting the plant, leaving it in green little heaps for the cartmen to load. In the early morning the carts are seen converging to the factory on every road, crawling along like huge green beetles. Here a cavalcade of twenty or thirty carts, there in clusters of twos or threes. When they reach the factory the loaders have several vats ready for the reception of the plant, while others are taking out the already steeped plant of yesterday; staggering under its weight, as, dripping with water, they toss it on the vast accumulating heap of refuse material.

Down in the vats below, the beating coolies are plashing, and shouting, and yelling, or the revolving wheel (where machinery is used) is scattering clouds of spray and foam in the blinding sunshine. The firemen stripped to the waist, are feeding the furnaces with the dried stems of last year's crop, which forms our only fuel. The smoke hovers in volumes over the boiling-house. The pinmen are busy sorting their pins, rolling hemp round them to make them fit the holes more exactly. Inside the boiling-house, dimly discernible through the clouds of stifling steam, the boilermen are seen with long rods, stirring slowly the boiling mass of bubbling blue. The clank of the levers resounds through the pressing-house, or the hoarse guttural 'hah, hah!' as the huge lever is strained and pulled at by the press-house coolies. The straining-table is being cleaned by the table 'mate' and his coolies, while the washerman stamps on his sheets and press-cloths to extract all the colour from them, and the cake-house boys run to and fro between the cutting-table and the cake-house with batches of cakes on their heads, borne on boards, like a baker taking his hot rolls from the oven, or like a busy swarm of ants taking the spoil of the granary to their forest haunt. Everywhere there is a confused jumble of sounds. The plash of water, the clank of machinery, the creaking of wheels, the roaring of the furnaces, mingle with the shouts, cries, and yells of the excited coolies; the vituperations of the drivers as some terrified or obstinate bullock plunges madly about; the objurgations of the 'mates' as some lazy fellow eases his stroke in the beating vats; the cracking of whips as the bullocks tear round the circle where the Persian wheel creaks and rumbles in the damp, dilapidated wheel-house; the dripping buckets revolving clumsily on the drum, the arriving and departing carts; the clang of the anvil, as the blacksmith and his men hammer away at some huge screw which has been bent; the hurrying crowds of cartmen and loaders with their burdens of fresh green plant or dripping refuse;—form such a medley of sights and sounds as I have never seen equalled in any other industry.

The planter has to be here, there, and everywhere. He sends carts to this village or to that, according as the crop ripens. Coolies must be counted and paid daily. The stubble must be ploughed to give the plant a start for the second growth whenever the weather will admit of it. Reports have to be sent to the agents and owners. The boiling must be narrowly watched, as also the beating and the straining. He has a large staff of native assistants, but if his *mahye* is to be successful, his eye must be over all. It is an anxious time, but the constant work is grateful, and when the produce is good, and everything working smoothly, it is perhaps the most enjoyable time of the whole year. Is it nothing to see the crop, on which so much care has been expended, which you have watched day by day through all the vicissitudes of the season, through drought, and flood, and blight; is it nothing to see it safely harvested, and your shelves filling day by day with fine sound cakes, the representatives of wealth, that will fill your pockets with commission, and build up your name as a careful and painstaking planter?

'What's your produce?' is now the first query at this season, when planters meet. Calculations are made daily, nay hourly, to see how much is being got per beegah, or how much per vat. The presses are calculated to weigh so much. Some days you will get a press a vat, some days it will mount up to two presses a vat, and at other times it will recede to half a press a vat, or even less. Cold wet weather reduces the produce. Warm sunny weather will send it up again. Short stunted plant from poor lands will often reduce your average per acre, to be again sent up as fresh, hardy, leafy plant comes in from some favourite village, where you have new and fertile lands, or where the plant from the rich zeraats laden with broad strong leaf is tumbled into the loading vat.

So far as I know, there seems to be no law of produce. It is the most erratic and incomprehensible thing about planting. One day your presses are full to straining, next day half of them lie empty. No doubt the state of the weather, the quality of your plant, the temperature of the water, the length of time steeping, and other things have an influence; but I know of no planter who can entirely and satisfactorily account for the sudden and incomprehensible fluctuations and variations which undoubtedly take place in the produce or yield of the plant. It is a matter of more interest to the planter than to the general public, but all I can say is, that if the circumstances attendant on any sudden change in the yielding powers of the plant were more accurately noted; if the chemical conditions of the water, the air, and the raw material itself, more especially in reference to the soil on which it grows, the time it takes in transit from the field to the vat, and other points, which will at once suggest themselves to a practical planter, were more carefully, methodically, and scientifically observed, some coherent theory resulting in plain practical results might be evolved.

Planters should attend more to this. I believe the chemical history of indigo has yet to be written. The whole manufacture, so far as chemistry is concerned, is yet crude and ill-digested. I know that by careful experiment, and close scientific investigation and observation, the preparation of indigo could be much improved. So far as the mechanical appliances for the manufacture go, the last ten years have witnessed amazing and rapid improvements. What is now wanted, is, that what has been done for the mere mechanical appliances, should be done for the proper understanding of the chemical changes and conditions in the constitution of the plant, and in the various processes of its manufacture [1].

---

[1] Since the above chapter was written Mons. P. I. Michea, a French chemist of some experience in Indigo matters, has patented an invention (the result of much study, experiment, and investigation), by the application of which an immense increase in the produce of the plant has been obtained during the last season, in several factories where it has been worked in Jessore, Purneah, Kishnaghur, and other places. This increase, varying according to circumstances, has in some instances reached the amazing extent of 30 to 47 per cent., and so far from being attended with a deterioration of quality the dye produced is said to be finer than that obtained under the old crude process described in the above chapter. This shows what a waste must have been going on, and what may yet be done, by properly organised scientific investigation. I firmly believe that with an intelligent application of the principles of chemistry and agricultural science, not only to the manufacture but to growth, cultivation, nature of the soil, application of manures, and other such departments

of the business, quite a revolution will set in, and a new era in the history of this great industry will be inaugurated. Less area for crop will be required, working expenses will be reduced, a greater out-turn, and a more certain crop secured, and all classes, planter and ryot alike, will be benefited.

Indian Factory Peon.

CHAPTER V.

Parewah factory.—A 'Bobbery Pack.'—Hunt through a village after a cat.—The pariah dog of India.—Fate of 'Pincher.'—Rampore hound.—Persian greyhound.—Caboolee dogs.—A jackal hunt.—Incidents of the chase.

AFTER living at Puttihee for two years, I was transferred to another out-factory in the same concern, called Parewah. There was here a very nice little three-roomed bungalow, with airy verandahs all round. It was a pleasant change from Puttihee, and the situation was very pretty. A small stream, almost dry in the hot weather, but a swollen, deep, rapid torrent in the rains, meandered past the factory. Nearing the bullock-house it suddenly took a sweep to the left in the form of a wide horseshoe, and in this bend or pocket was situated the bungalow, with a pretty terraced garden sloping gently to the stream. Thus the river was in full view from both the front and the back verandahs. In front, and close on the bank of the river, stood the kitchen, fowl-house, and offices. To the right of the compound were the stables, while behind the bungalow, and some distance down the stream, the wheel-house, vats, press-house, boiling-house, cake-house, and workshops were grouped together. I was but nine miles from the bead-factory, and the same distance from the station of Mooteeharree, while over the river, and but three miles off, I had the factory of Meerpore, with its hospitable manager as my nearest neighbour. His lands and mine lay contiguous. In fact some of his villages lay beyond some of mine, and he had to ride through part of my cultivation to reach them.

Not unfrequently we would meet in the zillah of a morning, when we would invariably make for the nearest patch of grass or jungle, and enjoy a hunt together. In the cool early mornings, when the heavy night dews still lie glittering on the grass, when the cobwebs seem strung with pearls, and faint lines of soft fleecy mist lie in the hollows by the watercourses; long ere the hot, fiery sun has left his crimson bed behind the cold grey horizon, we are out on our favourite horse, the wiry, long-limbed *syce* or groom trotting along behind us. The *mehter* or dog-keeper is also in attendance with a couple of greyhounds in leash, and a motley pack of wicked little terriers frisking and frolicking behind him. This mongrel collection is known as 'the Bobbery Pack,' and forms a certain adjunct to every assistant's bungalow in the district. I had one very noble-looking kangaroo hound that I had brought from Australia with me, and my 'bobbery pack' of terriers contained canine specimens of all sorts, sizes, and colours.

On nearing a village, you would see one black fellow, 'Pincher,' set off at a round trot ahead, with seemingly the most innocent air in the world. 'Tilly,' 'Tiny,' and 'Nipper' follow.

Then 'Dandy,' 'Curly,' 'Brandy,' and 'Nettle,' till spying a cat in the distance, the whole pack with a whimper of excitement dash off at a mad scramble, the hound straining meanwhile at the slip, till he almost pulls the *mehter* off his legs. Off goes the cat, round the corner of a hut with her tail puffed up to fully three times its normal size. Round in mad, eager pursuit rattle the terriers, thirsting for her blood. The *syce* dashes forward, vainly hoping to turn them from their quest. Now a village dog, roused from his morning nap, bounds out with a demoniac howl, which is caught up and echoed by all the curs in the village.

Meanwhile the row inside the hut is fiendish. The sleeping family rudely roused by the yelping pack, utter the most discordant screams. The women with garments fluttering behind them, rush out beating their breasts, thinking the very devil is loose. The wails of the unfortunate cat mingle with the short snapping barks of the pack, or a howl of anguish as pu s inflicts a caress on the face of some too careless or reckless dog. A howling village cur has rashly ventured too near. 'Pincher' has him by the hind leg before you could say 'Jack Robinson.' Leaving the dead cat for 'Toby' and 'Nettle' to worry, the whole pack now fiercely attack the luckless *Pariah* dog. A dozen of his village mates dance madly outside the ring, but are too wise or too cowardly to come to closer quarters. The kangaroo hound has now fairly torn the rope from the keeper's hand, and with one mighty bound is in the middle of the fight, scattering the village dogs right and left. The whole village is now in commotion, the *syce* and keeper shout the names of the terriers in vain. Oaths, cries, shouts, and screams mingle with the yelping and growling of the combatants, till riding up, I disperse the worrying pack with a few cracks of my hunting whip, and so on again over the zillah, leaving the women and children to recover their scattered senses, the old men to grumble over their broken slumbers, and the boys and young men to wonder at the pluck and dash of the *Belaitee Kookoòr*, or English dog.

The common Pariah dog, or village dog of India, is a perfect cur; a mangy, carrion-loving, yellow-fanged, howling brute. A most unlovely and unloving beast. As you pass his village he will bounce out on you with the fiercest bark and the most menacing snarl; but lo! if a terrier the size of a teacup but boldly go at him, down goes his tail like a pump-handle, he turns white with fear, and like the arrant coward that he is, tumbles on his back and fairly screams for mercy. I have often been amused to see a great hulking cowardly brute come out like an avalanche at 'Pincher,' expecting to make one mouthful of him. What a look of bewilderment he would put on, as my gallant little 'Pincher,' with a short, sharp, defiant bark would go boldly at him. The huge yellow brute would stop dead short on all four legs, and as the rest of my pack would come scampering round the corner, he would find himself the centre of a ring of indomitable assailants.

How he curses his short-sighted temerity. With one long howl of utter dismay and deadly fear, he manages to get away from the pack, leaving my little doggies to come proudly round my horse with their mouths full of fur, and each of their little tails as stiff as an iron ramrod.

That 'Pincher,' in some respects, was a very fiend incarnate. There was no keeping him in. He was constantly getting into hot water himself, and leading the pack into all sorts of mischief. He was as bold as brass and as courageous as a lion. He stole food, worried sheep and goats, and was never out of a scrape. I tried thrashing him, tying him up, half starving him, but all to no purpose. He would be into every hut in a village whenever he had the chance, overturning brass pots, eating up rice and curries, and throwing the poor villager's household into dismay and confusion. He would never leave a cat if he once saw it. I've seen him scramble through the roofs of more than one hut, and oust the cat from its fancied stronghold.

I put him into an indigo vat with a big dog jackal once, and he whipped the jackal single-handed. He did not kill it, but he worried it till the jackal shammed dead and would not 'come to the scratch.' 'Pincher's' ears were perfect shreds, and his scars were as numerous almost as his hairs. My gallant 'Pincher!' His was a sad end. He got eaten up by an alligator in the 'Dhans,' a sluggish stream in Bhaugulpore. I had all my pack in the boat with me, the stream was swollen and full of weeds. A jackal gave tongue on the bank, and 'Pincher' bounded over the side of the boat at once. I tried to 'grab' him, and nearly upset the boat in doing so. Our boat was going rapidly down stream, and 'Pincher tried to get ashore but got among the weeds. He gave a bark, poor gallant little dog, for help, but just then we saw a dark square snout shoot athwart the stream. A half-smothered sobbing cry from 'Pincher,' and the bravest little dog I ever possessed was gone for ever.

There is another breed of large, strong-limbed, big-boned dogs, called Rampore hounds. They are a cross breed from the original upcountry dog and the Persian greyhound. Some call them the Indian greyhound. They seem to be bred principally in the Rampore-Bareilly district, but one or more are generally to be found in every planter's pack. They are fast and strong enough, but I have often found them bad at tackling, and they are too fond of their keeper ever to make an affectionate faithful dog to the European.

Another somewhat similar breed is the *Tazi*. This, although not so large a dog as the Rhamporee, is a much pluckier animal, and when well trained will tackle a jackal with the utmost determination. He has a wrinkled almost hairless skin, but a very uncertain temper, and he is not very amenable to discipline. *Tazi* is simply the Persian word for a greyhound, and refers to no particular breed. The common name for a dog is *Kutta*, pronounced *Cootta*, but the Tazi has certainly been an importation from the North-west, hence the Persian name. The wandering Caboolees, who come down to the plains once a year with dried fruits, spices, and other products of field or garden, also bring with them the dogs of their native country for sale, and on occasion they bring lovely long-haired white Persian cats, very beautiful animals. These Caboolee dogs are tall, long-limbed brutes, generally white, with a long thin snout, very long silky-haired drooping ears, and generally wearing tufts of hair on their legs and tail, somewhat like the feathering of a spaniel, which makes them look rather clumsy. They cannot stand the heat of the plains at all well, and are difficult to tame, but fleet and plucky, hunting well with an English pack.

My neighbour Anthony at Meerpore had some very fine English greyhounds and bulldogs, and many a rattling burst have we had together after the fox or the jackal. Imagine a wide level plain, with one uniform dull covering of rice stubble, save where in the centre a mound rises some two acres in extent, covered with long thatching grass, a few scrubby acacia bushes, and other jungly brushwood. All round the circular horizon are dense forest masses of sombre looking foliage, save where some clump of palms uprear their stately heads, or the white shining walls of some temple, sacred to Shiva or Khristna glitter in the sunshine. Far to the left a sluggish creek winds slowly along through the plain, its banks fringed with acacias and wild rose jungle. On the far bank is a small patch of *Sal* forest jungle, with a thick rank undergrowth of ferns, thistles, and rank grass. As I am slowly riding along I hear a shout in the distance, and looking round behold Anthony advancing at a rapid hand gallop. His dogs and mine, being old friends, rapidly fraternise, and we determine on a hunt.

'Let's try the old patch, Anthony!'

'All right,' and away we go making straight for the mound. When we reach the grass the syces and keepers hold the hounds at the corners outside, while we ride through the grass urging on the terriers, who, quivering with excitement, utter short barks, and dash here and there among the thick grass, all eager for a find.

'Gone away, gone away!' shouts Anthony, as a fleet fox dashes out, closely followed by 'Pincher' and half a dozen others. The hounds are slipped, and away go the pack in full pursuit, we on our horses riding along, one on each side of the chase. The fox has a good start, but now the hounds are nearing him, when with a sudden whisk he doubles round the ridge encircling a rice field, the hounds overshoot him, and ere they turn the fox has put the breadth of a good field between himself and his pursuers. He is now making back again for the grass, but encounters some of the terriers who have tailed off behind. With panting chests and lolling tongues, they are pegging stolidly along, when fortune gives them this welcome chance. Redoubling their efforts, they dash at the fox. 'Bravo, Tilly! you tumbled him over that time;' but he is up and away again. Dodging, double-turning, and twisting, he has nearly run the gauntlet, and the friendly covert is close at hand, but the hounds are now up again and thirsting for his blood. 'Hurrah! Minnie has him!' cries Anthony, and riding up we divest poor Reynard of his brush, pat the dogs, ease the girths for a minute, and then again into the jungle for another beat.

This time a fat old jackal breaks to the left, long before the dogs are up. Yelling to the *mehters* not to slip the hounds, we gather the terriers together, and pound over the stubble and ridges. He is going very leisurely, casting an occasional scared look over his shoulder. 'Curly' and 'Legs,' two of my fastest terriers, are now in full view, they are laying themselves well to the ground, and Master Jackal thinks it's high time to increase his pace. He puts on a spurt, but condition tells. He is fat and pursy, and must have had a good feed last night on some poor dead bullock. He is shewing his teeth now. Curly makes his rush, and they both roll over together. Up hurries Legs, and the jackal gets a grip, gives him a shake, and then hobbles slowly on. The two terriers now hamper him terribly. One minute they are at his heels, and as soon as he turns, they are at his ear or shoulder. The rest of the pack are fast coming up.

Anthony has a magnificent bulldog, broad-chested, and a very Goliath among dogs. He is called 'Sailor.' Sailor always pounds along at the same steady pace; he never seems to get flurried. Sitting lazily at the door, he seems too indolent even to snap at a fly. He is a true philosopher, and nought seems to disturb his serenity. But see him after a jackal, his big red tongue hanging out, his eyes flashing fire, and his hair erected on his back like the bristles of a wild boar. He looks fiendish then, and he is a true bulldog.

There is no flinching with Sailor. Once he gets his grip it's no use trying to make him let go.

Up comes Sailor now.

He has the jackal by the throat.

A hoarse, rattling, gasping yell, and the jackal has gone to the happy hunting grounds.

The sun is now mounting in the sky. The hounds and terriers feel the heat, so sending them home by the keeper, we diverge on our respective roads, ride over our cultivation, seeing the ploughing and preparations generally, till hot, tired, and dusty, we reach home about 11.30, tumble into our bath, and feeling refreshed, sit down contentedly to breakfast. If the *dak* or postman has come in we get our letters and papers, and the afternoon is devoted to office work and accounts, hearing complaints and reports from the villages, or looking over any labour that may be going on in the zeraats or at the workshops. In the evening we ride over the zeraats again, give orders for the morrow's work, consume a little tobacco, have an early dinner, and after a little reading, retire soon to bed to dream of far away friends and the happy memories of home. Many an evening it is very lonely work. No friendly face, and no congenial society within miles of your factory. Little wonder that the arrival of a brother planter sends a thrill through the frame, and that his advent is welcomed as the most agreeable break to the irksome monotony of our lonely life.

CHAPTER VI.

Fishing in India.—Hereditary trades.—The boatmen and fishermen of India.—Their villages.—Nets.—Modes of fishing.—Curiosities relating thereto.—Catching an alligator with a hook.—Exciting capture.—Crocodiles.—Shooting an alligator.—Death of the man-eater.

NOT only in the wild jungles, on the undulating plains, and among the withered brown stubbles, does animal life abound in India; but the rivers, lakes, and creeks teem with fish of every conceivable size, shape, and colour. The varieties are legion. From the huge black porpoise, tumbling through the turgid stream of the Ganges, to the bright, sparkling, silvery shoals of delicate *chillooahs* or *poteeahs*, which one sees darting in and out among the rice stubbles in every paddy field during the rains. Here a huge *bhowarree* (pike), or ravenous *coira*, comes to the surface with a splash; there a *raho*, the Indian salmon, with its round sucker-like mouth, rises slowly to the surface, sucks in a fly and disappears as slowly as it rose; or a *pachgutchea*, a long sharp-nosed fish, darts rapidly by; a shoal of mullet with their heads out of the water swim athwart the stream, and far down in the cool depths of the tank or lake, a thousand different varieties disport themselves among the mazy labyrinths of the broad-leaved weeds.

During the middle, and about the end of the rains, is the best time for fishing; the whole country is then a perfect network of streams. Every rice field is a shallow lake, with countless thousands of tiny fish darting here and there among the rice stalks. Every ditch teems with fish, and every hollow in every field is a well stocked aquarium.

Round the edge of every lake or tank in the early morning, or when the fierce heat of the day begins to get tempered by the approaching shades of evening, one sees numbers of boys and men of the poorer classes, each with a couple of rough bamboo rods stuck in the ground in front of him, watching his primitive float with the greatest eagerness, and whipping out at intervals some luckless fish of about three or four ounces in weight with a tremendous haul, fit for the capture of a forty-pounder. They get a coarse sort of hook in the bazaar, rig up a roughly-twisted line, tie on a small piece of hollow reed for a float, and with a lively earth-worm for a bait, they can generally manage in a very short time to secure enough fish for a meal.

With a short light rod, a good silk line, and an English hook attached to fine gut, I have enjoyed many a good hour's sport at Parewah. I used to have a cane chair sent down to the bank of the stream, a *punkah*, or hand fan, plenty of cooling drinks, and two coolie boys in attendance to remove the fish, renew baits, and keep the punkah in constant swing. There I used to sit enjoying my cigar, and pulling in little fish at the rate sometimes of a couple a minute.

I remember hooking a turtle once, and a terrible job it was to land him. My light rod bent like a willow, but the tackle was good, and after ten minutes' hard work I got the turtle to the side, where my boys soon secured him. He weighed thirteen pounds. Sometimes you get among a colony of freshwater crabs.

E

They are little brown brutes, and strip your hooks of the bait as fast as you fling them in. There is nothing for it in such a case but to shift your station. Many of the bottom fish—the *ghurai*, the *saourie*, the *barnee* (eel), and others, make no effort to escape the hook. You see them resting at the bottom, and drop the bait at their very nose. On the whole, the hand fishing is uninteresting, but it serves to wile away an odd hour when hunting and shooting are hardly practicable.

Particular occupations in India are restricted to particular castes. All trades are hereditary. For example, a *tatmah*, or weaver, is always a weaver. He cannot become a blacksmith or carpenter. He has no choice. He must follow the hereditary trade. The peculiar system of land-tenure in India, which secures as far as possible a bit of land for every one, tends to perpetuate this hereditary selection of trades, by enabling every cultivator to be so far independent of his handicraft, thus restricting competition. There may be twenty *lohars*, or blacksmiths, in a village, but they do not all follow their calling. They till their lands, and are *de facto* petty farmers. They know the rudiments of their handicraft, but the actual blacksmith's work is done by the hereditary smith of the village, whose son in turn will succeed him when he dies, or if he leave no son, his fellow caste men will put in a successor.

Nearly every villager during the rains may be found on the banks of the stream or lake, angling in an amateur sort of way, but the fishermen of Behar *par excellence* are the *mullāhs;* they are also called *Gonhree, Beeu,* or *Muchooah.* In Bengal they are called *Nikaree,* and in some parts *Baeharee,* from the Persian word for a boat. In the same way *muchooah* is derived from *much,* a fish, and *mullah* means boatman, strictly speaking, rather than fisherman. All boatmen and fishermen belong to this caste, and their villages can be recognised at once by the instruments of their calling lying all around.

Perched high on some bank overlooking the stream or lake, you see innumerable festoons of nets hanging out to dry on tall bamboo poles, or hanging like lace curtains of very coarse texture from the roofs and eaves of the huts. Hauled up on the beach are a whole fleet of boats of different sizes, from the small *dugout*, which will hold only one man, to the huge *dinghy*, in which the big nets and a dozen men can be stowed with ease. Great heaps of shells of the freshwater mussel show the source of great supplies of bait; while overhead a great hovering army of kites and vultures are constantly circling round, eagerly watching for the slightest scrap of offal from the nets. When the rains have fairly set in, and the fishermen have got their rice fields all planted out, they are at liberty to follow their hereditary avocation. A day is fixed for a drag, and the big nets are overhauled and got in readiness. The head *mullah*, a wary grizzled old veteran, gives the orders. The big drag-net is bundled into the boat, which is quickly pushed off into the stream, and at a certain distance from shore the net is cast from the boat. Being weighted at the lower end it rapidly sinks, and, buoyed on the upper side with pieces of cork, it makes a perpendicular wall in the water. Several long bamboo poles are now run through the ropes along the upper side of the net, to prevent the net being dragged under water altogether by the weight of the fish in a great haul. The little boats, a crowd of which are in attendance, now dart out, surrounding the net on all sides, and the boatmen beating their oars on the sides of the boats, create such a clatter as to frighten the fish into the circumference of the big net. This is now being dragged slowly to shore by strong and willing arms. The women and children watch eagerly on the bank. At length the glittering haul is pulled up high and dry on the beach, the fish are divided among the men, the women fill their baskets, and away they hie to the nearest *bazaar*, or if it be not *bazaar* or market day, they hawk the fish through the nearest villages, like our fish-wives at home.

There is another common mode of fishing adopted in narrow lakes and small streams, which are let out to the fishermen by the Zemindars or landholders. A barricade made of light reeds, all matted together by string, is stuck into the stream, and a portion of the water is fenced in, generally in a circular form. The reed fence being quite flexible is gradually moved in, narrowing the circle. As the circle narrows, the agitation inside is indescribable; fish jumping in all directions—a moving mass of glittering scales and fins. The larger ones try to leap the barrier, and are caught by the attendant *mullahs*, who pounce on them with swift dexterity. Eagles and kites dart and swoop down, bearing off a captive fish in their talons. The reed fence is doubled back on itself, and gradually pushed on till the whole of the fish inside are jammed together in a moving mass. The weeds and dirt are then removed, and the fish put into baskets and carried off to market.

Others, again, use circular casting nets, which they throw with very great dexterity. Gathering the net into a bunch they rest it on the shoulder, then with a circular sweep round the head, they fling it far out.

Being loaded, it sinks down rapidly in the water. A string is attached to the centre of the net, and the fisherman hauls it in with whatever prey he may be lucky enough to secure.

As the waters recede during October, after the rains have ended, each runlet and purling stream becomes a scene of slaughter on a most reckless and improvident scale. The innumerable shoals of spawn and small fish that have been feeding in the rice fields, warned by some instinct seek the lakes and main streams. As they try to get their way back, however, they find at each outlet in each ditch and field a deadly wicker trap, in the shape of a square basket with a V-shaped opening leading into it, through which the stream makes its way. After entering this basket there is no egress except through the narrow opening, and they are trapped thus in countless thousands. Others of the natives in mere wantonness put a shelf of reeds or rushes in the bed of the stream, with an upward slope. As the water rushes along, the little fish are left high and dry on this shelf or screen, and the water runs off below. In this way scarcely a fish escapes, and as millions are too small to be eaten, it is a most serious waste. The attention of Government has been directed to the subject, and steps may be taken to stop such a reckless and wholesale destruction of a valuable food supply.

In some parts of Purneah and Bhaugulpore I have seen a most ingenious method adopted by the *mullahs*. A gang of four or five enter the stream and travel slowly downwards, stirring up the mud at the bottom with their feet. The fish, ascending the stream to escape the mud, get entangled in the weeds. The fishermen feel them with their feet amongst the weeds, and immediately pounce on them with their hands. Each man has a *gila* or earthen pot attached by a string to his waist and floating behind him in the water. I have seen four men fill their earthen pots in less than an hour by this ingenious but primitive mode of fishing. Some of them can use their feet almost as well for grasping purposes as their hands.

Another mode of capture is by a small net. A flat piece of netting is spread over a hoop, to which four or five pieces of bamboo are attached, rising up and meeting in the centre, so as to form a sort of miniature skeleton tent-like frame over the net. The hoop with the net stretched tight across is then pressed down flat on the bottom of the tank or stream. If any fish are beneath, their efforts to escape agitate the net. The motion is communicated to the fisherman by a string from the centre of the net which is rolled round the fisherman's thumb. When the jerking of his thumb announces a captive fish, he puts down his left hand and secures his victim. The *Banturs, Nepaulees,* and other jungle tribes, also often use the bow and arrow as a means of securing fish.

Seated on the branch of some overhanging tree, while his keen eye scans the depths below, he watches for a large fish, and as it passes, he lets fly his arrow with unerring aim, and impales the luckless victim. Some tribes fish at night, by torchlight, spearing the fish who are attracted by the light. In Nepaul the bark of the *Hill Sirees* is often used to poison a stream or piece of water. Pounded up and thrown in, it seems to have some uncommon effect on the fish. After water has been treated in this way, the fish, seemingly quite stupefied, rise to the surface, on which they float in great numbers, and allow themselves to be caught. The strangest part of it is that they are perfectly innocuous as food, notwithstanding this treatment.

Fish forms a very favourite article of diet with both Mussulmans and Hindoos. Many of the latter take a vow to touch no flesh of any kind. They are called *Kunthees* or *Boghuts*, but a *Boghut* is more of an ascetic than a *Kunthee*. However, the *Kunthee* is glad of a fish dinner when he can get it. They are restricted to no particular sect or caste, but all who have taken the vow wear a peculiar necklace, made generally of sandal-wood beads or *neem* beads round their throats. Hence the name, from *kunth* meaning the throat.

The right to fish in any particular piece of water, is let out by the proprietor on whose land the water lies, or through which it flows. The letting is generally done by auction yearly. The fishing is called a *shilkur*, from *shal*, a net. It is generally taken by some rich *Bunneah* (grain seller) or village banker, who sub-lets it in turn to the fishermen.

In some of the tanks which are not so let, and where the native proprietor preserves the fish, first-class sport can be had. A common native poaching dodge is this: if some oil cake be thrown into the water a few hours previous to your fishing, or better still, balls made of roasted linseed meal, mixed with bruised leaves of the 'sweet basil,' or *toolsee* plant, the fish assemble in hundreds round the spot, and devour the bait greedily. With a good eighteen-foot rod, fish of from twelve to twenty pounds are not uncommonly caught, and will give good play too. Fishing in the plains of India is, however, rather tame sport at the best of times.

You have heard of the famous *mahseer*—some of them over eighty or a hundred pounds weight? We have none of these in Behar, but the huge porpoise gives splendid rifle or carbine practice as he rolls through the turgid streams. They are difficult to hit, but I have seen several killed with ball; and the oil extracted from their bodies is a splendid dressing for harness. But the most exciting fishing I have ever seen was—What do you think?—Alligator fishing! Yes, the formidable scaly monster, with his square snout and terrible jaws, his ponderous body covered with armour, and his serrated tail, with which he could break the leg of a bullock, or smash an outrigger as easily as a whale could smash a jolly-boat.

I must try to describe one day's alligator fishing.

When I was down in Bhaugulpore, I went out frequently fishing in the various tanks and streams near my factory. My friend Pat, who is a keen sportsman and very fond of angling, wrote to me one day when he and his brother Willie were going out to the Teljuga, asking me to join their party. The Teljuga is the boundary stream between Tirhoot and Bhaugulpore, and its sluggish muddy waters teem with alligators— the regular square-nosed *mugger*, the terrible man-eater. The *nakar* or long-nosed species may be seen in countless numbers in any of the large streams, stretched out on the banks basking in the noonday sun. Going down the Koosee particularly, you come across hundreds sometimes lying on one bank. As the boat nears them, they slide noiselessly and slowly into the stream. A large excrescence forms on the tip of the long snout, like a huge sponge; and this is often all that is seen on the surface of the water as the huge brute swims about waiting for his prey. These *nakars*, or long-nosed specimens, never attack human beings —at least such cases are very very rare—but live almost entirely on fish. I remember seeing one catch a paddy-bird on one occasion near the junction of the Koosee with the Ganges. My boat was fastened to the shore near a slimy creek, that came oozing into the river from some dense jungle near. I was washing my hands and face on the bank, and the boatmen were fishing with a small hand-net, for our breakfast. Numbers of attenuated melancholy-looking paddy-birds were stalking solemnly and stiltedly along the bank, also fishing for *theirs*. I noticed one who was particularly greedy, with his long legs half immersed in the water, constantly darting out his long bill and bringing up a hapless struggling fish. All of a sudden a long snout and the ugly serrated ridgy back of a *nakar* was shot like lightning at the hapless bird, and right before our eyes the poor paddy was crunched up. As a rule, however, alligators confine themselves to a fish diet, and are glad of any refuse or dead animal that may float their way. But with the *mugger*, the *boach*, or square-nosed variety, 'all is fish that comes to his net.' His soul delights in young dog or live pork. A fat duck comes not amiss; and impelled by hunger he hesitates not to attack man. Once regaled with the flavour of human flesh, he takes up his stand near some ferry, or bathing ghaut, where many hapless women and children often fall victims to his unholy appetite, before his career is cut short.

    I remember shooting one ghastly old scaly villain in a tank near Ryseree. He had made this tank his home, and with that fatalism which is so characteristic of the Hindoo, the usual ablutions and bathings went on as if no such monster existed. Several woman having been carried off, however, at short intervals, the villagers asked me to try and rid them of their foe. I took a ride down to the tank one Friday morning, and found the banks a scene of great excitement. A woman had been carried off some hours before as she was filling her water jar, and the monster was now reposing at the bottom of the tank digesting his horrible meal. The tank was covered with crimson water-lilies in full bloom, their broad brown and green leaves showing off the crimson beauty of the open flower. At the north corner some wild rose bushes dropped over the water, casting a dense matted shade. Here was the haunt of the *mugger*. He had excavated a huge gloomy-looking hole, into which he retired when gorged with prey. My first care was to cut away some of these bushes, and then, finding he was not at home, we drove some bamboo stakes through the bank to prevent him getting into his *manu*, which is what the natives term the den or hole. I then sat down under a *goolar* tree, to wait for his appearance. The *goolar* is a species of fig, and the leaves are much relished by cattle and goats. Gradually the village boys and young men went off to their ploughing, or grass cutting for the cows' evening meal. A woman came down occasionally to fill her waterpot in evident fear and trembling. A swarm of *minas* (the Indian starling) hopped and twittered round my feet. The cooing of a pair of amatory pigeons overhead nearly lulled me to slumber. A flock of green parrots came swiftly circling overhead, making for the fig-tree at the south end of the tank. An occasional *raho* lazily rose among the water-lilies, and disappeared with an indolent flap of his tail. The brilliant king-fisher, resplendent in crimson and emerald, sat on the withered branch of a prostrate mango-tree close by, pluming his feathers and doubtless meditating on the vanity of life. Suddenly, close by the massive post which marks the centre of every Hindoo tank, a huge scaly snout slowly and almost imperceptibly rose to the surface, then a broad, flat, forbidding forehead, topped by two grey fishy eyes with warty-looking callosities for eyebrows. Just then an eager urchin who had been squatted by me for hours, pointed to the brute. It was enough. Down sank the loathsome creature, and we had to resume our attitude of expectation and patient waiting. Another hour passed slowly. It was the middle of the afternoon, and very hot. I had sent my *tokedar* off for a 'peg' to the factory, and was beginning to get very drowsy, when, right in the same spot, the repulsive head again rose slowly to the surface. I had my trusty No. 12 to my shoulder on the instant, glanced carefully along the barrels, but just then only the eyes of the brute were invisible. A moment of intense excitement followed, and then, emboldened by the extreme stillness, he showed his whole head above the surface. I pulled the trigger, and a Meade shell crashed through the monster's skull, scattering his brains in the water and actually sending one splinter of the skull to the opposite edge of the tank, where my little Hindoo boy picked it up and brought it to me.

There was a mighty agitation in the water; the water-lilies rocked to and fro, and the broad leaves glittered with the water drops thrown on them; then all was still. Hearing the report of my gun, the natives came flocking to the spot, and, telling them their enemy was slain, I departed, leaving instructions to let me know when the body came to the surface. It did so three days later. Getting some *chumars* and *domes* (two of the lowest castes, as none of the higher castes will touch a dead body under pain of losing caste), we hauled the putrid carcase to shore, and on cutting it open, found the glass armlets and brass ornaments of no less than five women and the silver ornaments of three children, all in a lump in the brute's stomach. Its skull was completely smashed and shattered to pieces by my shot. Its teeth were crusted with tartar, and worn almost to the very stumps. It measured nineteen feet.

But during this digression my friends Pat and Willie have been waiting on the banks of the 'Teljuga.' I reached their tents late at night, found them both in high spirits after a good day's execution among the ducks and teal, and preparations being made for catching an alligator next day. Up early in the morning, we beat some grass close by the stream, and roused out an enormous boar that gave us a three mile spin and a good fight, after Pat had given him first spear. After breakfast we got our tackle ready.

This was a large iron hook with a strong shank, to which was attached a stout iron ring. To this ring a long thick rope was fastened, and I noticed for several yards the strands were all loose and detached, and only knotted at intervals. I asked Pat the reason of this curious arrangement, and was told that if we were lucky enough to secure a *mugger*, the loose strands would entangle themselves amongst his formidable teeth, whereas were the rope in one strand only he might bite it through; the knottings at intervals were to give greater strength to the line. We now got our bait ready. On this occasion it was a live tame duck. Passing the bend of the hook round its neck, and the shank under its right wing, we tied the hook in this position with thread. We then made a small raft of the soft pith of the plantain-tree, tied the duck to the raft and committed it to the stream. Holding the rope as clear of the water as we could, the poor quacking duck floated slowly down the muddy current, making an occasional vain effort to get free. We saw at a distance an ugly snout rise to the surface for an instant and then noiselessly disappear.

'There's one!' says Pat in a whisper.

'Be sure and not strike too soon,' says Willie.

'Look out there, you lazy rascals!' This in Hindostanee to the grooms and servants who were with us.

Again the black mass rises to the surface, but this time nearer to the fated duck. As if aware of its peril it now struggles and quacks most vociferously. Nearer and nearer each time the black snout rises, and then each time silently disappears beneath the turgid muddy stream. Now it appears again; this time there are two, and there is another at a distance attracted by the quacking of the duck. We on the bank cower down and go as noiselessly as we can. Sometimes the rope dips on the water, and the huge snout and staring eyes immediately disappear. At length it rises within a few yards of the duck; then there is a mighty rush, two huge jaws open and shut with a snap like factory shears, and amid a whirl of foam and water and surging mud the poor duck and the hideous reptile disappear, and but for the eddying swirl and dense volumes of mud that rise from the bottom, nothing gives evidence of the tragedy that has been enacted. The other two disappointed monsters swim to and fro still further disturbing the muddy current.

'Give him lots of time to swallow,' yells Pat, now fairly mad with excitement.

The grooms and grass-cutters howl and dance. Willie and I dig each other in the ribs, and all generally act in an excited and insane way.

Pat now puts the rope over his shoulder, we all take hold, and with a 'one, two, three!' we make a simultaneous rush from the bank, and as the rope suddenly tightens with a pull and strain that nearly jerks us all on our backs, we feel that we have hooked the monster, and our excitement reaches its culminating point.

What a commotion now in the black depths of the muddy stream! The water, lashed by his powerful tail, surges and dashes in eddying whirls. He rises and darts backwards and forwards, snapping his horrible jaws, moving his head from side to side, his eyes glaring with fury. We hold stoutly on to the rope, although our wrists are strained and our arms ache. At length he begins to feel our steady pull, and inch by inch, struggling demoniacally, he nears the bank. When once he reaches it, however, the united efforts of twice our number would fail to bring him farther. Bleeding and foaming at the mouth, his horrid teeth glistening amid the frothy, blood-flecked foam, he plants his strong curved fore-legs against the shelving bank, and tugs and strains at the rope with devilish force and fury. It is no use—the rope has been tested, and answers bravely to the strain; and now with a long boar spear, Pat cautiously descends the bank, and gives him a deadly thrust under the fore arm. With a last fiendish glare of hate and defiance, he springs forward; we haul in the rope, Pat nimbly jumps back, and a pistol shot through the eye settles the monster for ever. This was the first alligator I ever saw hooked; he measured sixteen and a half feet exactly, but words can give no idea of half the excitement that attended the capture.

CHAPTER VII.

Native superstitions.—Charming a bewitched woman.—Exorcising ghosts from a field. — Witchcraft.—The witchfinder or 'Ojah.'—Influence of fear.— Snake bites.—How to cure them.—How to discover a thief.—Ghosts and their habits.—The 'Huddick' or native bone-setter.—Cruelty to animals by natives.

THE natives as a rule, and especially the lower classes, are excessively superstitious. They are afraid to go out after nightfall, believing that then the spirits of the dead walk abroad. It is almost impossible to get a coolie, or even a fairly intelligent servant, to go a message at night, unless you give him another man for company.

A belief in witches is quite prevalent, and there is scarcely a village in Behar that does not contain some withered old crone, reputed and firmly believed to be a witch. Others, either young or old are believed to have the evil eye; and, as in Scotland some centuries ago, there are also witch-finders and sorcerers, who will sell charms, cast nativities, give divinations, or ward off the evil efforts of wizards and witches by powerful spells. When a wealthy man has a child born, the Brahmins cast the nativity of the infant on some auspicious day. They fix on the name, and settle the date for the baptismal ceremony.

I remember a man coming to me on one occasion from the village of Kuppoorpuckree. He rushed up to where I was sitting in the verandah, threw himself at my feet, with tears streaming down his cheeks, and amid loud cries for pity and help, told me that his wife had just been bewitched. Getting him somewhat soothed and pacified, I learned that a reputed witch lived next door to his house; that she and the man's wife had quarrelled in the morning about some capsicums which the witch was trying to steal from his garden; that in the evening, as his wife was washing herself inside the *angana*, or little courtyard appertaining to his house, she was seized with cramps and shivering fits, and was now in a raging fever; that the witch had been also bathing at the time, and that the water from her body had splashed over this man's fence, and part of it had come in contact with his wife's body—hence undoubtedly this strange possession. He wished me to send peons at once, and have the witch seized, beaten, and expelled from the village. It would have been no use my trying to persuade him that no witchcraft existed. So I gave him a good dose of quinine for his wife, which she was to take as soon as the fit subsided. Next I got my old *moonshee*, or native writer, to write some Persian characters on a piece of paper; I then gave him this paper, muttering a bit of English rhyme at the time, and telling him this was a powerful spell. I told him to take three hairs from his wife's head, and a paring from her thumb and big toe nails, and at the rising of the moon to burn them outside the walls of his hut. The poor fellow took the quinine and the paper with the deepest reverence, made me a most lowly *salaam* or obeisance, and departed with a light heart. He carried out my instructions to the letter, the quinine acted like a charm on the feverish woman, and I found myself quite a famous witch-doctor.

There was a nice flat little field close to the water at Parewah, in which I thought I could get a good crop of oats during the cold weather. I sent for the 'dangur' mates, and asked them to have it dug up next day. They hummed and hawed and hesitated, as I thought, in rather a strange manner, but departed. In the evening back they came, to tell me that the dangurs would *not* dig up the field.

'Why?' I asked.

'Well you see, Sahib,' said old Teerbouan, who was the patriarch and chief spokesman of the village, 'this field has been used for years as a burning ghaut' (i.e. a place where the bodies of dead Hindoos were buried).

'Well?' said I.

'Well, Sahib, my men say that if they disturb this land, the "Bhoots" (ghosts) of all those who have been burned there, will haunt the village at night, and they hope you will not persist in asking them to dig up the land.'

'Very well, bring down the men with their digging hoes, and I will see.'

Accordingly, next morning, I went down on my pony, found the dangurs all assembled, but no digging going on. I called them together, told them that it was a very reasonable fear they had, but that I would cast such a spell on the land as would settle the ghosts of the departed for ever. I then got a branch of a *bael*[1] tree that grew close by, dipped it in the stream, and walking backwards round the ground, waved the dripping branch

---

[1] The *bael* or wood-apple is a sacred wood with Hindoos. It is enjoined in the Shastras that the bodies of the dead should be consumed in a fire fed by logs of bael-tree; but where it is not procurable in sufficient quantity, the natives compound with their consciences by lighting the funeral pyre with a branch from the bael-tree. It is a fine yellow-coloured, pretty durable wood, and makes excellent furniture. A very fine sherbet can be made from the fruit, which acts as an excellent corrective and stomachic.

round my head, repeating at the same time the first gibberish that came into my recollection. My incantation or spell was as follows, an old Scotch rhyme I had often repeated when a child at school—

> 'Eenerty, feenerty, fickerty, feg,
> Ell, dell, domun's egg;
> Irky, birky, story, rock,
> An, tan, toose, Jock;
> Black fish! white troot!
> "Gibbie Gaw, ye're oot."'

It had the desired effect. No sooner was my charm uttered, than, after a few encouraging words to the men, telling them that there was now no fear, that my charm was powerful enough to lay all the spirits in the country, and that I would take all the responsibility, they set to work with a will, and had the whole field dug up by the evening.

I have seen many such cases. A blight attacks the melon or cucumber beds; a fierce wind rises during the night, and shakes half the mangoes off the trees; the youngest child is attacked with teething convulsions; the plough-bullock is accidentally lamed, or the favourite cow refuses to give milk. In every case it is some 'Dyne,' or witch, that has been at work with her damnable spells and charms. I remember a case in which a poor little child had bad convulsions. The 'Ojah,' or witch-finder, in this case a fat, greasy, oleaginous knave, was sent for. Full of importance and blowing like a porpoise, he came and caused the child to be brought to him, under a tree near the village. I was passing at the time, and stopped out of curiosity. He spread a tattered cloth in front of him, and muttered some unintelligible gibberish, unceasingly making strange passes with his arms. He put down a number of articles on his cloth—which was villainously tattered and greasy—an unripe plantain, a handful of rice, of parched peas, a thigh bone, two wooden cups, some balls, &c., &c.; all of which he kept constantly lifting and moving about, keeping up the passes and muttering all the time.

The child was a sickly-looking, pining sort of creature, rocking about in evident pain, and moaning and fretting just as sick children do. Gradually its attention got fixed on the strange antics going on. The Ojah kept muttering away, quicker and quicker, constantly shifting the bone and cups and other articles on the cloth. His body was suffused with perspiration, but in about half an hour the child had gone off to sleep, and attended by some dozen old women, and the anxious father, was borne off in triumph to the house.

Another time one of Mr. D.'s female servants got bitten by a scorpion. The poor woman was in great agony, with her arm swelled up, when an Ojah was called in. Setting her before him, he began his incantations in the usual manner, but made frequent passes over her body, and over the bitten place. A gentle perspiration began to break out on her skin, and in a very short time the Ojah had thrown her into a deep mesmeric sleep. After about an hour she awoke perfectly free from pain. In this case no doubt the Ojah was a mesmerist.

The influence of fear on the ordinary native is most wonderful. I have known dozens of instances in which natives have been brought home at night for treatment in cases of snake-bite. They have arrived at the factory in a complete state of coma, with closed eyes, the pupils turned back in the head, the whole body rigid and cold, the lips pale white, and the tongue firmly locked between the teeth. I do not believe in recovery from a really poisonous bite, where the venom has been truly injected. I invariably asked first how long it was since the infliction of the bite; I would then examine the marks, and as a rule would find them very slight. When the patient had been brought some distance, I knew at once that it was a case of pure fright. The natives wrap themselves up in their cloths or blankets at night, and lie down on the floors of their huts. Turning about, or getting up for water or tobacco, or perhaps to put fuel on the fire, they unluckily tread on a snake, or during sleep they roll over on one. The snake gives them a nip, and scuttles off. They have not seen what sort of snake it is, but their imagination conjures up the very worst. After the first outcry, when the whole house is alarmed, the man sits down firmly possessed by the idea that he is mortally bitten. Gradually his fears work the effect a real poisonous bite would produce. His eye gets dull, his pulse grows feeble, his extremities cold and numb, and unless forcibly roused by the bystanders he will actually succumb to pure fright, not to the snake-bite at all. My chief care when a case of this sort was brought me, was to assume a cheery demeanour, laugh to scorn the fears of the relatives, and tell them he would be all right in a few hours if they attended to my directions. This not uncommonly worked by sympathetic influence on the patient himself. I believe, so long as all round him thought he was going to die, and expected no other result, the same effect was produced on his own mind. As soon as hope sprang up in the breasts of all around him, his spirit also caught the contagion. As a rule, he would now make an effort to articulate. I would then administer a good dose of sal volatile, brandy, eau-de-luce, or other strong stimulant, cut into the supposed bite, and apply strong nitric acid to the wound. This generally made him wince, and I would hail it as a token of certain recovery. By this time some confidence would return, and the supposed dying man would soon walk back sound and whole among his companions after profuse expressions of gratitude to his preserver.

I have treated dozens of cases in this way successfully, and only seen two deaths. One was a young woman, my chowkeydar's daughter; the other was an old man, who was already dead when they lifted him out of the basket in which they had slung him. I do not wish to be misunderstood. I believe that in all these cases of recovery it was pure fright working on the imagination, and not snake-bite at all. My opinion is shared by most planters, that there is no cure yet known for a cobra bite, or for that of any other poisonous snake, where the poison has once been fairly injected and allowed to mix with the blood [1].

[1] Deaths from actual snake bite are sadly numerous; but it appears from returns furnished to the Indian Government that Europeans enjoy a very happy exemption. During the last forty years it would seem that only two Europeans have been killed by snake bite, at least only two well substantiated cases. The poorer classes are the most frequent victims. Their universal habit of walking about unshod, and sleeping on the ground, penetrating into the grasses or jungles in pursuit of their daily avocations, no doubt conduces much to the frequency of such accidents. A good plan to keep snakes out of the bungalow is to leave a space all round the rooms, of about four inches, between the walls and the edge of the mats. Have this washed over about once a week with a strong solution of carbolic acid and water. The smell may be unpleasant for a short time, but it proves equally so to the snakes; and I have proved by experience that it keeps them out of the rooms. Mats should also be all firmly fastened down to the floor with bamboo battens, and furniture should be often moved, and kept raised a little from the ground, and the space below carefully swept every day. At night a light should always be kept burning in

There is another curious instance of the effects of fear on the native mind in the common method taken by an Ojah or Brahmin to discover a suspected thief. When a theft occurs, the Ojah is sent for, and the suspected parties are brought together. After various *muntras*, i.e. charms or incantations, have been muttered, the Ojah, who has meanwhile narrowly scrutinized each countenance, gives each of the suspected individuals a small quantity of dry rice to chew. If the thief be present, his superstitious fears are at work, and his conscience accuses him. He sees some terrible retribution for him in all these *muntras*, and his heart becomes like water within him, his tongue gets dry, his salivary glands refuse to act; the innocent munch away at their rice contentedly, but the guilty wretch feels as if he had ashes in his mouth. At a given signal all spit out their rice, and he whose rice comes out, chewed indeed, but dry as summer dust, is adjudged the thief. This ordeal is called *chowl chipao*, and is rarely unsuccessful. I have known several cases in my own experience in which a thief has been thus discovered.

The *bhoots*, or ghosts, are popularly supposed to have favourite haunts, generally in some specially selected tree; the *neem* tree is supposed to be the most patronised. The most intelligent natives share this belief with the poorest and most ignorant; they fancy the ghosts throw stones at them, cast evil influences over them, lure them into quicksands, and play other devilish tricks and cantrips. Some roads are quite shunned and deserted at night, for no other reason than

occupied bedrooms, and on no account should one get out of bed in the dark, or walk about the rooms at night without slippers or shoes.

that a ghost is supposed to haunt the place. The most tempting bribe would not make a native walk alone over that road after sunset.

Besides the witchfinder, another important village functionary who relies much on muntras and charms, is the *Huddick*, or cow doctor. He is the only veterinary surgeon of the native when his cow or bullock dislocates or breaks a limb, or falls ill. The Huddick passes his hands over the affected part, and mutters his *muntras*, which have most probably descended to him from his father. Usually knowing a little of the anatomical structure of the animal, he may be able to reduce a dislocation, or roughly to set a fracture; but if the ailment be internal, a draught of mustard oil, or some pounded spices and turmeric, or neem leaves administered along with the *muntra*, are supposed to be all that human skill and science can do.

The natives are cruel to animals. Half-starved bullocks are shamefully overworked. When blows fail to make the ill-starred brute move, they give a twist and wrench to the tail, which must cause the animal exquisite torture, and unless the hapless beast be utterly exhausted, this generally induces it to make a further effort. Ploughmen very often deliberately make a raw open sore, one on each rump of the plough-bullock. They goad the poor wretch on this raw sore with a sharp-pointed stick when he lags, or when they think he needs stirring up. Ponies, too, are always worked far too young; and their miserable legs get frightfully twisted and bent. The petty shopkeepers, sellers of brass pots, grain, spices, and other bazaar wares, who attend the various bazaars, or weekly and bi-weekly markets, transport their goods by means of these ponies.

The packs of merchandise are slung on rough pack-saddles, made of coarse sacking. Shambling along with knees bent together, sores on every joint, and frequently an eye knocked out, the poor pony's back gets cruelly galled; when the bazaar is reached, he is hobbled as tightly as possible, the coarse ropes cutting into the flesh, and he is then turned adrift to contemplate starvation on the burnt-up grass. Great open sores form on the back, on which a plaster of moist clay, or cowdung and pounded leaves, is roughly put. The wretched creature gets worn to a skeleton. A little common care and cleanliness would put him right, with a little kindly consideration from his brutal master, but what does the *Kulwar* or *Bunneah* care? he is too lazy.

This unfeeling cruelty and callous indifference to the sufferings of the lower animals is a crying evil, and every magistrate, European, and educated native, might do much to ease their burdens. Tremendous numbers of bullocks and ponies die from sheer neglect and ill treatment every year. It is now becoming so serious a trouble, that in many villages plough-bullocks are too few in number for the area of land under cultivation. The tillage suffers, the crops deteriorate, this reacts on prices, the ryot sinks lower and lower, and gets more into the grasp of the rapacious money-lender. In many villages I have seen whole tracts of land relapsed into *purtee*, or untilled waste, simply from want of bullocks to draw the plough. Severe epidemics, like foot and mouth disease and pleuro, occasionally sweep off great numbers; but, I repeat, that annually the lives of hundreds of valuable animals are sacrificed by sheer sloth, dirt, inattention, and brutal cruelty.

In some parts of India, cattle poisoning for the sake

NATIVE CRUELTY TO ANIMALS.

of the hides is extensively practised. The *Chumars*, that is, the shoemakers, furriers, tanners, and workers in leather and skins generally, frequently combine together in places, and wilfully poison cattle and buffaloes. There is actually a section in the penal code taking cognisance of the crime. The Hindoo will not touch a dead carcase, so that when a bullock mysteriously sickens and dies, the *Chumars* haul away the body, and appropriate the skin. Some luckless witch is blamed for the misfortune, when the rascally Chumars themselves are all the while the real culprits. The police, however, are pretty successful in detecting this crime, and it is not now of such frequent occurrence [1].

Highly as the pious Hindoo venerates the sacred bull of Shira, his treatment of his mild patient beasts of burden is a foul blot on his character. Were you to shoot a cow, or were a Mussulman to wound a stray bullock which might have trespassed, and be trampling down his opium or his tobacco crop, and ruining his fields, the Hindoos would rise *en masse* to revenge the insult offered to their religion. Yet they scruple not to goad their bullocks, beat them, half starve them, and

---

[1] Somewhat analogous to this is the custom which used to be a common one in some parts of Behar. *Koombars* and *Grannés*, that is, tile-makers and thatchers, when trade was dull or rain impending, would scatter peas and grain in the interstices of the tiles on the houses of the well-to-do. The pigeons and crows, in their efforts to get at the peas, would loosen and perhaps overturn a few of the tiles. The granné would be sent for to replace these, would condemn the whole roof as leaky, and the tiles as old and unfit for use, and would provide a job for himself and the tile-maker, the nefarious profits of which they would share together.

Cultivators of thatching-grass have been known deliberately and wantonly to set fire to villages simply to raise the price of thatch and bamboo.

let their gaping wounds fester and become corrupt. When the poor brute becomes old and unable to work, and his worn-out teeth unfit to graze, he is ruthlessly turned out to die in a ditch, and be torn to pieces by jackals, kites, and vultures. The higher classes and well-to-do farmers show much consideration for high-priced well-conditioned animals, but when they get old or unwell, and demand redoubled care and attention, they are too often neglected, till, from sheer want of ordinary care, they rot and die.

CHAPTER VIII.

Our annual race meet.—The arrivals.—The camps.—The 'ordinary.'—The course.—'They're off.'—The race.—The steeple-chase.—Incidents of the meet.—The ball.

OUR annual Race Meet is the one great occasion of the year when all the dwellers in the district meet. Our races in Chumparun generally took place some time about Christmas. Long before the date fixed on, arrangements would be made for the exercise of hearty hospitality. The residents in the 'station' ask as many guests as will fill their houses, and their 'compounds' are crowded with tents, each holding a number of visitors, generally bachelors. The principal managers of the factories in the district, with their assistants, form a mess for the racing week, and, not unfrequently, one or two ladies lend their refining presence to the several camps. Friends from other districts, from up country, from Calcutta, gather together; and as the weather is bracing and cool, and every one determined to enjoy himself, the meet is one of the pleasantest of reunions. There are always several races specially got up for assistants' horses, and long before, the youngsters are up in the early morning, giving their favourite nag a spin across the zeraats, or seeing the groom lead him out swathed in clothing and bandages, to get him into training for the Assistants' race.

As the day draws near, great cases of tinned meats, hampers of beer and wine, and goodly supplies of all sorts are sent into the station to the various camps. Tents of snowy white canvas begin to peep out at you from among the trees. Great oblong booths of blue indigo sheeting show where the temporary stables for the horses are being erected; and at night the glittering of innumerable camp-fires betokens the presence of a whole army of grooms, grass-cutters, peons, watchmen, and other servants cooking their evening meal of rice, and discussing the chances of the horses of their respective masters in the approaching races. On the day before the first racing, the planters are up early, and in buggy, dogcart, or on horseback, singly, and by twos and threes, from all sides of the district, they find their way to the station. The Planter's Club is the general rendezvous. The first comers, having found out their waiting servants, and consigned the smoking steeds to their care, seat themselves in the verandah, and eagerly watch every fresh arrival.

Up comes a buggy. 'Hullo, who's this?'

'Oh, it's "Giblets!" How do you do, "Giblets," old man?'

Down jumps 'Giblets,' and a general handshaking ensues.

'Here comes "Boach" and the "Moonshee,"' yells out an observant youngster from the back verandah.

The venerable buggy of the esteemed 'Boach' approaches, and another jubilation takes place; the handshaking being so vigorous that the 'Moonshee's' spectacles nearly come to grief. Now the arrivals ride and drive up fast and furious.

'Hullo, "Anthony!"'

'Aha, "Charley," how d'ye do?'

'By Jove, "Ferdie," where have you turned up from?'

'Has the "Skipper" arrived?'
'Have any of you seen "Jamie?"'
'Where's big "Mars'" tents?'
'Have any of ye seen my "Bearer?"'
'Has the "Bump" come in?' and so on.

Such a scene of bustle and excitement. Friends meet that have not seen each other for a twelvemonth. Queries are exchanged as to absent friends. The chances of the meeting are discussed. Perhaps a passing allusion is made to some dear one who has left our ranks since last meet. All sorts of topics are started, and up till and during breakfast there is a regular medley of tongues, a confused clatter of voices, dishes, and glasses, a pervading atmosphere of dense curling volumes of tobacco smoke.

To a stranger the names sound uncouth and meaningless, the fact being, that we all go by nicknames [1].

'Giblets,' 'Diamond Digger,' 'Mangelwurzel,' 'Goggle-eyed Plover,' 'Gossein' or holy man, 'Blind Bartimeus,' 'Old Boots,' 'Polly,' 'Bottle-nosed Whale,' 'Fin Mac-Coul,' 'Daddy,' 'The Exquisite,' 'The Mosquito,' 'Wee Bob,' and 'Napoleon,' are only a very few specimens of this strange nomenclature. These soubriquets quite usurp our baptismal appellations, and I have often been called 'Maori,' by people who did not actually know my real name.

By the evening, all, barring the very late arrivals,

---

[1] In such a limited society every peculiarity is noted; all our antecedents are known; personal predilections and little foibles of character are marked; eccentricities are watched, and no one, let him be as uninteresting as a miller's pig, is allowed to escape observation and remark. Some little peculiarity is hit upon, and a strange but often very happily expressive nickname stamps one's individuality and photographs him with a word.

have found out their various camps. There is a merry dinner, then each sahib, well muffled in ulster, plaid, or great coat, hies him to the club, where the 'ordinary' is to be held. The nights are now cold and foggy, and a tremendous dew falls. At the 'ordinary,' fresh greetings between those who now meet for the first time after long separation. The entries and bets are made for the morrow's races, although not much betting takes place as a rule; but the lotteries on the different races are rapidly filled, the dice circulate cheerily, and amid laughing, joking, smoking, noise, and excitement, there is a good deal of mild speculation. The 'horsey' ones visit the stables for the last time; and each retires to his camp bed to dream of the morrow.

Very early, the respective *bearers* rouse the sleepy *sahibs*. Table servants rush hurriedly about the mess tent, bearing huge dishes of tempting viands. Grooms, and *grasscuts* are busy leading the horses off to the course. The cold raw fog of the morning fills every tent, and dim grey figures of cowering natives, wrapped up over the eyes in blankets, with moist blue noses and chattering teeth, are barely discernible in the thick mist.

The racecourse is two miles from the club, on the other side of the lake, in the middle of a grassy plain, with a neat masonry structure at the further side, which serves as a grand stand. Already buggies, dogcarts in single harness and tandem, barouches, and waggonettes are merrily rolling through the thick mist, past the frowning jail, and round the corner of the lake. Natives in gaudy coloured shawls, and blankets, are pouring on to the racecourse by hundreds.

Bullock carts, within which are black-eyed, bold beauties, profusely burdened with silver ornaments, are drawn up in lines. *Ekkas*—small jingling vehicles with a dome-shaped canopy and curtains at the sides—drawn by gaily caparisoned ponies, and containing fat, portly Baboos, jingle and rattle over the ruts on the side roads.

Sweetmeat sellers, with trays of horrible looking filth, made seemingly of insects, clarified butter, and sugar, dodge through the crowd dispensing their abominable looking but seemingly much relished wares. Tall policemen, with blue jackets, red puggries, yellow belts, and white trousers, stalk up and down with conscious dignity.

A madcap young assistant on his pony comes tearing along across country. The weighing for the first race is going on; horses are being saddled, some vicious brute occasionally lashing out, and scattering the crowd behind him. The ladies are seated round the terraced grand stand; long strings of horses are being led round and round in a circle, by the *syces*; vehicles of every description are lying round the building.

Suddenly a bugle sounds; the judge enters his box; the ever popular old 'Bikram,' who officiates as starter, ambles off on his white cob, and after him go half-a-dozen handsome young fellows, their silks rustling and flashing through the fast rising mist.

A hundred field-glasses scan the start; all is silent for a moment.

'They're off!' shout a dozen lungs.

'False start!' echo a dozen more.

The gay colours of the riders flicker confusedly in a jumble. One horse careers madly along for half the distance, is with difficulty pulled up, and is then walked slowly back.

The others left at the post fret, and fidget, and curvet about. At length they are again in line. Down goes the white flag! 'Good start!' shouts an excited planter. Down goes the red flag. 'Off at last!' breaks like a deep drawn sigh from the crowd, and now the six horses, all together, and at a rattling pace, tear up the hill, over the sand at the south corner, and up, till at the quarter mile post 'a blanket could cover the lot.'

Two or three tails are now showing signals of distress; heels and whips are going. Two horses have shot ahead, a bay and a black. 'Jamie' on the bay, 'Paddy' on the black.

Still as marble sit those splendid riders, the horses are neck and neck; now the bay by a nose, now again the black. The distance post is passed with a rush like a whirlwind.

'A dead heat, by Jove!'

'Paddy wins!' 'Jamie has it!' 'Hooray, Pat!' 'Go it, Jamie!' 'Well ridden!' A subdued hum runs round the excited spectators. The ardent racers are nose and nose. One swift, sharp cut, the cruel whip hisses through the air, and the black is fairly 'lifted in,' a winner by a nose. The ripple of conversation breaks out afresh. The band strikes up a lively air, and the saddling for the next race goes on.

The other races are much the same; there are lots of entries: the horses are in splendid condition, and the riding is superb. What is better, everything is emphatically 'on the square.' No *pulling* and *roping* here, no false entries, no dodging of any kind. Fine, gallant, English gentlemen meet each other in fair and honest emulation, and enjoy the favourite national sport in perfection. The 'Waler' race, for imported Australians, brings out fine, tall, strong-boned, clean-limbed horses, looking blood all over. The country breds, with slender limbs, small heads, and glossy coats, look dainty and delicate as antelopes. The lovely, compact Arabs, the pretty-looking ponies, and the thick-necked, coarse-looking Cabools, all have their respective trials, and then comes the great event—the race of the day—the Steeplechase.

The course is marked out behind the grand stand, following a wide circle outside the flat course, which it enters at the quarter-mile post, so that the finish is on the flat before the grand stand. The fences, ditches, and water leap, are all artificial, but they are regular *howlers*, and no make-believes.

Seven horses are despatched to a straggling start, and all negotiate the first bank safely. At the next fence a regular *snorter* of a 'post and rail'—topped with brushwood—two horses swerve, one rider being deposited on his racing seat upon mother earth, while the other sails away across country in a line for home, and is next heard of at the stables. The remaining five, three 'walers' and two country-breds, race together to the water jump, where one waler deposits his rider, and races home by himself, one country-bred refuses, and is henceforth out of the race, and the other three, taking the leap in beautiful style, put on racing pace to the next bank, and are in the air together. A lovely sight! The country is now stiff, and the stride of the waler tells. He is leading the country-breds a 'whacker,' but he stumbles and falls at the last fence but one from home. His gallant rider, the undaunted 'Roley,' remounts just as the two country-breds pass him like a flash of light. 'Nothing venture, nothing win,' however, so in go the spurs, and off darts the waler like an arrow in pursuit. He is gaining fast, and tops the last hurdle leading to the straight just as the hoofs of the other two reach the ground.

It is now a matter of pace and good riding. It will be a close finish; the waler is first to feel the whip; there is a roar from the crowd; he is actually leading; whips and spurs are hard at work now; it is a mad, headlong rush; every muscle is strained, and the utmost effort made; the poor horses are doing their very best; amid a thunder of hoofs, clouds of dust, hats in air, waving of handkerchiefs from the grand stand, and a truly British cheer from the paddock, the 'waler' shoots in half a length ahead; and so end the morning's races.

Back to camp now, to bathe and breakfast. A long line of dust marks the track from the course, for the sun is now high in the heavens, the lake is rippling in placid beauty under a gentle breeze, and the long lines of natives, as well as vehicles of all sorts, form a quaint but picturesque sight. After breakfast calls are made upon all the camps and bungalows round the station. Croquet, badminton, and other games go on until dinner-time. I could linger lovingly over a camp dinner; the rare dishes, the sparkling conversation, the racy anecdote, and the general jollity and brotherly feeling; but we must all dress for the ball, and so about 9 P.M. the buggies are again in requisition for the ball room—the fine, large, central apartment in the Planters' club.

The walls are festooned with flowers, gay curtains, flags, and cloths. The floor is shining like silver, and as polished as a mirror. The band strikes up the Blue Danube waltz, and amid the usual bustle, flirtation, scandal, whispering, glancing, dancing, tripping, sipping, and hand-squeezing, the ball goes gaily on till the stewards announce supper. At this—to the wall-flowers—welcome announcement, we adjourn from the heated ball-room to the cool arbour-like supper tent, where every delicacy that can charm the eye or tempt the appetite is spread out.

Next morning early we are out with the hounds, and enjoy a rattling burst round by the racecourse, where the horses are at exercise. Perchance we have heard of a boar in the sugar-cane, and away we go with beaters to rouse the grisly monster from his lair. In the afternoon there is hockey on horseback, or volunteer drill, with our gallant adjutant putting us through our evolutions. In the evening there is the usual drive, dinner, music, and the ordinary, and so the meet goes on. A constant succession of gaieties keeps everyone alive, till the time arrives for a return to our respective factories, and another year's hard work.

CHAPTER IX.

Pig-sticking in India.—Varieties of boar.—Their size and height.—Ingenious mode of capture by the natives.—The 'Batan' or buffalo herd.—Pigs charging.—Their courage and ferocity.—Destruction of game.—A close season for game.

THE sport *par excellence* of India is pig-sticking. Call it hog-hunting if you will, I prefer the honest old-fashioned name. With a good horse under one, a fair country, with not too many pitfalls, and 'lots of pig,' this sport becomes the most exciting that can be practised. Some prefer tiger shooting from elephants, others like to stalk the lordly ibex on the steep Himalayan slopes, but anyone who has ever enjoyed a rattle after a pig over a good country, will recall the fierce delight, the eager thrill, the wild, mad excitement, that flushed his whole frame, as he met the infuriate charge of a good thirty-inch fighting boar, and drove his trusty spear well home, laying low the gallant grey tusker, the indomitable, unconquerable grisly boar. The subject is well worn; and though the theme is a noble one, there are but few I fancy who have not read the record of some gallant fight, where the highest skill, the finest riding, the most undaunted pluck, and the cool, keen, daring of a practised hand are not *always* successful against the headlong rush and furious charge of a Bengal boar at bay.

A record of planter life in India, however, such as this aims at being, would be incomplete without some reference to the gallant tusker, and so at the risk of tiring my readers, I must try to describe a pig-sticking party.

There are two distinct kinds of boar in India, the black and the grey. Their dispositions are very different, the grey being fiercer and more pugnacious. He is a vicious and implacable foe when roused, and always shews better fight than the black variety. The great difference, however, is in the shape of the skull; that of the black fellow being high over the frontal bone, and not very long in proportion to height, while the skull of the grey boar is never very high, but is long, and receding in proportion to height.

The black boar grows to an enormous size, and the grey ones are, generally speaking, smaller made animals than the black. The young of the two also differ in at least one important particular; those of the grey pig are always born striped, but the young of the black variety are born of that colour, and are not striped but a uniform black colour throughout. The two kinds of pig sometimes interbreed, but crosses are not common; and, from the colour, size, shape of the head, and general behaviour, one can easily tell at a glance what kind of pig gets up before his spear, whether it is the heavy, sluggish black boar, or the veritable fiery, vicious, fighting grey tusker.

Many stories are told of their enormous size, and a 'forty-inch tusker' is the established standard for a Goliath among boars. The best fighting boars, however, range from twenty-eight to thirty-two inches in height, and I make bold to say that very few of the present generation of sportsmen have ever seen a veritable wild boar over thirty-eight inches high.

G. S., who has had perhaps as much jungle experience as any man of his age in India, a careful observer, and a finished sportsman, tells me that the biggest *boar* he ever saw was only thirty-eight inches high; while the biggest *pig* he ever killed was a barren sow, with three-inch tusks sticking out of her gums; she measured thirty-nine-and-a-half inches, and fought like a demon. I have shot pig—in heavy jungle where spearing was impracticable—over thirty-six inches high, but the biggest pig I ever stuck to my own spear was only twenty-eight inches, and I do not think any pig has been killed in Chumparun, within the last ten or a dozen years at any rate, over thirty-eight inches.

In some parts of India, where pigs are numerous and the jungle dense, the natives adopt a very ingenious mode of hunting. I have frequently seen it practised by the cowherds on the Koosee *derahs*, i.e. the flat swampy jungles on the banks of the Koosee. When the annual floods have subsided, leaving behind a thick deposit of mud, wrack, and brushwood, the long thick grass soon shoots up to an amazing height, and vast herds of cattle and tame buffaloes come down to the jungles from the interior of the country, where natural pasture is scarce. They are attended by the owner and his assistants, all generally belonging to the *gualla*, or cowherd caste, although, of course, there are other castes employed. The owner of the herd gets leave to graze his cattle in the jungle, by paying a certain fixed sum per head. He fixes on a high dry ridge of land, where he runs up a few grass huts for himself and men, and there he erects lines of grass and bamboo screens, behind which his cattle take shelter at night from the cold south-east wind. There are also a few huts of exceedingly frail construction for himself and his people. This small colony, in the midst of the universal jungle covering the country for miles round, is called a *batan*.

At earliest dawn the buffaloes are milked, and then with their attendant herdsmen they wend their way to the jungle, where they spend the day, and return again to the batan at night, when they are again milked. The milk is made into *ghee*, or clarified butter, and large quantities are sent down to the towns by country boats. When we want to get up a hunt, we generally send to the nearest *batan* for *khubber*, i. e. news, information. The *Batanea*, or proprietor of the establishment, is well posted up. Every herdsman as he comes in at night tells what animals he has seen through the day, and thus at the *batan* you hear where tiger, and pig, and deer are to be met with; where an unlucky cow has been killed; in what ravine is the thickest jungle; where the path is free from clay, or quicksand; what fords are safest; and, in short, you get complete information on every point connected with the jungle and its wild inhabitants.

To these men the mysterious jungle reveals its most hidden secrets. Surrounded by his herd of buffaloes, the *gualla* ventures into the darkest recesses and the most tangled thickets. They have strange wild calls by which they give each other notice of the approach of danger, and when two or three of them meet, each armed with his heavy, iron-shod or brass-bound *lathee* or quarter staff, they will not budge an inch out of their way for buffalo or boar; nay, they have been known to face the terrible tiger himself, and fairly beat him away from the quivering carcase of some unlucky member of their herd. They have generally some favourite buffalo on whose broad back they perch themselves, as it browses through the jungle, and from this elevated seat they survey the rest of the herd, and note the incidents of jungle life. When they wish a little excitement, or a change from their milk and rice diet, there are hundreds of pigs around.

They have a broad, sharp spear-head, to which is attached a stout cord, often made of twisted hide or hair. Into the socket of the spear is thrust a bamboo pole or shaft, tough, pliant, and flexible. The cord is wound round the spear and shaft, and the loose end is then fastened to the middle of the pole. Having thus prepared his weapon, the herdsman mounts his buffalo, and guides it slowly, warily, and cautiously to the haunts of the pig. These are, of course, quite accustomed to see the buffaloes grazing round them on all sides, and take no notice until the *gualla* is within striking distance. When he has got close up to the pig he fancies, he throws his spear with all his force. The pig naturally bounds off, the shaft comes out of the socket, leaving the spearhead sticking in the wound. The rope uncoils of itself, but being firmly fastened to the bamboo, it brings up the pig at each bush, and tears and lacerates the wound, until either the spearhead comes out, or the wretched pig drops down dead from exhaustion and loss of blood. The *gualla* follows upon his buffalo, and frequently finishes the pig with a few strokes of his *lathee*. In any case he gets his pork, and it certainly is an ingenious and bold way of procuring it.

Wild pig are very destructive to crops. During the night they revel in the cultivated fields contiguous to the jungle, and they destroy more by rooting up than by actually eating. It is common for the ryot to dig a shallow pit, and ensconce himself inside with his matchlock beside him. His head being on a level with the ground, he can discern any animal that comes between him and the sky-line. When a pig comes in sight, he waits till he is within sure distance, and then puts either a bullet or a charge of slugs into him.

The pig is perhaps the most stubborn and courageous animal in India. Even when pierced with several spears, and bleeding from numerous wounds, he preserves a sullen silence. He disdains to utter a cry of fear and pain, but maintains a bold front to the last, and dies with his face to the foe, defiant and unconquered. When hard pressed he scorns to continue his flight, but wheeling round, he makes a determined charge, very frequently to the utter discomfiture of his pursuer.

I have seen many a fine horse fearfully cut by a charging pig, and a determined boar over and over again break through a line of elephants, and make good his escape. There is no animal in all the vast jungle that the elephant dreads more than a lusty boar. I have seen elephants that would stand the repeated charges of a wounded tiger, turn tail and take to ignominious flight before the onset of an angry boar.

His thick short neck, ponderous body, and wedge-like head are admirably fitted for crashing through the thick jungle he inhabits, and when he has made up his mind to charge, very few animals can withstand his furious rush. Instances are quite common of his having made good his charge against a line of elephants, cutting and ripping more than one severely. He has been known to encounter successfully even the kingly tiger himself. Can it be wondered, then, that we consider him a 'foeman worthy of our steel'?

To be a good pig-sticker is a recommendation that wins acceptance everywhere in India. In a district like Chumparun where nearly every planter was an ardent sportsman, a good rider, and spent nearly half his time on horseback, pig-sticking was a favourite pastime. Every factory had at least one bit of likely jungle close by, where a pig could always be found. When I first went to India we used to take out our pig-spear over the *zillah* with us as a matter of course, as we never knew when we might hit on a boar.

Things are very different now. Cultivation has much increased. Many of the old jungles have been reclaimed, and I fancy many more pigs are shot by natives than formerly. A gun can be had now for a few rupees, and every loafing 'ne'er do weel' in the village manages to procure one, and wages indiscriminate warfare on bird and beast. It is a growing evil, and threatens the total extinction of sport in some districts. I can remember when nearly every tank was good for a few brace of mallard, duck, or teal, where never a feather is now to be seen, save the ubiquitous paddy-bird. Jungles, where a pig was a certain find, only now contain a measly jackal, and not always that; and cover in which partridge, quail, and sometimes even florican were numerous, are now only tenanted by the great ground-owl, or a colony of field rats. I am far from wishing to limit sport to the European community. I would let every native that so wished sport his double barrels or handle his spear with the best of us, but he should follow and indulge in his sport with reason. The breeding seasons of all animals should be respected, and there should be no indiscriminate slaughter of male and female, young and old. Until all true sportsmen in India unite in this matter, the evil will increase, and bye-and-bye there will be no animals left to afford sport of any kind.

There are cases where wild animals are so numerous and destructive that extraordinary measures have to be taken for protection from their ravages, but these are very rare. I remember having once to wage a war of extermination against a colony of pigs that had taken possession of some jungle lands near Maharjnugger, a village on the Koosee. I had a deal of indigo growing on cleared patches at intervals in the jungles, and there the pigs would root and revel in spite of watchmen, till at last I was forced in sheer self-defence to begin a crusade against them. We got a line of elephants, and two or three friends came to assist, and in one day, and round one village only, we shot sixty-three full grown pigs. The villagers must have killed and carried away nearly double that number of young and wounded. That was a very extreme case, and in a pure jungle country; but in settled districts like Tirhoot and Chumparun the weaker sex should always be spared, and a close season for winged game should be insisted on. To the credit of the planters be it said, that this necessity is quite recognised; but every pot-bellied native who can beg, borrow, or steal a gun, or in any way procure one, is constantly on the look out for a pot shot at some unlucky hen-partridge or quail. A whole village will turn out to compass the destruction of some wretched sow that may have shewn her bristles outside the jungle in the daytime.

In districts where cultivated land is scarce and population scattered, it is almost impossible to enjoy pig-sticking. The breaks of open land between the jungles are too small and narrow to afford galloping space, and though you turn the pig out of one patch of jungle, he immediately finds safe shelter in the next.

On the banks of some of the large rivers, however, such as the Gunduch and the Bagmuttee, there are vast stretches of undulating sand, crossed at intervals by narrow creeks, and spotted by patches of close, thick jungle. Here the grey tusker takes up his abode with his harem. When once you turn him out from his lair, there is grand hunting room before he can reach the distant patch of jungle to which he directs his flight. In some parts the *jowah* (a plant not unlike broom in appearance) is so thick, that even the elephants can scarcely force their way through, but as a rule the beating is pretty easy, and one is almost sure of a find.

CHAPTER X.

Kuderent jungle.—Charged by a pig.—The biter bit.—'Mac' after the big boar.—The horse for pig-sticking.—The line of beaters.—The boar breaks.—'Away! Away!'—First spear.—Pig-sticking at Peeprah.—The old 'lungra' or cripple.—A boar at bay.—Hurrah for pig-sticking!

THERE was a very fine pig jungle at a place called Kuderent, belonging to a wealthy landowner who went by the name of the Mudhobunny Baboo. We occasionally had a pig-sticking meet here, and as the jungle was strictly preserved, we were never disappointed in finding plenty who gave us glorious sport. The jungles consisted of great grass plains, with thickly wooded patches of dense tree jungle, intersected here and there by deep ravines, with stagnant pools of water at intervals; the steep sides all thickly clothed with thorny clusters of the wild dog-rose. It was a difficult country to beat, and we had always to supplement the usual gang of beaters with as many elephants as we could collect. In the centre of the jungle was an eminence of considerable height, whence there was a magnificent view of the surrounding country.

Far in the distance the giant Himalayas towered into the still clear air, the guardian barriers of an unknown land. The fretted pinnacles and tremendous ridges, clothed in their pure white mantle of everlasting snow, made a magnificent contrast to the dark, misty, wooded masses formed by the lower ranges of hills. In the early morning, when the first beams of the rising sun had but touched the mountain tops, leaving the country below shrouded in the dim mists and vapours of retiring night, the sight was most sublime. In presence of such hills and distances, such wondrous combinations of colour, scenery on such a gigantic scale, even the most thoughtless become impressed with the majesty of nature.

Our camp was pitched on the banks of a clear running mountain stream, brawling over rocks and boulders; and to eyes so long accustomed to the never ending flatness of the rich alluvial plains, and the terrible sameness of the rice swamps, the stream was a source of unalloyed pleasure. There were only a few places where the abrupt banks gave facilities for fording, and when a pig had broken fairly from the jungle, and was making for the river (as they very frequently did), you would see the cluster of horsemen scattering over the plain like a covey of partridges when the hawk swoops down upon them. Each made for what he considered the most eligible ford, in hopes of being first up with the pig on the further bank, and securing the much coveted first spear.

When a pig is hard pressed, and comes to any natural obstacle, as a ditch, bank, or stream, he almost invariably gets this obstacle between himself and his pursuer; then wheeling round he makes his stand, showing wonderful sagacity in choosing the moment of all others when he has his enemy at most disadvantage. Experienced hands are aware of this, and often try to outflank the boar, but the best men I have seen generally wait a little, till the pig is again under weigh, and then clearing the ditch or bank, put their horses at full speed, which is the best way to make good your attack. The rush of the boar is so sudden, fierce, and determined, that a horse at half speed, or going slow, has no chance of escape; but a well trained horse at full speed meets the pig in his rush, the spear is delivered with unerring aim, and slightly swerving to the left, you draw it out as you continue your course, and the poor pig is left weltering in his blood behind you.

On one occasion I was very rudely made aware of this trait. It was a fine fleet young boar we were after, and we had had a long chase, but were now overhauling him fast. I had a good horse under me, and 'Jamie' and 'Giblets' were riding neck and neck. There was a small mango orchard in front surrounded by the usual ditch and bank. It was nothing of a leap; the boar took it with ease, and we could just see him top the bank not twenty spear lengths ahead. I was slightly leading, and full of eager anxiety and emulation. Jamie called on me to pull up, but I was too excited to mind him. I saw him and Giblets each take an outward wheel about, and gallop off to catch the boar coming out of the cluster of trees on the far side, as I thought. I could not see him, but I made no doubt he was in full flight through the trees. There was plenty of riding room between the rows, so lifting my game little horse at the bank, I felt my heart bound with emulation as I thought I was certain to come up first, and take the spear from two such noted heroes as my companions. I came up with the pig first, sure enough. *He* was waiting for *me*, and scarce giving my horse time to recover his stride after the jump, he came rushing at me, every bristle erect, with a vicious grunt of spite and rage. My spear was useless, I had it crosswise on my horse's neck; I intended to attack first, and finding my enemy turning the tables on me in this way was rather disconcerting. I tried to turn aside and avoid the charge, but a branch caught me across the face, and knocked my *puggree* off. In a trice the savage little brute was on me. Leaping up fairly from the ground, he got the heel of my riding boot in his mouth, and tore off the sole from the boot as if it had been so much paper. Jamie and Giblets were sitting outside watching the scene, laughing at my discomfiture. Fortunately the boar had poor tusks, and my fine little horse was unhurt, but I got out of that orchard as fast as I could, and ever after hesitated about attacking a boar when he had got a bank or ditch between him and me, and was waiting for me on the other side. The far better plan is to wait till he sees you are not pressing him, he then goes off at a surly sling trot, and you can resume the chase with every advantage in your favour. When the blood however is fairly up, and all one's sporting instincts roused, it is hard to listen to the dictates of prudence or the suggestions of caution and experience.

The very same day we had another instance. My manager, 'Young Mac,' as we called him, had started a huge old boar. He was just over the boar, and about to deliver his thrust, when his horse stumbled in a rat hole (it was very rotten ground), and came floundering to earth, bringing his rider with him. Nothing daunted, Mac picked himself up, lost the horse, but so eager and excited was he, that he continued the chase on foot, calling to some of us to catch his horse while he stuck his boar. The old boar was quite blown, and took in the altered aspect of affairs at a glance; he turned to charge, and we loudly called on Mac to 'clear out.' Not a bit of it, he was too excited to realise his danger, but Pat fortunately interposed his horse and spear in time, and no doubt saved poor Mac from a gruesome mauling. It was very plucky, but it was very foolish, for heavily weighted with boots, breeches, spurs, and spear, a man could have no chance against the savage onset of an infuriated boar.

In the long thick grass with which the plain was covered the riding was very dangerous. I remember seeing six riders come signally to grief over a blind ditch in this jungle. It adds not a little to the excitement, and really serious accidents are not so common as might be imagined. It is no joke however when a riderless horse comes ranging up alongside of you as you are sailing along, intent on war; biting and kicking at your own horse, he spoils your sport, throws you out of the chase, and you are lucky if you do not receive some ugly cut or bruise from his too active heels. There is the great beauty of a well trained Arab or country-bred; if you get a spill, he waits beside you till you recover your faculties, and get your bellows again in working order; if you are riding a Cabool, or even a waler, it is even betting that he turns to bite or kick you as you lie, or he rattles off in pursuit of your more firmly seated friends, spoiling their sport, and causing the most fearful explosions of vituperative wrath.

There is something to me intensely exciting in all the varied incidents of a rattling burst across country after a fighting old grey boar. You see the long waving line of staves, and spear heads, and quaint shaped axes, glittering and fluctuating above the feathery tops of the swaying grass. There is an irregular line of stately elephants, each with its towering howdah and dusky mahout, moving slowly along through the rustling reeds. You hear the sharp report of fireworks, the rattling thunder of the big *doobla* or drum, and the ear-splitting clatter of innumerable *tom-toms*. Shouts, oaths, and cries from a hundred noisy coolies, come floating down in bursts of clamour on the soft morning air. The din waxes and wanes as the excited beaters descry a 'sounder' of pig ahead; with a mighty roar that makes your blood tingle, the frantic coolies rally for the final burst. Like rockets from a tube, the boar and his progeny come crashing through the brake, and separate before you on the plain. With a wild cheer you dash after them in hot pursuit; no time now to think of pitfalls, banks, or ditches; your gallant steed strains his every muscle, every sense is on the alert, but you see not the bush and brake and tangled thicket that you leave behind you. Your eye is on the dusky glistening hide and the stiff erect bristles in front; the shining tusks and foam-flecked chest are your goal, and the wild excitement culminates as you feel your keen steel go straight through muscle, bone, and sinew, and you know that another grisly monster has fallen. As you ease your girths and wipe your heated brow, you feel that few pleasures of the chase come up to the noblest, most thrilling sport of all, that of pig-sticking.

The plain is alive with shouting beaters hurrying up to secure the gory carcase of the slaughtered foe. A riderless horse is far away, making off alone for the distant grove, where the snowy tents are glistening through the foliage. On the distant horizon a small cluster of eager sportsmen are fast overhauling another luckless tusker, and enjoying in all their fierce excitement the same sensations you have just experienced. Now is the time to enjoy the soothing weed, and quaff the grateful 'peg'; and as the syces and other servants come up in groups of twos and threes, you listen with languid delight to all their remarks on the incidents of the chase; and as, with their acute Oriental imaginations they dilate in terms of truly Eastern exaggeration on your wonderful pluck and daring, you almost fancy yourself really the hero they would make you out to be.

Then the reunion round the festive board at night, when every one again lives through all the excitement of the day. Talk of fox-hunting after pig-sticking, it is like comparing a penny candle to a lighthouse, or a donkey race to the 'Grand National'!

Peeprah Factory with its many patches of jungle, its various lakes and fine undulating country, was another favourite rendezvous for the votaries of pig-sticking. The house itself was quite palatial, built on the bank of a lovely horseshoe lake, and embosomed in a grove of trees of great rarity and beautiful foliage. It had been built long before the days of overland routes and Suez canals, when a planter made India his home, and spared no trouble nor expense to make his home comfortable. In the great garden were fruit trees from almost every clime; little channels of solid masonry led water from the well to all parts of the garden. Leading down to the lake was a broad flight of steps, guarded on the one side by an immense peepul tree, whose hollow trunk and wide stretching canopy of foliage had braved the storms of over half a century, on the other side by a most symmetrical almond tree, which, when in blossom, was the most beautiful object for miles around. A well-kept shrubbery surrounded the house, and tall casuarinas, and glossy dark green india-rubber and bhur trees, formed a thousand combinations of shade and colour. Here we often met to experience the warm, large-hearted hospitality of dear old Pat and his gentle little wife. At one time there was a pack of harriers, which would lead us a fine, sharp burst by the thickets near the river after a doubling hare; but as a rule a meet at Peeprah portended death to the gallant tusker, for the jungles were full of pigs, and only honest hard work was meant when the Peeprah beaters turned out.

The whole country was covered with patches of grass and thorny jungle. Knowing they had another friendly cover close by, the pigs always broke at the first beat, and the riding had to be fast and furious if a spear was to be won. There were some nasty drop jumps, and deep, hidden ditches, and accidents were frequent. In one of these hot, sharp gallops poor 'Bonnie Morn,' a favourite horse belonging to 'Jamie,' was killed. Not seeing the ditch, it came with tremendous force against the bank, and of course its back was broken. Even in its death throes it recognised its master's voice, and turned round and licked his hand. We were all collected round, and let who will sneer, there were few dry eyes as we saw this last mute tribute of affection from the poor dying animal.

THE DEATH OF 'BONNIE MORN.'

Alas, my 'Brave Bonnie!' the pride of my heart,
The moment has come when from thee I must part;
No more wilt thou hark to the huntsman's glad horn,
My brave little Arab, my poor 'Bonnie Morn.'

How proudly you bore me at bright break of day,
How gallantly 'led,' when the boar broke away!
But no more, alas! thou the hunt shall adorn,
For now thou art dying, my dear 'Bonnie Morn.'

He'd neigh with delight when I'd enter his stall,
And canter up gladly on hearing my call;
Rub his head on my shoulder while munching his corn,
My dear gentle Arab, my poor 'Bonnie Morn.'

Or out in the grass, when a pig was in view,
None so eager to start, when he heard a 'halloo';
Off, off like a flash, the ground spurning with scorn,
He aye led the van, did my brave 'Bonnie Morn.'

O'er *nullah* and ditch, o'er hedge, fence, or bank,
No matter, *he'd* clear it, aye in the front rank;
A brave little hunter as ever was born
Was my grand Arab fav'rite, my good 'Bonnie Morn.'

Or when in the 'ranks,' who so steady and still?
None better than 'Bonnie,' more 'up' in his drill;
His fine head erect—eyes flashing with scorn—
Right fit for a charger was staunch 'Bonnie Morn.'

And then on the 'Course,' who so willing and true?
Past the 'stand' like an arrow the bonnie horse flew;
No spur his good rider need ever have worn,
For he aye did his best, did my fleet 'Bonnie Morn.'

And now here he lies, the good little horse,
No more he'll career in the hunt or on 'course':
Such a charger to lose makes me sad and forlorn;
I *can't* help a tear, 'tis for poor 'Bonnie Morn.'

Ah! blame not my grief, for 'tis deep and sincere,
As a friend and companion I held 'Bonnie' dear;
No true sportsman ever such feelings will scorn
As I heave a deep sigh for my brave 'Bonnie Morn.'

And even in death, when in anguish he lay,
When his life's blood was drip—dripping—slowly away,
His last thought was still of the master he'd borne;
He neighed, licked my hand—and thus died 'Bonnie Morn.'

One tremendous old boar was killed here during one of our meets, which was long celebrated in our after-dinner talks on boars and hunting. It was called 'THE LUNGRA,' which means the cripple, because it had been wounded in the leg in some previous encounter, perhaps in its hot youth, before age had stiffened its joints and tinged its whiskers with grey. It was the most undaunted pig I have ever seen. It would not budge an inch for the beaters, and charged the elephants time after time, sending them flying from the jungle most ignominiously. At length its patience becoming exhausted, it slowly emerged from the jungle, coolly surveyed the scene and its surroundings, and then, disdaining flight, charged straight at the nearest horseman. Its hide was as tough as a Highland targe, and though L. delivered his spear, it turned the weapon aside as if it was merely a thrust from a wooden pole. The old *lungra* made good his charge, and ripped L's. horse on the shoulder. It next charged Pat, and ripped his horse, and cut another horse, a valuable black waler, across the knee, laming it for life. Rider after rider charged down upon the fierce old brute. Although repeatedly wounded none of the thrusts were very serious, and already it had put five horses *hors de combat*. It now took up a position under a big 'bhur' tree, close to some water, and while the boldest of us held back for a little, it took a deliberate mud bath under our very noses. Doubtless feeling much refreshed, it again took up its position under the tree, ready to face each fresh assailant, full of fight, and determined to die but not to yield an inch.

Time after time we rode at the dauntless cripple. Each time he charged right down, and our spears made little mark upon his toughened hide. Our horses too were getting tired of such a customer, and little inclined to face his charge. At length 'Jamie' delivered a lucky spear and the grey old warrior fell. It had kept us at bay for fully an hour and a half, and among our number we reckoned some of the best riders and boldest pig-stickers in the district.

Such was our sport in those good old days. Our meets came but seldom, so that sport never interfered with the interests of honest hard work; but meeting each other as we did, and engaging in exciting sport like pig-sticking, cemented our friendship, kept us in health, and encouraged all the hardy tendencies of our nature. It whetted our appetites, it roused all those robust virtues that have made Englishmen the men they are, it sent us back to work with lighter hearts and renewed energy. It built up many happy, cherished memories of kindly words and looks and deeds, that will only fade when we in turn have to bow before the hunter, and render up our spirits to God who gave them. Long live honest, hearty, true sportsmen, such as were the friends of those happy days. Long may Indian sportsmen find plenty of 'foemen worthy of their steel' in the old grey boar, the fighting tusker of Bengal.

Pig-stickers.

CHAPTER XI.

The sal forests.—The jungle goddess.—The trees in the jungle.—Appearance of the forests.—Birds.—Varieties of parrots.—A 'beat' in the forest.—The 'shekarry.'—Mehrman Singh and his gun.—The Banturs, a jungle tribe of wood-cutters.—Their habits.—A village feast.—We beat for deer.—Habits of the spotted deer.—Waiting for the game.—Mehrman Singh gets drunk.—Our bag.—Pea-fowl and their habits.—How to shoot them.—Curious custom of the Nepaulese.—How Juggroo was tricked, and his revenge.

TIRHOOT is too generally under cultivation and too thickly inhabited for much land to remain under jungle, and except the wild pig of which I have spoken, and many varieties of wild fowl, there is little game to be met with. It is, however, different in North Bhaugulpore, where there are still vast tracts of forest jungle, the haunt of the spotted deer, nilghau, leopard, wolf, and other wild animals. Along the banks of the Koosee, a rapid mountain river that rolls its flood through numerous channels to join the Ganges, there are immense tracts of uncultivated land covered with tall elephant grass, and giving cover to tigers, hog deer, pig, wild buffalo, and even an occasional rhinoceros, to say nothing of smaller game and wildfowl, which are very plentiful.

The sal forests in North Bhaugulpore generally keep to the high ridges, which are composed of a light, sandy soil, very friable, and not very fertile, except for oil and indigo seeds, which grow most luxuriantly wherever the forest land has been cleared. In the shallow valleys which lie between the ridges rice is chiefly cultivated, and gives large returns. The sal forests have been sadly thinned by unscientific and indiscriminate cutting, and very few fine trees now remain. The earth is teeming with insects, chief amongst which are the dreaded and destructive white ants. The high pointed nests of these destructive insects, formed of hardened mud, are the commonest objects one meets with in these forest solitudes.

At intervals, beneath some wide-spreading peepul or bhur tree, one comes on a rude forest shrine, daubed all over with red paint, and with gaudy festoons of imitation flowers, cut from the pith of the plantain tree, hanging on every surrounding bough. These shrines are sacred to *Chumpa buttee*, the Hindoo Diana, protectress of herds, deer, buffaloes, huntsmen, and herdsmen. She is the recognised jungle goddess, and is held in great veneration by all the wild tribes and half-civilized denizens of the gloomy sal jungle.

The general colour of the forest is a dingy green, save when a deeper shade here and there shows where the mighty bhur uprears its towering height, or where the crimson flowers of the *seemul* or cotton tree, and the bronze-coloured foliage of the *sunpul* (a tree very like the ornamental beech in shrubberies at home) imparts a more varied colour to the generally pervading dark green of the universal sal.

The varieties of trees are of course almost innumerable, but the sal is so out of all proportion more numerous than any other kind, that the forests well deserve their recognised name. The sal is a fine, hard wood of very slow growth. The leaves are broad and glistening, and in spring are beautifully tipped with a reddish bronze, which gradually tones down into the dingy green which is the prevailing tint. The *sheshum* or *sissoo*, a tree with bright green leaves much resembling the birch, the wood of which is invaluable for cart wheels and such-like work, is occasionally met with. There is the *kormbhe*, a very tough wood with a red stringy bark, of which the jungle men make a kind of touchwood for their matchlocks, and the *parass*, whose peculiarity is that at times it bursts into a wondrous wealth of bright crimson blossom without a leaf being on the tree. The *parass* tree in full bloom is gorgeous. After the blossom falls the dark-green leaves come out, and are not much different in colour from the sal. Then there is the *mhowa*, with its lovely white blossoms, from which a strong spirit is distilled, and on which the deer, pigs, and wild bear love to feast. The peculiar sickly smell of the *mhowa* when in flower pervades the atmosphere for a great distance round, and reminds one forcibly of the peculiar sweet, sickly smell of a brewery. The hill *sirres* is a tall feathery-looking tree of most elegant shape, towering above the other forest trees, and the natives strip it of its bark, which they use to poison streams. It seems to have some narcotic or poisonous principle, easily soluble in water, for when put in any quantity in a stream or piece of water, it causes all the fish to become apparently paralyzed and rise to the surface, where they float about quite stupified and helpless, and become an easy prey to the poaching 'Banturs' and 'Moosahurs' who adopt this wretched mode of fishing.

Along the banks of the streams vegetation gets very luxurious, and among the thick undergrowth are found some lovely ferns, broad-leaved plants, and flowers of every hue, all alike nearly scentless. Here is no odorous breath of violet or honeysuckle, no delicate perfume of primrose or sweetbriar, only a musty, dank, earthy smell which gets more and more pronounced as the mists rise along with the deadly vapours of the night. Sleeping in these forests is very unhealthy. There is a most fatal miasma all through the year, less during the hot months, but very bad during and immediately after the annual rains; and in September and October nearly every soul in the jungly tracts is smitten with fever. The vapour only rises to a certain height above the ground, and at the elevation of ten feet or so, I believe one could sleep in the jungles with impunity; but it is dangerous at all times to sleep in the forest, unless at a considerable elevation. The absence of all those delicious smells which make a walk through the woodlands at home so delightful, is conspicuous in the sal forests, and another of the most noticeable features is the extreme silence, the oppressive stillness that reigns.

You know how full of melody is an English wood, when thrush, blackbird, mavis, linnet, and a thousand warblers flit from tree to tree. How the choir rings out its full anthem of sweetest sound, till every bush and tree seems a centre of sweet strains, soft, low, liquid trills, and full ripe gushes of melody and song. But it is not thus in an Indian forest. There are actually few birds. As you brush through the long grass and trample the tangled undergrowth, putting aside the sprawling branches, or dodging under the pliant arms of the creepers, you may flush a black or grey partridge, raise a covey of quail, or startle a quiet family party of peafowl, but there are no sweet singers flitting about to make the vaulted arcades of the forest echo to their music.

The hornbill darts with a succession of long bounding flights from one tall tree to another. The large woodpecker taps a hollow tree close by, his gorgeous plumage glistening like a mimic rainbow in the sun. A flight of green parrots sweep screaming above your head, the *golden oriole* or mango bird, the *koel*, with here and there a red-tufted *bulbul*, make a faint attempt at a chirrup; but as a rule the deep silence is unbroken, save by the melancholy hoot of some blinking owl, and the soft monotonous coo of the ringdove or the green pigeon. The exquisite honey-sucker, as delicately formed as the petal of a fairy flower, flits noiselessly about from blossom to blossom. The natives call it the 'Muddpenah' or drinker of honey. There are innumerable butterflies of graceful shape and gorgeous colours; what few birds there are have beautiful plumage; there is a faint rustle of leaves, a faint, far hum of insect life; but it feels so silent, so unlike the woods at home. You are oppressed by the solemn stillness, and feel almost nervous as you push warily along, for at any moment a leopard, wolf, or hyena may get up before you, or you may disturb the siesta of a sounder of pig, or a herd of deer.

Up in those forests on the borders of Nepaul, which are called the *morung*, there are a great many varieties of parrot, all of them very beautiful. There is first the common green parrot, with a red beak, and a circle of salmon-coloured feathers round its neck; they are very noisy and destructive, and flock together to the fields where they do great damage to the crops. The *lutkun sooga* is an exquisitely-coloured bird, about the size of a sparrow. The *ghurāl*, a large red and green parrot, with a crimson beak. The *tota* a yellowish-green colour, and the male with a breast as red as blood; they call it the *amereet bhela*. Another lovely little parrot, the *taeteea sooga*, has a green body, red head, and black throat; but the most showy and brilliant of all the tribe is the *putsoogee*. The body is a rich living green, red wings, yellow beak, and black throat; there is a tuft of vivid red as a topknot, and the tail is a brilliant blue; the under feathers of the tail being a pure snowy white.

At times the silence is broken by a loud, metallic, bell-like cry, very like the yodel you hear in the Alps. You hear it rise sharp and distinct, 'Looralei!' and as suddenly cease. This is the cry of the *kookoor ghēt*, a bird not unlike a small pheasant, with a reddish-brown back and a fawn-coloured breast. The *sherra* is another green parrot, a little larger than the *putsoogee*, but not so beautifully coloured.

There is generally a green, slime-covered, sluggish stream in all these forests, its channel choked with rotting leaves and decaying vegetable matter. The water should never be drunk until it has been boiled and filtered. At intervals the stream opens out and forms a clear rush-fringed pool, and the trees receding on either bank leave a lovely grassy glade, where the deer and nilghau come to drink. On the glassy bosom of the pool in the centre, fine duck, mallard, and teal, can frequently be found, and the rushes round the margin are to a certainty good for a couple of brace of snipe.

Sometimes on a withered branch overhanging the stream, you can see perched the *ahur*, or great black fish-hawk. It has a grating, discordant cry, which it utters at intervals as it sits pluming its black feathers above the pool. The dark ibis and the ubiquitous paddy-bird are of course also found here; and where the land is low and marshy, and the stream crawls along through several channels, you are sure to come across a couple of red-headed *sarus*, serpent birds, a crane, and a solitary heron. The *moosahernee* is a black and white bird, I fancy a sort of ibis, and is good eating. The *dokahur* is another fine big bird, black body and white wings, and as its name (derived from *dokha*, a shell) implies, it is the shell-gatherer, or snail-eater, and gives good shooting.

When you have determined to beat the forest, you first get your coolies and villagers assembled, and send them some mile or two miles ahead, under charge of some of the head men, to beat the jungle towards you, while you look out for a likely spot, shady, concealed, and cool, where you wait with your guns till the game is driven up to you. The whole arrangements are generally made, of course under your own supervision, by your *Shekarry*, or gamekeeper, as I suppose you might call him. He is generally a thin, wiry, silent man, well versed in all the lore of the woods, acquainted with the name, appearance, and habits of every bird and beast in the forest. He knows their haunts and when they are to be found at home. He will track a wounded deer like a bloodhound, and can tell the signs and almost impalpable evidences of an animal's whereabouts, the knowledge of which goes to make up the genuine hunter.

When all is still around, and only the distant shouts of the beaters fall faintly at intervals on the ear, his keen hearing detects the light patter of hoof or paw on the crisp, withered leaves. His hawk-like glance can pick out from the deepest shade the sleek coat or hide of the leopard or the deer; and even before the animal has come in sight, his senses tell him whether it is young or old, whether it is alarmed, or walking in blind confidence. In fact, I have known a good shekarry tell you exactly what animal is coming, whether bear, leopard, fox, deer, pig, or monkey.

The best shekarry I ever had was a Nepaulee called 'Mehrman Singh.' He had the regular Tartar physiognomy of the Nepaulese. Small, oblique, twinkling eyes, high cheekbones, flattish nose, and scanty moustache. He was a tall, wiry man, with a remarkably light springy step, a bold erect carriage, and was altogether a fine, manly, independent fellow. He had none of the fawning obsequiousness which is so common to the Hindoo, but was a merry laughing fellow, with a keen love of sport and a great appreciation of humour. His gun was fearfully and wonderfully made. It was a long, heavy flint gun, with a tremendously heavy barrel, and the stock all splices and splinters, tied in places with bits of string. I would rather not have been in the immediate vicinity of the weapon when he fired it, and yet he contrived to do some good shooting with it.

He was wonderfully patient in stalking an animal or waiting for its near approach, as he never ventured on a long shot, and did not understand our objection to pot-shooting. His shot was composed of jagged little bits of iron, chipped from an old *kunthee*, or cooking-pot; and his powder was truly unique, being like lumps of charcoal, about the size of small raisins. A shekarry fills about four or five fingers' depth of this into his gun, then a handful of old iron, and with a little touch of English powder pricked in with a pin as priming, he is ready for execution on any game that may come within reach of a safe pot-shot. When the gun goes off there is a mighty splutter, a roar like that of a small cannon, and the slugs go hurtling through the bushes, carrying away twigs and leaves, and not unfrequently smashing up the game so that it is almost useless for the table.

The *Banturs*, who principally inhabit these jungles, are mostly of Nepaulese origin. They are a sturdy, independent people, and the women have fair skins, and are very pretty. Unchastity is very rare, and the infidelity of a wife is almost unknown. If it is found out, mutilation and often death are the penalties exacted from the unfortunate woman. They wear one long loose flowing garment, much like the skirt of a gown; this is tightly twisted round the body above the bosoms, leaving the neck and arms quite bare. They are fond of ornaments—nose, ears, toes and arms, and even ancles, being loaded with silver rings and circlets. Some decorate their nose and the middle parting of the hair with a greasy-looking red pigment, while nearly every grown-up woman has her arms, neck, and low down on the collar bone most artistically tattooed in a variety of close, elaborate patterns. The women all work in the clearings; sowing, and weeding, and reaping the rice, barley, and other crops. They do most of the digging where that is necessary, the men confining themselves to ploughing and wood-cutting. At the latter employment they are most expert; they use the axe in the most masterly manner, but their mode of cutting is fearfully wasteful; they always leave some three feet of the best part of the wood in the ground, very rarely cutting a tree close down to the root. Many of them are good charcoal-burners, and indeed their principal occupation is supplying the adjacent villages with charcoal and firewood. They use small narrow-edged axes for felling, but for lopping they invariably use the Nepaulese national weapon—the *kookree*. This is a heavy, curved knife, with a broad blade, the edge very sharp, and the back thick and heavy. In using it they slash right and left with a quick downward stroke, drawing the blade quickly toward them as they strike. They are wonderfully dexterous with the *kookree*, and will clear away brush and underwood almost as quickly as a man can walk. They pack their charcoal, rice, or other commodities, in long narrow baskets, which they sling on a pole carried on their shoulders, as we see the Chinese doing in the well known pictures on tea-chests. They are all Hindoos in religion, but are very fond of rice-whiskey. Although not so abstemious in this respect as the Hindoos of the plains, they are a much finer race both physically and morally. As a rule they are truthful, honest, brave, and independent. They are always glad to see you, laugh out merrily at you as you pass, and are wonderfully hospitable. It would be a nice point for Sir Wilfrid Lawson to reconcile the use of rice-whiskey with this marked superiority in all moral virtues in the whiskey-drinking, as against the totally-abstaining Hindoo.

To return to Mehrman Singh. His face was seamed with smallpox marks, and he had seven or eight black patches on it the first time I saw him, caused by the splintering of his flint when he let off his antediluvian gun. When he saw my breechloaders, the first he had ever beheld, his admiration was unbounded. He told me he had come on a leopard asleep in the forest one day, and crept up quite close to him. His faith in his old gun, however, was not so lively as to make him rashly attack so dangerous a customer, so he told me. 'Hum usko jans deydea oos wukt,' that is, 'I *gave* the brute its life that time, but,' he continued, 'had I had an English gun like this, your honour,

I

I would have blown the *soor* (*Anglice*, pig) to hell.' Old Mehrman was rather strong in his expletives at times, but I was not a little amused at the cool way he spoke of *giving* the leopard its life. The probability is, that had he only wounded the animal, he would have lost his own.

These Nepaulese are very fond of giving feasts to each other. Their dinner-parties, I assure you, are very often 'great affairs.' They are not mean in their arrangements, and the wants of the inner man are very amply provided for. Their crockery is simple and inexpensive. When the feast is prepared, each guest provides himself with a few broad leaves from the nearest sal tree, and forming these into a cup, he pins them together with thorns from the acacia. Squatting down in a circle, with half-a-dozen of these sylvan cups around, the attendant fills one with rice, another with *dhall*, a third with goat's-flesh, a fourth with *turkaree* or vegetables, a fifth with chutnee, pickle, or some kind of preserve. Curds, ghee, a little oil perhaps, sugar, plantains, and other fruit are not wanting, and the whole is washed down with copious draughts of fiery rice-whiskey, or where it can be procured, with palm-toddy. Not unfrequently dancing boys or girls are in attendance, and the horrid din of tom-toms, cymbals, a squeaking fiddle, or a twanging sitar, rattling castanets, and ear-piercing songs from the dusky *prima donna*, makes night hideous, until the grey dawn peeps over the dark forest line.

Early in January, 1875, my camp was at a place in the sal jungles called Lohurneah. I had been collecting rents and looking after my seed cultivation, and Pat and our sporting District Engineer having joined me, we determined to have a beat for deer.

Mehrman Singh had reported numerous herds in the vicinity of our camp. During the night we had been disturbed by the revellers at such a feast in the village as I have been describing. We had filled cartridges, seen to our guns, and made every preparation for the beat, and early in the morning the coolies and idlers of the forest villages all round were ranged in circles about our camp.

Swallowing a hasty breakfast we mounted our ponies, and followed by our ragged escort, made off for the forest. On the way we met a crowd of Banturs with bundles of stakes and great coils of strong heavy netting. Sending the coolies on ahead under charge of several headmen and peons, we plunged into the gloom of the forest, leaving our ponies and grooms outside. When we came to a likely-looking spot, the Banturs began operations by fixing up the nets on the stakes and between trees, till a line of strong net extended across the forest for several hundred yards. We then went ahead, leaving the nets behind us, and each took up his station about 200 yards in front. The men with the nets then hid themselves behind trees, and crouched in the underwood. With our kookries we cut down several branches, stuck them in the ground in front, and ensconced ourselves in this artificial shelter. Behind us, and between us and the nets, was a narrow cart track leading through the forest, and the reason of our taking this position was given me by Pat, who was an old hand at jungle shooting.

When deer are being driven, they are intensely suspicious, and of course frightened. They know every spot in the jungle, and are acquainted with all the paths, tracks, and open places in the forest. When they are nearing an open glade, or a road, they slacken their pace, and go slowly and warily forward, an old buck generally leading. When he has carefully reconnoitred and examined the suspected place in front, and found it clear to all appearance, they again put on the pace, and clear the open ground at their greatest speed. The best chance of a shot is when a path is in front of *them* and behind *you*, as then they are going slowly.

At first when I used to go out after them, I often got an open glade, or road, in *front* of me; but experience soon told me that Pat's plan was the best. As this was a beat not so much for real sport, as to show me how the villagers managed these affairs, we were all under Pat's direction, and he could not have chosen better ground. I was on the extreme left, behind a clump of young trees, with the sluggish muddy stream on my left. Our Engineer to my right was about one hundred yards off, and Pat himself on the extreme right, at about the same distance from H. Behind us was the road, and in the rear the long line of nets, with their concealed watchers. The nets are so set up on the stakes, that when an animal bounds along and touches the net, it falls over him, and ere he can extricate himself from its meshes, the vigilant Banturs rush out and despatch him with spears and clubs.

We waited a long time hearing nothing of the beaters, and watching the red and black ants hurrying to and fro. Huge green-bellied spiders oscillated backwards and forwards in their strong, systematically woven webs. A small mungoose kept peeping out at me from the roots of an old india-rubber tree, and aloft in the branches an amatory pair of hidden ringdoves were billing and cooing to each other. At this moment a stealthy step stole softly behind, and the next second Mr. Mehrman Singh crept quietly and noiselessly beside me, his face flushed with rapid walking, his eye flashing with excitement, his finger on his lip, and a look of portentous gravity and importance striving to spread itself over his speaking countenance. Mehrman had been up all night at the feast, and was as drunk as a piper. It was no use being angry with him, so I tried to keep him quiet and resumed my watch.

A few minutes afterwards he grasped me by the wrist, rather startling me, but in a low hoarse whisper warning me that a troop of monkeys was coming. I could not hear the faintest rustle, but sure enough in a minute or two a troop of over twenty monkeys came hopping and shambling along, stopping every now and then to sit on their hams, look back, grin, jabber, and show their formidable teeth, until Mehrman rose up, waved his cloth at them, and turned them off from the direction of the nets toward the bank of the stream.

Next came a fox, slouching warily and cautiously along; then a couple of lean, hungry-looking jackals; next a sharp patter on the crisp dry leaves, and several peafowl with resplendent plumage ran rapidly past. Another touch on the arm from Mehrman, and following the direction of his outstretched hand, I descried a splendid buck within thirty yards of me, his antlers and chest but barely visible above the brushwood. My gun was to my shoulder in an instant, but the shekarry in an excited whisper implored me not to fire. I hesitated, and just then the stately head turned round to look behind, and exposing the beautifully curving neck full to my aim, I fired, and had the satisfaction of seeing the fine buck topple over, seemingly hard hit.

A shot on my right, and two shots in rapid succession further on, shewed me that Pat and H. were also at work, and then the whole forest seemed alive with frightened, madly-plunging pig, deer, and other animals. I fired at, and wounded an enormous boar that came rushing past, and now the cries of the coolies in front as they came trooping on, mingled with the shouts of the men at the nets, where the work of death evidently was going on.

It was most exciting while it lasted, but, after all, I do not think it was honest sport. The only apology I could make to myself was, that the deer and pig were far too numerous, and doing immense damage to the crops, and if not thinned out, they would soon have made the growing of any crop whatever an impossibility.

The monkey being a sacred animal, is never molested by the natives, and the damage he does in a night to a crop of wheat or barley is astonishing. Peafowl too are very destructive, and what with these and the ravages of pig, deer, hares, and other plunderers, the poor ryot has to watch many a weary night, to secure any return from his fields.

On rejoining each other at the nets, we found that five deer and two pigs had been killed. Pat had shot a boar and a porcupine, the latter with No. 4 shot. H. accounted for a deer, and I got my buck and the boar which I had wounded in the chest; Mehrman Singh had followed him up and tracked him to the river, where he took refuge among some long swamp reeds. Replying to his call, we went up, and a shot through the head settled the old boar for ever. Our bag was therefore for the first beat, seven deer, four pigs, and a porcupine.

The coolies were now sent away out of the jungle, and on ahead for a mile or so, the nets were coiled up, our ponies regained, and off we set, to take another station. As we went along the river bank, frequently having to force our way through thick jungle, we started 'no end' of peafowl, and getting down we soon added a couple to the bag. Pat got a fine jack snipe, and I shot a *Jheela*, a very fine waterfowl with brown plumage, having a strong metallic, coppery lustre on the back, and a steely dark blue breast. The plumage was very thick and glossy, and it proved afterwards to be excellent eating.

Peafowl generally retire to the thickest part of the jungles during the heat of the day, but if you go out very early, when they are slowly wending their way back from the fields, where they have been revelling all night, you can shoot numbers of them. I used to go about twenty or thirty yards into the jungle, and walk slowly along, keeping that distance from the edge. My syce and pony would then walk slowly by the edges of the fields, and when the syce saw a peafowl ahead, making for the jungle, he would shout and try to make it rise. He generally succeeded, and as I was a little in advance and concealed by the jungle, I would get a fine shot as the bird flew overhead. I have shot as many as eight and ten in a morning in this way. I always used No. 4 shot with about $3\frac{1}{2}$ drams of powder.

Unless hard hit peafowl will often get away; they run with amazing swiftness, and in the heart of the jungle it is almost impossible to make them rise. A couple of sharp terriers, or a good retriever, will sometimes flush them, but the best way is to go along the edge of the jungle in the early morn, as I have described. The peachicks, about seven or eight months old, are deliciously tender and well flavoured. Old birds are very dry and tough, and require a great deal of that old-fashioned sauce, Hunger.

The common name for a peafowl is *mōr*, but the Nepaulese and Banturs call it *majoor*. Now *majoor* also means coolie, and a young fellow, S., was horrified one day hearing his attendant in the jungle telling him in the most excited way, '*Majoor, majoor,* Sahib; why don't you fire?' Poor S. thought it was a coolie the man meant, and that he must be going mad, wanting him to shoot a coolie, but he found out his mistake, and learnt the double meaning of the word, when he got home and consulted his *manager*.

The generic name for all deer is in Hindustani HURIN, but the Nepaulese call it CHEETER. The male spotted deer they call KUBRA, the female KUBREE. These spotted deer keep almost exclusively to the forests, and are very seldom found far away from the friendly cover of the sal woods. They are the most handsome, graceful looking animals I know, their skins beautifully marked with white spots, and the horns wide and arching. When properly prepared the skin makes a beautiful mat for a drawing room, and the horns of a good buck are a handsome ornament to the hall or the verandah. When bounding along through the forest, his beautifully spotted skin flashing through the dark green foliage, his antlers laid back over his withers, he looks the very embodiment of grace and swiftness. He is very timid, and not easily stalked.

In March and April, when a strong west wind is blowing, it rustles the myriads of leaves that, dry as tinder, encumber the earth. This perpetual rustle prevents the deer from hearing the footsteps of an approaching foe. They generally betake themselves then to some patch of grass, or long-crop outside the jungle altogether, and if you want them in those months, it is in such places, and not inside the forest at all, that you must search. Like all the deer tribe, they are very curious, and a bit of rag tied to a tree, or a cloth put over a bush, will not unfrequently entice them within range.

Old shekarries will tell you that as long as the deer go on feeding and flapping their ears, you may continue your approach. As soon as they throw up the head, and keep the ears still, their suspicions have been aroused, and if you want venison, you must be as still as a rock, till your game is again lulled into security. As soon as the ears begin flapping again, you may continue your stalk, but at the slightest noise, the noble buck will be off like a flash of lightning. You should never go out in the forest with white clothes, as you are then a conspicuous mark for all the prying eyes that are invisible to you. The best colour is dun brown, dark grey, or dark green. When you see a deer has become suspicious, and no cover is near, stand perfectly erect and rigid, and do not leave your legs apart. The 'forked-parsnip' formation of the 'human form divine' is detected at a glance, but there's just a chance that if your legs are drawn together, and you remain perfectly motionless, you may be mistaken for the stump of a tree, or at the best some less dangerous enemy than man.

As we rode slowly along, to allow the beaters to get ahead, and to let the heavily-laden men with the nets keep up with us, we were amused to hear the remarks of the syces and shekarries on the sport they had just witnessed. Pat's old man, Juggroo, a merry peep-eyed fellow, full of anecdote and humour, was rather hard on Mehrman Singh for having been up late the preceding night. Mehrman, whose head was by this time probably reminding him that there are 'lees to every cup,' did not seem to relish the humour. He began grasping one wrist with the other hand, working his hand slowly round his wrist, and I noticed that Juggroo immediately changed the subject. This, as I afterwards learned, is the invariable Nepaulese custom of showing anger. They grasp the wrist as I have said, and it is taken as a sign that, if you do not discontinue your banter, you will have a fight.

The Nepaulese are rather vain of their personal appearance, and hanker greatly after a good thick moustache. This, nature has denied them, for the hair on their faces is scanty and stubbly in the extreme. One day Juggroo saw his master putting some bandoline on his moustache, which was a fine, handsome, silky one. He asked Pat's bearer, an old rogue, what it was.

'Oh!' replied the bearer, 'that is the gum of the sal tree; master always uses that, and that is the reason he has such a fine moustache.'

Juggroo's imagination fired up at the idea.

'Will it make mine grow too?'

'Certainly.'

'How do you use it?'

'Just rub it on, as you see master do.'

Away went Juggroo to try the new recipe.

Now, the gum of the sal tree is a very strong resin, and hardens in water. It is almost impossible to get it off your skin, as the more water you use, the harder it gets.

Next day Juggroo's face presented a sorry sight. He had plentifully smeared the gum over his upper lip, so that when he washed his face, the gum *set*, making the lip as stiff as a board, and threatening to crack the skin every time the slightest muscle moved.

Juggroo *was* 'sold' and no mistake, but he bore it all in grim silence, although he never forgot the old bearer. One day, long after, he brought in some berries from the wood, and was munching them, seemingly with great relish. The bearer wanted to know what they were, Juggroo with much apparent *nonchalance* told him they were some very sweet, juicy, wild berries he had found in the forest. The bearer asked to try one.

Juggroo had *another* fruit ready, very much resembling those he was eating. It is filled with minute spikelets, or little hairy spinnacles, much resembling those found in ripe doghips at home. If these even touch the skin, they cause intense pain, stinging like nettles, and blistering every part they touch.

The unsuspicious bearer popped the treacherous berry into his mouth, gave it a crunch, and then with a howl of agony, spluttered and spat, while the tears ran down his cheeks, as he implored Juggroo by all the gods to fetch him some water.

Old Juggroo with a grim smile, walked coolly away, discharging a Parthian shaft, by telling him that these berries were very good for making the hair grow, and hoped he would soon have a good moustache.

A man from the village now came running up to tell us that there was a leopard in the jungle we were about to beat, and that it had seized, but failed to carry away, a dog from the village during the night. Natives are so apt to tell stories of this kind that at first we did not credit him, but turning into the village he showed us the poor dog, with great wounds on its neck and throat where the leopard had pounced upon it. The noise, it seems, had brought some herdsmen to the place, and their cries had frightened the leopard and saved the wretched dog. As the man said he could show us the spot where the leopard generally remained, we determined to beat him up; so sending a man off on horseback for the beaters to slightly alter their intended line of beat, we rode off, attended by the villager, to get behind the leopard's lair, and see if we could not secure him. These fierce and courageous brutes, for they are both, are very common in the sal jungles; and as I have seen several killed, both in Bhaugulpore and Oudh, I must devote a chapter to the subject.

CHAPTER XII.

The leopard.—How to shoot him.—Gallant encounter with a wounded one.—Encounter with a leopard in a dak bungalow.—Pat shoots two leopards.—Effects of the Express bullet.—The 'Sirwah Purrul,' or annual festival of huntsmen.—The Hindoo ryot.—Rice-planting and harvest.—Poverty of the ryot.—His apathy.—Village fires.—Want of sanitation.

WRITING principally for friends at home, who are not familiar with Indian life, I must narrate facts that, although well known in Indian circles, are yet new to the general reader in England. My object is of course to represent the life we lead in the far East, and to give a series of pictures of what is going on there. If I occasionally touch on what may to Indian readers seem well-worn ground, they will forgive me.

The leopard then, as a rule keeps to the wooded parts of India. In the long grassy jungles bordering the Koosee he is not generally met with. He is essentially a predatory animal, always on the outlook for a meal; round the villages, nestling amid their sal forests, he is continually on the prowl, looking out for a goat, a calf, or unwary dog. His appearance and habits are well known; he generally selects for his lair, a retired spot surrounded by dense jungle. The one we were after now had his home in a matted jungle, growing out of a pool of water, which had collected in a long hollow, forming the receptacle of the surface drainage from the adjacent slopes. This hollow stretched for miles towards the creek which we had been beating up; and the locality having moisture and other concurring elements in its favour, the vegetation had attained a luxuriance rarely seen in the dry uplands, where the west winds lick up the moisture, and the soil is arid and unpromising. The matted intertwining branches of the creepers had formed an almost impervious screen, and on the basis thus formed, amid the branches and creepers, the leopards had formed their lair. Beneath, was a still stagnant pool; above, was the leafy foliage. The tracks led down to a well-worn path.

Climbing like a cat, as the leopards can do, they found no difficulty in gaining a footing on the mass of vegetation. They generally select some retired spot like this, and are very seldom seen in the daytime. With the approach of night, however, they begin their wandering in quest of prey. In a beat such as we were having 'all is fish that comes to the net,' and leopards, if they are in the jungle, have to yield to the advance of the beaters, like the other denizens of the forest.

Experience tells you that the leopard is daring and ferocious. Old experienced hands warn you, that unless you can make sure of your shot, it is unwise to fire at a leopard approaching. It is better to wait till he has got past you, or at all events is 'broadside on.' If you only wound him as he is approaching, he will almost to a certainty make straight at you, but if you shoot him as he is going past, he will, maddened by pain and anger, go straight forward, and you escape his charge. He is more courageous than a tiger, and a very dangerous customer at close quarters. Up in one of the forests in Oudh, a friend of mine was out one day after leopard, with a companion who belonged to the forest department. My friend's companion fired at a leopard as it was approaching him, and wounded it severely. Nothing daunted, and recognising whence its hurt had come, it charged directly down on the concealed sportsman, and before he could half realise the position, sprang on him, caught his left arm in its teeth, and began mauling him with its claws. His presence of mind did not desert him; noticing close by the stump of a sal tree, that had been eaten by white ants till the harder parts of the wood alone remained, standing up hard and sharp like so many spikes of steel; and knowing that the leopard was already badly wounded, and in all probability struggling for his life, he managed to drag the struggling animal up to the stump; jammed his left arm yet further into the open mouth of the wounded beast, and being a strong man, by pure physical force dashed the leopard's brains out on the jagged edges of the stump. It was a splendid instance of presence of mind. He was horribly mauled of course; in fact I believe he lost his arm, but he saved his life. It shows the danger of only wounding a leopard, especially if he is coming towards you; always wait till he has passed your station, if it is practicable. If you *must* shoot, take what care you can that the shot be a sure one.

In some of the hill stations, and indeed in the villages on the plains, it is very common for a leopard to make his appearance in the house or verandah of an evening.

One was shot in Bhaugulpore station by the genial and respected chaplain, on a Sunday morning two or three years ago. As we went along, H. told us a humorous story of an Assistant in the Public Works Department, who got mauled by a leopard at Dengra Ghat, Dak Bungalow. It had taken up its quarters in a disused room, and this young fellow burning, with ardour to distinguish himself, made straight for the room in which he was known to be. He opened the door, followed by a motley crowd of retainers, discharged his gun, and the sequel proved that he was *not* a dead shot. He had only wounded the leopard. With a bound the savage brute was on him, but in the hurry and confusion, he had changed front. The leopard had him by the back. You can imagine the scene! He roared for help! The leopard was badly hit, and a plucky *bearer* came to his rescue with a stout *lathee*. Between them they succeeded in killing the wounded animal, but not before it had left its marks on a very sensitive portion of his frame. The moral is, if you go after leopard, be sure you kill him at once.

They seldom attack a strong, well-grown animal. Calves, however, goats, and dogs are frequently carried off by them. The young of deer and pig, too, fall victims, and when nothing else can be had, peafowl have been known to furnish them a meal. In my factory in Oudh I had a small, graceful, four-horned antelope. It was carried off by a leopard from the garden in broad daylight, and in face of a gang of coolies.

The most commonly practised mode of leopard shooting, is to tie a goat up to a tree. You have a *mychan* erected, that is, a platform elevated on trees above the ground. Here you take your seat. Attracted by the bleating of the goat, the prowling leopard approaches his intended victim. If you are on the watch you can generally detect his approach. They steal on with extreme caution, being intensely wary and suspicious. At a village near where we now were, I had sat up for three nights for a leopard, but although I knew he was prowling in the vicinity, I had never got a look at him. We believed this leopard to be the same brute.

I have already described our mode of beating. The jungle was close, and there was a great growth of young trees. I was again on the right, and near the edge of the forest. Beyond was a glade planted with rice. The incidents of the beat were much as you have just read. There was, however, unknown or at any rate unnoticed by us, more intense excitement. We knew that the leopard might at any moment pass before us. Pat was close to a mighty bhur tree, whose branches, sending down shoots from the parent stem, had planted round it a colony of vigorous supports. It was a magnificent tree with dense shade. All was solemn and still. Pat with his keen eye, his pulse bounding, and every sense on the alert, was keeping a careful look-out from behind an immense projecting buttress of the tree. All was deadly quiet. H. and myself were occupied watching the gambols of some monkeys in our front. The beaters were yet far off. Suddenly Pat heard a faint crackle on a dried leaf. He glanced in the direction of the sound, and his quick eye detected the glossy coats, the beautifully spotted hides of not *one* leopard, but *two*. In a moment the stillness was broken by the report of his rifle. Another report followed sharp and quick. We were on the alert, but to Pat the chief honour and glory belonged. He had shot one leopard dead through the heart. The female was badly hit and came bounding along in my direction. Of course we were now on the *qui vive*. Waiting for an instant, till I could get my aim clear of some intervening trees, I at length got a fair shot, and brought her down with a ball through the throat. H. and Pat came running up, and we congratulated ourselves on our success. By and bye Mehrman Singh and the rest of the beaters came up, and the joy of the villagers was gratifying. These were doubtless the two leopards we had heard so much about, for which I had sat up and watched. It was amusing to see some villager whose pet goat or valued calf had been carried off, now coming up, striking the dead body of the leopard, and abusing it in the most unmeasured terms. Such a crowding round as there was! such a noise, and such excitement!

While waiting for the horses to be brought, and while the excited mob of beaters and coolies carried off the dead animals to the camp to be skinned, we amused ourselves by trying our rifles at a huge tree that grew on the further side of the rice swamp. We found the effects of the 'Express' bullet to be tremendous. It splintered up and burst the bark and body of the tree into fragments. Its effects on an animal are even more wonderful. On looking afterwards at the leopard which had been shot, we found that my bullet had touched the base of the shoulder, near the collar-bone. It had gone downwards through the neck, under the collar-bone, and struck the shoulder. There it had splintered up and made a frightful wound, scattering its fragments all over the chest, and cutting and lacerating everything in its way.

For big game the 'Express' is simply invaluable. For all-round shooting perhaps a No. 12 smooth-bore is the best. It should be snap action with rebounding locks. You should have facilities and instruments for loading cartridges. A good cartridge belt is a good thing for carrying them, but go where you will now, where there is game to be killed, a No. 12 B. L. will enable you to participate in whatever shooting is going. Such a one as I have described would satisfy all the wishes of any young man who perhaps can only afford one gun.

As we rode slowly along, we learned many curious facts of jungle and native life from the followers, and by noticing little incidents happening before our eyes. Pat, who is so well versed in jungle life and its traditions, told us of a curious moveable feast which the natives of these parts hold annually, generally in March or April, which is called the *Sirwah Purrub.*

It seems to be somewhat like the old carnivals of the middle ages. I have read that in Sardinia, and Italy, and Switzerland something similar takes place. The *Sirwah Purrub* is a sort of festival held in honour of the native Diana—the *chumpa buttee* before referred to. On the appointed day all the males in the forest villages, without exception, go a-hunting. Old spears are furbished up; miraculous guns, of even yet more ancient lineage than Mehrman Singh's dangerous flintpiece, are brought out from dusty hiding-places. Battle-axes, bows and arrows, hatchets, clubs and weapons of all sorts, are looked up, and the motley crowd hies to the forest, the one party beating up the game to the other.

Some go fishing, others try to secure a quail or partridge, but it is a point of honour that something must be slain. If game be not plentiful they will even go to another village and slay a goat, which, rather than return empty-handed, they will bear in triumph home. The women meet the returning hunters, and if there has been a fortunate beat, there is a great feast in the village during the evening and far on into the night. The nets are used, and in this way they generally have some game to divide in the village on their return from the hunt. Ordinarily they seethe the flesh, and pour the whole contents of the cooking-pot into a mess of boiled rice. With the addition of a little salt, this is to them very palatable fare. They are very good cooks, with very simple appliances; with a little mustard oil or clarified butter, a few vegetables or a cut-up fish, they can be very successful. The food, however, is generally smoked from the cow-dung fire. If you are much out in these villages this smoke constantly hangs about, clinging to your clothes and flavouring your food, but the natives seem to like it amazingly.

In the cold mornings of December or January it hangs about like the peat smoke in a Highland village. Round every house are great stacks and piles of cow-dung cakes. Before every house is a huge pile of ashes, and the villagers cower round this as the evening falls, or before the sun has dissipated the mist of the mornings. During the day the village dogs burrow in the ashes. Hovering in a dense cloud about the roofs and eaves, and along the lower branches of the trees in filmy layers, the smoke almost chokes one to ride through it. I have seen a native sit till half-choked in a dense column of this smoke. He is too lazy to shift his position; the fumes of pungent smoke half smother him; tears run from his eyes; he splutters and coughs, and abuses the smoke, and its grandfather, and maternal uncle, and all its other known relatives; but he prefers semi-suffocation to the trouble of budging an inch.

Sometimes the energy of these people is surprising. To go to a fair or feast, or on a pilgrimage, they will walk miles upon miles, subsisting on parched peas or rice, and carrying heavy burdens. In company they sing and carol blithely enough. When alone they are very taciturn, man and woman walking together, the man first with his *lathee* or staff, the woman behind carrying child or bundle, and often looking fagged and tired enough.

Taking vegetables, or rice, or other commodities to the bazaar, the carrier often slings his burden to the two ends of a pole worn over the shoulder, much as Chinamen do. But they generally make their load into one bundle which they carry on the head, or which they sling, if not large and bulky, over their backs, rolled up in one of their cloths.

During the rice-planting season they toil in mud and water from earliest morn till late into twilight. Bending and stooping all the day, their lower extremities up to the knee sometimes in water, and the scorching sun beating on their backs, they certainly show their patient plodding industry, for it is downright honest hard work.

The young rice is taken from the nursery patch, where it has been sown thick some time previously. When the rice-field is ready—a sloppy, muddy, embanked little quagmire—the ryot gets his bundle of young rice-plants, and shoves in two or three at a time with his finger and thumb. These afterwards form the tufts of rice. Its growth is very rapid. Sometimes, in case of flood, the rice actually grows with the rise of the water, always keeping its tip above the stream. If wholly submerged for any length of time it dies. There are over a hundred varieties. Some are only suited for very deep marshy soils; others, such as the *sātee*, or sixty-days rice, can be grown on comparatively high land, and ripen early. If rain be scanty, the *sātee* and other rice crops have to be weeded. It is cut with a jagged-edged sort of reaping-hook called a *hussooa*. The cut bundles are carried from the fields by women, girls, and lads. They could not take carts in many instances into the swamps.

At such times you see every little dyke or embankment with a crowd of bustling villagers, each with a heavy bundle of grain on his head, hurrying to and fro like a stream of busy ants. The women, with clothes tucked up above the knee, plod and plash through the water. They go at a half run, a kind of fast trot, and hardly a word is spoken—garnering the rice crops is too important an operation to dawdle and gossip over. Each hurries off with his burden to the little family threshing-floor, dumps down his load, gives a weary grunt, straightens his back, gives a yawn, then off again to the field for another load. It is no use leaving a bundle on the field; where food is so eagerly looked for by such a dense population, where there are hungry mouths and empty stomachs in every village, a bundle of rice would be gone by the morning.

As in Greece, where every man has to watch his vineyard at night, so here, the *kureehan* or threshing-floor each has its watchman at night. For the protection of the growing crops, the villagers club together, and appoint a watchman or *chowkeydar*, whom they pay by giving him a small percentage on the yield; or a small fractional proportion of the area he has to guard, with its standing crop, may be made over to him as a recompense.

They thresh out the rice when it has matured a little on the threshing-floor. Four to six bullocks are tied in a line to a post in the centre, and round this they slowly pace in a circle. They are not muzzled, and the poor brutes seem rather to enjoy the unwonted luxury of feeding while they work. When there is a good wind, the grain is winnowed; it is lifted either in bamboo scoops or in the two hands. The wind blows the chaff or *bhoosa* on to a heap, and the fine fresh rice remains behind. The grain merchants now do a good business. Rice must be sold to pay the rent, the money-lender, and other clamouring creditors. The *bunniahs* will take repayment in kind. They put on the interest, and cheat in the weighments and measurements. So much has to be given to the weigh-man as a perquisite. If seed had been borrowed, it has now to be returned at a ruinous rate of interest. Some seed must be saved for next year, and an average *poor* ryot, the cultivator of but a little holding, very soon sees the result of his harvesting melt away, leaving little for wife and little ones to live on. He never gets free of the money-lender. He will have to go out and work hard for others, as well as get up his own little lands. No chance of a new bullock this year, and the old ones are getting worn out and thin. The wife must dispense with her promised ornament or dress. For the poor ryot it is a miserable hand-to-mouth existence when crops are poor. As a rule he is never out of debt. He lives on the scantiest fare; hunger often pinches him; he knows none of the luxuries of life. Notwithstanding all, the majority are patient, frugal, industrious, and to the full extent of their scanty means even charitable and benevolent. With the average ryot a little business goes a great way. There are some irreconcileable, discontented, worthless fellows in every village. All more or less count a lie as rather a good thing to be expert in; they lie naturally, simply, and instinctively : but with all his faults, and they are doubtless many, I confess to a great liking for the average Hindoo ryot.

At times, however, their apathy and laziness is amazing. They are very childish, petted, and easily roused. In a quarrel, however, they generally confine themselves to vituperation and abuse, and seldom come to blows.

As an instance of their fatalism or apathetic indolence, I can remember a village on the estate I was managing taking fire. It was quite close to the factory. I had my pony saddled at once, and galloped off for the burning village. It was a long, straggling one, with a good masonry well in the centre, shadowed by a mighty *peepul* tree. The wind was blowing the fire right along, and if no obstruction was offered, would sweep off every hut in the place. The only soul who was trying to do a thing was a young Brahmin watchman belonging to the factory. He had succeeded in removing some brass jars of his own, and was saving some grain. One woman was rocking to and fro, beating her breast and crying. There sat the rest of the apathetic villagers in groups, not lifting a finger, not stirring a step, but calmly looking on, while the devouring element was licking up hut after hut, and destroying their little all. In a few minutes some of my servants, syces, and factory men had arrived. I tied up the pony, ordered my men to pull down a couple of huts in the centre, and tried to infuse some energy into the villagers. Not a bit of it; they would *not* stir. They would not even draw a bucket of water. However, my men got earthen pots; I dug up fresh earth and threw it on the two dismantled huts, dragging away as much of the thatch and *debris* as we could.

The fire licked our faces, and actually got a footing on the first house beyond the frail opening we had tried to make, but we persevered, and ultimately stayed the fire, and saved about two thirds of the village. I never saw such an instance of complete apathy. Some of the inhabitants even had not untied the cattle in the sheds. They seemed quite prostrated. However, as we worked on, and they began to see that all was not yet lost, they began to buckle to; yet even then their principal object was to save their brass pots and cooking utensils, things that could not possibly burn, and which they might have left alone with perfect safety.

A Hindoo village is as inflammable as touchwood. The houses are generally built of grass walls, connected with thin battens of bamboo. The roof is bamboo and thatch. Thatch fences surround all the little court-yards. Leaves, refuse, cowdung fuel, and wood are piled up round every hut. At each door is an open air fire, which smoulders all day. A stray puff of wind makes an inquisitive visit round the corner, and before one can half realise the catastrophe, the village is on fire. Then each only thinks of his own goods; there is no combined effort to stay the flames. In the hot west winds of March, April, and May, these fires are of very frequent occurrence. In Bhaugulpore, I have seen, from my verandah, three villages on fire at one and the same time. In some parts of Oudh, among the sal forests, village after village is burnt down annually, and I have seen the same catastrophe visit the same village several times in the course of one year. These fires arise from pure carelessness, sheer apathy, and laziness.

Sanitary precautions too are very insufficient; practically there are none. Huge unsightly water-holes, filled during the rains with the drainage of all the dung-heaps and mounds of offal and filth that abound in the village, swelter under the hot summer sun. They get covered with a rank green scum, and if their inky depths be stirred, the foulest and most fearful odours issue forth. In these filthy pools the villagers often perform their ablutions; they do not scruple to drink the putrid water, which is no doubt a hotbed and regular nursery for fevers, and choleraic and other disorders.

Many home readers are but little acquainted with the Indian village system, and I shall devote a chapter to the description of a Hindoo village, with its functionaries, its institutions, its inhabitants, and the more marked of their customs and avocations.

CHAPTER XIII.

Description of a native village.—Village functionaries.—The barber.—Bathing habits.—The village well.—The school.—The children.—The village bazaar.—The landowner and his dwelling.—The 'Putwarrie' or village accountant.—The blacksmith.—The 'Punchayiet' or village jury system.—Our legal system in India.—Remarks on the administration of justice.

A TYPICAL village in Behar is a heterogeneous collection of thatched huts, apparently set down at random—as indeed it is, for every one erects his hut wherever whim or caprice leads him, or wherever he can get a piece of vacant land. Groves of feathery bamboos and broad-leaved plumy-looking plantains almost conceal the huts and buildings. Several small orchards of mango surround the village; the roads leading to and from it are merely well-worn cattle tracks,—in the rains a perfect quagmire, and in the hot weather dusty, and confined between straggling hedges of aloe or prickly pear. These hedges are festooned with masses of clinging luxuriant creepers, among which sometimes struggles up a custard apple, an avocado pear, or a wild plum-tree. The latter is a prickly straggling tree, called the *bhyre;* the wood is very hard, and is often used for making ploughs. The fruit is a little hard yellow crisp fruit, with a big stone inside, and very sweet; when it is ripe, the village urchins throw sticks up among the branches, and feast on the golden shower.

On many of the banks bordering the roads, thatching grass, or rather strong upright waving grass, with a beautiful feathery plume, is planted. This is used to make the walls of the houses, and these are then plastered outside and in with clay and cowdung. The tall hedge of dense grass keeps what little breeze there may be away from the traveller. The road is something like an Irish 'Boreen,' wanting only its beauty and freshness. On a hot day the atmosphere in one of these village roads is stifling and loaded with dust.

These houses with their grass walls and thatched roof are called *kutcha*, as opposed to more pretentious structures of burnt brick, with maybe a tiled sloping or flat plastered roof, which are called *pucca*. *Pucca* literally means 'ripe,' as opposed to *cutcha*, 'unripe'; but the rich Oriental tongue has adapted it to almost every kind of secondary meaning. Thus a man who is true, upright, respected, a man to be depended on, is called a *pucca* man. It is a word in constant use among Anglo-Indians. A *pucca* road is one which is bridged and metalled. If you make an engagement with a friend, and he wants to impress you with its importance, he will ask you, 'Now is that *pucca*?' and so on.

Other houses in the village are composed of unburnt bricks cemented with mud, or maybe composed of mud walls and thatched roof; these, being a compound sort of erection, are called *cutcha pucca*. In the *cutcha* houses live the poorer castes, the *Chumars* or workers in leathers, the *Moosahms*, *Doosadhs*, or *Gwallahs*.

The *Dornes*, or scavengers, feeders on offal, have to live apart in a *tolah*, which might be called a small suburb, by themselves. The *Dornes* drag from the village any animal that happens to die. They generally pursue the handicraft of basket making, or mat making, and the *Dorne tolah* can always be known by the pigs and fowls prowling about in search of food, and the *Dorne* and his family splitting up bamboo, and weaving mats and baskets at the doors of their miserable habitation. To the higher castes both pigs and fowls are unclean and an abomination. *Moosahms, Doosadhs,* and other poor castes, such as *Dangurs,* keep however an army of gaunt, lean, hungry-looking pigs. These may be seen rooting and wallowing in the marshes when the rice has been cut, or foraging among the mango groves, to pick up any stray unripe fruit that may have escaped the keen eyes of the hungry and swarming children.

There is yet another small *tolah* or suburb, called the *Kusbee tolah.* Here live the miserable outcasts who minister to the worst passions of our nature. These degraded beings are banished from the more respectable portions of the community; but here, as in our own highly civilised and favoured land, vice hovers by the side of virtue, and the Hindoo village contains the same elements of happiness and misery, profligacy and probity, purity and degradation, as the fine home cities that are a name in the mouths of men.

Every village forms a perfect little commonwealth; it contains all the elements of self-existence; it is quite a little commune, so far as social life is concerned. There is a hereditary blacksmith, washerman, potter, barber, and writer. The *dhobee,* or washerman, can always be known by the propinquity of his donkeys, diminutive animals which he uses to transport his bundle of unsavoury dirty clothes to the pool or tank where the linen is washed. On great country roads you may often see strings of donkeys laden with bags of grain, which they transport from far-away villages to the big bazaars; but if you see a laden donkey near a village, be sure the *dhobee* is not far off.

Here as elsewhere the *hajam*, or barber, is a great gossip, and generally a favourite. He uses no soap, and has a most uncouth-looking razor, yet he shaves the heads, beards, moustaches, and armpits of his customers with great deftness. The lower classes of natives shave the hair of the head and of the armpits for the sake of cleanliness and for other obvious reasons. The higher classes are very regular in their ablutions; every morning, be the water cold or warm, the Rajpoot and Brahmin, the respectable middle classes, and all in the village who lay any claim to social position, have their *goosal* or bath. Some hie to the nearest tank or stream; at all hours of the day, at any ferry or landing stage, you will see swarthy fine-looking fellows up to mid waist in the water, scrubbing vigorously their bronzed arms, and neck and chest. They clean their teeth with the end of a stick, which they chew at one extremity, till they loosen the fibres, and with this improvised toothbrush and some wood ashes for paste, they make them look as white and clean as ivory.

There is generally a large masonry well in the middle of the village, with a broad smooth *pucca* platform all round it. It has been built by some former father of the hamlet, to perpetuate his memory, to fulfil a vow to the gods, perhaps simply from goodwill to his fellow townsmen. At all events there is generally one such in every village. It is generally shadowed by a huge *bhur*, *peepul*, or tamarind tree. Here may always be seen the busiest sight in the village. Pretty young women chatter, laugh, and talk, and assume all sorts of picturesque attitudes as they fill their waterpots; the village matrons gossip, and sometimes quarrel, as they pull away at the windlass over the deep cool well. On the platform are a group of fat Brahmins nearly nude, their lighter skins contrasting well with the duskier hue of the lower classes. There are several groups. With damp drapery clinging to their glistening skins, they pour brass pots of cold water over their dripping bodies; they rub themselves briskly, and gasp again as the cool element pours over head and shoulders. They sit down while some young attendant or relation vigorously rubs them down the back; while sitting they clean their feet. Thus, amid much laughing and talking, and quaint gestures, and not a little expectoration, they perform their ablutions. Not unfrequently the more wealthy anoint their bodies with mustard oil, which at all events keeps out cold and chill, as they claim that it does, though it is not fragrant. Round the well you get all the village news and scandal. It is always thronged in the mornings and evenings, and only deserted when the fierce heat of midday plunges the village into a lethargic silence; unbroken save where the hum of the hand-mill, or the thump of the husking-post, tells where some busy damsel or matron is grinding flour, or husking rice, in the cool shadow of her hut, for the wants of her lord and master.

Education is now making rapid strides; it is fostered by government, and many of the wealthier landowners or Zemindars subscribe liberally for a schoolmaster in their villages. Near the principal street then, in a sort of lane, shadowed by an old mango-tree, we come on the village school. The little fellows have all discarded their upper clothes on account of the heat, and with much noise, swaying the body backwards and forwards, and monotonously intoning, they grind away at the mill of learning, and try to get a knowledge of books. Other dusky urchins figure away with lumps of chalk on the floor, or on flat pieces of wood to serve as copy-books. The din increases as the stranger passes: going into an English school, the stranger would probably cause a momentary pause in the hum that is always heard in school. The little Hindoo scholar probably wishes to impress you with a sense of his assiduity. He raises his voice, sways the body more briskly, keeps his one eye firmly fixed on his task, while with the other he throws a keen swift glance over you, which embraces every detail of your costume, and not improbably includes a shrewd estimate of your disposition and character.

Hindoo children never seem to me to be boys or girls; they are preternaturally acute and observant. You seldom see them playing together. They seem to be born with the gift of telling a lie with most portentous gravity. They wear an air of the most winning candour and guileless innocence, when they are all the while plotting some petty scheme against you. They are certainly far more precocious than English children; they realise the hard struggle for life far more quickly. The poorer classes can hardly be said to have any childhood; as soon as they can toddle they are sent to weed, cut grass, gather fuel, tend herds, or do anything that will bring them in a small pittance, and ease the burden of the struggling parents. I think the childen of the higher and middle classes very pretty; they have beautiful, dark, thoughtful eyes, and a most intelligent expression. Very young babies however are miserably nursed; their hair is allowed to get all tangled and matted into unsightly knots; their faces are seldom washed, and their eyes are painted with antimony about the lids, and are often rheumy and running with water. The use of the pocket handkerchief is sadly neglected.

There is generally one open space or long street in our village, and in a hamlet of any importance there is weekly or bi-weekly a bazaar or market. From early morning in all directions, from solitary huts in the forest, from struggling little crofts in the rice lands, from fishermen's dwellings perched on the bank of the river, from lonely camps in the grass jungle where the herd and his family live with their cattle, from all the petty Thorpes about, come the women with their baskets of vegetables, their bundles of spun yarn, their piece of woven cloth, whatever they have to sell or barter. There is a lad with a pair of wooden shoes, which he has fashioned as he was tending the village cows; another with a grass mat, or bamboo staff, or some other strange outlandish-looking article, which he hopes to barter in the bazaar for something on which his heart is set. The *bunniahs* hurry up their tottering, overladen ponies; the rice merchant twists his patient bullock's tail to make it move faster; the cloth merchant with his bale under his arm and measuring stick in hand, walks briskly along. Here comes a gang of charcoal-burners, with their loads of fuel slung on poles dangling from their shoulders. A *box wallah* with his attendant coolie, staggering under the weight of a huge box of Manchester goods, hurries by. It is a busy sight in the bazaar. What a cackling! What a confused clatter of voices! Here also the women are the chief contributors to the din of tongues. There is no irate husband here or moody master to tell them to be still. Spread out on the ground are heaps of different grain, bags of flour, baskets of meal, pulse, or barley; sweetmeats occupy the attention of nearly all the buyers.

All Hindoos indulge in sweets, which take the place of beer with us; instead of a 'nobbler,' they offer you a 'lollipop.' Trinkets, beads, bracelets, armlets, and anklets of pewter, there are in great bunches; fruits, vegetables, sticks of cane, skins full of oil, and sugar, and treacle. Stands with fresh 'paun' leaves, and piles of coarse looking masses of tobacco are largely patronised. It is like a hive of bees. The dust hovers over the moving mass; the smells are various, none of them 'blest odours of sweet Araby.' Drugs, condiments, spices, shoes, in fact, everything that a rustic population can require, is here. The *pice* jingle as they change hands; the haggling and chaffering are without parallel in any market at home. Here is a man apparently in the last madness of intense passion, in fierce altercation with another, who tries his utmost to outbluster his furious declamation. In a moment they are smiling and to all appearance the best friends in the world. The bargain has been concluded; it was all about whether the one could give three *brinjals* or four for one pice. It is a scene of indescribable bustle, noise, and confusion. By evening however, all will have been packed up again, and only the faint outlines of yet floating clouds of dust, and the hopping, cheeky crows, picking up the scattered litter and remnants of the market, will remain to tell that it has been bazaar day in our village.

Generally, about the centre of it, there is a more pretentious structure, with verandahs supported on wooden pillars. High walls surround a rather commodious courtyard. There are mysterious little doors, through which you can get a peep of crooked little stairs leading to the upper rooms or to the roof, from dusky inside verandahs. Half-naked, listless, indolent figures lie about, or walk slowly to and from the yard, with seemingly purposeless indecision. In the outer verandah is an old *palkee*, with evidences in the tarnished gilding and frayed and tattered hangings, that it once had some pretensions to fashionable elegance.

The walls of the buildings however are sadly cracked, and numerous young *peepul* trees grow in the crevices, their insidious roots creeping farther and farther into the fissures, and expediting the work of decay, which is everywhere apparent. It is the residence of the Zemindar, the lord of the village, the owner of the lands adjoining. Probably he is descended from some noble house of ancient lineage. His forefathers, possibly, led armed retainers against some rival in yonder far off village, where the dim outlines of a mud fort yet tell of the insecurity of the days of old. Now he is old, and fat, and lazy. Possibly he has been too often to the money-lender. His lands are mortgaged to their full value. Though they respect and look up to their old Zemindar, the villagers are getting independent; they are not so humble, and pay less and less of feudal tribute than in the old days, when the golden palanquin was new, when the elephant had splendid housings, when mace, and javelin, and matchlock-men followed in his train. Alas! the elephant was sold long ago, and is now the property of a wealthy *Bunniah* who has amassed money in the buying and selling of grain and oil. The Zemindar may be a man of progress and intelligence, but many are of this broken down and helpless type.

Holding the lands of the village by hereditary right, by grant, conquest, or purchase, he collects his rents from the villages through a small staff of *peons*, or un-official police. The accounts are kept by another important village functionary—the *putwarrie*, or village accountant. *Putwarries* belong to the writer or *Kayasth* caste. They are probably as clever, and at the same time as unscrupulous as any class in India. They manage the most complicated accounts between ryot and landlord with great skill. Their memories are wonderful, but they can always forget conveniently. Where ryots are numerous, the landlord's wants pressing, and frequent calls made on the tenantry for payment, often made in various kinds of grain and produce, the rates and prices of which are constantly changing, it is easy to imagine the complications and intricacies of a *putwarrie's* account. Each ryot pretty accurately remembers his own particular indebtedness, but woe to him if he pays the *putwarrie* the value of a 'red cent' without taking a receipt. Certainly there may be a really honest *putwarrie*, but I very much doubt it. The name stands for chicanery and robbery. On the one hand the landlord is constantly stirring him up for money, questioning his accounts, and putting him not unfrequently to actual bodily coercion. The ryot on the other hand is constantly inventing excuses, getting up delays, and propounding innumerable reasons why he cannot pay. He will try to forge receipts, he will get up false evidence that he has already paid, and the wretched *putwarrie* needs all his native and acquired sharpness, to hold his own. But all ryots are not alike, and when the *putwarrie* gets hold of some unwary and ignorant bumpkin whom he can plunder, he *does* plunder him systematically. All cowherds are popularly supposed to be cattle lifters, and a *putwarrie* after he has got over the stage of infancy, and has been indoctrinated into all the knavery that his elders can teach him, is supposed to belong to the highest category of villains. A popular proverb, much used in Behar, says :—

> 'Unda poortee, Cowa maro!
> Iinnum me, billar:
> Bara burris me, Kayashh marige!!
> Humesha mara gwar!!!'

This is translated thus : 'When the shell is breaking kill the crow, and the wild cat at its birth.' A *Kayasth*, writer, or *putwarrie*, may be allowed to live till he is twelve years old, at which time he is sure to have learned rascality. Then kill him; but kill *gwars* or cowherds any time, for they are invariably rascals. There is a deal of grim bucolic humour in this, and it very nearly hits the truth.

The *putwarrie*, then, is an important personage. He has his *cutcherry*, or office, where he and his tribe (for there are always numbers of his fellow caste men who help him in his books and accounts) squat on their mat on the ground. Each possesses the instruments of his calling in the shape of a small brass ink-pot, and an oblong box containing a knife, pencil, and several reeds for pens. Each has a bundle of papers and documents before him, this is called his *busta*, and contains all the papers he uses. There they sit, and have fierce squabbles with the tenantry. There is always some noise about a putwarrie's cutcherry. He has generally some half dozen quarrels on hand, but he trusts to his pen, and tongue, and clever brain. He is essentially a man of peace, hating physical contests, delighting in a keen argument, and an encounter with a plotting, calculating brain. Another proverb says that the putwarrie has as much chance of becoming a soldier as a sheep has of success in attacking a wolf.

The *lohar*, or blacksmith, is very unlike his prototype at home. Here is no sounding anvil, no dusky shop, with the sparks from the heated iron lighting up its dim recesses. There is little to remind one of Longfellow's beautiful poem. The *lohar* sits in the open air. His hammers and other implements of trade are very primitive. Like all native handicraftsmen he sits down at his work. His bellows are made of two loose bags of sheepskin, lifted alternately by the attendant coolie. As they lift they get inflated with air; they are then sharply forced down on their own folds, and the contained air ejected forcibly through an iron or clay nozzle, into the very small heap of glowing charcoal which forms the fire. His principal work is making and sharpening the uncouth-looking ploughshares, which look more like flat blunt chisels than anything else. They also make and keep in repair the *hussowahs*, or serrated sickles, with which the crops are cut. They are slow at their task, but many of them are ingenious workers in metal. They are very imitative, and I have seen many English tools and even gun-locks, made by a common native village blacksmith, that could not be surpassed in delicacy of finish by any English smith. It is foreign to our ideas of the brawny blacksmith, to hear that he sits to his work, but this is the invariable custom. Even carpenters and masons squat down to theirs. Cheap labour is but an arbitrary term, and a country smith at home might do the work of ten or twelve men in India; but it is just as well to get an idea of existing differences. On many of the factories there are very intelligent *mistrees*, which is the term for the master blacksmith. These men, getting but twenty-four to thirty shillings a month, and supplying themselves with food and clothing, are nevertheless

CARPENTERS AND BLACKSMITHS AT WORK

To face page 150.

competent to work all the machinery, attend to the engine, and do all the ironwork necessary for the factory. They will superintend the staff of blacksmiths; and if the sewing-machine of the *mem sahib*, the gunlock of the *luna sahib*, the lawn-mower, English pump, or other machine gets out of order, requiring any metal work, the *mistree* is called in, and is generally competent to put things to rights.

As I have said, every village is a self-contained little commune. All trades necessary to supplying the wants of the villagers are represented in it. Besides the profits from his actual calling, nearly every man except the daily labourer, has a little bit of land which he farms, so as to eke out his scanty income. All possess a cow or two, a few goats, and probably a pair of plough-bullocks.

When a dispute arises in the village, should a person be suspected of theft, should his cattle trespass on his neighbour's growing crop, should he libel some one against whom he has a grudge, or, proceeding to stronger measures, take the law into his own hands and assault him, the aggrieved party complains to the head man of the village. In every village the head man is the fountain of justice. He holds his office sometimes by right of superior wealth, or intelligence, or hereditary succession, not unfrequently by the unanimous wish of his fellow-villagers. On a complaint being made to him, he summons both parties and their witnesses. The complainant is then allowed to nominate two men, to act as assessors or jurymen on his behalf, his nominations being liable to challenge by the opposite party. The defendant next names two to act on his behalf, and if these are agreed to by both parties, these four, with the head man, form what is called a *punchayiet*, or council of five, in fact, a jury. They examine the witnesses, and each party to the suit conducts his own case. The whole village not unfrequently attends to hear what goes on. In a mere caste or private quarrel, only the friends of the parties will attend. Every case is tried in public, and all the inhabitants of the village can hear the proceedings if they wish. Respectable inhabitants can remark on the proceedings, make suggestions, and give an opinion. Public feeling is thus pretty accurately gauged and tested, and the *punchayiet* agree among themselves on the verdict. To the honour of their character for fair play be it said, that the decision of a *punchayiet* is generally correct, and is very seldom appealed against. Our complicated system of law, with its delays, its technicalities, its uncertainties, and above all its expense, its stamp duties, its court fees, its bribes to native underlings, and the innumerable vexations attendant on the administration of justice in our revenue and criminal courts, are repugnant to the villager of Hindostan. They are very litigious, and believe in our desire to give them justice and protection to life and property; but our courts are far too costly, our machinery of justice is far too intricate and complicated for a people like the Hindoos. 'Justice within the gate' is what they want. It is quite enough admission of the reality of our rule—that we are the paramount power—that they submit a case to us at all; and all impediments in the way of their getting cheap and speedy justice should be done away with. A codification of existing laws, a sweeping away of one half the forms and technicalities that at present bewilder the applicant for justice, and altogether a less legal and more equitable procedure, having a due regard to efficiency and the conservation of Imperial interests, should be the aim of our Indian rulers. More especially should this be the case in rural districts where large interests are concerned, where cases involve delicate points of law. Our present courts, divested of their hungry crowd of middlemen and retainers, are right enough; but I would like to see rural courts for petty cases established, presided over by leading natives, planters, merchants, and men of probity, which would in a measure supplement the *punchayiet* system, which would be easy of access, cheap in their procedure, and with all the impress of authority. It is a question I merely glance at, as it does not come within the scope of a book like this; but it is well known to every planter and European who has come much in contact with the rural classes of Hindostan, that there is a vast amount of smouldering disaffection, of deep-rooted dislike to, and contempt of, our present cumbrous costly machinery of law and justice.

If a villager wishes to level a withering sarcasm at the head of a plausible, talkative fellow, all promise and no performance, ready with tongue but not with purse or service, he calls him a *vakeel*, that is, a lawyer. If he has to cool his heels in your office, or round the factory to get some little business done, to neglect his work, to get his rent or produce account investigated, wherever there is worry, trouble, delay, or difficulty about anything concerning the relations between himself and the factory, the deepest and keenest expression of discontent and disgust his versatile and acute imagination can suggest, or his fluent tongue give utterance to is, that this is 'Adanlut lea mafich,' that is, 'Like a court of justice.' Could there be a stronger commentary on our judicial institutions?

The world is waking up now rapidly from the lethargic sleep of ages. Men's minds are keenly alive to what is passing; communications are much improved; the dissemination of news is rapid; the old race of besotted, ignorant tenants, and grasping, avaricious, domineering tyrants of landlords is fast dying out; and there could be no difficulty in establishing in such village or district courts as I have indicated. All educated respectable Europeans with a stake in the country should be made Justices of the Peace, with limited powers to try petty cases. There is a vast material—loyalty, educated minds, an honest desire to do justice, independence, and a genuine scorn of everything pettifogging and underhand—that the Indian Government would do well to utilise. The best friend of the Baboo cannot acquit him of a tendency to temporise, a hankering after finesse, a too fatal facility to fall under pecuniary temptation. The educated gentleman planter of the present day is above suspicion, and before showering titles and honours on native gentlemen, elevating them to the bench, and deluging the services with them, it might be worth our rulers' while to utilise, or try to utilise, the experience, loyalty, honour, and integrity of those of our countrymen who might be willing to place their services at the disposal of Government. 'India for the Indians' is a very good cry; it sounds well; but it will not do to push it to its logical issue. Unless Indians can govern India wisely and well, in accordance with modern national ideas, they have no more right to India than Hottentots have to the Cape, or the black fellows to Australia. In my opinion, Hindoos would never govern Hindostan half, quarter, nay, one tithe as well as Englishmen. Make more of your Englishmen in

India then, make not less of your Baboo if you please, but make more of your Englishmen. Keep them loyal and content. Treat them kindly and liberally. One Englishman contented, loyal, and industrious in an Indian district, is a greater pillar of strength to the Indian Government than ten dozen Baboos or Zemindars, let them have as many titles, decorations, university degrees, or certificates of loyalty from junior civilians as they may. Not India for the Indians, but India for Imperial Britain say I.

CHAPTER XIV.

A native village continued.—The watchman or 'chowkeydar.'—The temple.—Brahmins.—Idols.—Religion.—Humility of the poorer classes.—Their low condition.—Their apathy.—The police.—Their extortions and knavery.—An instance of police rascality.—Corruption of native officials.—The Hindoo unfit for self-government.

ONE more important functionary we have yet to notice, the watchman or *chowkeydar*. He is generally a *Doosadh*, or other low caste man, and perambulates the village at night, at intervals uttering a loud cry or a fierce howl, which is caught up and echoed by all the *chowkeydars* of the neighbouring villages. It is a weird, strange sound, cry after cry echoing far away, distance beyond distance, till it fades into faintness. At times it is not an unmusical cry, but when he howls out close to your tent, waking you from your first dreamless sleep, you do not feel it to be so. The *chowkeydar* has to see that no thieves enter the village by night. He protects the herds and property of the villagers. If a theft or crime occurs, he must at once report it to the nearest police station. If you lose your way by night, you shout out for the nearest *chowkeydar*, and he is bound to pass you on to the next village. These men get a small gratuity from government, but the villagers also pay them a small sum, which they assess according to individual means. The *chowkeydar* is generally a ragged, swarthy fellow with long matted hair, a huge iron-bound staff, and always a blue *puggra*. The blue is his official badge. Sometimes he has a brass badge, and carries a sword, a

HINDOO VILLAGE TEMPLES.

To face page 157.

curved, blunt weapon, the handle of which is so small that scarcely an Englishman's hand would be found to fit it. It is more for show than use, and in thousands of cases, it has become so fixed in the scabbard that it cannot be drawn.

In the immediate vicinity of each village, and often in the village itself, is a small temple sacred to Vishnu or Shiva. It is often perched high up on some bank, overlooking the lake or village tank. Generally there is some umbrageous old tree overshadowing the sacred fane, and seated near, reclining in the shade, are several oleaginous old Brahmins. If the weather be hot, they generally wear only the *dhote* or loin cloth made of fine linen or cotton, and hanging about the legs in not ungraceful folds. The Brahmin can be told by his sacred thread worn round the neck over the shoulder. His skin is much fairer than the majority of his fellow villagers. It is not unfrequently a pale golden olive, and I have seen them as fair as many Europeans. They are intelligent men with acute minds, but lazy and self-indulgent. Frequently the village Brahmin is simply a sensual voluptuary. This is not the time or place to descant on their religion, which, with many gross practices, contains not a little that is pure and beautiful. The common idea at home that they are miserable pagans, 'bowing down to stocks and stones,' is, like many of the accepted ideas about India, very much exaggerated. That the masses, the crude uneducated Hindoos, place some faith in the idol, and expect in some mysterious way that it will influence their fate for good or evil, is not to be denied, but the more intelligent natives, and most of the Brahmins, only look on the idol as a visible sign and symbol of the divinity. They want a vehicle to carry their thoughts upwards to God, and the idol is a means to assist their thoughts heavenward. As works of art their idols are not equal to the fine pictures and other symbols of the Greeks or the Roman Catholics, but they serve the same purpose. Where the village is very poor, and no pious founder has perpetuated his memory, or done honour to the gods by erecting a temple, the natives content themselves with a rough mud shrine, which they visit at intervals and daub with red paint. They deposit flowers, pour libations of water or milk, and in other ways strive to shew that a religious impulse is stirring within them. So far as I have observed, however, the vast mass of the poor toilers in India have little or no religion. Material wants are too pressing. They may have some dumb, vague aspirations after a higher and a holier life, but the fight for necessaries, for food, raiment, and shelter, is too incessant for them to indulge much in contemplation. They have a dim idea of a future life, but none of them can give you anything but a very unsatisfactory idea of their religion. They observe certain forms and ceremonies, because their fathers did, and because the Brahmins tell them. Of real, vital, practical religion, as we know it, they have little or no knowledge. Ask any common labourer or one of the low castes about immortality, about salvation, about the higher virtues, about the yearnings and wishes that every immortal soul at periods has, and he will simply tell you 'Khoda jane, hum greel admi,' i.e. 'God knows; I am only a poor man!' There they take refuge always when you ask them anything puzzling. If you are rating them for a fault, asking them to perform a complicated task, or inquiring your way in a strange neighbourhood, the first answer you get will, ten to one, be 'Hum greel admi.' It is said almost instinctively, and no doubt in many cases is the refuge of simple disinclination to think the matter out. Pure laziness suggests it. It is too much trouble to frame an answer, or give the desired information, and the 'greel admi' comes naturally to the lip. It is often deprecatory, meaning 'I am ignorant and uninformed,' you must not expect too 'much from a poor, rude, uncultivated man like me.' It is often, also, a delicate mode of flattery, which is truly oriental, implying, and often conveying in a tone, a look, a gesture, that though the speaker is 'greel,' poor, humble, despised, it is only by contrast to you, the questioner, who are mighty, exalted, and powerful. For downright fawning obsequiousness, or delicate, implied, fine-strung, subtle flattery, I will back a Hindoo sycophant against the courtier or place-hunter of every other nation. It is very annoying at times, if you are in a hurry, and particularly want a direct answer to a plain question, to hear the old old story, 'I am a poor man,' but there is nothing for it but patience. You must ask again plainly and kindly. The poorer classes are easily flurried; they will always give what information they have if kindly spoken to, but you must not fluster them. You must rouse their minds to think, and let them fairly grasp the purport of your inquiry, for they are very suspicious, often pondering over your object, carefully considering all the pros and cons as to your motive, inclination, or your position. Many try to give an answer that they think would be pleasing to you. If they think you are weary and tired, and you ask your distance from the place you may be wishing to reach, they will ridiculously underestimate the length of road. A man may have all the cardinal virtues, but if they think you do not like him, and you ask his character, they will paint him to you blacker than Satan himself. It is very hard to get the plain, unvarnished truth from a Hindoo. Many, indeed, are almost incapable of giving an intelligent answer to any question that does not nearly concern their own private and purely personal interests. They have a sordid, grubbing, vegetating life, many of them indeed are but little above the brute creation. They have no idea beyond the supply of the mere animal wants of the moment. The future never troubles them. They live their hard, unlovely lives, and experience no pleasures and no surprises. They have few regrets; their minds are mere blanks, and life is one long continued struggle with nature for bare subsistence. What wonder then that they are fatalists? They do not speculate on the mysteries of existence, they are content to be, to labour, to suffer, to die when their time comes like a dog, because it is *Kismet*—their fate. Many of them never strive to avert any impending calamity, such, for example, as sickness. A man sickens, he wraps himself in stolid apathy, he makes no effort to shake of his malady, he accepts it with sullen, despairing, pathetic resignation as his fate. His friends mourn in their dumb, despairing way, but they too accept the situation. He has no one to rouse him. If you ask him what is the matter, he only wails out, 'Hum kya kurre?' What can I do? I am unwell. No attempt whatever to tell you of the origin of his illness, no wish even for sympathy or assistance. He accepts the fact of his illness. He struggles not with Fate. It is so ordained. Why fight against it? Amen; so let it be. I have often been saddened to see poor toiling tenants struck down in this way.

Even if you give them medicine, they often have not energy enough to take it. You must see them take it before your eyes. It is *your* struggle not theirs. *You* must rouse them, by *your* will. *Your* energy must compel *them* to make an attempt to combat their weakness. Once you rouse a man, and infuse some spirit into him, he may resist his disease, but it is a hard fight to get him to TRY. What a meaning in that one word TRY! To ACT. To DO. The average poor suffering native Hindoo knows nothing of it.

Of course their moods vary. They have their 'high days and holidays,' feasts, processions, and entertainments; but on the whole the average ryot or small cultivator has a hard life.

In every village there are generally bits of uncultivated or jungle lands, on which the village herds have a right of pasture. The cow being a sacred animal, they only use her products, milk and butter. The urchins may be seen in the morning driving long strings of emaciated looking animals to the village pasture, which in the evening wend their weary way backwards through the choking dust, having had but 'short commons' all the day on the parched and scanty herbage.

The police are too often a source of annoyance, and become extortionate robbers, instead of the protectors of the poor. It seems to be inherent in the Oriental mind to abuse authority. I do not scruple to say that all the vast army of policemen, court peons, writers, clerks, messengers, and underlings of all sorts, about the courts of justice, in the service of government officers, or in any way attached to the retinue of a government official, one and all are undeniably shamelessly venal and corrupt. They accept a bribe much more quickly than an attorney a fee, or a hungry dog a shin of beef. If a policeman only enters a village he expects a feast from the head man, and will ask a present with unblushing effrontery as a perquisite of his office. If a theft is reported, the inspector of the nearest police-station, or *thanna* as it is called, sends one of his myrmidons, or, if the chance of bribes be good, he may attend himself. On arrival, ambling on his broken-kneed, wall-eyed pony, he seats himself in the verandah of the chief man of the village, who forthwith, with much inward trepidation, makes his appearance. The policeman assumes the air of a haughty conqueror receiving homage from a conquered foe. He assures the trembling wretch that, 'acting on information received,' he must search his dwelling for the missing goods, and that his women's apartments will have to be ransacked, and so annoys, goads, and insults the unfortunate man, that he is too glad to purchase immunity from further insolence by making the policeman a small present, perhaps a 'kid of the goats,' or something else. The guardian of the peace is then regaled with the best food in the house, after which he is 'wreathed with smiles.' If he sees a chance of a farther bribe, he takes his departure saying he will make his report to the *thanna*. He repeats his procedure with some of the other respectable inhabitants, and goes back a good deal richer than he came, to share the spoil with the *thannadar* or inspector.

Another man may then be sent, and the same course is followed, until all the force in the station have had their share. The ryot is afraid to resist. The police have tremendous powers for annoying and doing him harm. A crowd of subservient scoundrels always hangs round the station, dependents, relations, or accomplices.

These harry the poor man who is unwise enough to resist the extortionate demands of the police. They take his cattle to the pound, foment strife between him and his neighbours, get up frivolous and false charges against him, harass him in a thousand ways, and if all else fails, get him summoned as a witness in some case. You might think a witness a person to be treated with respect, to be attended to, to have every facility offered him for giving his evidence at the least cost of time and trouble possible, consistent with the demands of justice, and the vindication of law and authority.

Not so in India with the witness in a police case, when the force dislike him. If he has not previously satisfied their leech-like rapacity, he is tormented, tortured, bullied, and kicked 'from pillar to post,' till his life becomes a burden to him. He has to leave all his avocations, perhaps at the time when his affairs require his constant supervision. He has to trudge many a weary mile to attend the Court. The police get hold of him, and keep him often in real durance. He gets no opportunity for cooking or eating his food. His daily habits are upset and interfered with. In every little vexatious way (and they are masters of the art of petty torture) they so worry and goad him, that the very threat of being summoned as a witness in a police case, is often enough to make the horrified well-to-do native give a handsome gratuity to be allowed to sit quietly at home.

This is no exaggeration. It is the every day practice of the police. They exercise a real despotism. They have set up a reign of terror. The nature of the ryot is such, that he will submit to a great deal to avoid having to leave his home and his work. The police take full advantage of this feeling, and being perfectly unscrupulous, insatiably rapacious, and leagued together in villany, they make a golden harvest out of every case put into their hands. They have made the name of justice stink in the nostrils of the respectable and well-to-do middle classes of India.

The District Superintendents are men of energy and probity, but after all they are only mortal. What with accounts, inspections, reports, forms, and innumerable writings, they cannot exercise a constant vigilance and personal supervision over every part of their district. A district may comprise many hundred villages, thousands of inhabitants, and leagues of intricate and densely peopled country. The mere physical exertion of riding over his district would be too much for any man in about a week. The subordinate police are all interested in keeping up the present system of extortion, and the inspectors and sub-inspectors, who wink at malpractices, come in for their share of the spoil. There is little combination among the peasantry. Each selfishly tries to save his own skin, and they know that if any one individual were to complain, or to dare to resist, he would have to bear the brunt of the battle alone. None of his neighbours would stir a finger to back him; he is too timid and too much in awe of the official European, and constitutionally too averse to resistance, to do aught but suffer in silence. No doubt he feels his wrongs most keenly, and a sullen feeling of hate and wrong is being garnered up, which may produce results disastrous for the peace and wellbeing of our empire in the East.

As a case in point, I may mention one instance out of many which came under my own observation. I had a *moonshee*, or accountant, in one of my outworks in Purneah. Formerly, when the police had come through the factory, he had been in the habit of giving them a present and some food. Under my strict orders, however, that no policemen were to be allowed near the place unless they came on business, he had discontinued paying his black mail. This was too glaring an infringement of what they considered their vested rights to be passed over in silence. Example might spread. My man must be made an example of. I had a case in the Court of the Deputy Magistrate some twenty miles or so from the factory. The moonshee had been named as a witness to prove the writing of some papers filed in the suit. They got a citation for him to appear, a mere summons for his attendance as a witness. Armed with this, they appeared at the factory two or three days before the date fixed on for hearing the cause. I had just ridden in from Purneah, tired, hot, and dusty, and was sitting in the shade of the verandah with young D., my assistant. One policeman first came up, presented the summons, which I took, and he then stated that it was a *warrant* for the production of my moonshee, and that he must take him away at once. I told the man it was merely a summons, requiring the attendance of the moonshee on a certain date, to give evidence in the case. He was very insolent in his manner. It is customary when a Hindoo of inferior rank appears before you, that he removes his shoes, and stands before you in a respectful attitude. This man's headdress was all disarranged, which in itself is a sign of disrespect. He spoke loudly and insolently; kept his shoes on; and sat down squatting on the grass before me. My assistant was very indignant, and wanted to speak to the man; but rightly judging that the object was to enrage me, and trap me into committing some overt act, that would be afterwards construed against me, I kept my temper, spoke very firmly but temperately, told him my moonshee was doing some work of great importance, that I could not spare his services then, but that I would myself see that the summons was attended to. The policeman became more boisterous and insolent. I offered to give him a letter to the magistrate, acknowledging the receipt of the summons, and I asked him his own name, which he refused to give. I asked him if he could read, and he said he could not. I then asked him if he could not read, how could he know what was in the paper which he had brought, and how he knew my moonshee was the party meant. He said a chowkeydar had told him so. I asked where was the chowkeydar, and seeing from my coolness and determination that the game was up, he shouted out, and from round the corner of the huts came another policeman, and two village chowkeydars from a distance. They had evidently been hiding, observing all that passed, and meaning to act as witnesses against me, if I had been led by the first scoundrel's behaviour to lose my temper. The second man was not such a brute as the first, and when I proceeded to ask their names and all about them, and told them I meant to report them to their superintendent, they became somewhat frightened, and tried to make excuses.

I told them to be off the premises at once, offering to take the summons, and give a receipt for it, but they now saw that they had made a mistake in trying to bully me, and made off at once. Mark the sequel. The day before the case was fixed on for hearing, I sent off the moonshee who was a witness of my own, and his evidence was necessary to my proving my case. I supplied him with travelling expenses, and he started.

On his way to the Court he had to pass the *thanna*, or police-station. The police were on the watch. He was seized as he passed. He was confined all that night and all the following day. For want of his evidence I lost my case, and having thus achieved one part of their object to pay me off, they let my moonshee go, after insult and abuse, and with threats of future vengeance should he ever dare to thwart or oppose them. This was pretty 'hot' you think, but it was not all. Fearing my complaint to the superintendent, or to the authorities, might get them into trouble, they laid a false charge against me, that I had obstructed them in the discharge of their duty, that I had showered abuse on them, used threatening language, and insulted the majesty of the law by tearing up and spitting upon the respected summons of Her Majesty. On this complaint I was accordingly summoned into Purneah. The charge was a tissue of the most barefaced lies, but I had to ride fifty-four miles in the burning sun, ford several rivers, and undergo much fatigue and discomfort. My work was of course seriously interfered with. I had to take in my assistant as witness, and one or two of the servants who had been present. I was put to immense trouble, and no little expense, to say nothing of the indignation which I naturally felt, and all because I had set my face against a well known evil, and was determined not to submit to impudent extortion. Of course the case broke down. They contradicted themselves in almost every particular. The second constable indeed admitted that I had offered them a letter to the magistrate, and had not moved out of the verandah during the colloquy. I was honourably acquitted, and had the satisfaction of seeing the lying rascals put into the dock by the indignant magistrate and prosecuted summarily for getting up a false charge and giving false evidence. It was a lesson to the police in those parts, and they did not dare to trouble me much afterwards; but it is only one instance out of hundreds I could give, and which every planter has witnessed of the barefaced audacity, the shameless extortion, the unblushing lawlessness of the rural police of India.

It is a gigantic evil, but surely not irremediable. By adding more European officers to the force; by educating the people and making them more intelligent, independent, and self-reliant, much may be done to abate the evil, but at present it is admittedly a foul ulcer on the administration of justice under our rule. The menial who serves a summons, gets a decree of Court to execute, or is entrusted with any order of an official nature, expects to be bribed to do his duty. If he does not get his fee, he will throw such impediments in the way, raise such obstacles, and fashion such delays, that he completely foils every effort to procure justice through a legal channel. No wonder a native hates our English Courts. Our English officials, let it be plainly understood, are above suspicion. It needs not my poor testimony to uphold their character for high honour, loyal integrity, and zealous eagerness to do 'justly, and to walk uprightly.' They are unwearied in their efforts to get at truth, and govern wisely; but our system of law is totally unsuited for Orientals. It is made a medium for chicanery and trickery of the most atrocious form. Most of the native underlings are utterly venal and corrupt. Increased pay does not mean decrease of knavery. Cheating, and lying, and taking bribes, and abuse of authority are ingrained into their very souls;

and all the cut and dry formulas of namby pamby philanthropists, the inane maunderings of stay-at-home sentimentalists, the wise saws of self-opinionated theorists, who know nothing of the Hindoo as he really shews himself to us in daily and hourly contact with him, will ever persuade me that native, as opposed to English rule, would be productive of aught but burning oppression and shameless venality, or would end in anything but anarchy and chaos.

It sounds very well in print, and increases the circulation of a paper or two among the Baboos, to cry out that our task is to elevate the oppressed and ignorant millions of the East, to educate them into self-government, to make them judges, officers, lawgivers, governors over all the land. To vacate our place and power, and let the Baboo and the Bunneah, to whom we have given the glories of Western civilization, rule in our place, and guide the fortunes of these toiling millions who owe protection and peace to our fostering rule. It is a noble sentiment to resign wealth, honour, glory, and power; to give up a settled government; to alter a policy that has welded the conflicting elements of Hindostan into one stable whole; to throw up our title of conqueror, and disintegrate a mighty empire. For what? A sprinkling of thinly-veneered, half-educated natives, want a share of the loaves and fishes in political scrambling, and a few inane people of the 'man and brother' type, cry out at home to let them have their way.

No. Give the Hindoo education, equal laws, protection to life and property; develop the resources of the country; foster all the virtues you can find in the native mind; but till you can give him the energy, the integrity, the singleness of purpose, the manly, honourable straightforwardness of the Anglo-Saxon; his scorn of meanness, trickery, and fraud; his loyal single-heartedness to do right; his contempt for oppression of the weak; his self-dependence; his probity. But why go on? When you make Hindoos honest, truthful, God-fearing Englishmen, you can let them govern themselves; but as soon 'may the leopard change his spots,' as the Hindoo his character. He is wholly unfit for self-government; utterly opposed to honest, truthful, stable government at all. Time brings strange changes, but the wisdom which has governed the country hitherto, will surely be able to meet the new demand that may be made upon it in the immediate present, or in the far distant future.

CHAPTER XV.

Jungle wild fruits.—Curious method of catching quail.—Quail nets.—Quail caught in a blacksmith's shop.—Native wrestling.—The trainer.—How they train for a match.—Rules of wrestling.—Grips.—A wrestling match.—Incidents of the struggle.—Description of a match between a Brahmin and a blacksmith.—Sparring for the grip.—The blacksmith has it.—The struggle.—The Brahmin getting the worst of it.—Two to one on the little 'un !—The Brahmin plays the waiting game, turns the tables *and* the blacksmith.—Remarks on wrestling.

A PECULIARITY in the sombre sal jungles is the scarcity of wild fruit. At home the woods are filled with berries and fruit-bearing bushes. Who among my readers has not a lively recollection of bramble hunting, nutting, or merry expeditions for blueberries, wild strawberries, raspberries, and other wild fruits? You might walk many a mile through the sal jungles without meeting fruit of any kind, save the dry and tasteless wild fig, or the sickly mhowa.

There are indeed very few jungle fruits that I have ever come across. There is one acid sort of plum called the *Omra*, which makes a good preserve, but is not very nice to eat raw. The *Gorkah* is a small red berry, very sweet and pleasant, slightly acid, not unlike a red currant in fact, and with two small pips or stones. The Nepaulese call it *Bunchooree*. It grows on a small stunted-looking bush, with few branches, and a pointed leaf, in form resembling the acacia leaf, but not so large.

The *Glaphur* is a brown, round fruit; the skin

rather crisp and hard, and of a dull earthy colour, not unlike that of a common boiled potato. The inside is a stringy, spongy-looking mass, with small seeds embedded in a gummy viscid substance. The taste is exactly like an almond, and it forms a pleasant mouthful if one is thirsty.

Travelling one day along one of the glades I have mentioned as dividing the strips of jungle, I was surprised to see a man before me in a field of long stubble, with a cloth spread over his head, and two sticks projecting in front at an obtuse angle to his body, forming horn-like projections, on which the ends of his cloth twisted spirally, were tied. I thought from his curious antics and movements, that he must be mad, but I soon discovered that there was method in his madness. He was catching quail. The quail are often very numerous in the stubble fields, and the natives adopt very ingenious devices for their capture. This was one I was now witnessing. Covering themselves with their cloth as I have described, the projecting ends of the two sticks representing the horns, they simulate all the movements of a cow or bull. They pretend to paw up the earth, toss their make-believe horns, turn round and pretend to scratch themselves, and in fact identify themselves with the animal they are representing; and it is irresistibly comic to watch a solitary performer go through this *al fresco* comedy. I have laughed often at some cunning old herdsman, or shekarry. When they see you watching them, they will redouble their efforts, and try to represent an old bull, going through all his pranks and practices, and throw you into convulsions of laughter.

Round two sides of the field, they have previously put fine nets, and at the apex they have a large cage with a decoy quail inside, or perhaps a pair. The quail is a running bird, disinclined for flight except at night; in the day-time they prefer running to using their wings. The idiotic looking old cow, as we will call the hunter, has all his wits about him. He proceeds very slowly and warily, his keen eye detects the coveys of quail, which way they are running; his ruse generally succeeds wonderfully. He is no more like a cow, than that respectable animal is like a cucumber; but he paws, and tosses, and moves about, pretends to eat, to nibble here, and switch his tail there, and so manœuvres as to keep the running quail away from the unprotected edges of the field. When they get to the verge protected by the net, they begin to take alarm; they are probably not very certain about the peculiar looking 'old cow' behind them, and running along the net, they see the decoy quails evidently feeding in great security and freedom. The V shaped mouth of the large basket cage looks invitingly open. The puzzling nets are barring the way, and the 'old cow' is gradually closing up behind. As the hunter moves along, I should have told you, he rubs two pieces of dry hard sticks gently up and down his thigh with one hand, producing a peculiar crepitation, a crackling sound, not sufficient to startle the birds into flight, but alarming them enough to make them get out of the way of the 'old cow.' One bolder than the others, possibly the most timid of the covey, irritated by the queer crackling sound, now enters the basket, the others follow like a flock of sheep; and once in, the puzzling shape of the entrance prevents their exit. Not unfrequently the hunter bags twenty or even thirty brace of quail in one field, by this ridiculous looking but ingenious method.

The small quail net is also sometimes used for the

capture of hares. The natives stretch the net in the jungle, much as they do the large nets for deer described in a former chapter; forming a line, they then beat up the hares, of which there are no stint. My friend Pat once made a novel haul. His *lobarkhanna* or blacksmith's shop was close to a patch of jungle, and Pat often noticed numbers of quail running through the loose chinks and crevices of the walls, in the morning when anyone went into the place for the first time; this was at a factory called Rajpore. Pat came to the conclusion, that as the blacksmith's fires smouldered some time after work was discontinued at night, and as the atmosphere of the hut was warmer and more genial than the cold, foggy, outside air, for it was in the cold season, the quail probably took up their quarters in the hut for the night, on account of the warmth and shelter. One night therefore he got some of his servants, and with great caution and as much silence as possible, they let down a quantity of nets all round the lobarkhanna, and in the morning they captured about twenty quails.

The quail is very pugnacious, and as they are easily trained to fight, they are very common pets with the natives, who train and keep them to pit them against each other, and bet what they can afford on the result. A quail fight, a battle between two trained rams, a cock fight, even an encounter between trained tamed buffaloes, are very common spectacles in the villages; but the most popular sport is a good wrestling match.

The dwellers in the Presidency towns, and indeed in most of the large stations, seldom see an exhibition of this kind; but away in the remote interior, near the frontier, it is very popular pastime, and wrestling is a favourite with all classes. Such manly sport is rather opposed to the commonly received idea at home, of the mild Hindoo. In nearly every village of Behar however, and all along the borders of Nepaul, there is, as a rule, a bit of land attached to the residence of some head man, or the common property of the commune, set apart for the practice of athletic sports, chief of which is the favourite *khoosthee* or wrestling. There is generally some wary old veteran, who has won his spurs, or laurels, or belt, or whatever you choose to call it, in many a hard fought and well contested tussle for the championship of his little world; he is 'up to every dodge,' and knows every feint and guard, every wile and tactic of the wrestling ground. It is generally in some shady grove, secluded and cool; here of an evening when the labours of the day are over, the most stalwart sons of the hamlet meet, to test each others skill and endurance in a friendly *shake*. The old man puts them through the preliminary practice, shows them every trick at his command, and attends strictly to their training and various trials. The ground is dug knee deep, and forms a soft, good holding stand. I have often looked on at this evening practice, and it would astonish a stranger, who cannot understand strength, endurance, and activity being attributed to a 'mere nigger,' to see the severe training these young lads impose upon themselves. They leap into the air, and suddenly assume a sitting position, then leap up again and squat down with a force that would seem to jerk every bone in their bodies out of its place; this gets up the muscles of the thighs. Some lie down at full length, only touching the ground with the extreme tips of their toes, their arms doubled up under them, and sustaining the full weight of the body on the extended palms of the hands. They then sway themselves backwards and forwards to their full length, never shifting hand or toe, till they are bathed in perspiration; they keep up a uniform steady backward and forward movement, so as to develop the muscles of the arms, chest, and back. They practice leaping, running, and lifting weights. Some standing at their full height, brace up the muscles of the shoulder and upper arm, and then leaping up, allow themselves to fall to earth on the tensely strung muscles of the shoulder. This severe exercise gets the muscles into perfect form, and few, very few indeed of our untrained youths, could cope in a dead lock, or fierce struggle, with a good village Hindoo or Mussulman in active training, and having any knowledge of the tricks of the wrestling school. No hitting is allowed. The Hindoo system of wrestling is the perfection of science and skill; mere dead weight of course will always tell in a close grip, but the catches, the holds, the twists and dodges that are practised, allow for the fullest development of cultivated skill, as against mere brute force. The system is purely a scientific one. The fundamental rule is 'catch where you can,' only you must not clutch the hair or strike with the fists.

The loins are tightly girt with a long waist-belt or *kummerbund* of cloth, which, passed repeatedly between the limbs and round the loins, sufficiently braces up and protects that part of the body. In some matches you are not allowed to clutch this waist cloth or belt, in some villages it is allowed; the custom varies in various places, but what is a fair grip, and what is not, is always made known before the competitors engage. A twist, or grip, or dodge, is known as a *paench*. This literally means a screw or twist, but in wrestling phraseology, means any grip by which you can get such an advantage over your opponent as to defeat him. For every paench there is a counter paench. A throw is considered satisfactory when BOTH shoulders of your opponent touch the ground simultaneously. The old *khalifa* or trainer takes a great interest in the progress of his *chailas* or pupils. *Chaila* really means disciple or follower. Every khalifa has his favourite paenches or grips, which have stood him in good stead in his old battling days; he teaches these paenches to his pupils, so that when you get young fellows from different villages to meet, you see a really fine exhibition of wrestling skill. There is little tripping, as amongst our wrestlers at home; a dead-lock is uncommon. The rival wrestlers generally bound into the ring, slapping their thighs and arms with a loud resounding slap. They lift their legs high up from the ground with every step, and scheme and manœuvre sometimes for a long while to get the best corner; they try to get the sun into their adversaries eyes; they scan the appearance and every movement of their opponent. The old wary fellows take it very coolly, and if they can't get the desired side of the ground, they keep hopping about like a solemn old ostrich, till the impetuosity or impatience of their foe leads him to attack. They remind you for all the world of a pair of game cocks, their bodies are bent, their heads almost touching. There is a deal of light play with the hands, each trying to get the other by the wrist or elbow, or at the back of the head round the neck. If one gets the other by a finger even, it is a great advantage, as he would whip nimbly round, and threaten to break the impounded finger; this would be considered quite fair. One will often suddenly drop on his knees and try to reach the ankles of his adversary. I have seen a slippery customer, stoop suddenly down, grasp up a handful of dust, and throw it into the eyes of his opponent. It was done with the quickness of thought, but it was detected, and on an appeal by the sufferer, the knave was well thrashed by the onlookers.

There are many professionals who follow no other calling. Wrestlers are kept by Rajahs and wealthy men, who get up matches. Frequently one village will challenge another, like our village cricket clubs. The villagers often get up small subscriptions, and purchase a silver armlet or bracelet, the prize him who shall hold his own against all comers. The 'Champion's Belt' scarcely calls forth greater competition, keener rivalry, or better sport. It is at once the most manly and most scientific sport in which the native indulges. A disputed fall sometimes terminates in a general free fight, when the backers of the respective men lay on the stick to each other with mutual hate and hearty lustiness.

It is not by any means always the strongest who wins. The man who knows the most paenches, who is agile, active, cool, and careful, will not unfrequently overthrow an antagonist twice his weight and strength. All the wrestlers in the country-side know each other's qualifications pretty accurately, and at a general match got up by a Zemindar or planter, or by public subscription, it is generally safe to let them handicap the men who are ready to compete for the prizes. We used generally to put down a few of the oldest professors, and let them pit couples against each other; the sport to the onlookers was most exciting. Between the men themselves as a rule, the utmost good humour reigns, they strive hard to win, but they accept a defeat with smiling resignation. It is only between rival village champions, different caste men, or worse still, men of differing religions, such as a Hindoo and a Mahommedan, that there is any danger of a fight. A disturbance is a rare exception, but I have seen a few wrestling matches end in a regular general scrimmage, with broken heads, and even fractured limbs. With good management however, and an efficient body of men to guard against a breach of the peace, this need never occur.

It rarely takes much trouble to get up a match. If you tell your head men that you would like to see one, say on a Saturday afternoon, they pass the word to the different villages, and at the appointed time, all the finest young fellows and most of the male population, led by their head man, with the old trainer in attendance, are at the appointed place. The competitors are admitted within the enclosure, and round it the rows of spectators packed twenty deep squat on the ground, and watch the proceedings with deep interest.

While the *Punchayiet*, a picked council, are taking down the names of intending competitors, finding out about their form and performances, and assigning to each his antagonist, the young men throw themselves with shouts and laughter into the ring, and go through all the evolutions and postures of the training ground. They bound about, try all sorts of antics and contortions, display wonderful agility and activity; it is a pretty sight to see, and one can't help admiring their vigorous frames, and graceful proportions. They are handsome, well made, supple, wiry fellows, although they be NIGGERS, and Hodge and Giles at home would not have a chance with them in a fair wrestling bout, conducted according to their own laws and customs.

The entries are now all made, places and pairs are arranged, and to the ear-splitting thunder of two or three tom-toms, two pair of strapping youngsters step into the ring; they carefully scan each other, advance, shake hands, or salaam, leisurely tie up their back hair, slap their muscles, rub a little earth over their shoulders and arms, so that their adversary may have a fair grip, then step by step slowly and gradually they near each other. A few quick passages are now interchanged; the lithe supple fingers twist and intertwine, grips are formed on arm and neck. The postures change each moment, and are a study for an anatomist or sculptor. As they warm to their work they get more reckless; they are only the raw material, the untrained lads. There is a quick scuffle, heaving, swaying, rocking, and struggling, and the two victors, leaping into the air, and slapping their chests, bound back into the gratified circle of their comrades, while the two discomfited athletes, forcing a rueful smile, retire and 'take a back seat.' Two couple of more experienced hands now face each other. There is pretty play this time, as the varying changes of the contest bring forth ever varying displays of skill and science. The crowd shout as an advantage is gained, or cry out 'Hi, hi' in a doubtful manner, as their favourite seems to be getting the worst of it. The result however is much the same; after a longer or shorter time, two get fairly thrown and retire. If there is any dispute, it is at once referred to the judges, who sit grimly watching the struggle, and comparing the paenches displayed, with those they themselves have practised in many a well-won fight. On a reference being made, both combatants retain their exact hold and position, only cease straining. As soon as the matter is settled, they go at it again till victory determine in favour of the lucky man. In no similar contest in England I am convinced would there be so much fairness, quietness, and order. The only stimulants in the crowd are betel nut and tobacco. All is orderly and calm, and at any moment a word from the sahib will quell any rising turbulence. It is now time for a still more scientific exhibition.

Pat has a man, a tall, wiry, handsome Brahmin, who has never yet been beaten. Young K. has long been jealous of his uniform success, and on several occasions has brought an antagonist to battle with Pat's champion. To-day he has got a sturdy young blacksmith, whom rumour hath much vaunted, and although he is not so tall as Pat's wrestler, his square, deep chest and stalwart limbs, give promise of great strength and endurance.

As the two men strip and bound into the ring, there is the usual hush of anticipation. Keen eyes scan the appearance of the antagonists. They are both models of manly beauty. The blacksmith, though more awkward in his motions, has a cool, determined look about him. The Brahmin, conscious of his reputation, walks quickly up, with a smile of rather ostentatious condescension on his finely cut features, and offers his hand to the blacksmith. The little man is evidently suspicious. He thinks this may be a deeply laid trap to get a grip upon him. Nor does he like the bland patronising manner of 'Roopnarain,' so he surlily draws back, at which there is a roar of laughter from the crowd, in which we cannot help joining.

K. now comes forward, and pats his 'fancy man' on the back. The two wrestlers thereupon shake hands, and then in the usual manner both warily move backwards and forwards, till amid cries from the onlookers, the blacksmith makes a sudden dash at the practised old player, and in a moment has him round the waist.

He evidently depended on his superior strength. For a moment he fairly lifted Roopnarain clean off his legs, swayed him to and fro, and with a mighty strain tried to throw him to the ground. Bending to the notes, Roopnarain allowed himself to yield, till his feet touched the ground, then crouching like a panther, he bounded forward, and getting his leg behind that of the blacksmith, by a deft side twist he nearly threw him over. The little fellow, however, steadied himself on the ground with one hand, recovered his footing, and again had the Brahmin firmly locked in his tenacious hold. Roopnarain did not like the grip. These were not the tactics he was accustomed to. While the other tugged and strained, he, quietly yielding his lithe lissome frame to every effort, tried hard with obstinate endeavour to untwist the hands that held him firmly locked. It was beautiful play to see the mute hands of both the wrestlers feeling, tearing, twisting at each other, but the grasp was too firm, and, taking advantage of a momentary movement, Roopnarain got his elbow under the other's chin, then leaning forward, he pressed his opponent's head backward, and the strain began to tell. He fought fiercely, he struggled hard, but the determined elbow was not to be baulked, and to save himself from an overthrow the blacksmith was forced to relax his hold, and sprang nimbly back beyond reach, to mature another attack. Roopnarain quietly walked round, rubbed his shoulders with earth, and with the same mocking smile, stood leaning forward, his hands on his knees, waiting for a fresh onset.

This time the young fellow was more cautious. He found he had no novice to deal with, and the Brahmin was not at all anxious to precipitate matters. By a splendid feint, after some pretty sparring for a grip, the youngster again succeeded in getting a hold on the Brahmin, and wheeling round quick as lightning, got behind Roopnarain, and with a dexterous trip threw the tall man heavily on his face. He then tried to get him by the ankle, and bending his leg up backwards, he would have got a purchase for turning him on his back. The old man was, however, 'up to this move.' He lay extended flat on his chest, his legs wide apart. As often as the little one bent down to grasp his ankle, he would put out a hand stealthily, and silently as a snake, and endeavour to get the little man's leg in his grasp. This necessitated a change of position, and round and round they spun, each trying to get hold of the other by the leg or foot. The blacksmith got his knee on the neck of the Brahmin, and by sheer strength tried several times with a mighty heave to turn his opponent. It was no use, however, it is next to impossible to throw a man when he is lying flat out as the Brahmin now was. It is difficult enough to turn the dead weight of a man in that position, and when he is straining every nerve to resist the accomplishment of your object it becomes altogether impracticable. The excitement in the crowd was intense. The very drummer—I ought to call him a tom-tomer—had ceased to beat his tom-tom. Pat's lips were firmly pressed together, and K. was trembling with suppressed excitement. The heaving chests and profuse perspiration bedewing the bodies of both combatants, told how severe had been their exertions. The blacksmith seemed gathering himself up for a mighty effort, when, quick as light, the Brahmin drew his limbs together, was seen to arch his back, and with a sudden backward movement, seemed to glide from under his dashing assailant, and quicker than it takes me to write it, the positions were reversed.

The Brahmin was now above, and the blacksmith taking in the altered aspect of affairs at a glance, threw himself flat on the ground, and tried the same tactics as his opponent. The different play of the two men now came strongly into relief. Instead of exhausting himself with useless efforts, Roopnarain, while keeping a wary eye on every movement of his prostrate foe, contented himself while he took breath, with coolly and and yet determinedly making his grip secure. Putting out one leg then within reach of his opponent's hand, as a lure, he saw the blacksmith stretch forth to grasp the tempting hold.

Quicker than the dart of the python, the fierce onset of the kingly tiger, the sudden flash of the forked and quivering lightning, was the grasp made at the outstretched arm by the practised Brahmin. His tenacious fingers closed tightly round the other's wrist. One sudden wrench, and he had the blacksmith's arm bent back and powerless, held down on the little fellow's own shoulders. Pat smiled a derisive smile, K. uttered what was not a benison, while the Brahmins in the crowd, and all Pat's men, raised a truly Hindoo howl. The position of the men was now this. The stout little man was flat on his face, one of his arms bent helplessly round on his own back. Roopnarain, calm and cool as ever, was astride the prostrate blacksmith, placidly surveying the crowd. The little man writhed, and twisted, and struggled, he tried with his legs to entwine himself with those of the Brahmin. He tried to spin round; the Brahmin was watching with the eye of a hawk for a grip of the other arm, but it was closely drawn in, and firmly pressed in safety under the heaving chest of the blacksmith. The muscles were of steel; it could not be dislodged: that was seen at a glance. The calmness and placidity of the old athlete was surprising, it was wonderful. Still bending the imprisoned arm further back, he put his knee on the neck of the poor little hero, game as a pebble through it all, and by a strong steady strain tried to bend him over, till we thought either the poor fellow's neck must break, or his arm be torn from its socket.

He endured all without a murmur. Not a chance did he throw away. Once or twice he made a splendid effort, once he tried to catch the Brahmin again by the leg. Roopnarain pounced down, but the arm was as quickly within its shield. It was now but a question of time and endurance. Every dodge that he was master of did the Brahmin bring into play. They were both in perfect training, muscles as hard as steel, every nerve and sinew strained to the utmost tension. Roopnarain actually tried tickling his man, but he would not give him a chance. At length he got his hand in the bent elbow of the free arm, and slowly, and laboriously forced it out. There were tremendous spurts and struggles, but patient determination was not to be baulked. Slowly the arm came up over the back, the struggle was tremendous, but at length both the poor fellow's arms were tightly pinioned behind his back. He was powerless now. The Brahmin drew the two arms backwards, towards the head of the poor little fellow, and he was bound to come over or have both his arms broken. With a hoarse cry of sobbing pain and shame, the brave little man came over, both shoulders on the mould, and the scientific old veteran was again the victor.

This is but a very faint description of a true wrestling bout among the robust dwellers in these remote villages. It may seem cruel, but it is to my mind the perfection of muscular strength and skill, combined with keen subtle, intellectual acuteness. It brings every faculty of mind and body into play, it begets a healthy, honest love of fair play, and an admiration of endurance and pluck, two qualities of which Englishmen certainly can boast. Strength without skill and training will not avail. It is a fine manly sport, and one which should be encouraged by all who wish well to our dusky fellow subjects in the far off plains and valleys of Hindostan.

CHAPTER XVI.

Indigo seed growing.—Seed buying and buyers.—Tricks of sellers.—Tests for good seed.—The threshing-floor.—Seed cleaning and packing.—Staff of servants.—Despatching the bags by boat.—The 'Pooneah' or rent day.—Purneah planters—their hospitality.—The rent day a great festival.—Preparation.—Collection of rents.—Feast to retainers.—The reception in the evening.—Tribute.—Old customs.—Improvisatores and bards.—Nautches.—Dancing and music.—The dance of the Dangurs.—Jugglers and itinerary showmen.—'Bara Roopes,' or actors and mimics.—Their different styles of acting.

BESIDES indigo planting proper, there is another large branch of industry in North Bhaugulpore, and along the Nepaul frontier there, and in Purneah, which is the growing of indigo seed for the Bengal planters. The system of advances and the mode of cultivation is much the same as that followed in indigo planting proper. The seed is sown in June or July, is weeded and tended all through the rains, and cut in December. The planters advance about four rupees a beegah to the ryot, who cuts his seed-plant, and brings it into the factory threshing ground, where it is beaten out, cleaned, weighed, and packed in bags. When the seed has been threshed out and cleaned, it is weighed, and the ryot or cultivator gets four rupees for every maund—a maund being eighty pounds avoirdupois. The previous advance is deducted. The rent or loan account is adjusted, and the balance made over in cash.

Others grow the seed on their own account, without

taking advances, and bring it to the factory for sale. If prices are ruling high, they may get much more than four rupees per maund for it, and they adopt all kinds of ingenious devices to adulterate the seed, and increase its weight. They mix dust with it, seeds of weeds, even grains of wheat, and mustard, pea, and other seeds. In buying seed, therefore, one has to be very careful, to reject all that looks bad, or that may have been adulterated. They will even get old useless seed, the refuse stock of former years, and mixing this with leaves of the neem tree and some turmeric powder, give it a gloss that makes it look like fresh seed.

When you suspect that the seed has been tampered with in this manner, you wet some of it, and rub it on a piece of fresh clean linen, so as to bring off the dye. Where the attempt has been flagrant, you are sometimes tempted to take the law into your own hands, and administer a little of the castigation which the cheating rascal so richly deserves. In other cases it is necessary to submit the seed to a microscopic examination. If any old, worn seeds are detected, you reject the sample unhesitatingly. Even when the seed appears quite good, you subject it to yet another test. Take one or two hundred seeds, and putting them on a damp piece of the pith of a plantain tree, mixed with a little earth, set them in a warm place, and in two days you will be able to tell what percentage has germinated, and what is incapable of germination. If the percentage is good, the seed may be considered as fairly up to the sample, and it is purchased. There are native seed buyers, who try to get as much into their hands as they can, and rig the market. There are also European buyers, and there is a keen rivalry in all the bazaars.

The threshing-floor, and seed-cleaning ground presents a busy sight when several thousand maunds of seed are being got ready for despatch by boats. The dirty seed, full of dust and other impurities, is heaped up in one corner. The floor is in the shape of a large square, nicely paved with cement, as hard and clean as marble. Crowds of nearly nude coolies, hurry to and fro with scoops of seed resting on their shoulders. When they get in line, at right angles to the direction in which the wind is blowing, they move slowly along, letting the seed descend on the heap below, while the wind winnows it, and carries the dust in dense clouds to leeward. This is repeated over and over again, till the seed is as clean as it can be made. It is put through bamboo sieves, so formed that any seed larger than indigo cannot pass through. What remains in the sieve is put aside, and afterwards cleaned, sorted, and sold as food, or if useless, thrown away or given to the fowls. The men and boys dart backwards and forwards, there is a steady drip, drip, of seed from the scoops, dense clouds of dust, and incessant noise and bustle. Peons or watchmen are stationed all around to see that none is wasted or stolen. Some are filling sacks full of the cleaned seed, and hauling them off to the weighman and his clerk. Two maunds are put in every sack, and when weighed the bags are hauled up close to the *godown* or store-room. Here are an army of men with sailmaker's needles and twine. They sew up the bags, which are then hauled away to be marked with the factory brand. Carts are coming and going, carrying bags to the boats, which are lying at the river bank taking in their cargo, and the returning carts bring back loads of wood from the banks of the river. In one corner, under a shed, sits the sahib chaffering with a party of *paikars* (seed merchants), who have brought seed for sale.

Of course he decries the seed, says it is bad, will not hear of the price wanted, and laughs to scorn all the fervent protestations that the seed was grown on their own ground, and has never passed through any hands but their own. If you are satisfied that the seed is good, you secretly name your price to your head man, who forthwith takes up the work of depreciation. You move off to some other department of the work. The head man and the merchants sit down, perhaps smoke a *hookah*, each trying to outwit the other, but after a keen encounter of wits perhaps a bargain is made. A pretty fair price is arrived at, and away goes the purchased seed, to swell the heap at the other end of the yard. It has to be carefully weighed first, and the weighman gets a little from the vendor as his perquisite, which the factory takes from him at the market rate.

You have buyers of your own out in the *dehaat* (district), and the parcels they have bought come in hour by hour, with invoices detailing all particulars of quantity, quality, and price. The loads from the seed depôts and outworks, come rolling up in the afternoon, and have all to be weighed, checked, noted down, and examined. Every man's hand is against you. You cannot trust your own servants. For a paltry bribe they will try to pass a bad parcel of seed, and even when you have your European assistants to help you, it is hard work to avoid being over-reached in some shape or other.

You have to keep up a large staff of writers, who make out invoices and accounts, and keep the books.

Your correspondence alone is enough work for one man, and you have to tally bags, count coolies, see them paid their daily wage, attend to lawsuits that may be going on, and yet find time to superintend the operations of the farm, and keep an eye to your rents and revenues from the villages. It is a busy, an anxious time. You have a vast responsibility on your shoulders, and when one takes into consideration the climate you have to contend with, the home comforts and domestic joys you have to do without, the constant tension of mind and irritation of body from dust, heat, insects, lies, bribery, robbers, and villany of every description, that meets you on all hands, it must be allowed that a planter at such a time has no easy life.

The time at which you despatch the seed is also the very time when you are preparing your land for spring sowings. This requires almost as much surveillance as the seed-buying and despatching. You have not a moment you can call your own. If you had subordinates you could trust, who would be faithful and honest, you could safely leave part of the work to them, but from very sad experience I have found that trusting to a native is trusting to a very rotten stick. They are certainly not all bad, but there are just enough exceptions to prove the rule.

One peculiar custom prevailed in this border district of North Bhaugulpore, which I have not observed elsewhere. At the beginning of the financial year, when the accounts of the past season had all been made up and arranged, and the collection of the rents for the new year was beginning, the planters and Zemindars held what was called the *Pooneah*. It is customary for all cultivators and tenants to pay a proportion of their rent in advance. The Pooneah might therefore be called 'rent-day.' A similar day is set apart for the same purpose in Tirhoot, called *tousee* or collections, but it is not attended by the same ceremonious observances, and quaint customs, as attach to the Pooneah on the border land.

When every man's account has been made up and checked by the books, the Pooneah day is fixed on. Invitations are sent to all your neighbouring friends, who look forward to each other's annual Pooneah as a great gala day. In North Bhaugulpore and Purneah, nearly all the planters and English-speaking population belong to old families who have been born in the district, and have settled and lived there long before the days of quick communication with home. Their rule among their dependants is patriarchal. Everyone is known among the natives, who have seen him since his birth living amongst them, by some pet name. The old men of the villages remember his father and his father's father, the younger villagers have had him pointed out to them on their visits to the factory as 'Willie Baba,' 'Freddy Baba,' or whatever his boyish name may have been, with the addition of 'Baba,' which is simply a pet name for a child. These planters know every village for miles and miles. They know most of the leading men in each village by name. The villagers know all about them, discuss their affairs with the utmost freedom, and not a single thing, ever so trivial, happens in the planter's home but it is known and commented on in all the villages that lie within the *ilaka* (jurisdiction) of the factory.

The hospitality of these planters is unbounded. They are most of them much liked by all the natives round. I came a 'stranger amongst them,' and in one sense, and not a flattering sense, they tried 'to take me in,' but only in one or two instances, which I shall not specify here. By nearly all I was welcomed and kindly treated, and I formed some very lasting friendships among them. Old traditions of princely hospitality still linger among them. They were clannish in the best sense of the word. The kindness and attention given to aged or indigent relations was one of their best traits. I am afraid the race is fast dying out. Lavish expenditure, and a too confiding faith in their native dependants has often brought the usual result. But many of my readers will associate with the name of Purneah or Bhaugulpore planter, recollections of hospitality and unostentatious kindness, and memories of glorious sport and warm-hearted friendships.

On the Pooneah day then, or the night before, many of these friends would meet. The day has long been known to all the villages round, and nothing could better shew the patriarchal semi-feudal style in which they ruled over their villages than the customs in connection with this anniversary. Some days before it, requisitions have been made on all the villages in any way connected with the factory, for various articles of diet. The herdsmen have to send a tribute of milk, curds, and *ghee* or clarified butter. Cultivators of root crops or fruit send in samples of their produce, in the shape of huge bundle of plantains, immense jack-fruits, or baskets of sweet potatoes, yams, and other vegetables. The *koomhar* or potter has to send in earthen pots and jars. The *mochee* or worker in leather, brings with him a sample of his work in the shape of a pair of shoes. These are pounced on by your servants and *omlah*, the omlah being the head men in the office. It is a fine time for them. Wooden shoes, umbrellas, brass pots, fowls, goats, fruits, in fact all the productions of your country side are sent or brought in. It is the old feudal tribute of the middle ages back again. During the day the *cutcherry* or office is crowded with the more respectable villagers, paying in rents and settling accounts. The noise and bustle are great, but an immense quantity of work is got through.

The village putwarries and head men are all there with their voluminous accounts. Your rent-collector, called a *tehseeldar*, has been busy in the villages with the tenants and putwarries, collecting rent for the great Pooneah day. There is a constant chink of money, a busy hum, a scratching of innumerable pens. Under every tree, 'neath the shade of every hut, busy groups are squatted round some acute accountant. Totals are being totted up on all hands. From greasy recesses in the waistband a dirty bundle is slowly pulled forth, and the desired sum reluctantly counted out.

From early morn till dewy eve this work goes on, and you judge your Pooneah to have been a good or bad one by the amount you are able to collect. Peons, with their brass badges flashing in the sun, and their red puggrees shewing off their bronzed faces and black whiskers, are despatched in all directions for defaulters. There is a constant going to and fro, a hurrying and bustling in the crowd, a hum as of a distant fair pervading the place, and by evening the total of the day's collections is added up, and while the sahib and his friends take their sherry and bitters, the omlah and servants retire to wash and feast, and prepare for the night's festivities.

During the day, at the houses of the omlah, culinary preparations on a vast scale have been going on. The large supplies of grain, rice, flour, fruit, vegetables, &c., which were brought in as *salamee* or tribute, supplemented by additions from the sahib's own stores, have been made into savoury messes. Curries, and cakes, boiled flesh, and roast kid, are all ready, and the crowd, having divested themselves of their head-dress and outer garments, and cleaned their hands and feet by copious ablutions, sit down in a wide circle. The large leaves of the water-lily are now served out to each man, and perform the office of plates. Huge baskets of *chupatties*, a flat sort of 'griddle-cake,' are now brought round, and each man gets four or five doled out. The cooking and attendance is all done by Brahmins. No inferior caste would answer, as Rajpoots and other high castes will only eat food that has been cooked by a Brahmin or one of their own class. The Brahmin attendants now come round with great *dekchees* or cooking-pots, full of curried vegetables, boiled rice, and similar dishes. A ladle-full is handed out to each man, who receives it on his leaf. The rice is served out by the hands of the attendants. The guests manipulate a huge ball of rice and curry mixed between the fingers of the right hand, pass this solemnly into their widely-gaping mouths, with the head thrown back to receive the mess, like an adjutant-bird swallowing a frog, and then they masticate with much apparent enjoyment. Sugar, treacle, curds, milk, oil, butter, preserves, and chutnees are served out to the more wealthy and respectable. The amount they can consume is wonderful. Seeing the enormous supplies, you would think that even this great crowd could never get through them, but by the time repletion has set in, there is little or nothing left, and many of the inflated and distended old farmers could begin again and repeat 'another of the same' with ease. Each person has his own *lotah*, a brass drinking vessel, and when all have eaten they again wash their hands, rinse out their mouths, and don their gayest apparel.

The gentlemen in the bungalow now get word that the evening's festivities are about to commence. Lighting our cigars, we sally out to the *shamiana* which has been erected on the ridge, surrounding the deep tank which supplies the factory during the manufacturing season with water. The *shamiana* is a large canopy or wall-less tent. It is festooned with flowers and green plantain trees, and evergreens have been planted all round it. Flaring flambeaux, torches, Chinese lanterns, and oil lamps flicker and glare, and make the interior almost as bright as day. When we arrive we find our chairs drawn up in state, one raised seat in the centre being the place of honour, and reserved for the manager of the factory.

When we are seated, the *malee* or gardener advances with a wooden tray filled with sand, in which are stuck heads of all the finest flowers the garden can afford, placed in the most symmetrical patterns, and really a pretty tasteful piece of workmanship. Two or three old Brahmins, principal among whom is 'Hureehar Jha,' a wicked old scoundrel, now advance, bearing gay garlands of flowers, muttering a strange gibberish in Sanskrit, supposed to be a blessing, but which might be a curse for all we understood of it, and decking our wrists and necks with these strings of flowers. For this service they get a small gratuity. The factory omlah headed by the dignified, portly *gornasta* or confidential adviser, dressed in snowy turbans and spotless white, now come forward. A large brass tray stands on the table in front of you. They each present a *salamee* or *nuzzur*, that is, a tribute or present, which you touch, and it is then deposited with a rattling jingle on the brass plate. The head men of villages, putwarries, and wealthy tenants, give two, three, and sometimes even four rupees. Every tenant of respectability thinks it incumbent on him to give something. Every man as he comes up makes a low salaam, deposits his *salamee*, his name is written down, and he retires. The putwarries present two rupees each, shouting out their names, and the names of their villages. Afterwards a small assessment is levied on the villagers, of a 'pice' or two 'pice' each, about a halfpenny of our money, and which recoups the putwarree for his outlay.

This has nothing to do with the legitimate revenue of the factory. It never appears in the books. It is quite a voluntary offering, and I have never seen it in any other district. In the meantime the *Rajbhats*, a wandering class of hereditary minstrels or bards, are singing your praises and those of your ancestors in ear-splitting strains. Some of them have really good voices, all possess the gift of improvisation, and are quick to seize on the salient points of the scene before them, and weave them into their song, sometimes in a very ingenious and humorous manner. They are often employed by rich natives, to while away a long night with one of their treasured rhythmical tales or songs. One or two are kept in the retinue of every Rajah or noble, and they possess a mine of legendary information, which would be invaluable to the collector of folk-lore and antiquarian literature.

At some of the Pooneahs the evening's gaiety winds up with a *nautch* or dance, by dancing girls or boys. I always thought this a most sleep-inspiring exhibition. It has been so often described that I need not trouble my readers with it. The women are gaily dressed in brocades and gauzy textures, and glitter with spangles and tawdry ornaments. The musical accompaniment of clanging zither, asthmatic fiddle, timber-toned drum, clanging cymbal, and harsh metallic triangle, is a sore affliction, and when the dusky prima donna throws back her head, extends her chest, gets up to her high note, with her hand behind her ear, and her poura-stained mouth and teeth wide expanded like the jaws of a fangless wolf, and the demoniac instruments and performers redouble their din, the noise is something too dreadful to experience often. The native women sit mute and hushed, seeming to like it. I have heard it said that the Germans eat ants. Finlanders relish penny candles. The Nepaulese gourmandise on putrid fish. I am fond of mouldy cheese, and organ-grinders are an object of affection with some of our home community. I *know* that the general run of natives delight in a nautch. Tastes differ, but to me it is an inexplicable phenomenon.

Amid all this noise we sit till we are wearied. Parin-leaves and betel nut are handed round by the servants. There is a very sudorific odour from the crowd. All are comfortably seated on the ground. The torches flare, and send up volumes of smoke to the ornamented roof of the canopy. The lights are reflected in the deep glassy bosom of the silent tank. The combined sounds and odours get oppressive, and we are glad to get back to the bungalow, to consume our 'peg' and our 'weed' in the congenial company of our friends.

In some factories the night closes with a grand dance by all the inhabitants of the *dangur tola*. The men and women range themselves in two semicircles, standing opposite each other. The tallest of both lines at the one end, diminishing away at the other extremity to the children and little ones who can scarcely toddle. They have a wild, plaintive song, with swelling cadences and abrupt stops. They go through an extraordinary variety of evolutions, stamping with one foot and keeping perfect time. They sway their bodies, revolve, march, and countermarch, the men sometimes opening their ranks, and the women going through, and *vice versa*. They turn round like the winding convolutions of a shell, increase their pace as the song waxes quick and shrill, get excited, and finish off with a resounding stamp of the foot, and a guttural cry which seems to exhaust all the breath left in their bodies. The men then get some liquor, and the women a small money present. If the sahib is very liberal he gives them a pig on which to feast, and the *dangurs* go away very happy and contented. Their dance is not unlike the *corroborry* of the Australian aborigines. The two races are not unlike each other too in feature, although I cannot think that they are in any way connected.

Next morning there is a jackal hunt, or cricket, or pony races, or shooting matches, or sport of some kind, while the rent collection still goes on. In the afternoon we have grand wrestling matches amongst the natives for small prizes, and generally witness some fine exhibitions of athletic skill and endurance.

Some wandering juggler may have been attracted by

the rumour of the gathering. A tight-rope dancer, a snake charmer, an itinerant showman with a performing goat, monkey, or dancing bear, may make his appearance before the admiring crowd.

At times a party of mimes or actors come round, and a rare treat is not seldom afforded by the *bara roopees*. *Bara* means twelve, and *roop* is an impersonation, a character. These 'twelve characters' make up in all sorts of disguises. Their wardrobe is very limited, yet the number of people they personate, and their genuine acting talent would astonish you. With a projecting tooth and a few streaks of clay, they make up a withered, trembling old hag, afflicted with palsy, rheumatism, and a hacking cough. They make friends with your bearer, and an old hat and coat transforms them into a planter, a missionary, or an officer. They whiten their faces, using false hair and moustache, and while you are chatting with your neighbour, a strange sahib suddenly and mysteriously seats himself by your side. You stare, and look at your host, who is generally in the secret, but a stranger, or new comer, is often completely taken in. It is generally at night that they go through their personations, and when they have dressed for their part, they generally choose a moment when your attention is attracted by a cunning diversion. On looking up you are astounded to find some utter stranger standing behind your chair, or stalking solemnly round the room.

They personate a woman, a white lady, a sepoy policeman, almost any character. Some are especially good at mimicking the Bengalee Baboo, or the merchant from Cabool or Afghanistan with his fruits and cloths. A favourite *roop* with them is to paint one half of the face like a man. Everything is complete down to moustache, the folds of the puggree, the *lathee* or staff, indeed to the slightest detail. You would fancy you saw a stalwart, strapping Hindoo before you. He turns round, and lo, a bashful maiden. Her eyes are stained with *henna* (myrtle juice) or antimony. Her long hair neatly smoothed down is tied into a knot at the back, and glistens with the pearl-like ornaments. The taper arm is loaded with armlets and bracelets. The very toes are bedecked with rings. The bodice hides the taper waist and budding bosom, the tiny ear is loaded with jewelled ear-rings, the very nose is not forgotten, but is ornamented with a golden circle, bearing on its circumference a pearl of great price. The art, the posturing, the mimicry, is really admirable. A good *bara roopee* is well worth seeing, and amply earns the two or three rupees he gets as his reward.

The Pooneah seldom lasts more than the two days, but it is quite unique in its feudal character, and is one of the old-fashioned observances; a relic of the time when the planter was really looked upon as the father of his people, and when a little sentiment and mutual affection mingled with the purely business relations of landlord and tenant.

I delighted my ryots by importing some of our own country recreations, and setting the ploughmen to compete against each other. I stuck a greasy bamboo firmly into the earth, putting a bag of copper coins at the top. Many tried to climb it, but when they came to the grease they came down 'by the run.' One fellow however filled his *kummerbund* with sand, and after much exertion managed to secure the prize. Wheeling the barrow blindfold also gave much amusement, and we made some boys bend their foreheads down to a stick and run round till they were giddy. Their ludicrous efforts then to jump over some water-pots, and run to a thorny bush, raised tumultuous peals of laughter. The poor boys generally smashed the pots, and ended by tumbling into the thorns.

CHAPTER XVII.

The Koosee jungles.—Ferries.—Jungle roads.—The rhinoceros.—We go to visit a neighbour.—We lose our way and get belated.—We fall into a quicksand.—No ferry boat.—Camping out on the sand.—Two tigers close by.—We light a fire.—The boat at last arrives.—Crossing the stream.—Set fire to the boatman's hut.—Swim the horses.—They are nearly drowned.—We again lose our way in the jungle.—The towing path, and how boats are towed up the river.—We at last reach the factory.—News of rhinoceros in the morning.—Off we start, but arrive too late.—Death of the rhinoceros.—His dimensions.— Description. — Habits.— Rhinoceros in Nepaul. — The old 'Major Captān.'—Description of Nepaulese scenery.—Immigration of Nepaulese.—Their fondness for fish.—They eat it putrid.—Exclusion of Europeans from Nepaul.—Resources of the country.—Must sooner or later be opened up.—Influences at work to elevate the people.—Planters and factories chief of these.—Character of the planter. — His claims to consideration from government.

IN the vast grass jungles that border the banks of the Koosee, stretching in great plains without an undulation for miles on either side, intersected by innumerable water-beds and dried up channels, there is plenty of game of all sorts. It is an impetuous, swiftly-flowing stream, dashing directly down from the mighty hills of Nepaul. So swift is its current and so erratic its course, that it frequently bursts its banks, and careers through the jungle, forming a new bed, and carrying away cattle and wild animals in its headlong rush.

The *ghauts* or ferries are constantly changing, and a long bamboo with a bit of white rag affixed, shows where the boats and boatmen are to be found. In many instances the track is a mere cattle path, and hundreds of cross openings, leading into the tall jungle grass, are apt to bewilder and mislead the traveller. During the dry season these jungles are the resort of great herds of cattle and tame buffaloes, which trample down the dry stalks, and force their way into the innermost recesses of the wilderness of grass, which grows ten to twelve feet high. If you once lose your path you may wander for miles, until your weary horse is almost unable to stumble on. In such a case, the best way is to take it coolly, and halloo till a herdsman or thatch-cutter comes to your rescue. The knowledge of the jungles displayed by these poor ignorant men is wonderful; they know every gully and watercourse, every ford and quicksand, and they betray not the slightest sign of fear, although they know that at any moment they may come across a herd of wild buffalo, a savage rhinoceros, or even a royal tiger.

The tracks of rhinoceros are often seen, but although I have frequently had these pointed out to me when out tiger shooting, I only saw two while I lived in that district.

The first occasion was after a night of discomfort such as I have fortunately seldom experienced. I had been away at a neighbouring factory in Purneah, some eighteen or twenty miles from my bungalow. My companion had been my predecessor in the management, and was supposed to be well acquainted with the country. We had gone over to one of the outworks across the river, and I had received charge of the place from him. It was a lonely solitary spot; the house was composed of grass walls plastered with mud, and had not been used for some time. F. proposed that we should ride over to see H., to whom he would introduce me, as he would be one of my nearest neighbours, and would give us a comfortable dinner and bed, which there was no chance of our procuring where we were.

We plunged at once into the mazy labyrinths of the jungle, and soon emerged on the high sandy downs, stretching mile beyond mile along the southern bank of the ever-changing river. Having lost our way, we got to the factory after dark, but a friendly villager volunteered his services as guide, and led us safely to our destination. After a cheerful evening with H., we persuaded him to accompany us back next day. He took out his dogs, and we had a good course after a hare, killing two jackals, and sending back the dogs by the sweeper. At Burgamma, the outwork, we stopped to *tiffin* on some cold fowl we had brought with us. The old factory head man got us some milk, eggs, and *chupatties*; and about three in the afternoon we started for the head factory. In an evil moment F. proposed that, as we were near another outwork called *Fusseah*, we should diverge thither, I could take over charge, and we could thus save a ride on another day. Not knowing anything of the country I acquiesced, and we reached Fusseah in time to see the place, and do all that was needful. It was a miserable tumbledown little spot, with four pair of vats; it had formerly been a good working factory, but the river had cut away most of its best lands, and completely washed away some of the villages, while the whole of the cultivation was fast relapsing into jungle.

'Debnarain Singh' the *gomorsta* or head man, asked us to stay for the night, as he said we could never get home before dark. F. however scouted the idea, and we resumed our way. The track, for it could not be called a road, led us through one or two jungle villages completely hidden by the dense bamboo clumps and long jungle grass. You can't see a trace of habitation till you are fairly on the village, and as the rice-fields are bordered with long strips of tall grass, the whole country presents the appearance of a uniform jungle. We got through the rice swamps, the villages, and the grass in safety, and as it was getting dark, emerged on the great plain of undulating ridgy sandbanks, that form the bed of the river during the annual floods. We had our *syces* (grooms) and two peons with us. We had to ride over nearly two miles of sand before we could reach the *ghat* where we expected the ferry-boats, and, the main stream once crossed, we had only two miles further to reach the factory. We were getting both tired and hungry; a heavy dew was falling, and the night was raw and chill. It was dark, there was no moon to light our way, and the stars were obscured by the silently creeping fog, rising from the marshy hollows among the sand. All at once F., who was leading, called out that we were off the path, and before I could pull up, my poor old tired horse was floundering in a quicksand up to the girths; I threw myself off and tried to wheel him round. H. was behind us, and we cried to him to halt where he was. I was sinking at every movement up to the knees, when the syce came to my rescue, and took charge of the horse. F.'s syce ran to extricate his master and horse; the two peons kept calling, 'Oh! my father, my father,' the horses snorted, and struggled desperately in the tenacious and treacherous quicksand; but after a prolonged effort, we all got safely out, and rejoined H. on the firm ridge.

We now hallooed and shouted for the boatmen, but beyond the swish of the rapid stream to our right, or the plash of a falling bank as the swift current undermined it, no sound answered our repeated calls. We were wet and weary, but to go either backward or forward was out of the question. We were off the path, and the first step in any direction might lead us into another quicksand, worse perhaps than that from which we had just extricated ourselves. The horses were trembling in every limb. The syces cowered together and shivered with the cold. We ordered the two peons to try and reach the ghat, and see what had become of the boats, while we awaited their return where we were. The fog and darkness soon swallowed them up, and putting the best face on our dismal circumstances that we could, we lit our pipes and extended our jaded limbs on the damp sand.

For a time we could hear the shouts of the peons as they hallooed for the boatmen, and we listened anxiously for the response, but there was none. We could hear the purling swish of the rapid stream, the crumbling banks falling into the current with a distant splash. Occasionally a swift rushing of wings overhead told us of the arrowy flight of diver or teal. Far in the distance twinkled the gleam of a herdsman's fire, the faint tinkle of a distant bell, or the subdued barking of a village dog for a moment, alone broke the silence.

At times the hideous chorus of a pack of jackals woke the echoes of the night. Then, at no great distance, rose a hoarse booming cry, swelling on the night air, and subsiding into a lengthened growl. The syces started to their feet, the horses snorted with fear; and as the roar was repeated, followed closely by another to our left, and seemingly nearer, H. exclaimed 'By Jove! there's a couple of tigers.'

Sure enough, so it was. It was the first time I had heard the roar of the tiger in his own domain, and I must confess that my sensations were not altogether pleasant. We set about collecting sticks and what roots of grass we could find, but on the sand-flats everything was wet, and it was so dark that we had to grope about on our hands and knees, and pick up whatever we came across.

With great difficulty we managed to light a small fire, and for about half-an-hour were nearly smothered by trying with inflated cheeks to coax it into a blaze. The tigers continued to call at intervals, but did not seem to be approaching us. It was a long weary wait, we were cold, wet, hungry, and tired; F., the cause of our misfortunes, had taken off his saddle, and with it for a pillow was now fast asleep. H. and I cowered over the miserable sputtering flame, and longed and wished for the morning. It was a miserable night, the hours seemed interminable, the dense volumes of smoke from the water-sodden wood nearly choked us. At last, after some hours spent in this miserable manner, we heard a faint halloo in the distance; it was now past eleven at night. We returned the hail, and bye-and-bye the peons returned bringing a boatman with them. The lazy rascals at the ghat where we had proposed crossing, had gone home at nightfall, leaving their boats on the further bank. Our trusty peons, had gone five miles up the river, through the thick jungle, and brought a boat down with them from the next ghat to that where we were.

We now warily picked our way down to the edge of the bank. The boat seemed very fragile, and the current looked so swift and dangerous, that we determined to go across first ourselves, get the larger boat from the other side, light a fire, and then bring over the horses. We embarked accordingly, leaving the syces and horses behind us. The peons and boatman pulled the boat a long way up stream by a rope, then shooting out we were carried swiftly down stream, the dark shadow of the further bank seeming at a great distance. The boatman pushed vigorously at his bamboo pole, the water rippled and gurgled, and frothed and eddied around. Half-a-dozen times we thought our boat would topple over, but at length we got safely across, far below what we had proposed as our landing place.

We found the boats all right, and the boatman's hut, a mere collection of dry grass and a few old bamboos. As it could be replaced in an hour, and the material lay all around, we fired the hut, which soon blazed up, throwing a weird lurid glow on bank and stream, and disclosing far on the other bank our weary nags and shivering syces, looking very bedraggled and forlorn indeed. The leaping and crackling of the flames, and the genial warmth, invigorated us a little, and while I stayed behind to feed the fire, the others recrossed to bring the horses over.

With the previous fright however, their long waiting, the blazing fire, and being unaccustomed to boats at night, the poor scared horses refused to enter the boat. The boats are flat-bottomed or broadly bulging, with a bamboo platform strewn with grass in the centre. As a rule, they have no protecting rails, and even in the daytime, when the current is strong and eddies numerous, they are very dangerous for horses. At all events, the poor brutes would not be led on to the platform, so there was nothing for it but to swim them across. The boat was therefore towed a long way up the bank, which on the farther side was nearly level with the current, but where the hut had stood was steep and slushy, and perhaps twenty feet high. This was where the deepest water ran, and where the current was swiftest. If the horses therefore missed the landing ghat or stage, which was cut sloping into the bank, there was a danger of their being swept away altogether and lost. However, we determined on making the attempt. Entering the water, and holding the horses tightly by the head, with a leading rope attached, to be paid out in case of necessity; the boat shot out, the horses pawed the water, entering deeper and deeper, foot by foot, into the swiftly rushing silent stream. So long as they were in their depth, and had footing, they were alright, but when they reached the middle of the river, the current, rushing with frightful velocity, swept them off their feet, and boat and horses began to go down stream. The horses, with lips apart showing their teeth firmly set, the lurid glare of the flame lighting up their straining eyeballs, the plashing of the water, the dark rapid current flowing noiselessly past; the rocking heaving boat, the dusky forms of syces, peons, and boatman, standing out clear in the ruddy fire-light against the utter blackness of the night, composed a weird picture I can never forget.

The boat shot swiftly past the ghat, and came with a thump against the bank. It swung round into the stream again, but the boatman had luckily managed to scramble ashore, and his efforts and mine united, hauling on the mooring-rope, sufficed to bring her in to the bank. The three struggling horses were yet in the current, trying bravely to stem the furious rush of the river. The syces and my friends were holding hard to the tether-ropes, which were now at their full stretch. It was a most critical moment. Had they let go, the horses would have been swept away to form a meal for the alligators. They managed, however, to get in close to the bank, and here, although the water was still over their backs, they got a slight and precarious footing, and inch by inch struggled after the boat, which we were now pulling up to the landing place.

After a sore struggle, during which we thought more than once the gallant nags would never emerge from the water, they staggered up the bank, dripping, trembling, and utterly overcome with their exertions. It was my first introduction to the treacherous Koosee, and I never again attempted to swim a horse across at night. We led the poor tired creatures up to the fire, heaping on fresh bundles of thatching-grass, of which there was plenty lying about, the syces then rubbed them down, and shampooed their legs, till they began to take a little heart, whinnying as we spoke to them and caressed them.

After resting for nearly an hour, we replaced the saddles, and F., who by this time began to mistrust his knowledge of the jungles by night, allowed one of the peons, who was sure he knew every inch of the road, to lead the way. Leaving the smouldering flames to flicker and burn out in solitude, we again plunged into the darkness of the night, threading our way through the thick jungle grass, now loaded with dewy moisture, and dripping copious showers upon us from its high walls at either side of the narrow track. We crossed a rapid little stream, an arm of the main river, turned to the right, progressed a few hundred yards, turned to the left, and finally came to a dead stop, having again lost our way.

We heaped execrations on the luckless peon's head, and I suggested that we should make for the main stream, follow up the bank till we reached the next ghat, where I knew there was a cart-road leading to the factory. Otherwise we might wander all night in the jungles, perhaps get into another quicksand, or come to some other signal grief. We accordingly turned round. We could hear the swish of the river at no great distance, and soon, stumbling over bushes and bursting through matted chumps of grass, dripping with wet, and utterly tired and dejected, we reached the bank of the stream.

Here we had no difficulty in following the path. The river is so swift, that the only way boats are enabled to get up stream to take down the inland produce, is by having a few coolies or boatmen to drag the boat up against the current by towing-lines. This is called *gooning*. The goon-ropes are attached to the mast of the boat. At the free end is a round bit of bamboo. The towing-coolie places this against his shoulder, and slowly and laboriously drags the boat up against the current. We were now on this towing-path, and after riding for nearly four miles we reached the ghat, struck into the cart-road, and without further misadventure reached the factory about four in the morning, utterly fagged and worn out.

About eight in the morning my bearer woke me out of a deep sleep, with the news that there was a *gaerha*, that is, a rhinoceros, close to the factory. We had some days previously heard it rumoured that there were *two* rhinoceroses in the *Battabarree* jungles, so I at once roused my soundly-sleeping friends. Swallowing a hasty morsel of toast and a cup of coffee, we mounted our ponies, sent our guns on ahead, and rode off for the village where the rhinoceros was reported. As we rode hurriedly along we could see natives running in the same direction as ourselves, and one of my men came up panting and breathless to confirm the news about the rhinoceros, with the unwelcome addition that Premnarain Singh, a young neighbouring Zemindar, had gone in pursuit of it with his elephant and guns. We hurried on, and just then heard the distant report of a shot, followed quickly by two more. We tried to take a short cut across country through some rice-fields, but our ponies sank in the boggy ground, and we had to retrace our way to the path.

By the time we got to the village we found an excited crowd of over a thousand natives, dancing and gesticulating round the prostrate carcase of the rhinoceros. The Baboo and his party had found the poor brute firmly imbedded in a quicksand. With organised effort they might have secured the prize alive, and could have sold him in Calcutta for at least a thousand rupees, but they were too excited, and blazed away three shots into the helpless beast. 'Many hands make light work,' so the crowd soon had the dead animal extricated, rolled him into the creek, and floated him down to the village, where we found them already beginning to hack and hew the flesh, completely spoiling the skin, and properly completing the butchery. We were terribly vexed that we were too late, but endeavoured to stop the stupid destruction that was going on. The body measured eleven feet three inches from the snout to the tail, and stood six feet nine. The horn was six and a half inches long, and the girth a little over ten feet. We put the best face on the matter, congratulated the Baboo with very bad grace, and asked him to get the skin cut up properly.

Cut in strips from the under part of the ribs and along the belly, the skin makes magnificent riding-whips. The bosses on the shoulder and sides are made into shields by the natives, elaborately ornamented and much prized. The horn, however, is the most coveted acquisition. It is believed to have peculiar virtues, and is popularly supposed by its mere presence in a house to mitigate the pains of maternity. A rhinoceros horn is often handed down from generation to generation as a heirloom, and when a birth is about to take place the anxious husband often gets a loan of the precious treasure, after which he has no fears for the safe issue of the labour.

The flesh of the rhinoceros is eaten by all classes. It is one of the five animals that a Brahmin is allowed to eat by the *Shastras*. They were formerly much more common in these jungles, but of late years very few have been killed. When they take up their abode in a piece of jungle they are not easily dislodged. They are fierce, savage brutes, and do not scruple to attack an elephant when they are hard pressed by the hunter. When they wish to leave a locality where they have been disturbed, they will make for some distant point, and march on with dogged and inflexible purpose. Some have been known to travel eighty miles in the twenty-four hours, through thick jungle, over rivers, and through swamp and quicksand. Their sense of hearing is very acute, and they are very easily roused to fury. One peculiarity often noticed by sportsmen is, that they always go to the same spot when they want to obey the calls of nature. Mounds of their dung are sometimes seen in the jungle, and the tracks shew that the rhinoceros pays a daily visit to this one particular spot.

In Nepaul, and along the *terai* or wooded slopes of the frontier, they are more numerous; but 'Jung Bahadur,' the late ruler of Nepaul, would allow no one to shoot them but himself. I remember the wailing lament of a Nepaul officer with whom I was out shooting, when I happened to fire at and wound one of the protected beasts. It was in Nepaul, among a cluster of low woody hills, with a brawling stream dashing through the precipitous channel worn out of the rocky, boulder-covered dell. The rhinoceros was up the hill slightly above me, and we were beating up for a tiger that we had seen go ahead of the line.

In my eagerness to bag a 'rhino' I quite forgot the interdict, and fired an Express bullet into the shoulder of the animal, as he stood broadside on, staring stupidly at me. He staggered, and made as if he would charge down the hill. The old 'Major Captān,' as they called our sporting host, was shouting out to me not to fire. The *mahouts* and beaters were petrified with horror at my presumption. I fancy they expected an immediate order for my decapitation, or for my ears to be cut off at the very least, but feeling I might as well be 'in for a pound as for a penny,' I fired again, and tumbled the huge brute over, with a bullet through the skull behind the ear. The old officer was horror-stricken, and would allow no one to go near the animal. He would not even let me get down to measure it, being terrified lest the affair should reach the ears of his formidable lord and ruler, that he hurried us off from the scene of my transgression as quickly as he could.

The old Major Captān was a curious character. The government of Nepaul is purely military. All executive and judicial functions are carried on by military officers. After serving a certain time in the army, they get rewarded for good service by being appointed to the executive charge of a district. So far as I could make out, they seem to farm the revenue much as is done in Turkey. They must send in so much to the Treasury, and anything over they keep for themselves. Their administration of justice is rough and ready. Fines, corporal punishment, and in the case of heinous crimes, mutilation and death are their penalties. There is a tax of *kind* on all produce, and licenses to cut timber bring in a large revenue. A protective tariff is levied on all goods or produce passing the frontier from British territory, and no European is allowed to travel in the country, or to settle and trade there. In the lower valleys there are magnificent stretches of land suitable for indigo, tea, rice, and other crops. The streams are numerous, moisture is plentiful, the soil is fertile, and the slopes of the hills are covered with splendid timber, a great quantity of which is cut and floated down the Gunduch, Bagmuttee, Koosee, and other streams during the rainy season. It is used principally for beams, rafters, and railway sleepers.

The people are jealous of intrusion and suspicious of strangers, but as I was with an official, they generally came out in great numbers to gaze as we passed through a village. The country does not seem so thickly populated as in our territory, and the cultivators had a more well-to-do look. They possess vast numbers of cattle. The houses have conical roofs, and great quadrangular sheds, roofed with a flat covering of thatch, are erected all round the houses, for the protection of the cattle at night. The taxes must weigh heavily on the population. The executive officer, when he gets charge of a district, removes all the subordinates who have been acting under his predecessor. When I asked the old Major if this would not interfere with the efficient administration of justice, and the smooth working of his revenue and executive functions, he gave a funny leer, almost a wink, and said it was much more satisfactory to have men of your own working under you, the fact being, that with his own men he could more securely wring from the ryots the uttermost farthing they could pay, and was more certain of getting his own share of the spoil.

With practically irresponsible power, and only answerable directly to his immediate military superior, an unscrupulous man may harry and harass a district pretty much as he chooses. Our old Major seemed to be civil and lenient, but in some districts the exactions and extortions of the rulers have driven many of the hard-working Nepaulese over the border into our territory. Our landholders or Zemindars, having vast areas of untilled land, are only too glad to encourage this immigration, and give the exiles, whom they find hard-working industrious tenants, long leases on easy terms. The new-comers are very independent, and strenuously resist any encroachment on what they consider their rights. If an attempt is made to raise their rent, even equitably, the land having increased in value, they will resist the attempt 'tooth and nail,' and take every advantage the law affords to oppose it. They are very fond of litigation, and are mostly able to afford the expense of a lawsuit. I generally found it answer better to call them together and reason quietly with them, submitting any point in dispute to an arbitration of parties mutually selected.

Nearly all the rivers in Nepaul are formed principally from the melting of the snow on the higher ranges. A vast body of water descends annually into the plains from the natural surface drainage of the country, but the melting of the snows is the main source of the river system. Many of the hill streams, and it is particularly observable at some seasons in the Koosee, have a regular daily rise and fall. In the early morning you can often ford a branch of the river, which by midday has become a swiftly-rolling torrent, filling the channel from bank to bank. The water is intensely cold, and few or no fish are to be found in the mountain streams of Nepaul. When the Nepaulese come down to the plains on business, pleasure, or pilgrimage their great treat is a mighty banquet of fish. For two or three *annas* a fish of several pounds weight can easily be purchased. They revel on this unwonted fare, eating to repletion, and very frequently making themselves ill in consequence. When Jung Bahadur came down through Chumparun to attend the *durbar* of the lamented Earl Mayo, cholera broke out in his camp, brought on simply by the enormous quantities of fish, often not very fresh or wholesome, which his guards and camp followers consumed.

Large quantities of dried fish are sent up to Nepaul, and exchanged for rice and other grain, or horns, hides, and blankets. The fish-drying is done very simply in the sun. It is generally left till it is half putrid and taints the air for miles. The sweltering, half-rotting mass, packed in filthy bags, and slung on ponies or bullocks, is sent over the frontier to some village bazaar in Nepaul. The track of a consignment of this horrible filth can be recognised from very far away. The perfume hovers on the road, and as you are riding up and get the first sniff of the putrid odour, you know at once that the Nepaulese market is being recruited by a *fresh* accession of very *stale* fish. If the taste is at all equal to the smell, the rankest witches broth ever brewed in reeking cauldron would probably be preferable. Over the frontier there seems to be few roads, merely bullock tracks. Most of the transporting of goods is done by bullocks, and intercommunication must be slow and costly. I believe that near Katmandoo, the capital, the roads and bridges are good, and kept in tolerable repair. There is an arsenal where they manufacture modern munitions of war. Their soldiers are well disciplined, fairly well equipped, and form excellent fighting material.

Our policy of annexation, so far as India is concerned, may perhaps be now considered as finally abandoned. We have no desire to annex Nepaul, but surely this system of utter isolation, of jealous exclusion at all hazards of English enterprise and capital, might be broken down to a mutual community of interest, a full and free exchange of products, and a reception by Nepaul without fear and distrust of the benefits our capitalists and pioneers could give the country by opening out its resources, and establishing the industries of the West on its fertile slopes and plains. I am no politician, and know nothing of the secret springs of policy that regulate our dealings with Nepaul, but it does seem somewhat weak and puerile to allow the Nepaulese free access to our territories, and an unprotected market in our towns for all their produce, while the British subject is rigorously excluded from the country, his productions saddled with a heavy protective duty, and the representative of our Government himself, treated more as a prisoner in honourable confinement, than as the accredited ambassador of a mighty empire.

I may be utterly wrong. There may be weighty reasons of State for this condition of things, but it is a general feeling among Englishmen in India that, *we* have to do all the GIVE and our Oriental neighbours do all the TAKE. The un-official English mind in India does not see the necessity for the painfully deferential attitude we invariably take in our dealings with native states. The time has surely come, when Oriental mistrust of our intentions should be stoutly battled with. There is room in Nepaul for hundreds of factories, for tea-gardens, fruit-groves, spice-plantations, woollen-mills, saw-mills, and countless other industries. Mineral products are reported of unusual richness. In the great central valley the climate approaches that of England. The establishment of productive industries would be a work of time, but so long as this ridiculous policy of isolation is maintained, and the exclusion of English tourists, sportsmen, or observers carried out in all its present strictness, we can never form an adequate idea of the resources of the country. The Nepaulese themselves cannot progress. I am convinced that a frank and unconstrained intercourse between Europeans and natives would create no jealousy and antagonism, but would lead to the development of a country singularly blessed by nature, and open a wide field for Anglo-Saxon energy and enterprise. It does seem strange, with all our vast territory of Hindostan accurately mapped out and known, roads and railways, canals and embankments, intersecting it in all directions, that this interesting corner of the globe, lying contiguous to our territory for hundreds of miles, should be less known than the interior of Africa, or the barren solitudes of the ice-bound Arctic regions.

In these rich valleys hundreds of miles of the finest and most fertile lands in Asia lie covered by dense jungle, waiting for labour and capital. For the present we have enough to do in our own possessions to reclaim the uncultured wastes; but considering the rapid increase of population, the avidity with which land is taken up, the daily increasing use of all modern labour-saving appliances, the time must very shortly come when capital and energy will need new outlets, and one of the most promising of these is in Nepaul. The rapid changes which have come over the face of rural India, especially in these border districts, within the last twenty years, might well make the most thoughtless pause. Land has increased in value more than two-fold. The price of labour and of produce has kept more than equal pace. Machinery is whirring and clanking, where a few years ago a steam whistle would have startled the natives out of their wits. With cheap, easy, and rapid communication, a journey to any of the great cities is now thought no more of than a trip to a distant village in the same district was thought of twenty years ago. Everywhere are the signs of progress. New industries are opening up. Jungle is fast disappearing. Agriculture has wonderfully improved; and wherever an indigo factory has been built, progress has taken the place of stagnation, industry and thrift that of listless indolence and shiftless apathy. A spirit has moved in the valley of dry bones, and has clothed with living flesh the gaunt skeletons produced by ignorance, disease, and want. The energy and intelligence of the planter has breathed on the stagnant waters of the Hindoo intellect the breath of life, and the living tide is heaving, full of activity, purging by its resistless ever-moving pulsations the formerly stagnant mass of its impurities, and making it a life-giving sea of active industry and progress.

Let any unprejudiced observer see for himself if it

be not so; let him go to those districts where British capital and energy are not employed; let him leave the planting districts, and go up to the wastes of Oudh, or the purely native districts of the North-west, where there are no Europeans but the officials in the *station*. He will find fewer and worse roads, fewer wells, worse constructed houses, much ruder cultivation, less activity and industry; more dirt, disease, and desolation; less intelligence; more intolerance; and a peasantry morally, mentally, physically, and in every way inferior to those who are brought into daily contact with the Anglo-Saxon planters and gentlemen, and have imbibed somewhat of their activity and spirit of progress. And yet these are the men whom successive Lieutenant-Governors, and Governments generally, have done their best to thwart and obstruct. They have been misrepresented, held up to obloquy, and foully slandered; they have been described as utterly base, fattening on the spoils of a cowed and terror-ridden peasantry. Utterly unscrupulous, fearing neither God nor man, hesitating at no crime, deterred by no consideration from oppressing their tenantry, and compassing their interested ends by the vilest frauds.

Such was the picture drawn of the indigo planter not so many years ago. There may have been much in the past over which we would willingly draw the veil, but at the present moment I firmly believe that the planters of Behar—and I speak as an observant student of what has been going on in India—have done more to elevate the peasantry, to rouse them into vitality, and to improve them in every way, than all the other agencies that have been at work with the same end in view.

The Indian Government to all appearance must always work in extremes. It never seems to hit the happy medium. The Lieutenant-Governor for the time being impresses every department under him too strongly with his own individuality. The planters, who are an intelligent and independent body of men, have seemingly always been obnoxious to the ideas of a perfectly despotic and irresponsible ruler. In spite however of all difficulties and drawbacks, they have held their own. I know that the poor people and small cultivators look up to them with respect and affection. They find in them ready and sympathizing friends, able and willing to shield them from the exactions of their own more powerful and uncharitable fellow-countrymen. Half, nay nine-tenths, of the stories against planters, are got up by the money-lenders, the petty Zemindars, and wealthy villagers, who find the planter competing with them for land and labour, and raising the price of both. The poor people look to the factory as a never failing resource when all else fails, and but for the assistance it gives in money, or seed, or plough bullocks and implements of husbandry, many a struggling hard-working tenant would inevitably go to the wall, or become inextricably entangled in the meshes of the Bunneah and money-lender.

I assert as a fact that the great majority of villagers in Behar would rather go to the factory, and have their sahib adjudicate on their dispute, than take it into Court. The officials in the indigo districts know this, and as a rule are very friendly with the planters. But not long since, an official was afraid to dine at a planter's house, fearing he might be accused of planter proclivities. In no other country in the world would the same jealousy of men who open out and enrich a country, and who are loyal, intelligent, and educated citizens, be displayed; but there are high quarters in which the old feeling of the East India Company, that all who were not in the service must be adventurers and interlopers, seems not wholly to have died out.

That there have been abuses no one denies; but for years past the majority of the planters in Tirhoot, Chupra, and Chumparun, and in the indigo districts generally, not merely the managers, but the proprietors and agents have been laudably and loyally stirring, in spite of failures, reduced prices, and frequent bad seasons, to elevate the standard of their peasantry, and establish the indigo system on a fair and equitable basis. During the years when I was an assistant and manager on indigo estates, the rates for payment of indigo to cultivators nearly doubled, although prices for the manufactured article remained stationary. In well managed factories, the forcible seizure of carts and ploughs, and the enforcement of labour, which is an old charge against planters, was unknown; and the payment of tribute, common under the old feudal system, and styled *furmaish*, had been allowed to fall into desuetude. The NATIVE Zemindars or landholders however, still jealously maintain their rights, and harsh exactions were often made by them on the cultivators on the occasions of domestic events, such as births, marriages, deaths, and such like, in the families of the landowners. For years these exactions or feudal payments by the ryot to the Zemindar have been commuted by the factories into a lump sum in cash, when villages have been taken in farm, and this sum has been paid to the Zemindar as an enhanced rent.

In the majority of cases it has not been levied from the cultivators, but the whole expense has been borne by the factory. In individual instances resort may have been had to unworthy tricks to harass the ryots, the factory middle-men having often been oppressors and tyrants; but as a body, the indigo planters of the present day have sternly set their faces to put down these oppressions, and have honestly striven to mete out even-handed justice to their tenants and dependants. With the spread of education and intelligence, the development of agricultural knowledge and practical science, and the vastly improved communication by roads, bridges, and ferries, in bringing about all of which the planting community themselves have been largely instrumental, there can be little doubt that these old fashioned charges against the planters as a body will cease, and public opinion will be brought to bear on any one who may promote his own interests by cruelty or rapacity, instead of doing his business on an equitable commercial basis, giving every man his due, relying on skill, energy, industry, and integrity, to promote the best interests of his factory; gaining the esteem and affection of his people by liberality, kindness, and strict justice.

It can never be expected that a ryot can grow indigo at a loss to himself, or at a lower rate of profit than that which the cultivation of his other ordinary crops would give him, without at least some compensating advantages. With all his poverty and supposed stupidity, he is keenly alive to his own interests, quite able to hold his own in matters affecting his pocket. I have no hesitation in saying that the steady efforts which have been made by all the best planters to treat the ryot fairly, to give him justice, to encourage him with liberal aid and sympathy, and to put their mutual relations on a fair business footing, are now bearing fruit, and will result in the cultivation and manufacture of indigo in Upper Bengal becoming, as it deserves to become, one of the most firmly established, fairly conducted, and justly administered industries in India. That it may be so is, as I know, the earnest wish, as it has long been the dearest object, of my best friends among the planters of Behar.

CHAPTER XVIII.

The tiger.—His habitat.—Shooting on foot.—Modes of shooting.—A tiger hunt on foot.—The scene of the hunt.—The beat.—Incidents of the hunt.—Fireworks.—The tiger charges.—The elephant bolts.—The tigress will not break.—We kill a half-grown cub.—Try again for the tigress.—Unsuccessful.—Exaggerations in tiger stories.—My authorities.—The brothers S.—Ferocity and structure of the tiger.—His devastations.—His frame-work, teeth, &c.—A tiger at bay.—His unsociable habits.—Fight between tiger and tigress.—Young tigers.—Power and strength of the tiger.—Examples.—His cowardice.—Charge of a wounded tiger.—Incidents connected with wounded tigers.—A spined tiger.—Boldness of young tigers.—Cruelty.—Cunning.—Night scenes in the jungle.—Tiger killed by a wild boar.—His cautious habits.—General remarks.

IN the foregoing chapters I have tried to perform my promise, to give a general idea of our daily life in India; our toils and trials, our sports, our pastimes, and our general pursuits. No record of Indian sport, however, would be complete without some allusion to the kingly tiger, and no one can live long near the Nepaul frontier, without at some time or other having an encounter with the royal robber—the striped and whiskered monarch of the jungle.

He is always to be found in the Terai forests, and although very occasionally indeed met with in Tirhoot, where the population is very dense, and waste lands infrequent, he is yet often to be encountered in the solitudes of Oudh or Goruchpore, has been shot at and killed near Bettiah, and at our pig-sticking ground near Kuderent. In North Bhaugulpore and Purneah he may be said to be ALWAYS at home, as he can be met there, if you search for him, at all seasons of the year.

In some parts of India, notably in the Deccan, and in some districts on the Bombay side, and even in the Soonderbunds near Calcutta, sportsmen and shekarries go after the tiger on foot. I must confess that this seems to me a mad thing to do. With every advantage of weapon, with the most daring courage, and the most imperturbable coolness, I think a man no fair match for a tiger in his native jungles. There are men now living who have shot numbers of tigers on foot, but the numerous fatal accidents recorded every year, plainly shew the danger of such a mode of shooting.

In Central India, in the North-west, indeed in most districts where elephants are not easily procurable, it is customary to erect *mychans* or bamboo platforms on trees. A line of beaters, with tom-toms, drums, fireworks, and other means for creating a din, are then sent into the jungle, to beat the tigers up to the platform on which you sit and wait. This is often a successful mode if you secure an advantageous place, but accidents to the beaters are very common, and it is at best a weary and vexatious mode of shooting, as after all your trouble the tiger may not come near your *mychan*, or give you the slightest glimpse of his beautiful skin.

I have only been out after tiger on foot on one occasion. It was in the sal jungles in Oudh. A neighbour of mine, a most intimate and dear friend, whom I had nicknamed the 'General,' and a young friend, Fullerton, were with me. A tigress and cub were reported to be in a dense patch of *nurkool* jungle, on the banks of the creek which divided the General's cultivation from mine. The nurkool is a tall feathery-looking cane, very much relished by elephants. It grows in dense brakes, and generally in damp boggy ground, affording complete shade and shelter for wild animals, and is a favourite haunt of pig, wolf, tiger, and buffalo.

We had only one elephant, the use of which Fullerton had got from a neighbouring Baboo. It was not a staunch animal, so we put one of our men in the howdah, with a plentiful supply of bombs, a kind of native firework, enclosed in a clay case, which burns like a huge squib, and sets fire to the jungle. Along with the elephant we had a line of about one hundred coolies, and several men with drums and tom-toms. Fullerton took the side nearest the river, as it was possible the brute might sneak out that way, and make her escape along the bank. The General's shekarry remained behind, in rear of the line of beaters, in case the tigress might break the line, and try to escape by the rear. My *Gomasta*, the General, and myself, then took up positions behind trees all along the side of the glade or dell in which was the bit of nurkool jungle.

It was a small basin, sloping gently down to the creek from the sal jungle, which grew up dark and thick all around. A margin of close sward, as green and level as a billiard-table, encircled the glade, and in the basin the thick nurkool grew up close, dense, and high, like a rustling barrier of living green. In the centre was the decaying stump of a mighty forest monarch, with its withered arms stretching out their bleached and shattered lengths far over the waving feathery tops of the nurkool below.

The General and I cut down some branches, which we stuck in the ground before us. I had a fallen log in front of me, on which I rested my guns. I had a naked *kookree* ready to hand, for we were sure that the tigress was in the swamp, and I did not know what might happen. I did not half like this style of shooting, and wished I was safely seated on the back of 'JORROCKS,' my faithful old Bhaugulpore elephant. The General whistled as a sign for the beat to begin. The coolies dashed into the thicket. The stately elephant slowly forced his ponderous body through the crashing swaying brake. The rattle of the tom-toms and rumble of the drums, mingled with the hoarse shouts and cries of the beaters, the fiery rush of sputtering flame, and the loud report as each bomb burst, with the huge volumes of blinding smoke, and the scent of gunpowder that came on the breeze, told us that the bombs were doing their work. The jungle was too green to burn; but the fireworks raised a dense sulphurous smoke, which penetrated among the tall stems of the nurkool, and by the waving and crashing of the tall swaying canes, the heaving of the howdah, with the red puggree of the peon, and the gleaming of the staves and weapons, we could see that the beat was advancing.

As they neared the large withered tree in the centre of the brake, the elephant curled up his trunk and trumpeted. This was a sure sign there was game afoot. We could see the peon in the howdah leaning over the front bar, and eagerly peering into the recesses of the thicket before him. He lit one of the bombs, and hurled it right up against the bole of the tree. It hissed and sputtered, and the smoke came curling over the reeds in dense volumes. A roar followed that made the valley ring again. We heard a swift rush. The elephant turned tail, and fled madly away, crashing through the matted brake that crackled and tore under his tread. The howdah swayed wildly, and the peon clung tenaciously on to the top bar with all his desperate might. The *mahout*, or elephant-driver, tried in vain to check the rush of the frightened brute, but after repeated sounding whacks on the head he got her to stop, and again turn round. Meantime the cries and shouting had ceased, and the beaters came pouring from the jungle by twos and threes, like the frightened inhabitants of some hive or ant-heap. Some in their hurry came tumbling out headlong, others with their faces turned backwards to see if anything was in pursuit of them, got entangled in the reeds, and fell prone on their hands and knees. One fellow had just emerged from the thick cover, when another terrified compatriot dashed out in blind unreasoning fear close behind him. The first one thought the tiger was on him. With one howl of anguish and dismay he fled as fast as he could run, and the General and I, who had witnessed the episode, could not help uniting in a resounding peal of laughter, that did more to bring the scared coolies to their senses than anything else we could have done.

There was no doubt now of the tiger's whereabouts. One of the beaters gave us a most graphic description of its appearance and proportions. According to him it was bigger than an elephant, had a mouth as wide as a coal scuttle, and eyes that glared like a thousand suns. From all this we inferred that there was a full grown tiger or tigress in the jungle. We re-formed the line of beaters, and once more got the elephant to enter the patch. The same story was repeated. No sooner did they get near the old tree, than the tigress again charged with a roar, and our valiant coolies and the chicken-hearted elephant vacated the jungle as fast as their legs could carry them. This happened twice or thrice. The tigress charged every time, but would not leave her safe cover. The elephant wheeled round at every charge, and would not shew fight. Fullerton got into the howdah, and fired two shots into the spot where the tigress was lying. He did not apparently wound her, but the reports brought her to the charge once more, and the elephant, by this time fairly tired of the game, and thoroughly demoralised with fear, bolted right away, and nearly cracked poor Fullerton's head against the branch of a tree.

We could plainly see, that with only one elephant we could never dislodge the tigress, so making the coolies beat up the patch in lines, we shot several pig and a hogdeer, and adjourned for something to eat by the bank of the creek. We had been trying to oust the tigress for over four hours, but she was as wise as she was savage, and refused to become a mark for our bullets in the open. After lunch we made another grand attempt. We promised the coolies double pay if they roused the tigress to flight. The elephant was forced again into the nurkool very much against his will, and the mahout was promised a reward if we got the tigress. The din this time was prodigious, and strange to say they got quite close up to the big withered tree without the usual roar and charge. This seemed somewhat to stimulate the beaters and the old elephant. The coolies redoubled their cries, smote among the reeds with their heavy staves, and shouted encouragement to each other. Right in the middle of the line, as it seemed to us from the outside, there was then a fierce roar and a mighty commotion. Cries of fear and consternation arose, and forth poured the coolies again, helter skelter, like so many rabbits from a warren when the weasel or ferret has entered the burrow. Right before me a huge old boar and a couple of sows came plunging forth. I let them get on a little distance from the brake, and then with my 'Express' I rolled over the tusker and one of his companions, and just then the General shouted out to me, 'There's the tiger!'

I looked in the direction of his levelled gun, and there at the edge of the jungle was a handsome half-grown tiger cub, beautifully marked, his tail switching angrily from side to side, and his twitching retracted lips and bristling moustache drawn back like those of a vicious cat, showing his gleaming polished fangs and teeth.

The General had a fine chance, took a steady aim, and shot the young savage right through the heart. The handsome young tiger gave one convulsive leap into the air and fell on his side stone dead. We could not help a cheer, and shouted for Fullerton, who soon came running up. We got some coolies together, but they were frightened to go near the dead animal, as we could plainly hear the old vixen inside snarling and snapping, for all the world like an angry terrier. We heard her half-suppressed growl and snarl. She was evidently in a fine temper. How we wished for a couple of staunch elephants to hunt her out of the cane. It was no use, however, the elephant would not go near the jungle again. The coolies were thoroughly scared, and had got plenty of pork and venison to eat, so did not care for anything else. We collected a lot of tame buffaloes, and tried to drive them through the jungle, but the coolies had lost heart, and would not exert themselves; so we had to content ourselves with the cub, who measured six feet three inches (a very handsome skin it was), and very reluctantly had to leave the savage mother alone. I never saw a brute charge so persistently as she did. She always rushed forward with a succession of roars, and was very wary and cunning. She never charged home, she did not even touch the elephant or any of the coolies, but evidently trusted to frighten her assailants away by a bold show and a fierce outcry.

We went back two days after with five elephants, which with great difficulty we had got together[1], and thoroughly beat the patch of nurkool, killed a lot of pig and a couple of deer, shot an alligator, and destroyed over thirty of its eggs, which we discovered on the bank of the creek; and returning in the evening shot a nilghau and a black buck, but the tigress had disappeared. She was gone, and we grumbled sorely at our bad luck. That was the only occasion I was ever after tiger on foot. It was doubtless intensely exciting work, and both tigress and cub must have passed close to us several times, hidden by the jungle. We were only about thirty paces from the edge of the brake, and both animals must have seen us, although the dense cover hid them from our sight. I certainly prefer shooting from the howdah.

Although it is beyond the scope of this book to enter into a detailed account of the tiger, discussing his structure, habits, and characteristics, it may aid the reader if I give a sketchy general outline of some

[1] This was at the time the Prince of Wales was shooting in Nepaul, not very far from where I was then stationed. Most of the elephants in the district had been sent up to his Royal Highness's camp, or were on their way to take part in the ceremonies of the grand *Durbar* in Delhi.

of the more prominent points of interest connected with the monarch of the jungle, the cruel, cunning, ferocious king of the cat tribe, the beautiful but dreaded tiger.

I should prefer to shew his character by incidents with which I have myself been connected, but as many statements have been made about tigers that are utterly absurd and untrue, and as tiger stories generally contain a good deal of exaggeration, and a natural scepticism unconsciously haunts the reader when tigers and tiger shooting are the topics, it may be as well to state once for all, that I shall put down nothing that cannot be abundantly substantiated by reference to my own sporting journals, on those of the brothers S., friends and fellow-sportsmen of my own. To G. S. I am under great obligations for many interesting notes he has given me about tiger shooting. Joe, his brother, was long our captain in our annual shooting parties. Their father and *his* brother, the latter still alive and a keen shot, were noted sportsmen at a time when game was more plentiful, shooting more generally practised, and when to be a good shot meant more than average excellence. The two brothers between them have shot, I daresay, more than four hundred and fifty male and female tigers, and serried rows of skulls ranged round the billiard-rooms in their respective factories, bear witness to their love of sport and the deadly accuracy of their aim. Under their auspices I began my tiger shooting, and as they knew every inch of the jungles, had for years been observant students of nature, were acquainted with all the haunts and habits of every wild creature, I acquired a fund of information about the tiger which I knew could be depended on. It was the result of actual observation and experience, and in most instances it was corroborated by my own experience in my more limited sphere of action. Every incident I adduce, every deduction I draw, every assertion I make regarding tigers and tiger shooting can be plentifully substantiated, and abundantly testified to, by my brother sportsmen of Purneah and Bhaugulpore. From their valuable information I have got most of the material for this part of my book.

Of the order FERAE, the family *felidae*, there is perhaps no animal in the wide range of all zoology, so eminently fitted for destruction as the tiger. His whole structure and appearance, combining beauty and extreme agility with prodigious strength, his ferocity, and his cunning, mark him out as the very type of a beast of prey. He is the largest of the cat tribe, the most formidable race of quadrupeds on earth. He is the most bloodthirsty in habit, and the most dreaded by man. Whole tracts of fertile fields, reclaimed from the wild luxuriance of matted jungle, and waving with golden grain, have been deserted by the patient husbandmen, and allowed to relapse into tangled thicket and uncultured waste on account of the ravages of this formidable robber. Whole villages have been depopulated by tigers, the mouldering door-posts, and crumbling rafters, met with at intervals in the heart of the solitary jungle, alone marking the spot where a thriving hamlet once sent up the curling smoke from its humble hearths, until the scourge of the wilderness, the dreaded 'man-eater,' took up his station near it, and drove the inhabitants in terror from the spot. Whole herds of valuable cattle have been literally destroyed by the tiger. His habitat is in those jungles, and near those localities, which are most highly prized by the herdsmen of India for their pastures, and the numbers of cattle that yearly fall before his thirst for blood, and his greed for living prey, are almost incredible. I have scarcely known a day pass, during the hot months, on the banks of the Koosee, that news of a *kill* has not been sent in from some of the villages in my *ilaka*, and as a tiger eats once in every four or five days, and oftener if he can get the chance, the number of animals that fall a prey to his insatiable appetite, over the extent of Hindostan, must be enormous. The annual destruction of tame animals by tigers alone is almost incredible, and when we add to this the wild buffalo, the deer, the pig, and other untamed animals, to say nothing of smaller creatures, we can form some conception of the destruction caused by the tiger in the course of a year.

His whole frame is put together to effect destruction. In cutting up a tiger you are impressed with this. His tendons are masses of nerve and muscle as hard as steel. The muscular development is tremendous. Vast bands and layers of muscle overlap each other. Strong ligaments, which you can scarcely cut through, and which soon blunt the sharpest knife, unite the solid, freely-playing, loosely-jointed bones. The muzzle is broad, and short, and obtuse. The claws are completely retractile. The jaws are short. There are two false molars, two grinders above, and the same number below. The upper carnivorous tooth has three lobes, and an obtuse heel; the lower has two lobes, pointed and sharp, and no heel. There is one very small tuberculous tooth above as an auxiliary, and then the strong back teeth. The muscles of the jaws are of tremendous power. I have come across the remains of a buffalo killed by a tiger, and found all the large bones, even the big strong bones of the pelvis and large joints, cracked and crunched like so many walnuts, by the powerful jaws of the fierce brute.

The eye is peculiarly brilliant, and when glaring with fury it is truly demoniac. With his bristles rigid, the snarling lips drawn back, disclosing the formidable fangs, the body crouching for his spring, and the lithe tail puffed up and swollen, and lashing restlessly from side to side, each muscle tense and strung, and an undulating movement perceptible like the motions of a huge snake, a crouching tiger at bay is a sight that strikes a certain chill to the heart of the onlooker. When he bounds forward, with a roar that reverberates among the mazy labyrinths of the interminable jungle, he tests the steadiest nerve and almost daunts the bravest heart.

In their habits they are very unsociable, and are only seen together during the amatory season. When that is over the male tiger betakes him again to his solitary predatory life, and the tigress becomes, if possible, fiercer than he is, and buries herself in the gloomiest recesses of the jungle. When the young are born, the male tiger has often been known to devour his offspring, and at this time they are very savage and quarrelsome. Old G., a planter in Purneah, once came across a pair engaged in deadly combat. They writhed and struggled on the ground, the male tiger striking tremendous blows on the chest and flanks of his consort, and tearing her skin in strips, while the tigress buried her fangs in his neck, tearing and worrying with all the ferocity of her nature. She was battling for her young. G. shot both the enraged combatants, and found that one of the cubs had been mangled, evidently by his unnatural father. Another, which he picked up in a neighbouring bush, was unharmed, but did not survive long. Pairs have often been shot in the same jungle, but seldom in close proximity, and it accords with all experience that they betray an aversion to each other's society, except at the one season. This propensity of the father to devour his offspring seems to be due to jealousy or to blind unreasoning hate. To save her offspring the female always conceals her young, and will often move far from the jungle which she usually frequents.

When the cubs are able to kill for themselves, she seems to lose all pleasure in their society, and by the time they are well grown she usually has another batch to provide for. I have, however, shot a tigress with a full-grown cub—the hunt described in the last chapter is an instance—and on several occasions, my friend George has shot the mother with three or four full-grown cubs in attendance. This is however rare, and only happens I believe when the mother has remained entirely separate from the company of the male.

The strength of the tiger is amazing. The fore paw is the most formidable weapon of attack. With one stroke delivered with full effect he can completely disable a large buffalo. On one occasion, on the Koosee *derahs*, that is, the plains bordering the river, an enraged tiger, passing through a herd of buffaloes, broke the backs of two of the herd, giving each a stroke right and left as he went along. One blow is generally sufficient to kill the largest bullock or buffalo. Our captain, Joe, had once received *khubber*, that is, news or information, of a kill by a tiger. He went straight to the *baithan*, the herd's head-quarters, and on making enquiries, was told that the tiger was a veritable monster.

'Did you see it?' asked Joe.

'I did not,' responded the *goala* or cowherd.

'Then how do you know it was so large?'

'Because,' said the man, 'it killed the biggest buffalo in my herd, and the poor brute only gave one groan.'

George once tracked a tiger, following up the drag of a bullock that he had carried off. At one place the brute came to a ditch, which was measured and found to be five feet in width. Through this there was no drag, but the traces continued on the further side. The inference is, that the powerful thief had cleared the ditch, taking the bullock bodily with him at a bound. Others have been known to jump clear out of a cattle pen, over a fence some six feet high, taking on one occasion a large-sized calf, and another time a sheep.

Another wounded tiger, with two bullets in his flanks, the wound being near the root of the tail, cleared a *nullah*, or dry watercourse, at one bound. The nullah was stepped by George, and found to be twenty-three paces wide. It is fortunate, with such tremendous powers for attack, that the tiger will try as a rule to slink out of the way if he can. He almost always avoids an encounter with man. His first instinct is flight. Only the exciting incidents of the chase are as a rule put upon record. A narrative of tiger shooting therefore is apt in this respect to be a little misleading. The victims who meet their death tamely and quietly (and they form the majority in every hunt),—those that are shot as they are tamely trying to escape—are simply enumerated, but the charging tiger, the old vixen that breaks the line, and scatters the beaters to right and left, that rouses the blood of the sportsmen to a fierce excitement, these are made the most of. Every incident is detailed and dwelt upon, and thus the idea has gained ground, that ALL tigers are courageous, and wait not for attack, but in most instances take the initiative. It is not the case. Most of the tigers I have seen killed would have escaped if they could. It is only when brought to bay, or very hard pressed, or in defence of its young, that a tiger or tigress displays its native ferocity. At such a moment indeed, nothing gives a better idea of savage determined fury and fiendish rage. With ears thrown back, brows contracted, mouth open, and glaring yellow eyes scintillating with fury, the cruel claws plucking at the earth, the ridgy hairs on the back stiff and erect as bristles, and the lithe lissome body quivering in every muscle and fibre with wrath and hate, the beast comes down to the charge with a defiant roar, which makes the pulse bound and the breath come short and quick. It requires all a man's nerve and coolness, to enable him to make steady shooting.

Roused to fury by a wound, I have seen tigers wheel round with amazing swiftness, and dash headlong, roaring dreadfully as they charged, full upon the nearest elephant, scattering the line and lacerating the poor creature on whose flanks or head they may have fastened, their whole aspect betokening pitiless ferocity and fiendish rage.

Even in death they do not forget their savage instincts. I knew of one case in which a seemingly dead tiger inflicted a fearful wound upon an elephant that had trodden on what appeared to be his inanimate carcase. Another elephant, that attacked and all but trampled a tiger to death, was severely bitten under one of the toe-nails. The wound mortified, and the unfortunate beast died in about a week after its infliction. Another monster, severely wounded, fell into a pool of water, and seized hold with its jaws of a hard knot of wood that was floating about. In its death agony, it made its powerful teeth meet in the hard wood, and not until it was being cut up, and we had divided the muscles of the jaws, could we extricate the wood from that formidable clench. In rage and fury, and mad with pain, the wounded tiger will often turn round and savagely bite the wound that causes its agony, and they very often bite their paws and shoulders, and tear the grass and earth around them.

A tiger wounded in the spine, however, is the most exciting spectacle. Paralysed in the limbs, he wheels round, roaring and biting at everything within his reach. In 1874 I shot one in the spine, and watched his furious movements for some time before I put him out of his misery. I threw him a pad from one of the elephants, and the way he tore and gnawed it gave me some faint idea of his fury and ferocity. He looked the very personification of impotent viciousness; the incarnation of devilish rage.

Urged by hunger the tiger fearlessly attacks his prey. The most courageous are young tigers about seven or eight feet long. They invariably give better sport than larger and older animals, being more ready to charge, and altogether bolder and more defiant. Up to the age of two years they have probably been with the mother, have never encountered a reverse or defeat, and having become bold by impunity, hesitate not to fly at any assailant whatever.

Like all the cat tribe, they are very cruel in disposition, often most wantonly so. Having disabled his prey with the first onset, the tiger plays with it as a cat does with a mouse, and, unless very sharp set by hunger, he always indulges this love of torture. His attacks are by no means due only to the cravings of his appetite. He often slays the victims of a herd, in the wantonness of sport, merely to indulge his murderous propensities. Even when he has had a good meal he will often go on adding fresh victims, seemingly to gratify his sense of power, and his love of slaughter. In teaching her cubs to kill for themselves, the mother often displays great cruelty, frequently killing at a time five or six cows from one herd. The young savages are apt pupils, and 'try their prentice hand' on calves and weakly members of the herd, killing from the mere love of murder.

Their cunning is as remarkable as their cruelty; what they lack in speed they make up in consummate subtlety. They take advantage of the direction of the wind, and of every irregularity of the ground. It is amazing what slight cover will suffice to conceal their lurking forms from the observation of the herd. During the day they generally retreat to some cool and shady spot, deep in the recesses of the jungle. Where the soft earth has been worn away with ragged hollows and deep shady water-courses, where the tallest and most impenetrable jungle conceals the winding and impervious paths, hidden in the gloom and obscurity of the densely-matted grass, the lordly tiger crouches, and blinks away the day. With the approach of night, however, his mood undergoes a change. He hears the tinkle of the bells, borne by some of the members of a retreating herd, that may have been feeding in close proximity to his haunt all day long, and from which he has determined to select a victim for his evening meal. He rouses himself and yawns, stretches himself like the great cruel cat he is, and then crawls and creeps silently along, by swampy watercourses, and through devious labyrinths known to himself alone. He hangs on the outskirts of the herd, prowling along and watching every motion of the returning cattle. He makes his selection, and with infinite cunning and patience contrives to separate it from the rest. He waits for a favourable moment, when, with a roar that sends the alarmed companions of the unfortunate victim scampering together to the front, he springs on his unhappy prey, deprives it of all power of resistance with one tremendous stroke, and bears it away to feast at his leisure on the warm and quivering carcase.

He generally kills as the shades of evening are falling, and seldom ventures on a foraging expedition by day. After nightfall it is dangerous to be abroad in the jungles. It is then that dramas are acted of thrilling interest, and unimaginable sensation scenes take place. Some of the old shekarries and field-watchers frequently dig shallow pits, in which they take their stand. Their eye is on the level of the ground, and any object standing out in relief against the sky line can be readily detected. If they could relate their experiences, what absorbing narratives they could write. They see the tiger spring upon his terror-stricken prey, the mother and her hungry cubs prowling about for a victim, or two fierce tigers battling for the favours of some sleek, striped, remorseless, bloodthirsty forest-fiend. In pursuit of their quarry, they steal noiselessly along, and love to make their spring unawares. They generally select some weaker member of a herd, and are chary of attacking a strong big-boned, horned animal. They sometimes 'catch a Tartar,' and instances are known of a buffalo not only withstanding the attack of a tiger successfully, but actually gaining the victory over his more active assailant, whose life has paid the penalty of his rashness.

Old G. told me, he had come across the bodies of a wild boar and an old tiger, lying dead together near Burgamma. The boar was fearfully mauled, but the clean-cut gaping gashes in the striped hide of the tiger, told how fearfully and gallantly he had battled for his life.

In emerging from the jungle at night, they generally select the same path or spot, and approach the edge of the cover with great caution. They will follow the same track for days together. Hence in some places the tracks of the tigers are so numerous as to lead the tyro to imagine that dozens must have passed, when in truth the tracks all belong to one and the same brute. So acute is their perception, so narrowly do they scrutinize every minute object in their path, so suspicious is their nature, that anything new in their path, such as a pitfall, a screen of cut grass, a *mychan*, that is, a stage from which you might be intending to get a shot, nay, even the print of a footstep—a man's, a horse's, an elephant's—is often quite enough to turn them from a projected expedition, or at any rate to lead them to seek some new outlet from the jungle. In any case it increases their wariness, and under such circumstances it becomes almost impossible to get a shot at them from a pit or shooting-stage. Their vision, their sense of smell, of hearing, all their perceptions are so acute, that I think lying in wait for them is chiefly productive of weariness and vexation of spirit. It is certainly dangerous, and the chances of a successful shot are so problematical, while the *disagreeables*, and discomforts, and dangers are so real and tangible, that I am inclined to think this mode of attack 'hardly worth the candle.'

With all his ferocity and cruelty, however, I am

of opinion that the tiger is more cowardly than courageous. He will always try to escape a danger, and fly from attack, rather than attack in return or wait to meet it, and wherever he can, in pursuit of his prey, he will trust rather to his cunning than to his strength, and he always prefers an ambuscade to an open onslaught.

CHAPTER XIX.

The tiger's mode of attack.—The food he prefers.—Varieties of prey.—Examples.—What he eats first.—How to tell the kill of a tiger.—Appetite fierce.—Tiger choked by a bone.—Two varieties of tiger.—The royal Bengal.—Description.—The hill tiger.—His description.—The two compared.—Length of the tiger.—How to measure tigers.—Measurements.—Comparison between male and female.—Number of young at a birth.—The young cubs.—Mother teaching cubs to kill.—Education and progress of the young tiger.—Wariness and cunning of the tiger.—Hunting incidents shewing their powers of concealment.—Tigers taking to water.—Examples.—Swimming powers.—Caught by floods.—Story of the Soonderbund tigers.

THE tiger's mode of attack is very characteristic of his whole nature. To see him stealthily crouching, or crawling silently and sneakingly after a herd of cattle, dodging behind every clump of bushes or tuft of grass, running swiftly along the high bank of a watercourse, and sneaking under the shadowing border of a belt of jungle, is to understand his cunning and craftiness. His attitude, when he is crouching for the final bound, is the embodiment of suppleness and strength. All his actions are graceful, and half display and half conceal beneath their symmetry and elegance the tremendous power and deadly ferocity that lurks beneath. For a short distance he is possessed of great speed, and with a few short agile bounds he generally manages to overtake his prey. If baffled in his first attack, he retires growling to lie in wait for a less fortunate victim. His onset being so fierce and sudden, the animal he selects for his prey is generally taken at a great disadvantage, and is seldom in a position to make any strenuous or availing resistance.

Delivering the numbing blow with his mighty fore paw, he fastens on the throat of the animal he has felled, and invariably tries to tear open the jugular vein. This is his practice in nearly every case, and it shews a wonderful instinct for selecting the most deadly spot in the whole body of his luckless prey. When he has got hold of his victim by the throat, he lies down, holding on to the bleeding carcase, snarling and growling, and fastening and withdrawing his claws, much as a cat does with a rat or mouse. Some writers say he then proceeds to drink the blood, but this is just one of those broad general assertions which require proof. In some cases he may quench his thirst and gratify his appetite for blood by drinking it from the gushing veins of his quivering victim, but in many cases I know from observation, that the blood is not drunk. If the tiger is very hungry he then begins his feast, tearing huge fragments of flesh from the dead body, and not unusually swallowing them whole. If he is not particularly hungry, he drags the carcase away, and hides it in some well-known spot. This is to preserve it from the hungry talons and teeth of vultures and jackals. He commonly remains on guard near his *cache* until he has acquired an appetite. If he cannot conveniently carry away his quarry, because of its bulk, or the nature of the ground, or from being disturbed, he returns to the place at night and satisfies his appetite.

Tigers can sneak crouchingly along as fast as they can trot, and it is wonderful how silently they can steal on their prey. They seem to have some stray provident fits, and on occasions make provision for future wants. There are instances on record of a tiger dragging a *kill* after him for miles, over water, and through slush and weeds, and feasting on the carcase days after he has killed it. It is a fact, now established beyond a doubt, that he will eat carrion and putrid flesh, but only from necessity and not from choice.

On one occasion my friends put up a tigress during the rains, when there are few cattle in the *derahs* or plains near the river. She had killed a pig, and was eagerly devouring the carcase when she was disturbed. Snarling and growling, she made off with a leg of pork in her mouth, when a bullet ended her career. They seem to prefer pork and venison to almost any other kind of food, and no doubt pig and deer are their natural and usual prey. The influx, however, of vast herds of cattle, and the consequent presence of man, drive away the wild animals, and at all events make them more wary and more difficult to kill. Finding domestic cattle unsuspicious, and not very formidable foes, the tiger contents himself at a pinch with beef, and judging from his ravages he comes to like it. Getting bolder by impunity, he ventures in some straits to attack man. He finds him a very easy prey; he finds the flesh too, perhaps, not unlike his favourite pig. Henceforth he becomes a 'man-eater,' the most dreaded scourge and pestilent plague of the district. He sometimes finds an old boar a tough customer, and never ventures to attack a buffalo unless it be grazing alone, and away from the rest of the herd. When buffaloes are attacked, they make common cause against their crafty and powerful foe, and uniting together in a crescent-shaped line, their horns all directed in a living *cheval-de-frise* against the tiger, they rush tumultuously at him, and fairly hunt him from the jungle. The pig, having a short thick neck, and being tremendously muscular, is hard to kill; but the poor inoffensive cow, with her long neck, is generally killed at the first blow, or so disabled that it requires little further effort to complete the work of slaughter.

Two friends of mine once shot an enormous old tiger on a small island in the middle of the river, during the height of the annual rains. The brute had lost nearly all its hair from mange, and was an emaciated sorry-looking object. From the remains on the island—the skin, scales, and bones—they found that he must have slain and eaten several alligators during his enforced imprisonment on the island. They will eat alligators when pressed by hunger, and they have been known to subsist on turtles, tortoises, iguanas, and even jackals. Only the other day in Assam, a son of Dr. B. was severely mauled by a tiger which sprang into the verandah after a dog. There were three gentlemen in the verandah, and, as you may imagine, they were taken not a little by surprise. They succeeded in bagging the tiger, but not until poor B. was very severely hurt.

After tearing the throat open, they walk round the prostrate carcase of their prey, growling and spitting like 'tabby' cats. They begin their operations in earnest, invariably on the buttock. A leopard generally eats the inner portion of the thigh first. A wolf tears open the belly, and eats the intestines first. A vulture, hawk, or kite, begins on the eyes; but a tiger invariably begins on the buttocks, whether of buffalo, cow, deer, or pig. He then eats the fatty covering round the intestines, follows that up with the liver and udder, and works his way round systematically to the fore-quarters, leaving the head to the last. It is frequently the only part of an animal that they do not eat.

A 'man-eater' eats the buttocks, shoulders, and breasts first. So many carcases are found in the jungle of animals that have died from disease or old age, or succumbed to hurts and accidents, that the whitened skeletons meet the eye in hundreds. But one can always tell the kill of a tiger, and distinguish between it and the other bleached heaps. The large bones of a tiger's kill are always broken. The broad massive rib bones are crunched in two as easily as a dog would snap the drumstick of a fowl. Vultures and jackals, the scavengers of the jungle, are incapable of doing this; and when you see the fractured large bones, you can always tell that the whiskered monarch has been on the war-path. George S. writes me :—

'I have known a tiger devour a whole bullock to his own cheek in one day. Early in the morning a man came to inform me he had seen a tiger pull down a bullock. I went after the fellow late in the afternoon, and found him in a bush not more than twenty feet square, the only jungle he had to hide in for some distance round, and in this he had polished off the bullock, nothing remaining save the head. The jungle being so very small, and he having lain the whole day in it, nothing in the way of vultures or jackals could have assisted him in finishing off the bullock.'

When hungry they appear to bolt large masses of flesh without masticating it. The same correspondent writes :—

'We cut out regular "fids" once from a tiger's stomach, also large pieces of bone. Joe heard a tremendous roaring one night, which continued till near morning, not far from Nipunneah. He went out at dawn to look for the tiger, which he found was dead. The brute had tried to swallow the knee-joint of a bullock, and it had stuck in his gullet. This made him roar from pain, and eventually choked him.'

As there are two distinct varieties of wild pig in India, so there seems to be little doubt that there are two distinct kinds of tigers. As these have frequently crossed we find many hybrids. I cannot do better than again quote from my obliging and observant friend George. The two kinds he designates as 'The Royal Bengal,' and 'The Hill Tiger,' and goes on to say:—

'As a rule the stripes of a Royal Bengal are single and dark. The skull is widely different from that of his brother the Hill tiger, being low in the crown, wider in the jaws, rather flat in comparison, and the brain-pan longer with a sloping curve at the end, the crest of the brain-pan being a concave curve.

'The Hill tiger is much more massively built; squat and thick set, heavier in weight and larger in bulk, with shorter tail, and very large and powerful neck, head, and shoulders. The stripes generally are double, and of a more brownish tinge, with fawn colour between the double stripes. The skull is high in the crown, and not quite so wide. The brain-pan is shorter, and the crest slightly convex or nearly straight, and the curve at the end of the skull rather abrupt.

'They never grow so long as the "Bengal," yet look twice as big.

'The crosses are very numerous, and vary according

to pedigree, in stripes, skulls, form, weight, bulk, and tail. This I find most remarkable when I look at my collection of over 160 skulls.

'The difference is better marked in tigers than in tigresses. The Bengal variety are not as a rule as ferocious as the Hill tiger. Being more supple and cunning, they can easier evade their pursuers by flight and manœuvre than their less agile brothers. The former, owing to deficiency of strength, oftener meet with discomfiture, and consequently are more wary and cunning; while the latter, prone to carry everything before them, trust more to their strength and courage, anticipating victory as certain.

'In some the stripes are doubled throughout, in others only partially so, while in some they are single throughout, and some have manes to a slight extent.'

I have no doubt this classification is correct. The tigers I have seen in Nepaul near the hills, were sometimes almost a dull red, and at a distance looked like a huge dun cow, while those I have seen in the plains during our annual hunts, were of a bright tawny yellow, longer, more lanky, and not shewing half such a bold front as their bulkier and bolder brethren of the hills.

The length of the tiger has often given rise to fierce discussions among sportsmen. The fertile imagination of the slayer of a solitary 'stripes,' has frequently invested the brute he has himself shot, or seen shot, or perchance heard of as having been shot by a friend, or the friend of a friend, with a fabulous length, inches swelling to feet, and dimensions growing at each repetition of the yarn, till, as in the case of boars, the twenty-eight incher becomes a forty inch tusker, and the eight foot tiger stretches to twelve or fourteen feet.

Purists again, sticklers for stern truth, haters of bounce or exaggeration, have perhaps erred as much on the other side; and in their eagerness to give the exact measurement, and avoid the very appearance of exaggeration, they actually stretch their tape line and refuse to measure the curves of the body, taking it in straight lines. This I think is manifestly unfair.

Our mode of measurement in Purneah was to take the tiger as he lay before he was put on the elephant, and measure from the tip of the nose, over the crest of the skull, along the undulations of the body, to the tip of the tail. That is, we followed the curvature of the spine along the dividing ridge of the back, and always were careful and fair in our attempts. I am of opinion that a tiger over ten feet long is an exceptionally long one, but when I read of sportsmen denying altogether that even that length can be attained, I can but pity the dogmatic scepticism that refuses credence to well ascertained and authenticated facts. I believe also that tigers are not got nearly so large as in former days. I believe that much longer and heavier tigers—animals larger in every way—were shot some twenty years ago than those we can get now, but I account for this by the fact that there is less land left waste and uncultivated. There are more roads, ferries, and bridges, more improved communications, and in consequence more travelling. Population and cultivation have increased; firearms are more numerous; sport is more generally followed; shooting is much more frequent and deadly; and, in a word, tigers have not the same chances as they had some twenty years ago of attaining a ripe old age, and reaching the extremest limit of their growth. The largest tigers being also the most suspicious and wary, are only found in the remotest recesses of the impenetrable jungles of Nepaul and the Terai, or in those parts of the Indian wilds where the crack of the European rifle is seldom or never heard.

It has been so loudly asserted, and so boldly maintained that no tiger was ever shot reaching, when fairly measured (that is, measured with the skin on, as he lay), ten feet, that I will let Mr. George again speak for himself. Referring to the royal Bengal, he says:—

'These grow to great lengths. They have been shot as long as twelve feet seven inches (my father shot one that length) or longer; twelve feet seven inches, twelve feet six inches, twelve feet three inches, twelve feet one inch, and twelve feet, have been shot and recorded in the old sporting magazines by gentlemen of undoubted veracity in Purneah.

'I have seen the skin of one twelve feet one inch, compared with which the skin of one I have by me *that measured as he lay* (the italics are mine) eleven feet one inch, looks like the skin of a cub. The old skin looks more like that of a huge antediluvian species in comparison with the other.

'The twelve footer was so heavy that my uncle (C. A. S.) tells me no number of mahouts could lift it. Several men, if they could have approached at one and the same time, might have been able to do so, but a sufficient number of men could not lay hold simultaneously to move the body from the ground.

'Eventually a number of bamboos had to be cut, and placed in an incline from the ground to the elephant's saddle while the elephant knelt down, and up this incline the tiger had to be regularly hauled and shoved, and so fastened on the elephant.

'He (the tiger) mauled four elephants, one of whom died the same day, and one other had a narrow *butch*, i.e. escape, of its life.

In another communication to me, my friend goes over the same ground, but as the matter is one of interest to sportsmen and naturalists, I will give the extract entire. It proceeds as follows:—

'Tigers grow to great lengths, some assert to even fourteen feet. I do not say they do not, but such cases are very rare, and require authentication. The longest I have seen, measured as he lay, eleven feet one inch (see "Oriental Sporting Magazine," for July, 1871, p. 308). He was seven feet nine inches from tip of nose to root of tail; root of tail one foot three inches in circumference; round chest four feet six inches; length of head one foot two inches; fore arm two feet two inches; round the head two feet ten inches; length of tail three feet four inches.

'Besides this, I have shot another eleven feet, and one ten feet eleven inches.

'The largest tigress I have shot was at Sahareah, which measured ten feet two inches. I shot another ten feet exactly.' (See O. S. M., Aug., 1874, p. 358.)

'I have got the head of a tiger, shot by Joe, which measured eleven feet five inches. It was shot at Baraila.

'The male is much bigger built in every way—length, weight, size, &c., than the female. The males are more savage, the females more cunning and agile. The arms, body, paws, head, skull, claws, teeth, &c., of the female, are smaller. The tail of tigress longer; hind legs more lanky; the prints look smaller and more contracted, and the toes nearer together. It is said that though a large tiger may venture to attack a buffalo, the tigress refrains from doing so, but I have found this otherwise in my experience.

'I have kept a regular log of all tigers shot by me. The average length of fifty-two tigers recorded in my journal is nine feet six and a half inches (cubs excluded), and of sixty-eight tigresses (cubs excluded), eight feet four inches.

'The average of tigers and tigresses is eight feet ten and a quarter inches. This is excluding cubs I have taken alive.'

As to measurements, he goes on to make a few remarks, and as I cannot improve on them I reproduce the original passage :—

'Several methods have been recommended for measuring tigers. I measure them on the ground, or when brought to camp before skinning, and run the tape tight along the line, beginning at the tip of the nose, along the middle of the skull, between the ears and neck, then along the spine to the end of the tail, taking any curves of the body.

'No doubt measurements of skull, body, tail, legs, &c., ought all to be taken, to give an adequate idea of the tiger, and for comparing them with one another, but this is not always feasible.'

Most of the leading sportsmen in India now-a-days are very particular in taking the dimensions of every limb of the dead tiger. They take his girth, length, and different proportions. Many even weigh the tiger when it gets into camp, and no doubt this test is one of the best that can be given for a comparison of the sizes of the different animals slain.

Another much disputed point in the natural history of the animal, a point on which there has been much acrimonious discussion, is the number of young that are given at a birth. Some writers have asserted, and stoutly maintained, that two cubs, or at the most three, is the extreme number of young brought forth at one time.

This may be the ordinary number, but the two gentlemen I have already alluded to have assured me, that on frequent occasions they have picked up four actually born, and have cut out five several times, and on one occasion six, from the womb of a tigress.

I have myself picked up four male cubs, all in one spot, with their eyes just beginning to open, and none of their teeth through the gums. One had been trampled to death by buffaloes, the other three were alive and scatheless, huddled into a bush, like three immense kittens. I kept the three for a considerable time, and eventually took them to Calcutta and sold them for a very satisfactory price.

It seems clear, however, that the tigress frequently has four and even five cubs. It is rare, indeed to find her accompanied by more than two well grown cubs, very seldom three; and the inference is, that one or two of the young tigers succumb in very early life.

The young ones do not appear to grow very quickly; they are about a foot long when they are born; they are born blind, with very minute hair, almost none in fact, but with the stripes already perfectly marked on the soft supple skin; they open their eyes when they are eight or ten days old, at which time they measure about a foot and a half. At the age of nine months they have attained to five feet in length, and are waxing mischievous. Tiger cubs a year old average about five feet eight inches, tigresses some three inches or so less. In two years they grow respectively to—the male seven feet six inches, and the female seven feet. At about this time they leave the mother, if they have not already done so, and commence depredations on their own account. In fact, their education has been well attended to. The mother teaches them to kill when they are about a year old. A young cub that measured only six feet, and whose mother had been shot in one of the annual beats, was killed while attacking a full grown cow in the government pound at Dumdaha police station. When they reach the length of six feet six inches they can kill pretty easily, and numbers have been shot by George and other Purneah sportsmen close to their 'kills.'

They are most daring and courageous when they have just left their mother's care, and are cast forth to fight the battle of life for themselves. While with the old tigress their lines have been cast in not unpleasant places, they have seldom known hunger, and have experienced no reverses. Accustomed to see every animal succumb to her well planned and audacious attacks, they fancy that nothing will withstand their onslaught. They have been known to attack a line of elephants, and to charge most determinedly, even in this adolescent stage.

Bye-and-bye, however, as they receive a few rude shocks from buffaloes, or are worsted in a hand-to-hand encounter with some tough old bull, or savage old grey boar, more especially if they get an ugly rip or two from the sharp tusks of an infuriated fighting tusker, they begin to be less aggressive, they learn that discretion may be the better part of valour, and their cunning instincts are roused. In fact, their education is progressing, and in time they instinctively discover every wile and dodge and cunning stratagem, and display all the wondrous subtelty of their race in procuring their prey.

Old tigers are invariably more wary, cautious, and suspicious than young ones, and till they are fairly put to it by hunger, hurt, or compulsion, they endeavour to keep their stripes concealed. When brought to bay, however, there is little to reproach them with on the score of cowardice, and it will be matter of rejoicing if you or your elephants do not come off second best in the encounter. Even in the last desperate case, a cunning old tiger will often make a feint, or sham rush, or pretended charge, when his whole object is flight. If he succeed in demoralising the line of elephants, roaring and dashing furiously about, he will then try in the confusion to double through, unless he is too badly wounded to be able to travel fast, in which case he will fight to the end.

Old fellows are well acquainted with every maze and thicket in the jungles, and they no sooner hear the elephants enter the 'bush' or 'cover' than they make off for some distant shelter. If there is no apparent chance of this being successful, they try to steal out laterally and outflank the line, or if that also is impossible, they hide in some secret recess like a fox, or crouch low in some clumpy bush, and trust to you or your elephant passing by without noticing their presence.

It is marvellous in what sparse cover they will manage to lie up. So admirably do their stripes mingle with the withered and charred grass-stems and dried up stalks, that it is very difficult to detect the dreaded robber when he is lying flat, extended, close to the ground, so still and motionless that you cannot distinguish a tremor or even a vibration of the grass in which he is crouching.

On one occasion George followed an old tiger through some stubble about three feet high. It had been well trampled down too by tame buffaloes. The tiger had been tracked into the field, and was known to be in it. George was within ten yards of the cunning brute, and although mounted on a tall elephant, and eagerly scanning the thin cover with his sharpest glance, he could not discern the concealed monster. His elephant was within four paces of it, when it sprang up at the charge, giving a mighty roar, which however also served as its death yell, as a bullet from George's trusty gun crashed through its ribs and heart.

Tigers can lay themselves so flat on the ground, and lie so perfectly motionless, that it is often a very easy thing to overlook them. On another occasion, when the Purneah Hunt were out, a tigress that had been shot got under some cover that was trampled down by a line of about twenty elephants. The sportsmen knew that she had been severely wounded, as they could tell by the gouts of blood, but there was no sign of the body. She had disappeared. After a long search, beating the same ground over and over again, an elephant trod on the dead body lying under the trampled canes, and the mahout got down and discovered her lying quite dead. She was a large animal and full grown.

On another occasion George was after a fine male tiger. He was following up fast, but coming to a broad nullah, full of water, he suddenly lost sight of his game. He looked up and down the bank, and on the opposite bank, but could see no traces of the tiger. Looking down, he saw in the water what at first he took to be a large bull-frog. There was not a ripple on the placid stagnant surface of the pool.

He marvelled much, and just then his mahout pointed to the supposed bull-frog, and in an excited whisper implored George to fire. A keener look convinced George that it really was the tiger. It was totally immersed all but the face, and lying so still that not the faintest motion or ripple was perceptible. He fired and inflicted a terrible wound. The tiger bounded madly forward, and George gave it its quietus through the spine as it tried to spring up the opposite bank.

A nearly similar case occurred to old Mr. C., one of the veteran sportsmen of Purneah. A tiger had bolted towards a small tank or pond, and though the line followed up in hot pursuit, the brute disappeared. Old C., keener than the others, was loth to give up the pursuit, and presently discerned a yellowish reflection in the clear water. Peering more intently, he could discover the yellowish tawny outline of the cunning animal, totally immersed in the water, save its eyes, ears, and nose. He shot the tiger dead, and it sank to the bottom like a stone. So perfectly had it concealed itself, that the other sportsmen could not for the life of them imagine what old C. had fired at, till his mahout got down and began to haul the dead animal out of the water.

Tigers are not at all afraid of water, and are fast and powerful swimmers. They swim much after the fashion of a horse, only the head out of the water, and they make scarcely any ripple.

'In another case,' writes George, 'though not five yards from the elephant, and right under me, a tiger was swimming with so slight a ripple that I mistook it for a rat, until I saw the stripes emerge, when I perforated his jacket with a bullet.'

Only their head remaining out of water when they

are swimming, they are very hard to hit, as shooting at an object on water is very deceptive work as to judging distance, and a tiger's head is but a small object to aim at when some little way off.

Old C. had another adventure with a cunning rogue, which all but ended disastrously. He was in hot pursuit of the tiger, and, finding no safety on land, it took to swimming in a broad unfordable piece of water, a sort of deep lagoon. Old C. procured a boat that was handy, and got a coolie to paddle him out after the tiger. He fired several shots at the exposed head of the brute, but missed. He thought he would wait till he got nearer and make a sure shot, as he had only one bullet left in the boat. Suddenly the tiger turned round, and made straight for the boat. Here was a quandary. Even if he killed the tiger with his single bullet it might upset the boat; the lagoon was full of alligators, to say nothing of weeds, and there was no time to get his heavy boots off. He felt his life might depend on the accuracy of his aim. He fired, and killed the tiger stone dead within four or five yards of the boat.

On one occasion, when out with our worthy district magistrate, Mr. S., I came on the tracks of what to all appearance, was a very large tiger. They led over the sand close to the water's edge, and were very distinct. I could see no returning marks, so I judged that the tiger must have taken to the water. The stream was rapid and deep, and midway to the further bank was a big, oblong-shaped, sandy islet, some five or six hundred yards long, and having a few scrubby bushes growing sparsely on it. We put our elephants into the rapid current, and got across. The river here was nearly a quarter of a mile wide on each side of the islet. As we emerged from the stream on to the island we found fresh tracks of the tiger. They led us completely round the circumference of the islet. The tiger had evidently been in quest of food. The prints were fresh and very well defined. Finding that all was barren on the sandy shore, he entered the current again, and following up we found his imprint once more on the further bank, several hundred yards down the stream.

One tiger was killed stone dead by a single bullet during one of our annual hunts, and falling back into the water, it sank to the bottom like lead. Being unable to find the animal, we beat all round the place, till I suggested it might have been hit and fallen into the river. One of the men was ordered to dive down, and ascertain if the tiger was at the bottom. The river water is generally muddy, so that the bottom cannot be seen. Divesting himself of puggree, and girding up his loins, the diver sank gently to the bottom, but presently reappeared in a palpable funk, puffing and blowing, and declaring that the tiger was certainly at the bottom. The foolish fellow thought it might be still alive. We soon disabused his mind of that idea, and had the dead tiger hauled up to dry land.

Surprised by floods, a tiger has been known to remain for days on an ant-hill, and even to take refuge on the branch of some large tree, but he takes to water readily, and can swim for over a mile, and he has been known to remain for days in from two to three feet depth of water.

A time-honoured tiger story with old hands, used to tell how the Soonderbund tigers got carried out to sea. If the listener was a new arrival, or a *gobe mouche*, they would explain that the tigers in the Soonderbunds often get carried out to sea by the retiring tide. It would sweep them off as they were swimming from island to island in the vast delta of Father Ganges. Only the young ones, however, suffered this lamentable fate. The older and more wary fellows, taught perhaps by sad experience, used always to dip their tails in, before starting on a swim, so as to ascertain which way the tide was flowing. If it was the flow of the tide they would boldly venture in, but if it was ebb tide, and there was the slightest chance of their being carried out to sea, they would patiently lie down, meditate on the fleeting vanity of life, and like the hero of the song—

'Wait for the turn of the tide.'

Without venturing an opinion on this story, I may confidently assert, that the tiger, unlike his humble prototype the domestic cat, is not really afraid of water, but will take to it readily to escape a threatened danger, or if he can achieve any object by 'paddling his own canoe.'

CHAPTER XX.

No regular breeding season.—Beliefs and prejudices of the natives about tigers.—Bravery of the 'gwalla,' or cowherd caste.—Claw-marks on trees.—Fondness for particular localities.—Tiger in Mr. F.'s howdah.—Springing powers of tigers.—Lying close in cover.—Incident —Tiger shot with No. 4 shot.—Man clawed by a tiger.—Knocked its eye out with a sickle.—Same tiger subsequently shot in same place.—Tigers easily killed.—Instances.—Effect of shells on tiger and buffalo.—Best weapon and bullets for tiger.—Poisoning tigers denounced.—Natives prone to exaggerate in giving news of tiger.—Anecdote.—Beating for tiger.—Line of elephants.—Padding dead game.—Line of seventy-six elephants.—Captain of the hunt.—Flags for signals in the line.—'Naka,' or scout ahead.—Usual time for tiger shooting on the Koosee.—Firing the jungle.—The line of fire at night.—Foolish to shoot at moving jungle.—Never shoot down the line.—Motions of different animals in the grass.

TIGERS seem to have no regular breeding season. As a rule the male and female come together in the autumn and winter, and the young ones are born in the spring and summer. All the young tigers I have ever heard of have been found in March, April, and May, and so on through the rains.

The natives have many singular beliefs and prejudices about tigers, and they are very often averse to give the slightest information as to their whereabouts. To a stranger they will either give no information at all, pleading entire ignorance, or they will wilfully mislead him, putting him on a totally wrong track. If you are well known to the villagers, and if they have confidence in your nerve and aim, they will eagerly tell you everything they know, and will accompany you on your elephant, to point out the exact spot where the tiger was last seen. In the event of a 'find' they always look for *backsheesh*, even though your exertions may have rid their neighbourhood of an acknowledged scourge.

The *gwalla*, or cowherd caste, seem to know the habits of the yellow striped robber very accurately. Accompanied by their herd they will venture into the thickest jungle, even though they know that it is infested by one or more tigers. If any member of the herd is attacked, it is quite common for the *gwalla* to rush up, and by shouts and even blows try to make the robber yield up his prey. This is no exaggeration, but a simple fact. A cowherd attacked by a tiger has been known to call up his herd by cries, and they have succeeded in driving off his fierce assailant. No tiger will willingly face a herd of buffaloes or cattle united for mutual defence. Surrounded by his trusty herd, the *gwalla* traverses the densest jungle and most tiger-infested thickets without fear.

They believe that to rub the fat of the tiger on the loins, and to eat a piece of the tongue or flesh, will cure impotency; and tiger fat, rubbed on a painful part of the body, is an accepted specific for rheumatic affections. It is a firmly settled belief, that the whiskers and teeth, worn on the body, will act as a charm, making the wearer proof against the attacks of tigers. The collar-bone too, is eagerly coveted for the same reason.

During the rains tigers are sometimes forced, like others of the cat tribe, to take to trees. A Mr. McI. shot two large full grown tigers in a tree at Gunghara, and a Baboo of my acquaintance bagged no less than eight in trees during one rainy season at Rampoor.

Tigers generally prefer remaining near water, and

drink a great deal, the quantity of raw meat they devour being no doubt provocative of thirst.

The marks of their claws are often seen on trees in the vicinity of their haunts, and from this fact many ridiculous stories have got abroad regarding their habits. It has even been regarded by some writers as a sort of rude test, by which to arrive at an approximate estimate of the tiger's size. A tiger can stretch himself out some two or two and a half feet more than his measurable length. You have doubtless often seen a domestic cat whetting its claws on the mat, or scratching some rough substance, such as the bark of a tree; this is often done to clean the claws, and to get rid of chipped and ragged pieces, and it is sometimes mere playfulness. It is the same with the tiger, the scratching on the trees is frequently done in the mere wantonness of sport, but it is often resorted to to clear the claws from pieces of flesh, that may have adhered to them during a meal on some poor slaughtered bullock. These marks on the trees are a valuable sign for the hunter, as by their appearance, whether fresh or old, he can often tell the whereabouts of his quarry, and a good tracker will even be able to make a rough guess at its probable size and disposition.

Like policemen, tigers stick to certain beats; even when disturbed, and forced to abandon a favourite spot, they frequently return to it; and although the jungle may be wholly destroyed, old tigers retain a partiality for the scenes of their youthful depredations; they are often shot in the most unlikely places, where there is little or no cover, and one would certainly never expect to find them; they migrate with the herds, and retire to the hills during the annual floods, always coming back to the same jungle when the rains are over.

Experienced shekarries know this trait of the tiger's character well, and can tell you minutely the colour and general appearance of the animals in any particular jungle; they are aware of any peculiarity, such as lameness, scars, &c., and their observations must be very keen indeed, and amazingly accurate, as I have never known them wrong when they committed themselves to a positive statement.

An old planter residing at Sultanpore, close on the Nepaul border, a noted sportsman and a crack shot, was charged on one occasion by a large tiger; the brute sprang right off the ground on to the elephant's head; his hind legs were completely off the ground, resting on the elephant's chest and neck; Mr. F. retained sufficient presence of mind to sit close down in his howdah; the tiger's forearm was extended completely over the front bar, and so close that it touched his hat. In this position he called out to his son who was on another elephant close by, to fire at the tiger; he was cool enough to warn him to take a careful aim, and not hit the elephant. His son acted gallantly up to his instructions, and shot the tiger through the heart, when it dropped down quite dead, to Mr. F.'s great relief.

Some sportsmen are of opinion, that the tiger when charging never springs clear from the ground, but only rears itself on its hind legs; this however is a mistake. I saw a tiger leap right off the ground, and spring on to the rump of an elephant carrying young Sam S. The elephant proved staunch, and remained quite quiet, and Sam, turning round in his howdah, shot his assailant through the head.

I may give another incident, to shew how closely tigers will sometimes stick to cover; they are sometimes as bad to dislodge as a quail or a hare; they will crouch down and conceal themselves till you almost trample on them. One day a party of the Purneah Club were out; they had shot two fine tigers out of several that had been seen; the others were known to have gone ahead into some jungle surrounded by water, and easy to beat. Before proceeding further it was proposed accordingly to have some refreshment. The *tiffin* elephant was directed to a tree close by, beneath whose shade the hungry sportsmen were to plant themselves; the elephant had knelt down, one or two boxes had actually been removed, several of the servants were clearing away the dried grass and leaves. H. W. S. came up on the opposite side of the tree, and was in the act of leaping off his elephant, when an enormous tiger got up at his very feet, and before the astounded sportsmen could handle a gun, the formidable intruder had cleared the bushes with a bound, and disappeared in the thick jungle.

The following adventure bears me out in my remark, that tigers get attached to, and like to remain in, one place. Mr. F. Simpson, a thorough-going sportsman of the good old type, had been out one day in the Koosee derahs; he had had a long and unsuccessful beat for tiger, and had given up all hope of bagging one that day; he thought therefore that he might as well turn his attention to more ignoble game. Extracting his bullets, he replaced them with No. 4 shot. In a few minutes a peacock got up in front of him, and he fired. The report roused a very fine tiger right in front of his elephant; to make the best of a bad bargain, he gave the retreating animal the full benefit of his remaining charge of shot, and peppered it well. About a year after, close to this very place, C. A. S. bagged a fine tiger. On examination, the marks of a charge of shot were found in the flanks, and on removing the pads of the feet, numbers of pellets of No. 4 shot were found embedded in them. It was evidently the animal that had been peppered a year before, and the pellets had worked their way downwards to the feet.

On another occasion, a man came to the factory where George was then residing, to give information of a tiger. He bore on his back numerous bleeding scratches, ample evidence of the truth of his story. While cutting grass in the jungle, with a blanket on his back, the day being rainy, he had been attacked by a tiger from the rear. The blanket is generally folded several times, and worn over the head and back. It is a thick heavy covering, and in the first onset the tiger tore the blanket from the man's body, which was probably the means of saving his life. The man turned round, terribly scared, as may be imagined. In desperation he struck at the tiger with his sickle, and according to his own account, he succeeded in putting out one of its eyes. He said it was a young tiger, and his bleeding wounds, and the persistency with which he stuck to his story, impressed George with the belief that he was telling the truth. A search for the tiger was made. The man's blanket was found, torn to shreds, but no tiger, although the footprints of one were plainly visible. But some months after, near the same spot, George shot a half grown tiger with one of its eyes gone, which had evidently been roughly torn from the socket. This was doubtless the identical brute that had attacked the grass-cutter.

It is sometimes wonderful how easily a large and powerful tiger may be killed. The most vulnerable parts are the back of the head, through the neck, and broadside on the chest. The neck is the most deadly spot of all, and a shot behind the shoulder, or on the spine, is sure to bring the game to bag. I have seen several shot with a single bullet from a smooth-bore, and on one occasion, George tells me he saw a tigress killed with a single smooth-bore bullet at over a hundred yards. The bullet was a *ricochet*, and struck the tigress below the chest, and travelled towards the heart, but without touching it. She fell twenty yards from where she had been hit. Another, which on skinning we found had been shot through the heart, with a single smooth-bore bullet at a distance of one hun- and fifty yards, travelled for thirty yards before falling dead. Meiselback, a neighbour of mine, shot three tigers successively, on one occasion, with a No. 18 Joe Manton smooth-bore. Each of the three was killed by a single bullet, one in the head, one in the neck, and one through the heart, the bullet entering behind the shoulder.

On the other hand, I once fired no less than six Jacob's shells into a tiger, all behind the shoulder, before I could stop him. The shells seemed to explode on the surface the moment they came in contact with the body. There was a tremendous surface wound, big enough to put a pumpkin into, but very little internal hurt. On another occasion (April 4, 1874) during one of the most exciting and most glorious moments of my sporting life—buffaloes charging the line in all directions, burning jungle all around us, and bullets whistling on every side—I fired TWELVE shells into a large bull before I killed him. As every shell hit him, I heard the sharp detonation, and saw the tiny puff of smoke curl outward from the ghastly wound. The poor maddened brute would drop on his knees, stagger again to his feet, and, game to the last, attempt to charge my elephant. I was anxious really to test the effect of the Jacob's shell as against the solid conical bullet, and carefully watched the result of each shot. My weapon was a beautifully finished No. 12 smooth-bore, made expressly to order for an officer in the Royal Artillery, from whom I bought it. From that day I never fired another Jacob's shell.

My remarks about the tiger springing clear off the ground when charging, are amply borne out by the experience of some of my sporting friends. I could quote pages, but will content myself with one extract. It is a point of some importance, as many good old sportsmen pooh-pooh the idea, and maintain that the tiger merely stretches himself out to his fullest length, and if he does leave the ground, it is by a purely physical effort, pulling himself up by his claws.

My friend George writes me: 'In several cases I have known and seen the tiger spring, and leave the ground. In one case the tiger sprang from fully five yards off. He crouched at the distance of a few paces, as if about to spring, and then sprang clean on to the head of Joe's *tusker*. An eight feet nine inch tigress once got on to the head of my elephant, which was ten feet seven inches in height. Every one present saw her leave the ground. Once, when after a tiger in small stubble, about six feet high, I saw one bound over a bush so clean that I could see every bit of him.' And so on.

For long range shooting the rifle is doubtless the best weapon. The Express is the most deadly. The smooth-bore is the gun for downright honest sport. Shells and hollow pointed bullets are the things, as one sportsman writes me, 'for mutilation and cowardly murder, and for spoiling the skin.' Poison is the resource of the poacher. No sportsman could descend so low. Grant that the tiger is a scourge, a pest, a nuisance, a cruel and implacable foe to man and beast; pile all the vilest epithets of your vocabulary on his head, and say that he deserves them all, still he is what opportunity and circumstance have made him. He is as nature fashioned him; and there are bold spirits, and keen sights, and steady nerves enough, God wot, among our Indian sportsmen, to cope with him on more equal and sportsmanlike terms than by poisoning him like a mangy dog. On this point, however, opinions differ. I do not envy the man who would prefer poisoning a tiger to the keen delight of patiently following him up, ousting him from cover to cover, watching his careful endeavours to elude your search; perhaps at the end of a long and fascinating beat, feeling the electric excitement thrill every nerve and fibre of your body, as the magnificent robber comes bounding down at the charge, the very embodiment of ferocity and strength, the perfection of symmetry, the acme of agility and grace.

Natives are such notorious perverters of the truth, and so often hide what little there may be in their communications under such floods of Oriental hyperbole and exaggeration, that you are often disappointed in going out on what you consider trustworthy and certain information. They often remind me of the story of the Laird of Logan. He was riding slowly along a country road one day, when another equestrian joined him. Logan's eye fixed itself on a hole in the turf bank bounding the road, and with great gravity, and in trust-inspiring accents, he said, 'I saw a *tod* (or fox) gang in there.'

'Did you, really;' cried the new comer.

'I did,' responded the laird.

'Will you hold my horse till I get a spade,' cried the now excited traveller.

The laird assented. Away hurried the man, and soon returned with a spade. He set manfully to work to dig out the fox, and worked till the perspiration streamed down his face. The laird sat stolidly looking on, saying never a word; and as he seemed to be nearing the confines of the hole, the poor digger redoubled his exertions. When at length it became plain that there was no fox there, he wiped his streaming brow, and rather crossly exclaimed, 'I'm afraid there's no tod here.'

'It would be a wonder if there was,' rejoined the laird, without the movement of a muscle, 'it's ten years since I saw him gang in there.'

So it is sometimes with a native. He will fire your ardour, by telling you of some enormous tiger, to be found in some jungle close by, but when you come to enquire minutely into his story, you find that the tiger was seen perhaps the year before last, or that it *used* to be there, or that somebody else had told him of its being there.

Some tigers, too, are so cunning and wary, that they will make off long before the elephants have come near. I have seen others rise on their hind legs just like a hare or a kangaroo, and peer over the jungle trying to make out one's whereabouts. This is of course only in short light jungle.

The plan we generally adopt in beating for tiger on or near the Nepaul border, is to use a line of elephants to beat the cover. It is a fine sight to watch the long line of stately monsters moving slowly and steadily forward. Several howdahs tower high above the line, the polished barrels of guns and rifles glittering in the fierce rays of the burning and vertical sun. Some of the shooters wear huge hats made from the light pith of the solah plant, others have long blue or white puggrees wound round their heads in truly Oriental style. These are very comfortable to wear, but rather trying to the sight, as they afford no protection to the eyes. For riding they are to my mind the most comfortable head-dress that can be worn, and they are certainly more graceful than the stiff unsightly solah hat.

Between every two howdahs are four or five pad elephants. These beat up all the intervening bushes, and carry the game that may be shot. When a pig, deer, tiger, or other animal has been shot, and has received its *coup de grace*, it is quickly bundled on to the pad, and there secured. The elephant kneels down to receive the load, and while game is being padded the whole line waits, till the operation is complete, as it is bad policy to leave blanks. Where this simple precaution is neglected, many a tiger will sneak through the opening left by the pad elephant, and so silently and cautiously can they steal through the dense cover, and so cunning are they and acute, that they will take advantage of the slightest gap, and the keenest and best trained eye will fail to detect them.

In most of our hunting parties on the Koosee, we had some twenty or thirty elephants, and frequently six or eight howdahs. These expeditions were very pleasant, and we lived luxuriously. For real sport ten elephants and two or three tried comrades—not more—is much better. With a short, easily-worked line, that can turn and double, and follow the tiger quickly, and dog his every movement, you can get far better sport, and bring more to bag, than with a long unwieldy line, that takes a considerable time to turn and wheel, and in whose onward march there is of necessity little of the silence and swiftness which are necessary elements in successful tiger shooting.

I have been out with a line of seventy-six elephants and fourteen howdahs. This was on 16th March 1875. It was a magnificent sight to see the seventy-six huge brutes in the river together, splashing the water along their heated sides to cool themselves, and sending huge waves dashing against the crumbling banks of the rapid stream. It was no less magnificent to see their slow stately march through the swaying, crashing jungle. What an idea of irresistible power and ponderous strength the huge creatures gave us, as they heaved through the tangled brake, crushing everything in their resistless progress. It was a sight to be remembered, but as might have been expected, we found the jungles almost untenanted. Everything cleared out before us, long ere the line could reach its vicinity. We only killed one tiger, but next day we separated, the main body crossing the stream, while my friends and myself, with only fourteen elephants, rebeat the same jungle and bagged two.

In every hunt, one member is told off to look after the forage and grain for the elephants. One attends to the cooking and requirements of the table, one acts as paymaster and keeper of accounts, while the most experienced is unanimously elected captain, and takes general direction of every movement of the line. He decides on the plan of operations for the day, gives each his place in the line, and for the time, becomes an irresponsible autocrat, whose word is law, and against whose decision there is no appeal.

Scouts are sent out during the night, and bring in reports from all parts of the jungle in the early morning, while we are discussing *chota baziree*, our early morning meal. If tiger is reported, or a kill has been discovered, we form line in silence, and without noise bear down direct on the spot. In the captain's howdah are three flags. A blue flag flying means that only tiger or rhinoceros are to be shot at. A red flag signifies that we are to have general firing, in fact that we may blaze away at any game that may be afoot, and the white flag shews us that we are on our homeward way, and then also may shoot at anything we can get, break the line, or do whatever we choose. On the flanks are generally posted the best shots of the party. The captain, as a rule, keeps to the centre of the line. Frequently one man and elephant is sent on ahead to some opening or dry water-bed, to see that no cunning tiger sneaks away unseen. This vedette is called *naka*. All experienced sportsmen employ a naka, and not unfrequently where the ground is difficult, two are sent ahead. The naka is a most important post, and the holder will often get a lucky shot at some wary veteran trying to sneak off, and may perhaps bag the only tiger of the day. The mere knowledge that there is an elephant on ahead, will often keep tigers from trying to get away. They prefer to face the known danger of the line behind, to the unknown danger in front, and in all cases where there is a big party a naka should be sent on ahead.

Tigers can be, and are, shot on the Koosee plains all the year round, but the big hunts take place in the months of March, April, and May, when the hot west winds are blowing, and when the jungle has got considerably trampled down by the herds of cattle grazing in the tangled wilderness of tall grass. Innumerable small paths shew where the cattle wander backward and forward through the labyrinths of the jungle. In the howdah we carry ample supplies of vesuvians. We light and drop these as they blaze into the dried grass and withered leaves as we move along, and soon a mighty wall of roaring flame behind us, attests the presence of the destroying element. We go diagonally up wind, and the flames and smoke thus surge and roar and curl and roll, in dense blinding volumes, to the rear and leeward of our line. The roaring of the flames sounds like the maddened surf of an angry sea, dashing in thunder against an iron-bound coast. The leaping flames mount up in fiery columns, illuminating the fleecy clouds of smoke with an unearthly glare. The noise is deafening; at times some of the elephants get quite nervous at the fierce roar of the flames behind, and try to bolt across country. The fire serves two good purposes. It burns up the old withered grass, making room for the fresh succulent sprouts to spring, and it keeps all the game in front of the line, driving the animals before us, as they are afraid to break back and face the roaring wall of flame. A seething, surging sea of flame, several miles long, encircling the whole country in its fiery belt, sweeping along at night with the roar of a storm-tossed sea; the flames flickering, swelling, and leaping up in the dark night, the fiery particles rushing along amid clouds of lurid smoke, and the glare of the serpent-like line reddening the horizon, is one of those magnificent spectacles that can only be witnessed at rare intervals among the experiences of a sojourn in India. Words fail to depict its grandeur, and the utmost skill of Doré could not render on canvas, the weird, unearthly magnificence of a jungle fire, at the culmination of its force and fury.

In beating, the elephants are several yards apart, and, standing in the howdah, you can see the slightest motion of the grass before you, unless indeed it be virgin jungle, quite untrodden, and perhaps higher than your elephant; in such high dense cover, tigers will sometimes lie up and allow you to go clean past them. In such a case you must fire the jungle, and allow the blaze to beat for you. It is common for young, over eager sportsmen, to fire at moving jungle, trusting to a lucky chance for hitting the moving animal; this is useless waste of powder; they fail to realize the great length of the swaying grass, and invariably shoot over the game; the animal hears the crashing of the bullet through the dense thicket overhead, and immediately stops, and you lose all idea of his whereabouts. When you see an animal moving before you in long jungle, it should be your object to follow him slowly and patiently, till you can get a sight of him, and see what sort of beast he is. Firing at the moving grass is worse than useless. Keep as close behind him as you can, make signs for the other elephants to close in; stick to your quarry, never lose sight of him for an instant, be ready to seize the first moment, when more open jungle, or some other favourable chance, may give you a glimpse of his skin.

Another caution should be observed. Never fire down the line. It is astonishing how little will divert a bullet, and a careless shot is worse than a dozen charging tigers. If a tiger does break back, let him get well away behind the line, and then blaze at him as hard as you like. It is particularly unpleasant to hear a bullet come singing and booming down the line, from some excited dunderhead on the far left or right.

A tiger slouching along in front moves pretty fast, in a silent swinging trot; the tops of the reeds or grass sway very gently, with a wavering, side to side motion. A pig rushes boldly through, and a deer will cause the grass to rock violently to and fro. A buffalo or rhinoceros is known at once by the crashing of the dry stalks, as his huge frame plunges along; but the tiger can never be mistaken. When that gentle, undulating, noiseless motion is once seen, be ready with your trusty gun, and remove not your eye from the spot, for the mighty robber of the jungle is before you.

CHAPTER XXI.

Howdahs and howdah-ropes.—Mussulman custom.—Killing animals for food.—Mysterious appearance of natives when an animal is killed.—Fastening dead tigers to the pad.—Present mode wants improving.—Incident illustrative of this.—Dangerous to go close to wounded tigers.—Examples.—Footprints of tigers.—Call of the tiger.—Natives and their powers of description.—How to beat successfully for tiger.—Description of a beat.—Disputes among the shooters.—Awarding tigers.—Cutting open the tiger.—Native idea about the liver of the tiger.—Signs of a tiger's presence in the jungle.—Vultures.—Do they scent their quarry or view it?—A vulture carrion feast.

THE best howdahs are light, single-seated ones, with strong, light frames of wood and cane-work, and a moveable seat with a leather strap, adjustable to any length, on which to lean back. They should have a strong iron rail all round the top, covered with leather, with convenient grooves to receive the barrels of the guns, as they rest in front, ready to either hand. In front there should be compartments for different kinds of cartridges; and pockets and lockers under the seat, and at the back, or wherever there is room. Outside should be a strong iron step, to get out and in by easily, and a strong iron ring, through which to pass the rope that binds the howdah to the elephant.

You cannot be too careful with your howdah ropes. A chain is generally used as an auxiliary to the rope, which should be of cotton, strong and well twisted, and should be overhauled daily, to see that there is no chafing. It is passed round the foot-bars of the howdah, and several times round the belly of the elephant.

Another rope acts as a crupper behind, being passed through rings in the terminal frame-work of the howdah, and under the elephant's tail; it frequently causes painful sores there, and some drivers give it a hitch round the tail, in the same way as you would hitch it round a post. Another steadying rope goes round the elephant's breast, like a chest-band. 'A merciful man is merciful to his beast.' You should always, therefore, have a sheet of soft well oiled leather to go between the chest and belly ropes and the elephant's hide; this prevents chafing, and is a great relief to the poor old *hathi*, as they call the elephant. *Hatnee* is the female elephant. *Duntar* is a fellow with large tusks, and *mukna* is an elephant with small downward growing tusks.

Many of the old fashioned howdahs are far too heavy; a firm, strong howdah should not weigh more than 28lbs. In most of the old fashioned ones, there is a seat for an attendant. If your attendant be a Mussulman, he hurries down as soon as you shoot a deer, to cut its throat. The Mohammedan religion enjoins a variety of rules on its professors in regard to the slaying of animals for food. Chief of these is a prohibition against eating the flesh of an animal that has died a natural death; the throat of every animal intended to be eaten should be cut, and at the moment of applying the knife, *Bismillah* should be said, that is, 'In the name of God.' If therefore your mahout, or attendant, belong to the religion of the *Koran*, he will hurry down to cut the throat of a wounded deer if possible before life is extinct; if it be already dead, he will leave it alone for the Hindoos, who have no such scruples.

A number of *moosahurs, banturs, gwallas*, and other idlers, from the jungle villages, generally follow in the wake of the line. If you shoot many pigs, they carry off the dead bodies, and hold high carnival in their homes in the evening. To see them rush on a slain buffalo, and hack it to pieces, is a curious sight; they fight for pieces of flesh like so many vultures. Sportsmen generally content themselves with the head of a buffalo, but not a scrap of the carcase is ever wasted. The natives are attracted to the spot, like ants to a heap of grain, or wasps to an old sugar barrel; they seem to spring out of the earth, so rapidly do they make their appearance. If you were to kill a dozen buffaloes, I believe all the flesh would be taken away to the neighbouring villages within an hour.

This appearance of men in the jungles is wonderful. You may think yourself in the centre of a vast wilderness, not a sign of human habitation for miles around; on all sides stretches a vast ocean of grass, the resort of ferocious wild animals, seemingly untrodden by a human foot. You shoot a deer, a pig, or other animal whose flesh is fit for food; the man behind you gives a cry, and in ten minutes you will have a group of brawny young fellows around your elephant, eager to carry away the game. The way these natives thread the dense jungle is to me a wonder; they seem to know every devious path and hidden recess, and they traverse the most gloomy and dangerous solitudes without betraying the slightest apprehension.

In fastening dead game to the pad of the carrying elephant great care is necessary. Some elephants are very timid, and indeed all elephants are mistrustful and suspicious of anything behind them. They are pretty courageous in facing anything before them, but they do not like a rustling or indeed any motion in their rear. I have seen a dog put an elephant to flight, and if you have a lazy *hathi*, a good plan is to walk a horse behind him. He will then shuffle along at a prodigious pace, constantly looking round from side to side, and no doubt in his heart anathematising the horse that forces the running so persistently.

The present method of roughly lashing on dead game anyhow requires altering. Some ingenious sportsman could surely devise a system of slings by which the dead weight of the game could be more equally distributed. At present the dead bodies are hauled up at random, and fastened anyhow. The pad gets displaced, the elephant must stop till the burden is rearranged; the ropes, especially on a hot day, cut into the skin and rub off the hair, and many a good skin is quite spoiled by the present rough method of tying on the pad.

One day, in taking off a dead tiger from the pad, near George's bungalow, the end of the rope (a new one) remained somehow fixed to the neck of the elephant. When he rose up, being relieved of the weight, he dragged the dead tiger with him. This put the elephant into a horrible funk, and despite all the efforts of the driver he started off at a trot, hauling the tiger after him. Every now and then he would turn round, and tread and kick the lifeless carcase. At length the rope gave way, and the elephant became more manageable, but not before a fine skin had been totally ruined, all owing to this primitive style of fastening by ropes to the pad. A proper pad, with leather straps and buckles, that could be hauled as tight as necessary —a sort of harness arrangement, could easily be devised, to secure dead game on the pad. I am certain it would save time in the hunting-field, and protect many a fine skin, that gets abraded and marked by the present rough and ready lashing.

It is always dangerous to go too close up to a wounded

tiger, and one should never rashly jump to the conclusion that a tiger is dead because he appears so. Approach him cautiously, and make very certain that he is really and truly dead, before you venture to get down beside the body. It is a bad plan to take your elephant close up to a dead tiger at all. I have known cases, where good staunch elephants have been spoiled for future sport, by being rashly taken up to a wounded tiger. In rolling about, the tiger may get hold of the elephants, and inflict injuries that will demoralise them, and make them quite unsteady on subsequent occasions.

I have known cases where a tiger left for dead has had to be shot over again. I have seen a man get down to pull a seemingly dead tiger into the open, and get charged. Fortunately it was a dying effort, and I put a bullet through the skull before the tiger could reach the frightened peon. We have been several times grouped round a dying tiger, watching him breathe his last, when the brute has summoned up strength for a final effort, and charged the elephants.

On one occasion W. D. had got down beside what he thought a dead tiger, had rolled him over, and, tape in hand, was about to measure the animal, when he staggered to his feet with a terrific growl, and made away through the jungle. He had only been stunned, and fortunately preferred running to fighting, or the consequences might have been more tragic; as it was, he was quickly followed up and killed. But instances like these might be indefinitely multiplied, all teaching, that seemingly dead tigers should be approached with the utmost respect. Never venture off your elephant without a loaded revolver.

In beating for tiger, we have seen that the appearance of the kill, whether fresh or old, whether much torn and mangled or comparatively untouched, often affords valuable indications to the sportsman. The footprints are not less narrowly looked for, and scrutinized. If we are after tiger, and following them up, the captain will generally get down at any bare place, such as a dry nullah, the edge of a tank or water hole, or any other spot where footprints can be detected. Fresh prints can be very easily distinguished. The impression is like that made by a dog, only much larger, and the marks of the claws are not visible. The largest footprint I have heard of was measured by George S., and was found to be eight and a quarter inches wide from the outside of the first to the outside of the fourth toe. If a tiger has passed very recently, the prints will be fresh-looking, and if on damp ground there can be no mistaking them. If it has been raining recently, we particularly notice whether the rain has obliterated the track at all, in any place; which would lead us to the conclusion that the tiger had passed before it rained. If the water has lodged in the footprint, the tiger has passed after the shower. In fresh prints the water will be slightly puddly or muddy. In old prints it will be quite clear; and so on.

The call of the male tiger is quite different from that of the female. The male calls with a hoarse harsh cry, something between the grunt of a pig and the bellow of a bull; the call of the tigress is more like the prolonged mew of a cat much intensified. During the pairing season the call is sharper and shorter, and ends in a sudden break. At that time, too, they cry at more frequent intervals. The roar of the tiger is quite unlike the call. Once heard it is not easily forgotten. The natives who live in the jungles can tell one tiger from another by colour, size, &c., and they can even distinguish one animal from another by his call. It is very absurd to hear a couple of natives get together and describe the appearance of some tiger they have seen.

In describing a pig, they refer to his height, or the length of his tusks. They describe a fish by putting their fists together, and saying he was so thick, *itna mota*. The head of a tiger is always the most conspicuous part of the body seen in the jungle. They therefore invariably describe him by his head. One man will hold his two hands apart about two feet, and say that the head was *itna burra*, that is, so big. The other, not to be outdone, gives rein to his imagination, and adds another foot. The first immediately fancies discredit will attach to his veracity, and vehemently asserts that there must in that case have been two tigers; and so they go on, till they conclusively prove, that two tigers there must have been, and indeed, if you let them go on, they will soon assure you that, besides the pair of tigers, there must be at least a pair of half-grown cubs. Their imaginations are very fertile, and you must take the information of a native as to tigers with a very large pinch of salt.

For successful tiger shooting much depends on the beating. When after tiger, general firing should on no account be allowed, and the line should move forward as silently as possible. In light cover, extending over a large area, the elephants should be kept a considerable distance apart, but in thick dense cover the line should be quite close, and beat up slowly and thoroughly, as a tiger may lay up and allow the line to pass him. On no account should an elephant be let to lag behind, and no one should be allowed to rush forward or go in advance. The elephants should move along, steady and even, like a moving wall, the fastest being on the flanks, and accommodating their pace to the general rate of progress. No matter what tempting chances at pig or deer you may have, you must on no account fire except at tiger.

The captain should be in the centre, and the men on the flanks ought to be constantly on the *qui vive*, to see that no cunning tiger outflanks the line. The attention should never wander from the jungle before you, for at any moment a tiger may get up—and I know of no sport where it is necessary to be so continuously on the alert. Every moment is fraught with intense excitement, and when a tiger does really show his stripes before you, the all-absorbing eager excitement of a lifetime is packed in a few brief moments. Not a chance should be thrown away, a long, or even an uncertain shot, is better than none, and if you make one miss, you may not have another chance again that day: for the tiger is chary of showing his stripes, and thinks discretion the better part of valour.

All the line of course are aware, as a rule, when a tiger is on the move, and a good captain (and Joe S., who generally took the direction of our beats, could not well be matched) will wheel the line, double, turn, march, and countermarch, and fairly run the tiger down. At such a time, although you may not actually see the tiger, the excitement is tremendous. You stand erect in the howdah, your favourite gun ready; your attendant behind is as excited as yourself, and sways from side to side to peer into the gloomy depths of the jungle; in front, the mahout wriggles on his seat, as if by his motion he could urge the elephant to a quicker advance. He digs his toes savagely into his elephant behind the ear; the line is closing up; every eye is fixed on the moving jungle ahead. The roaring of the flames behind, and the crashing of the dried reeds as the elephants force their ponderous frames through the intertwisted stems and foliage, are the only sounds that greet the ear. Suddenly you see the tawny yellow hide, as the tiger slouches along. Your gun rings out a reverberating challenge, as your fatal bullet speeds on its errand. To right and left the echoes ring, as shot after shot is fired at the bounding robber. Then the line closes up, and you form a circle round the stricken beast, and watch his mighty limbs quiver in the death-agony, and as he falls over dead, and powerless for further harm, you raise the heartfelt, pulse-stirring cheer, that finds an echo in every brother sportsman's heart.

Disputes sometimes arise as to whose bullet first drew blood. These are settled by the captain, and from his decision there is no appeal. Many sportsmen put peculiar marks on their bullets, by which they can be recognised, which is a good plan. In an exciting scrimmage every one blazes at the tiger, not one bullet perhaps in five or six takes effect, and every one is ready to claim the skin, as having been pierced with his particular bullet. Disputes are not very common, but an inspection of the wounds, and the bullets found in the body, generally settle the question. After hearing all the pros and cons, the captain generally succeeds in awarding the tiger to the right man.

After a successful day, the news rapidly spreads through the adjacent country, and we may take the line a little out of our way to make a sort of triumphal procession through the villages. On reaching the camp there is sure to be a great crowd waiting to see the slain tigers, the despoilers of the people's flocks and herds.

It is then you hear of all the depredations the dead robber has committed, and it is then you begin to form some faint conception of his enormous destructive powers. Villager after villager unfolds a tale of some favourite heifer, or buffalo, or cow having been struck down, and the copious vocabulary of Hindostanee Billingsgate is almost exhausted, and floods of abuse poured out on the prostrate head.

On cutting open the tiger, parasites are frequently found in the flesh. These are long, white, thread-like worms, and are supposed by some to be Guinea worms. Huge masses of undigested bone and hair are sometimes taken from the intestines, shewing that the tiger does not waste much time on mastication, but tears and eats the flesh in large masses. The liver is found to have numbers of separate lobes, and the natives say that this is an infallible test of the age of a tiger, as a separate lobe forms on the liver for each year of the tiger's life. I have certainly found young tigers having but two and three lobes, and old tigers I have found with six, seven, and even eight, but the statement is entirely unsupported by careful observation, and requires authentication before it can be accepted.

A reported kill is a pretty certain sign that there are tigers in the jungle, but there are other signs with which one soon gets familiar. When, for example, you hear deer calling repeatedly, and see them constantly on the move, it is a sign that tiger are in the neighbourhood. When cattle are reluctant to enter the jungle, restless, and unwilling to graze, you may be sure tiger are somewhere about, not far away. A kill is often known by the numbers of vultures that hover about in long, sailing, steady circles. What multitudes of vultures there are. Over head, far up in the liquid ether, you see them circling round and round like dim specks in the distance; farther and farther away, till they seem like bees, then lessen and fade into the infinitude of space. No part of the sky is ever free from their presence. When a kill has been perceived, you see one come flying along, strong and swift in headlong flight. With the directness of a thunderbolt he speeds to where his loathsome meal lies sweltering in the noonday sun. As he comes nearer and nearer, his repulsive looking body assumes form and substance. The cruel, ugly bald head, drawn close in between the strong pointed shoulders, the broad powerful wings, with their wide sweep, measured and slow, bear him swiftly past. With a curve and a sweep he circles round, down come the long bony legs, the bald and hideous neck is extended, and with talons quivering for the rotting flesh, and cruel beak agape, he hurries on to his repast, the embodiment of everything ghoul-like and ghastly. In his wake comes another, then twos and threes, anon tens and twenties, till hundreds have collected, and the ground is covered with the hissing, tearing, fiercely clawing crowd. It is a horrible sight to see a heap of vultures battling over a dead bullock. I have seen them so piled up that the under ones were nearly smothered to death; and the writhing contortions of the long bare necks, as the fierce brutes battled with talons and claws, were like the twisting of monster snakes, or the furious writhing of gorgons and furies over some fated victim.

It has been a much debated point with sportsmen

and naturalists, whether the eye or the sense of smell guides the vulture to his feast of carrion. I have often watched them. They scan the vast surface spread below them with a piercing and never tiring gaze. They observe each other. When one is seen to cease his steady circling flight, far up in mid air, and to stretch his broad wings earthwards, the others know that he has espied a meal, and follow his lead; and these in turn are followed by others, till from all quarters flock crowds of these scavengers of the sky. They can detect a dog or jackal from a vast height, and they know by intuition that, where the carcase is there will the dogs and jackals be gathered. I think there can be no doubt that the vision is the sense they are most indebted to for directing them to their food.

On one occasion I remember seeing a tumultuous heap of them, battling fiercely, as I have just tried to describe, over the carcases of two tigers we had killed near Dumdaha. The dead bodies were hidden partially in a grove of trees, and for a long time there were only some ten or a dozen vultures near. These gorged themselves so fearfully, that they could not rise from the ground, but lay with wings expanded, looking very aldermanic and apoplectic. Bye-and-bye, however, the rush began, and by the time we had struck the tents, there could not have been fewer than 150 vultures, hissing and spitting at each other like angry cats; trampling each other to the dust to get at the carcases; and tearing wildly with talon and beak for a place. In a very short time nothing but mangled bones remained. A great number of the vultures got on to the rotten limb of a huge mango tree. One other proved the last straw, for down came the rotten branch and several of the vultures, tearing at each other, fell heavily to the ground, where they lay quite helpless. As an experiment we shot a miserable mangy Pariah dog, that was prowling about the ground seeking garbage and offal. He was shot stone dead, and for a time no vulture ventured near. A crow was the first to begin the feast of death. One of the hungriest of the vultures next approached, and in a few minutes the yet warm body of the poor dog was torn into a thousand fragments, till nothing remained but scattered and disjointed bones.

CHAPTER XXII.

We start for a tiger hunt on the Nepaul frontier.—Indian scenery near the border.—Lose our way.—Cold night.—The river by night.—Our boat and boatmen.—Tigers calling on the bank.—An anxious moment.—Fire at and wound the tigress.—Reach camp.—The Nepaulee's adventure with a tiger.—The old Major.—His appearance and manners.—The pompous Jemadar.—Nepaulese proverb.—Firing the jungle.—Start a tiger and shoot him.—Another in front.—Appearance of the fires by night.—The tiger escapes.—Too dark to follow up.—Coolie shot by mistake during a former hunt.

EARLY in 1875 a military friend of mine was engaged in inspecting the boundary pillars near my factory, between our territory and that of Nepaul. Some of the pillars had been cut away by the river, and the survey map required a little alteration in consequence. Our district magistrate was in attendance, and sent me an invitation to go up and spend a week with them in camp. I had no need to send on tents, as they had every requisite for comfort. I sent off my bed and bedding on Geerdharee Jha's old elephant, a timid, useless brute, fit neither for beating jungle nor for carrying a howdah. My horse I sent on to the ghat or crossing, some ten miles up the river, and after lunch I started. It was a fine cool afternoon, and it was not long ere I reached the neighbouring factory of Imāmnugger. Here I had a little refreshment with Old Tom, and after exchanging greetings, I resumed my way, over a part of the country with which I was totally unacquainted.

I rode on, past villages nestling in the mango groves, past huge tanks, excavated by the busy labour of generations long since departed; past decaying temples, overshadowed by mighty tamarind trees, with the *pepul* and *pakur* insinuating their twining roots amid the shattered and crumbling masonry. In one large village I passed through the bustling bazaar, where the din, and dust, and mingled odours, were almost overpowering. The country was now assuming quite an undulating character. The banks of the creeks were steep and rugged, and in some cases the water actually tumbled from rock to rock, with a purling pleasant ripple and plash, a welcome sound to a Scotch ear, and a pleasant surprise after the dull, dead, leaden, noiseless flow of the streams further down on the plains.

Far in front lay the gloomy belt of Terai, or border forest, here called the *morung*, where the British territories had their extreme limit in that direction. Behind this belt, tier on tier, rose the mighty ranges of the majestic Himalayas, towering up in solemn grandeur from the bushy masses of forest-clad hills till their snow-capped summits seemed to pierce the sky. The country was covered by green crops, with here and there patches of dingy rice-stubble, and an occasional stretch of dense grass jungle. Quail, partridge, and plover rose from the ground in coveys, as my horse cantered through; and an occasional peafowl or florican scudded across the track as I ambled onward. I asked at a wretched little accumulation of weavers' huts where the ghat was, and if my elephant had gone on. To both my queries I received satisfactory replies, and as the day was now drawing in, I pushed my nag into a sharp canter and hurried forward.

I soon perceived the bulky outline of my elephant ahead, and on coming up, found that my men had come too far up the river, had missed the ghat to which

I had sent my spare horse, and were now making for another ferry still higher up. My horse was jaded, so I got on the elephant, and made one of the peons lead the horse behind. It was rapidly getting dark, and the mahout, or elephant driver, a miserable low caste stupid fellow, evidently knew nothing of the country, and was going at random. I halted at the next village, got hold of the chowkedar, and by a promise of backsheesh, prevailed on him to accompany us and show us the way. We turned off from the direct northerly direction in which we had been going, and made straight for the river, which we could see in the distance, looking chill and grey in the fast fading twilight. We now got on the sandbanks, and had to go cautiously for fear of quicksands. By the time we reached the ghat it was quite dark and growing very cold.

We were quite close to the hills, a heavy dew was falling, and I found that I should have to float down the river for a mile, and then pole up stream in another channel for two miles before I could reach camp.

I got my horse into the boat, ordering the elephant driver to travel all night if he could, as I should expect my things to be at camp early in the morning, and the boatmen pushed off the unwieldy ferry-boat, floating us quietly down the rapid 'drumly' stream. All is solemnly still and silent on an Indian river at night. The stream is swift but noiseless. Vast plains and heaps of sand stretch for miles on either bank. There are no villages near the stream. Faintly, far away in the distance, you hear a few subdued sounds, the only evidences of human habitation. There is the tinkle of a cow-bell, the barking of a pariah dog, the monotonous dub-a-dub-dub of a timber-toned tom-tom, muffled and slightly mellowed by the distance. The faint far cries, and occasional halloos of the herd-boys calling to each other, gradually cease, but the monotonous dub-a-dub-dub continues till far into the night.

It was now very cold, and I was glad to borrow a blanket from my peon. At such a time the pipe is a great solace. It soothes the whole system, and plunges one into an agreeable dreamy speculative mood, through which all sorts of fantastic notions resolve. Fancies chase each other quickly, and old memories rise, bitter or sweet, but all tinged and tinted by the seductive influence of the magic weed. Hail, blessed pipe! the invigorator of the weary, the uncomplaining faithful friend, the consoler of sorrows, and the dispeller of care, the much-prized companion of the solitary wayfarer!

Now a jackal utters a howl on the bank, as our boat shoots past, and the diabolical noise is echoed from knoll to knoll, and from ridge to ridge, as these incarnate devils of the night join in and prolong the infernal chorus. An occasional splash, as a piece of the bank topples over into the stream, rouses the cormorant and gull from their placid dozing on the sandbanks. They squeak and gurgle out an unintelligible protest, then cosily settle their heads again beneath the sheltering wing, and sleep the slumber of the dreamless. A sharp sudden plump, or a lazy surging sound, accompanied by a wheezy blowing sort of hiss, tells us that a *seelun* is disporting himself; or that a fat old 'porpus' is bearing his clumsy bulk through the rushing current.

The bank now looms out dark and mysterious, and as we turn the point another long stretch of the river opens out, reflecting the merry twinkle of the myriad stars, that glitter sharp and clear millions of miles overhead. There is now a clattering of bamboo poles. With a grunt of disgust, and a quick catching of the breath, as the cold water rushes up against his thighs, one of the boatmen splashes overboard, and they commence slowly and wearily pushing the boat up stream. We touch the bank a dozen times. The current swoops down and turns us round and round. The men have to put their shoulders under the gunwale, and heave and strain with all their might. The long bamboo poles are plunged into the dark depths of the river, and the men puff, and grunt, and blow, as they bend almost to the bottom of the boat while they push. It is a weary progress. We are dripping wet with dew. Quite close on the bank we hear the hoarse wailing call of a tigress. The call of the tiger comes echoing down between the banks. The men cease poling. I peer forward into the obscurity. My syce pats, and speaks soothingly to the trembling horse, while my peon with excited fingers fumbles at the straps of my gun-case. For a moment all is intensely still.

I whisper to the boatmen to push out a little into the stream. Again the tigress calls, this time so close to us that we could almost fancy we could feel her breath. My gun is ready. The syce holds the horse firmly by the head, and as we leave the bank, we can distinctly see the outline of some large animal, standing out a dark bulky mass against the skyline. I take a steady aim and fire. A roar of astonishment, wrath, and pain follows the report. The horse struggles and snorts, the boatman calls out 'Oh, my father!' and ejaculates 'hi-hi-hi!' in tones of piled up anguish and apprehension, the peon cries exultantly ' Wah wah! khodawund, lug, gea,' that bullet has told; oh your highness! and while the boat rocks violently to and fro, I abuse the boatmen, slang the syce, and rush to grasp a pole, while the peon seizes another; for we are drifting rapidly down stream, and may at any moment strike on a bank and topple over. We can hear by the growling and commotion on the bank, that my bullet has indeed told, and that something is hit. We soon get the frightened boatmen quieted down, and after another hour's weary work we spy the white outline of the tents above the bank. A lamp shines out a bright welcome; and although it is nearly twelve at night, the Captain and the magistrate are discussing hot toddy, and waiting my arrival. My spare horse had come on from the ghat, the syce had told them I was coming, and they had been indulging in all sorts of speculations over my non-arrival.

A good supper, and a reeking jorum, soon banished all recollections of my weary journey, and men were ordered to go out at first break of dawn, and see about the wounded tiger. In the morning I was gratified beyond expression to find a fine tigress, measuring 8 feet 3 inches, had been brought in, the result of my lucky night shot; the marks of a large tiger were found about the spot, and we determined to beat up for him, and if possible secure his skin, as we already had that of his consort.

Captain S. had some work to finish, and my elephant and bearer had not arrived, so our magistrate and myself walked down to the sandbanks, and amused ourselves for an hour shooting sandpipers and plover; we also shot a pair of mallard and a couple of teal, and then went back to the tents, and were soon busily discussing a hunter's breakfast. While at our meal, my elephant and things arrived, and just then also, the 'Major Captān,' or Nepaulese functionary, my old friend, came up with eight elephants, and we hurried out to greet the fat, merry-featured old man.

What a quaint, genial old customer he looked, as he bowed and salaamed to us from his elevated seat, his face beaming, and his little bead-like eyes twinkling with pleasure. He was full of an adventure he had as he came along. After crossing a brawling mountain-torrent, some miles from our camp, they entered some dense kair jungle. The kair is I believe a species of mimosa; it is a hard wood, growing in a thick scrubby form, with small pointed leaves, a yellowish sort of flower, and sharp thorns studding its branches; it is a favourite resort for pig, and although it is difficult to beat on account of the thorns, tigers are not unfrequently found among the gloomy recesses of a good kair scrub.

As they entered this jungle, some of the men were loitering behind. When the elephants had passed about half way through, the men came rushing up pell mell, with consternation on their faces, reporting that a huge tiger had sprung out on them, and carried off one of their number. The Major and the elephants hurried back, and met the man limping along, bleeding from several scratches, and with a nasty bite in his shoulder, but otherwise more frightened than hurt. The tiger had simply knocked him down, stood over him for a minute, seized him by the shoulder, and then dashed on through the scrub, leaving him behind half dead with pain and fear.

It was most amusing to hear the fat little Major relate the story. He went through all the by-play incident to the piece, and as he got excited, stood right up on his narrow pad. His gesticulations were most vehement, and as the elephant was rather unsteady, and his footing to say the least precarious, he seemed every moment as if he must topple over. The old warrior however, was equal to the occasion; without for an instant abating the vigour of his narrative, he would clutch at the greasy, matted locks of his mahout, and steady himself, while he volubly described incident after incident. As he warmed with his subject, and tried to shew us how the tiger must have pounced on the man, he would let go and use his hands in illustration; the old elephant would give another heave, and the fat little man would make another frantic grab at the patient mahout's hair. The whole scene was most comical, and we were in convulsions of laughter.

The news however foreboded ample sport; we now had certain *khubber* of at least two tigers; we were soon under weigh; the wounded man had been sent back to the Major's head-quarters on an elephant, and in time recovered completely from his mauling. As we jogged along, we had a most interesting talk with the Major Captān. He was wonderfully well informed, considering he had never been out of Nepaul. He knew all about England, our army, our mode of government, our parliament, and our Queen; whenever he alluded to Her Majesty he salaamed profoundly, whether as a tribute of respect to her, or in compliment to us as loyal subjects, we could not quite make out. He described to us the route home by the Suez canal, and the fun of his talk was much heightened by his applying the native names to everything; London was *Shuhur*, the word meaning 'a city,' and he told us it was built on the *Thamāss nuddee*, by which he meant the Thames river.

Our magistrate had a Jemadar of Peons with him, a sort of head man among the servants. This man, abundantly bedecked with ear-rings, finger-rings, and other ornaments, was a useless, bullying sort of fellow; dressed to the full extent of Oriental foppishness, and because he was the magistrate's servant, he thought himself entitled to order the other servants about in the most lordly way. He was now making himself peculiarly officious, shouting to the drivers to go here and there, to do this and do that, and indulging in copious torrents of abuse, without which it seems impossible for a native subordinate to give directions on any subject. We were all rather amused, and could not help bursting into laughter, as, inflated with a sense of his own importance, he began abusing one of the native drivers of the Nepaulee chief; this man did not submit tamely to his insolence. To him the magistrate was nobody, and the pompous Jemadar a perfect nonentity. He accordingly turned round and poured forth a perfect flood of invective. Never was collapse more utter. The Jemadar took a back seat at once, and no more that day did we hear his melodious voice in tones of imperious command.

The old Major chuckled, and rubbed his fat little hands, and leaning over to me said, 'at home a lion, but abroad a lamb,' for, surrounded by his women at home, the man would twirl his moustaches, look fierce and fancy himself a very tiger; but, no sooner did he go abroad, and mix with men as good, if not better than himself, than he was ready to eat any amount of humble pie.

We determined first of all to beat for the tiger whose tracks had been seen near where I had fired my lucky shot the preceding night. A strong west wind was blowing, and dense clouds of sand were being swept athwart our line, from the vast plains of fine white sand bordering the river for miles. As we went along we fired the jungle in our rear, and the strong wind carried the flames raging and roaring through the dense jungle with amazing fury. One elephant got so frightened at the noise behind him, that he fairly bolted for the river, and could not be persuaded back into the line.

Disturbed by the fire, we saw numerous deer and pig, but being after tiger we refrained from shooting at them. The Basinattea Tuppoo, which was the scene of our present hunt, were famous jungles, and many a tiger had been shot there by the Purneah Club in bygone days. The annual ravages of the impetuous river, had however much changed the face of the country; vast tracts of jungle had been obliterated by deposits of sand from its annual incursions. Great skeletons of trees stood everywhere, stretching out bare and unsightly branches, all bending to the south, shewing the mighty power of the current, when it made its annual progress of devastation over the surrounding country. Now, however, it was like a thin streak of silver, flashing back the fierce rays of the meridian sun. Through the blinding clouds of fine white sand we could at times, during a temporary lull, see its ruffled surface. And we were glad when we came on the tracks of the tiger, which led straight from the stream, in the direction of some thick tree jungle at no great distance. We gladly turned our backs to the furious clouds of dust and gusts of scorching wind, and led by a Nepaulee tracker, were soon crashing heavily through the jungle.

When hunting with elephants, the Nepaulese beat in a dense line, the heads of the elephants touching each other. In this manner we were now proceeding, when S. called out, 'There goes the tiger.'

We looked up, and saw a very large tiger making off for a deep watercourse, which ran through the jungle some 200 yards ahead of the line. We hurried up as fast as we could, putting out a fast elephant on either flank, to see that the cunning brute did not sneak either up or down the nullah, under cover of the high banks. This, however, was not his object. We saw him descend into the nullah, and almost immediately top the further bank, and disappear into the jungle beyond.

Pressing on at a rapid jolting trot, we dashed after him in hot pursuit. The jungle seemed somewhat lighter on ahead. In the distance we could see some dangurs at work breaking up land, and to the right was a small collection of huts with a beautiful riband of green crops, a perfect oasis in the wilderness of sand and parched up grass. Forming into line we pressed on. The tiger was evidently lying up, probably deterred from breaking across the open by the sight of the dangurs at work. My heart was bounding with excitement. We were all intensely eager, and thought no more of the hot wind and blinding dust. Just then Captain S. saw the brute sneaking along to the left of the line, trying to outflank us, and break back. He fired two shots rapidly with his Express, and the second one, taking effect in the neck of the tiger, bowled him over as he stood. He was a mangy-looking brute, badly marked, and measured eight feet eleven inches. He did not have a chance of charging, and probably had little heart for a fight.

We soon had him padded, and then proceeded straight north, to the scene of the Major's encounter with the tiger in the morning. The jungle was well trampled down; there were numerous streams and pools of water, occasional clumps of bamboos, and abrupt ridgy undulations. It was the very jungle for tiger, and

x

elated by our success in having bagged one already, we were all in high spirits. The line of fire we could see far in the distance, sweeping on like the march of fate, and we could have shot numerous deer, but reserved our fire for nobler game. It was getting well on in the afternoon when we came up to the kair jungle. We beat right up to where the man had been seized, and could see the marks of the struggle distinctly enough. We beat right through the jungle with no result, and as it was now getting rather late, the old Major signified his desire to bid us good evening. As this meant depriving us of eight elephants, we prevailed on him to try one spare straggling corner that we had not gone through. He laughed the idea to scorn of getting a tiger there, saying there was no cover. One elephant, however, was sent while we were talking. Our elephants were all standing in a group, and the mahout on his solitary elephant was listlessly jogging on in a purposeless and desultory manner, when we suddenly heard the elephant pipe out a shrill note of alarm, and the mahout yelled 'Bagh! Bagh!' tiger! tiger! The Captain was again the lucky man. The tiger, a much finer and stronger built animal than the one we had already killed, was standing not eighty paces off, shewing his teeth, his bristles erect, and evidently in a bad temper. He had been crouching among some low bushes, and seeing the elephant bearing directly down on him, he no doubt imagined his retreat had been discovered. At all events there he was, and he presented a splendid aim. He was a noble-looking specimen as he stood there grim and defiant. Captain S. took aim, and lodged an Express bullet in his chest. It made a fearful wound, and the ferocious brute writhed and rolled about in agony. We quickly surrounded him, and a bullet behind the ear from my No. 16 put an end to his misery.

The old Major now bade us good evening, and after padding the second tiger, and much elated at our success, we began to beat homewards, shooting at everything that rose before us. A couple of tremendous pig got up before me, and dashed through a clear stream that was purling peacefully in its pebbly bed. As the boar was rushing up the farther bank, I deposited a pellet in his hind quarters. He gave an angry grunt and tottered on, but presently pulled up, and seemed determined to have some revenge for his hurt. As my elephant came up the bank, the gallant boar tried to charge, but already wounded and weak from loss of blood, he tottered and staggered about. My elephant would not face him, so I gave him another shot behind the shoulder, and padded him for the *moosahurs* and sweepers in camp. Just then one of the policemen started a young hog-deer, and several of the men got down and tried to catch the little thing alive. They soon succeeded, and the cries of the poor little *butcha*, that is 'young one,' were most plaintive.

The wind had now subsided, there was a red angry glare, as the level rays of the setting sun shimmered through the dense clouds of dust that loaded the atmosphere. It was like the dull, red, coppery hue which presages a storm. The vast morung jungle lay behind us, and beyond that the swelling wooded hills, beginning to show dark and indistinct against the gathering gloom. A long line of cattle were wending their way homeward to the batan, and the tinkle of the big copper bell fell pleasingly on our ears. In the distance, we could see the white canvas of the tents gleaming in the rays of the setting sun. A vast circular line of smouldering fire, flickering and flaring fitfully, and surmounted by huge volumes of curling smoke, shewed the remains of the fierce tornado of flame that had raged at noon, when we lit the jungle. The jungle was very light, and much trodden down, our three howdah elephants were not far apart, and we were chatting cheerfully together and discussing the incidents of the day. My bearer was sitting behind me in the back of the howdah, and I had taken out my ball cartridge from my No. 12 breechloader, and had replaced them with shot. Just then my mahout raised his hand, and in a hoarse excited whisper called out,

'Look, sahib, a large tiger!'

'Where?' we all exclaimed, getting excited at once. He pointed in front to a large object, looking for all the world like a huge dun cow.

'Why, you fool, that is a bullock.' I exclaimed.

My bearer, who had also been intently gazing, now said.

'No, sahib! that is a tiger, and a large one.'

At that moment, it turned partly round, and I at once saw that the men were right, and that it was a veritable tiger, and seemingly a monster in size. I at once called to Captain S. and the magistrate, who had by this time fallen a little behind.

'Look out, you fellows! here's a tiger in front.'

At first they thought I was joking, but a glance confirmed the truth of what I had said. When I first saw the brute, he was evidently sneaking after the cattle, and was about sixty paces from me. He was so intent on watching the herd, that he had not noticed our approach. He was now, however, evidently alarmed and making off. By the time I called out, he must have been over eighty yards away. I had my No. 12 in my hand, loaded with shot; it was no use; I put it down and took up my No. 16; this occupied a few seconds; I fired both barrels; the first bullet was in excellent line but rather short, the second went over the animal's back, and neither touched him. It made him, however, quicken his retreat, and when Captain S. fired, he must have been fully one hundred and fifty yards away; as it was now somewhat dusky, he also missed. He fired another long shot with his rifle, but missed again. Oh that unlucky change of cartridges in my No. 12! But for that—but there—we are always wise after the event. We never expected to see a tiger in such open country, especially as we had been over the same ground before, firing pretty often as we came along.

We followed up of course, but it was now fast getting dark, and though we beat about for some time, we could not get another glimpse of the tiger. He was seemingly a very large male, dark-coloured, and in splendid condition. We must have got him, had it been earlier, as he could not have gone far forward, for the lines of fire were beyond him, and we had him between the fire and the elephants. We got home about 6. 30, rather disappointed at missing such a glorious prize, so true is it that a sportsman's soul is never satisfied. But we had rare and most unlooked-for luck, and we felt considerably better after a good dinner, and indulged in hopes of getting the big fellow next morning.

In the same jungles, some years ago, a very sad accident occurred. A party were out tiger-shooting, and during one of the beats, a cowherd hearing the noise of the advancing elephants, crouched behind a bush, and covered himself with his blanket. At a distance he looked exactly like a pig, and one of the shooters mistook him for one. He fired, and hit the poor herd in the hip. As soon as the mistake was perceived, everything was done for the poor fellow. His wound was dressed as well as they could do it, and he was sent off to the doctor in a dhoolie, a sort of covered litter, slung on a pole and carried on men's shoulders. It was too late, the poor coolie died on the road, from shock and loss of blood. Such mistakes occur very seldom, and this was such a natural one, that no one could blame the unfortunate sportsman, and certainly no one felt keener regret than he did. The coolie's family was amply provided for, which was all that remained to be done.

This is the only instance I know, where fatal results have followed such an accident. I have known several cases of beaters peppered with shot, generally from their own carelessness, and disregard of orders, but a salve in the shape of a few rupees has generally proved the most effective ointment. I have known some rascals say, they were sorry they had not been lucky enough to be wounded, as they considered a punctured cuticle nothing to set against the magnificent douceur of four or five rupees. One impetuous scamp, being told not to go in front of the line during a beat near Burgamma, replied to the warning caution of his jemadar,

'Oh never mind, if get shot I will get backsheesh.'

Whether this was a compliment to the efficacy of our treatment (by the silver ointment), or to the inaccuracy and harmlessness of our shooting, I leave the reader to judge.

Our bag during this lucky day, including the tigress killed by my shot on the river bank, was as follows: three tigers, one boar, four deer, including the young one taken alive, eight sandpipers, nine plovers, two mallards, and two teal.

CHAPTER XXIII.

We resume the beat.—The hog-deer.—Nepaulese villages.—Village granaries.—Tiger in front.—A hit! a hit!—Following up the wounded tiger.—Find him dead.—Tiffin in the village.—The Patair jungle.—Search for tiger.—Gone away!—An elephant steeplechase in pursuit.—Exciting chase.—The Morung jungle.—Magnificent scenery.—Skinning the tiger.—Incidents of tiger hunting.

NEXT morning, both the magistrate and myself felt very ill, headachy and sick, with violent vomiting and retching; Captain S. attributed it to the fierce hot wind and exposure of the preceding day, but we, the sufferers, blamed the *dekchees* or cooking pots. These *dekchees* are generally made of copper, coated or tinned over with white metal once a month or oftener; if the tinning is omitted, or the copper becomes exposed by accident or neglect, the food cooked in the pots sometimes gets tainted with copper, and produces nausea and sickness in those who eat it. I have known, within my own experience, cases of copper poisoning that have terminated fatally. It is well always thoroughly to inspect the kitchen utensils, particularly when in camp; unless carefully watched and closely supervised, servants get very careless, and let food remain in these copper vessels. This is always dangerous, and should never be allowed.

In consequence of our indisposition, we did not start till the forenoon was far advanced, and the hot west wind had again begun to sweep over the prairie-like stretches of sand and withered grass. We commenced beating up by the Batan or cattle stance, near which we had seen the big tiger, the preceding evening. S. however became so sick and giddy, that he had to return to camp, and Captain S. and I continued the beat alone. Having gone over the same ground only yesterday, we did not expect a tiger so near to camp, more especially as the fire had made fearful havoc with the tall grass. Hog-deer were very numerous; they are not as a rule easily disturbed; they are of a reddish brown colour, not unlike that of the Scotch red deer, and rush through the jungle, when alarmed, with a succession of bounding leaps; they make very pretty shooting, and when young, afford tender and well-flavoured venison. One hint I may give. When you shoot a buck, see that he is at once denuded of certain appendages, else the flesh will get rank and disagreeable to eat. The bucks have pretty antlers, but are not very noble looking. The does are somewhat lighter in colour, and do not seem to consort together in herds like antelopes; there are rarely more than five in a group, though I have certainly seen more on several occasions.

This morning we were unlucky with our deer. I shot three, and Captain S. shot at and wounded three, not one of which however did we bag. This part of the country is exclusively inhabited by Parbutteas, the native name for Nepaulese settled in British territory. Over the frontier line, the villages are called Pahareeas, signifying mountaineers or hillmen, from Pahar, a mountain. We beat up to a Parbuttea village, with its conical roofed huts; men and women were engaged in plaiting long coils of rice straw into cable looking ropes. A few split bamboos are fastened into the ground, in a circle, and these ropes are then coiled round, in and out, between the stakes; this makes a huge circular vat-shaped repository, open at both ends;

it is then lifted up and put on a platform coated with mud, and protected from rats and vermin by the pillars being placed on smooth, inverted earthen pots. The coils of straw are now plastered outside and in with a mixture of mud, chaff, and cowdung, and allowed to dry; when dried the hut is filled with grain, and securely roofed and thatched. This forms the invariable village granary, and looks at a distance not unlike a stack or rick of corn, round a farm at home. By the abundance of these granaries in a village, one can tell at a glance whether the season has been a good one, and whether the frugal inhabitants of the clustering little hamlet are in pretty comfortable circumstances. If they are under the sway of a grasping and unscrupulous landlord, they not unfrequently bury their grain in clay-lined chambers in the earth, and have always enough for current wants, stored up in the sun-baked clay repositories mentioned in a former chapter.

Beyond the village we entered some thick Patair jungle. Its greenness was refreshing after the burnt up and withered grass jungle. We were now in a hollow bordering the stream, and somewhat protected from the scorching wind, and the stinging clouds of fine sand and red dust. The brook looked so cool and refreshing, and the water so clear and pellucid, that I was about to dismount to take a drink and lave my heated head and face, when a low whistle to my right made me look in that direction, and I saw the Captain waving his hand excitedly, and pointing ahead. He was higher up the bank than I was, and in very dense Patair; a ridge ran between his front of the line and mine, so that I could only see his howdah, and the bulk of the elephant's body was concealed from me by the grass on this ridge.

I closed up diagonally across the ridge; S. still waving to me to hurry up; as I topped it, I spied a large tiger slouching along in the hollow immediately below me. He saw me at the same instant, and bounded on in front of S. His Express was at his shoulder on the instant; he fired, and a tremendous spurt of blood shewed a hit, a hit, a palpable hit. The tiger was nowhere visible, and not a cry or a motion could we hear or see, to give us any clue to the whereabouts of the wounded animal. We followed up however, quickly but cautiously, expecting every instant a furious charge.

We must have gone at least a hundred yards, when right in front of me I descried the tiger, crouching down, its head resting on its fore paws, and to all appearance settling for a spring. It was about twenty yards from me, and taking a rather hasty aim, I quickly fired both barrels straight at the head. I could only see the head and paws, but these I saw quite distinctly. My elephant was very unsteady, and both my bullets went within an inch of the tiger's head, but fortunately missed completely. I say fortunately, for finding the brute still remaining quite motionless, we cautiously approached, and found it was stone dead. The perfect naturalness of the position, however, might well have deceived a more experienced sportsman. The beast was lying crouched on all fours, as if in the very act of preparing to spring. The one bullet had killed it; the wound was in the lungs, and the internal bleeding had suffocated it, but here was a wonderful instance of the tiger's tenacity of life, even when sorely wounded, for it had travelled over a hundred and thirty yards after S. had shot it.

It was lucky I missed, for my bullets would have

spoiled the skull. She was a very handsome, finely marked tigress, a large specimen, for on applying the tape we found she measured exactly nine feet. Before descending to measure her, we were joined by the old Major Captān, whose elephants we had for some time descried in the distance. His congratulations were profuse, and no doubt sincere, and after padding the tigress, we hied to the welcome shelter of one of the village houses, where we discussed a hearty and substantial tiffin.

During tiffin, we were surrounded by a bevy of really fair and buxom lasses. They wore petticoats of striped blue cloth, and had their arms and shoulders bare, and their ears loaded with silver ornaments. They were merry, laughing, comely damsels, with none of the exaggerated shyness, and affected prudery of the women of the plains. We were offered plantains, milk, and chuppaties, and an old patriarch came out leaning on his staff, to revile and abuse the tigress. From some of the young men we heard of a fresh kill to the north of the village, and after tiffin we proceeded in that direction, following up the course of the limpid stream, whose gurgling ripple sounded so pleasantly in our ears.

Far ahead to the right, and on the further bank of the stream, we could see dense curling volumes of smoke, and leaping pyramids of flame, where a jungle fire was raging in some thick acacia scrub. As we got nearer, the heat became excessive, and the flames, fanned into tremendous fury by the fierce west wind, tore through the dry thorny bushes. Our elephants were quite unsteady, and did not like facing the fire. We made a slight detour, and soon had the roaring wall of flame behind us. We were now entering on a moist, circular, basin-shaped hollow. Among the patair roots were the recent marks of great numbers of wild pigs, where they had been foraging among the stiff clay for these esculents. The patair is like a huge bulrush, and the elephants are very fond of its succulent, juicy, cool-looking leaves. Those in our line kept tearing up huge tufts of it, thrashing out the mud and dirt from the roots against their forelegs, and with a grunt of satisfaction, making it slowly disappear in their cavernous mouths. There was considerable noise, and the jungle was nearly as high as the howdahs, presenting the appearance of an impenetrable screen of vivid green. We beat and rebeat, across and across, but there was no sign of the tiger. The banks of the nullah were very steep, rotten looking, and dangerous. We had about eighteen elephants, namely, ten of our own, and eight belonging to the Nepaulese. We were beating very close, the elephants' heads almost touching. This is the way they always beat in Nepaul. We thought we had left not a spot in the basin untouched, and Captain S. was quite satisfied that there could be no tiger there. It was a splendid jungle for cover, so thick, dense, and cool. I was beating along the edge of the creek, which ran deep and silent, between the gloomy sedge-covered banks. In a placid little pool I saw a couple of widgeon all unconscious of danger, their glossy plumage reflected in the clear water. I called to Captain S. 'We are sold this time Captain, there's no tiger here!'

'I am afraid not,' he answered.

'Shall I bag those two widgeon?' I asked.

'All right,' was the response.

Putting in shot cartridge, I shot both the widgeon,

but we were all astounded to see the tiger we had so carefully and perseveringly searched for, bound out of a crevice in the bank, almost right under my elephant. Off he went with a smothered roar, that set our elephants hurrying backwards and forwards. There was a commotion along the whole line. The jungle was too dense for us to see anything. It was one more proof how these hill tigers will lie close, even in the midst of a line.

S. called out to me to remain quiet, and see if we could trace the tiger's progress by any rustling in the cover. Looking down we saw the kill, close to the edge of the water. A fast elephant was sent on ahead, to try and ascertain whether the tiger was likely to break beyond the circle of the little basin-shaped valley. We gathered round the kill; it was quite fresh; a young buffalo. The Major told us that in his experience, a male tiger always begins on the neck first. A female always at the hind quarters. A few mouthfuls only had been eaten, and according to the Major, it must have been a tigress, as the part devoured was from the hind quarters.

While we were talking over these things, a frenzied shout from the driver of our naka elephant caused us to look in his direction. He was gesticulating wildly, and bawling at the top of his voice, 'Come, come quickly, sahibs, the tiger is running away.'

Now commenced such a mad and hurried scramble as I have never witnessed before or since, from the back of an elephant. As we tore through the tangled dense green patair, the broad leaves crackled like crashing branches, the huge elephants surged ahead like ships rocking in a gale of wind, and the mahouts and attendants on the pad elephants, shouted and urged on their shuffling animals, by excited cries and resounding whacks.

In the retinue of the Major, were several men with elephant spears or goads. These consist of a long, pliant, polished bamboo, with a sharp spike at the end, which they call a *jhetha*. These men now came hurrying round the ridge, among the opener grass, and as we emerged from the heavy cover, they began goading the elephants behind and urging them to their most furious pace. On ahead, nearly a quarter of a mile away, we could see a huge tiger making off for the distant morung, at a rapid sling trot. His lithe body shone before us, and urged us to the most desperate efforts. It was almost a bare plateau. There was scarcely any cover, only here and there a few stunted acacia bushes. The dense forest was two or three miles ahead, but there were several nasty steep banks, and precipitous gullies with deep water rushing between. Attached to each Nepaulee pad, by a stout curiously-plaited cord, ornamented with fancy knots and tassels of silk, was a small pestle-shaped instrument, not unlike an auctioneer's hammer. It was quaintly carved, and studded with short, blunt, shining, brass nails or spikes. I had noticed these hanging down from the pads, and had often wondered what they were for. I was now to see them used. While the mahouts in front rained a shower of blows on the elephants head, and the spear-men pricked him up from behind with their jhethas, the occupant of the pad, turning round with his face to the tail, belaboured the poor hathee with the auctioneer's hammer. The blows rattled on the elephant's rump. The brutes trumpeted with pain, but they *did* put on the pace, and travelled as I never imagined an elephant *could* travel. Past bush and brake, down precipitous ravine, over the stones, through the thorny scrub, dashing down a steep bank here, plunging madly through a deep stream there, we shuffled along. We must have been going fully seven miles an hour. The pestle-shaped hammer is called a *lohath*, and most unmercifully were they wielded. We were jostled and jolted, till every bone ached again. Clouds of dust were driven before our reeling waving line. How the Nepaulese shouted and capered. We were all mad with excitement. I shouted with the rest. The fat little Major kicked his heels against the sides of his elephant, as if he were spurring a Derby winner to victory. Our usually sedate captain yelled—actually yelled!—in an agony of excitement, and tried to execute a war dance of his own on the floor of his howdah. Our guns rattled, the chains clanked and jangled, the howdahs rocked and pitched from side to side. We made a desperate effort. The poor elephants made a gallant race of it. The foot men perspired and swore, but it was not to be. Our striped friend had the best of the start, and we gained not an inch upon him. To our unspeakable mortification, he reached the dense cover on ahead, where we might as well have sought for a needle in a haystack. Never, however, shall I forget that mad headlong scramble. Fancy an elephant steeple-chase. Reader, it was sublime; but we ached for it next day.

The old Major and his fleet racing elephants now left us, and our jaded beasts took us slowly back in the direction of our camp. It was a fine wild view on which we were now gazing. Behind us the dark gloomy impenetrable morung, the home of ever-abiding fever and ague. Behind that the countless multitude of hills, swelling here and receding there, a jumbled heap of mighty peaks and fretted pinnacles, with their glistening sides and dark shadowless ravines, their mighty scaurs and their abrupt serrated edges showing out clearly and boldly defined against the evening sky. Far to the right, the shining river—a riband of burnished steel, for its waters were a deep steely blue—rolled its swift flood along amid shining sandbanks. In front, the vast undulating plain, with grove, and rill, and smoking hamlet, stretched at our feet in a lovely panorama of blended and harmonious colour. We were now high up above the plain, and the scene was one of the finest I have ever witnessed in India. The wind had gone down, and the oblique rays of the sun lit up the whole vast panorama with a lurid light, which was heightened in effect by the dust-laden atmosphere, and the volumes of smoke from the now distant fires, hedging in the far horizon with curtains of threatening grandeur and gloom. That far away canopy of dust and smoke formed a wonderful contrast to the shining snow-capped hills behind. Altogether it was a day to be remembered. I have seen no such strange and unearthly combination of shade and colour in any landscape before or since.

On the way home we bagged a florican and a very fine mallard, and reached the camp utterly fagged, to find our worthy magistrate very much recovered, and glad to congratulate us on our having bagged the tigress. After a plunge in the river, and a rare camp dinner—such a meal as only an Indian sportsman can procure—we lay back in our cane chairs, and while the fragrant smoke from the mild Manilla curled lovingly about the roof of the tent, we discussed the day's proceedings, and fought our battles over again.

A rather animated discussion arose about the length of the tiger—as to its frame merely, and we wondered what difference the skin would make in the length of the animal. As it was a point we had never heard mooted before, we determined to see for ourselves. We accordingly went out into the beautiful moonlight, and superintended the skinning of the tigress. The skin was taken off most artistically. We had carefully measured the animal before skinning. She was exactly nine feet long. We found the skin made a difference of only four inches, the bare skeleton from tip of nose to extreme point of tail measuring eight feet eight inches.

As an instance of tigers taking to trees, our worthy magistrate related that in Rajmehal he and a friend had wounded a tiger, and subsequently lost him in the jungle. In vain they searched in every conceivable direction, but could find no trace of him. They were about giving up in despair, when S., raising his hat, happened to look up, and there, on a large bough directly overhead, he saw the wounded tiger lying extended at full length, some eighteen feet from the ground. They were not long in leaving the dangerous vicinity, and it was not long either ere a well-directed shot brought the tiger down from his elevated perch.

These after-dinner stories are not the least enjoyable part of a tiger-hunting party. Round the camp table in a snug, well-lighted tent, with all the 'materials' handy, I have listened to many a tale of thrilling adventure. S. was full of reminiscences, and having seen a deal of tiger shooting in various parts of India, his recollections were much appreciated. To shew that the principal danger in tiger shooting is not from the tiger himself, but from one's elephant becoming panic-stricken and bolting, he told how a Mr. Aubert, a Benares planter, lost his life. A tiger had been 'spined' by a shot, and the line gathered round the prostrate monster to watch its death-struggle. The elephant on which the unfortunate planter sat got demoralised and attempted to bolt. The mahout endeavoured to check its rush, and in desperation the elephant charged straight down, close past the tiger, which lay writhing and roaring under a huge overhanging tree. The elephant was rushing directly under this tree, and a large branch would have swept howdah and everything it contained clean off the elephant's back, as easily as one would brush off a fly. To save himself Aubert made a leap for the branch, the elephant forging madly ahead; and the howdah, being smashed like match-wood, fell on the tiger below, who was tearing and clawing at everything within his reach. Poor Aubert got hold of the branch with his hands, and clung with all the desperation of one fighting for his life. He was right above the wounded tiger, but his grasp on the tree was not a firm one. For a moment he hung suspended above the furious animal, which, mad with agony and fury, was a picture of demoniac rage. The poor fellow could hold no longer, and fell right on the tiger. It was nearly at its last gasp, but it caught hold of Aubert by the foot, and in a final paroxysm of pain and rage chawed the foot clean off, and the poor fellow died next day from the shock and loss of blood. He was one of four brothers who all met untimely deaths from accidents. This one was killed by the tiger, another was thrown from a vehicle and killed on the spot, the third was drowned, and the fourth shot by accident.

Our bag to-day was one tiger, one florican, one mallard,

and two widgeon. On cutting the tiger open, we found that the bullet had entered on the left side, and, as we suspected, had entered the lungs. It had, however, made a terrible wound. We found that it had penetrated the heart and liver, gone forward through the chest, and smashed the right shoulder. Notwithstanding this fearful wound, shewing the tremendous effects of the Express bullet, the tiger had gone on for the distance I have mentioned, after which it must have fallen stone-dead. It was a marvellous instance of vitality, even after the heart, liver, and lungs had been pierced. The liver had six lobes, and it was then I heard for the first time, that with the natives this was an infallible sign of the age of a tiger. The old Major firmly believed it, and told us it was quite an accepted article of faith with all native sportsmen. Facts subsequently came under my own observation which seemed to give great probability to the theory, but it is one on which I would not like to give a decided opinion, till after hearing the experiences of other sportsmen.

CHAPTER XXIV.

Camp of the Nepaulee chief.—Quicksands.—Elephants crossing rivers.
—Tiffin at the Nepaulee camp.—We beat the forest for tiger.—Shoot
a young tiger.—Red ants in the forest.—Bhowras or ground bees.
—The *ursus labialis* or long-lipped bear.—Recross the stream.—
Florican.—Stag running the gauntlet of flame.—Our bag.—Start
for factory.—Remarks on elephants.—Precautions useful for protection from the sun in tiger shooting.—The *puggree*.—Cattle
breeding in India, and wholesale deaths of cattle from disease.—
Nathpore.—Ravages of the river.—Mrs. Gray, an old resident in the
jungles.—Description of her surroundings.

NEXT morning we started beating due east, setting fire to the jungle as we went along. The roaring and crackling of the flames startled the elephant on which Captain S. was riding, and going away across country at a furious pace, it was with difficulty that it could be stopped. We crossed the frontier line a short distance from camp, and entered a dense jungle of thorny acacia, with long dry grass almost choking the trees. They were dry and stunted, and when we dropped a few lights amongst such combustible material, the fire was splendid beyond description. How the flames surged through the withered grass. We were forced to pause and admire the magnificent sight. The wall of flame tore along with inconceivable rapidity, and the blinding volumes of smoke obscured the country for miles. The jungle was full of deer and pig. One fine buck came bounding along past our line, but I stopped him with a single bullet through the neck. He fell over with a tremendous crash, and turning a complete somersault broke off both his horns with the force of the fall.

We beat down a shallow sandy watercourse, and could see the camp of the old Major on the high bank beyond. Farther down the stream there was a small square fort, the whitewashed walls of which flashed back the rays of the sun, and grouped round it were some ruinous looking huts, several snowy tents, and a huge shamiana or canopy, under which we could see a host of attendants spreading carpets, placing chairs, and otherwise making ready for us. The banks of the stream were very steep, but the guide at length brought us to what seemed a safe and fordable passage. On the further side was a flat expanse of seemingly firm and dry sand, but no sooner had our elephants begun to cross it, than the whole sandbank for yards began to rock and tremble; the water welled up over the footmarks of the elephants, and S. called out to us, Fussun, Fussun! quicksand, quicksand! We scattered the elephants, and tried to hurry them over the dangerous bit of ground with shouts and cries of encouragement.

The poor animals seemed thoroughly to appreciate the danger, and shuffled forward as quickly as they could. All got over in safety except the last three. The treacherous sand, rendered still more insecure by the heavy tread of so many ponderous animals, now gave way entirely, and the three hapless elephants were left floundering in the tenacious hold of the dreaded fussun. Two of the three were not far from the firm bank, and managed to extricate themselves after a short struggle; but the third had sunk up to the shoulders, and could scarcely move. All hands immediately began cutting long grass and forming it into bundles. These were thrown to the sinking elephant.

He rolled from side to side, the sand quaking and undulating round him in all directions. At times he would roll over till nearly half his body was invisible. Some of the Nepaulese ventured near, and managed to undo the harness-ropes that were holding on the pad. The sagacious brute fully understood his danger, and the efforts we were making for his assistance. He managed to get several of the big bundles of grass under his feet, and stood there looking at us with a most pathetic pleading expression, and trembling, as if with an ague, from fear and exhaustion.

The old Major came down to meet us, and a crowd of his men added their efforts to ours, to help the unfortunate elephant. We threw in bundle after bundle of grass, till we had the yielding sand covered with a thick passage of firmly bound fascines, on which the hathee, staggering and floundering painfully, managed to reach firm land. He was so completely exhausted that he could scarcely walk to the tents, and we left him there to the care of his attendants. This is a very common episode in tiger hunting, and does not always terminate so fortunately. In running water, the quicksand is not so dangerous, as the force of the stream keeps washing away the sand, and does not allow it to settle round the legs of the elephant; but on dry land, a dry fussun, as it is called, is justly feared; and many a valuable animal has been swallowed up in its slow, deadly, tenacious grasp.

In crossing sand, the heaviest and slowest elephants should go first, preceded by a light, nimble pioneer. If the leading elephant shows signs of sinking, the others should at once turn back, and seek some safer place. In all cases the line should separate a little, and not follow in each other's footsteps. The indications of a quicksand are easily recognised. If the surface of the sand begins to oscillate and undulate with a tremulous rocking motion, it is always wise to seek some other passage. Looking back, after elephants have passed, you will often see what was a perfectly dry flat, covered with several inches of water. When water begins to ooze up in any quantity, after a few elephants have passed, it is much safer to make the remainder cross at some spot farther on.

In crossing a deep swift river, the elephants should enter the water in a line, ranged up and down the river. That is, the line should be ranged along the bank, and enter the water at right angles to the current, and not in Indian file. The strongest elephants should be up stream, as they help to break the force of the current for the weaker and smaller animals down below. It is a fine sight to see some thirty or forty of these huge animals crossing a deep and rapid river. Some are reluctant to strike out, when they begin to enter the deepest channel, and try to turn back; the mahouts and 'mates' shout, and belabour them with bamboo poles. The trumpeting of the elephants, the waving of the trunks, disporting, like huge water-snakes, in the perturbed current, the splashing of the bamboos, the dark bodies of the natives swimming here and there round the animals, the unwieldy boat piled high with howdahs and pads, the whole heap surmounted by a group of sportsmen with their gleaming weapons, and variegated puggrees, make up a picturesque and memorable sight. Some of the strong swimmers among the elephants seem to enjoy the whole affair immensely. They dip their huge heads entirely under the current, the sun flashes on the dark hide, glistening with the dripping water; the enormous head emerges again slowly, like some monstrous antediluvian creation, and with a succession of these ponderous appearances and disappearances, the mighty brutes forge through the surging water. When they reach a shallow part, they pipe with pleasure, and send volumes of fluid splashing against their heaving flanks, scattering the spray all round in mimic rainbows.

At all times the Koosee was a dangerous stream to cross, but during the rains I have seen the strongest and best swimming elephants taken nearly a mile down stream; and in many instances they have been drowned, their vast bulk and marvellous strength being quite unable to cope with the tremendous force of the raging waters.

When we had got comfortably seated under the shamiana, a crowd of attendants brought us baskets of fruit and a very nice cold collation of various Indian dishes and curries. We did ample justice to the old soldier's hospitable offerings, and then betel-nut, cardamums, cloves, and other spices, and pawri leaves, were handed round on a silver salver, beautifully embossed and carved with quaint devices. We lit our cigars, our beards and handkerchiefs were anointed with attar of roses; and the old Major then informed us that there was good khubber of tiger in the wood close by.

The trees were splendid specimens of forest growth, enormously thick, beautifully umbrageous, and growing very close together. There was a dense undergrowth of tangled creeper, and the most lovely ferns and tropical plants in the richest luxuriance, and of every conceivable shade of amber and green. It was a charming spot. The patch of forest was separated from the unbroken line of morung jungle by a beautifully sheltered glade of several hundred acres, and further broken in three places by avenue-looking openings, disclosing peeps of the black and gloomy-looking mass of impenetrable forest beyond.

In the first of these openings we were directed to take up a position, while the pad elephants and a crowd of beaters went to the edge of the patch of forest and began beating up to us. Immense numbers of genuine jungle fowl were calling in all directions, and flying right across the opening in numerous coveys. They are beautifully marked with black and golden plumes round the neck, and I determined to shoot a few by and bye to send home to friends, who I knew would prize them as invaluable material in dressing hooks for fly-fishing. The crashing of the trees, as the elephants forced their way through the thick forest, or tore off huge branches as they struggled amid the matted vegetation, kept us all on the alert. The first place was however a blank, and we moved on to the next. We had not long to wait, for a fierce din inside the jungle, and the excited cries of the beaters, apprised us that game of some sort was afoot. We were eagerly watching, and speculating on the cause of the uproar, when a very fine half-grown tiger cub sprang out of some closely growing fern, and dashed across the narrow opening so quickly, that ere we had time to raise a gun, he had disappeared in some heavy jhamun jungle on the further side of the path.

We hurried round as fast as we could to intercept him, should he attempt to break on ahead; and leaving some men to rally the mahouts, and let them know that there was a tiger afoot, we were soon in our places, and ready to give the cub a warm reception, should he again show his stripes. It was not long ere he did so. I spied him stealing along the edge of the jungle, evidently intending to make a rush back past the opening he had just crossed, and outflank the line of beater elephants. I fired and hit him in the forearm; he rolled over roaring with rage, and then descrying his assailants, he bounded into the open, and as well as his wound would allow him, came furiously down at the charge. In less time however than it takes to write it, he had received three bullets in his body, and tumbled down a lifeless heap. We raised a cheer which brought the beaters and elephants quickly to the spot. In coming through a thickly wooded part of the forest, with numerous long and pliant creepers intertwisted into a confused tangle of rope-like ligaments, the old Juddeah elephant tore down one of the long lines, and dislodged an angry army of venomous red ants on the occupants of the guddee, or cushioned seat on the elephant's pad. The ants proved formidable assailants. There were two or three Baboos or native gentlemen, holding on to the ropes, chewing pān, and enjoying the scene, but the red ants were altogether more than they had bargained for. Recognising the Baboos as the immediate cause of their disturbance, they attacked them with indomitable courage. The mahout fairly yelled with pain, and one of the Baboos, smarting from the fiery bites of the furious insects, toppled clean backwards into the undergrowth, showing an undignified pair of heels. The other two danced on the guddee, sweeping and thrashing the air, the cushion, and their clothes, with their cummerbunds, in the vain effort to free themselves of their angry assailants. The guddee was literally covered with ants; it looked an animated red mass, and the wretched Baboos made frantic efforts to shake themselves clear. They were dreadfully bitten, and reaching the open, they slid off the elephant, and even on the ground continued their saltatory antics before finally getting rid of their ferocious assailants.

In forest shooting the red ant is one of the most dreaded pests of the jungle. If a colony gets dislodged from some overhanging branch, and is landed in your howdah, the best plan is to evacuate your stronghold as quickly as you can, and let the attendants clear away the invaders. Their bite is very painful, and they take such tenacious hold, that rather than quit their grip, they allow themselves to be decapitated and leave their head and formidable forceps sticking in your flesh.

Other dreaded foes in the forest jungle are the Bhowra or ground bees, which are more properly a kind of hornet. If by evil chance your elephant should tread on their mound-like nest, instantly an angry swarm of venomous and enraged hornets comes buzzing about your ears. Your only chance is to squat down, and envelope yourself completely in a blanket. Old sportsmen, shooting in forest jungle, invariably take a blanket with them in the howdah, to ensure themselves protection in the event of an attack by these blood-thirsty creatures. The thick matted creepers too are a great nuisance, for which a bill-hook or sharp kookree is an invaluable adjunct to the other paraphernalia of the march. I have seen a mahout swept clean off the elephant's back by these tenacious creepers, and the elephants themselves are sometimes unable to break through the tangle of sinewy, lithe cords, which drape the huge forest trees, hanging in slender festoons from every branch. Some of them are prickly, and as the elephant slowly forces his way through the mass of pendent swaying cords, they lacerate and tear the mahout's clothes and skin, and appropriate his puggree. As you crouch down within the shelter of your howdah, you can't help pitying the poor wretch, and incline to think that, after all, shooting in grass jungle has fewer drawbacks and is preferable to forest shooting.

One of the drivers reported that he had seen a bear in the jungle, and we saw the earth of one not far from where the young tiger had fallen; it was the lair of the sloth bear or *Ursus labialis*, so called from his long pendent upper lip. His spoor is very easily distinguished from that of any other animal; the ball of the foot shows a distinct round impression, and about an inch to an inch and a half further on, the impression of the long curved claws are seen. He uses these long curved claws to tear up ant hills, and open hollow decaying trees, to get at the honey within, of which he is very fond. We went after the bear, and were not long in discovering his whereabouts, and a well-directed shot from S. added him to our bag. The best bear shooting in India perhaps is in CHOTA NAGPOOR, but this does not come within the limits of my present volume. We now beat slowly through the wood, keeping a bright look out for ants and hornets, and getting fine shooting at the numerous jungle fowl which flew about in amazing numbers.

The forest trees in this patch of jungle were very fine. The hill seerees, with its feathery foliage and delicate clusters of white bugle-shaped blossom; the semul or cotton tree, with its wonderful wealth of magnificent crimson flowers; the birch-looking sheeshum or sissod; the sombre looking sal; the shining, leathery-leafed bhur, with its immense over-arching limbs, and the crisp, curly-leafed elegant-looking jhamun or Indian olive, formed a paradise of sylvan beauty, on which the eye dwelt till it was sated with the woodland loveliness.

In recrossing the dhar or water-course, we took care to avoid the quicksands, and as we did not expect to fall in with another tiger, we indulged in a little general firing. I shot a fine buck through the spine, and we bagged several deer, and no less than five florican; this bird is allied to the bustard family, and has beautiful drooping feathers, hanging in plumy pendants of deep black and pure white, intermingled in the most graceful and showy manner. The male is a magnificent bird, and has perhaps as fine plumage as any bird on the border; the flesh yields the most delicate eating of any game bird I know; the slices of mingled brown and white from the breast are delicious. The birds are rather shy, generally getting up a long way in front of the line, and moving with a slow, rather clumsy, flight, not unlike the flight of the white earth owl. They run with great swiftness, and are rather hard to kill, unless hit about the neck and head. There are two sorts, the lesser and the greater, the former also called the bastard florican. Altogether they are noble looking birds, and the sportsman is always glad to add as many florican as he can to his bag.

We were now nearing the locality of the fierce fire of the morning; it was still blazing in a long extended line of flame, and we witnessed an incident without parallel in the experience of any of us. I fired at and wounded a large stag; it was wounded somewhere in the side, and seemed very hard hit indeed. Maddened probably by terror and pain, it made straight for the line of fire, and bounded unhesitatingly right into the flame. We saw it distinctly go clean though the flames, but we could not see whether it got away with its life, as the elephants would not go up to the fire. At all events, the stag went right through his fiery ordeal, and was lost to us. We started numerous hares close to camp, and S. bowled over several. They are very common in the short grass jungle, where the soil is sandy, and are frequently to be found among thin jowah jungle; they afford good sport for coursing, but are neither so fleet, nor so large, nor such good eating as the English hare. In fact, they are very dry eating, and the best way to cook them is to jug them, or make a hunter's pie, adding portions of partridge, quail, or plover, with a few mushrooms, and a modicum of ham or bacon if these are procurable.

We reached camp pretty late, and sent off venison, birds, and other spoils to Mrs. S. and to Inamputte factory. Our bag shewed a diversity of spoil, consisting of one tiger, seven hog-deer, one bear (*Ursus labialis*), seventeen jungle fowl, five florican, and six hares. It was no bad bag considering that during most of the day we had been beating solely for tiger. We could have shot many more deer and jungle fowl, but we never try to shoot more than are needed to satisfy the wants of the camp. Were we to attempt to shoot at all the deer and pig that we see, the figures would reach very large totals. As a rule therefore, the records of Indian sportsmen give no idea of the vast quantities of game that are put up and never fired at. It would be the very wantonness of destruction, to shoot animals not wanted for some specific purpose, unless indeed, you were raging an indiscriminate war of extermination, in a quarter where their numbers were a nuisance and prejudicial to crops. In that case, your proceedings would not be dignified by the name of sport.

After a few more days shooting, the incidents of which were pretty much like those I have been describing, I started back for the factory. I sent my horse on ahead, and took five elephants with me to beat up for game on the homeward route. Close to camp a fine buck got up in front of me. I broke both his forelegs with my first shot, but the poor brute still managed to hobble along. It was in some very dense patair jungle, and I had considerable difficulty in bringing him to bag. When we reached the ghat or ferry, I ordered Geerdharree Jha's mahout to cross with his elephant. The brute, however, refused to cross the river alone, and in spite of all the driver could do, she insisted on following the rest. I got down, and some of the other drivers got out the hobbles and bound them round her legs. In spite of these she still seemed determined to follow us. She shook the bedding and other articles with which she was loaded off her back, and made a frantic effort to follow us through the deep sand. The iron chains cut into her legs, and, afraid that she might do herself an irreparable injury, I had her tied up to a tree, and left her trumpeting and making an indignant lamentation at being separated from the rest of the line.

The elephant seems to be quite a social animal. I have frequently seen cases where, after having been in company together for a lengthened hunt, they have manifested great reluctance to separate. In leaving the line, I have often noticed the single elephant looking back at his comrades, and giving vent to his disappointment and disapproval, by grunts and trumpetings of indignant protest. We left the refractory hathee tied up to her tree, and as we crossed the long rolling billows of burning sand that lay athwart our course, she was soon lost to view. I shot a couple more hog-deer, and got several plover and teal in the patches of water that lay in some of the hollows among the sandbanks. I fired at a huge alligator basking in the sun, on a sandbank close to the stream. The bullet hit him somewhere in the forearm, and he made a tremendous sensation header into the current. From the agitation in the water, he seemed not to appreciate the leaden message which I had sent him.

We found the journey through the soft yielding sand very fatiguing, and especially trying to the eyes. When not shooting, it is a very wise precaution to wear eye-preservers or 'goggles.' They are a great relief to the eyes, and the best, I think, are the neutral tinted. During the west winds, when the atmosphere is loaded with fine particles of irritating sand and dust, these goggles are very necessary, and are a great protection to the sight.

Another prudent precaution is to have the back of one's shirt or coat slightly padded with cotton and quilted. The heat prevents one wearing thick clothes, and there is no doubt that the action of the direct rays of the burning sun all down the back on the spinal cord, is very injurious, and may be a fruitful cause of sunstroke. It is certainly productive of great lassitude and weariness. I used to wear a thin quilted sort of shield made of cotton-drill, which fastened round the shoulders and waist. It does not incommode one's action in any particular, and is, I think, a great protection against the fierce rays of the sun. Many prefer the puggree as a head-piece. It is undeniably a fine thing when one is riding on horseback, as it fits close to the head, does not catch the wind during a smart trot or canter, and is therefore not easily shaken off. For riding I think it preferable to all other headdresses. A good thick puggree is a great protection to the back of the head and neck, the part of the body which of all others requires protection from the sun. It feels rather heavy at first, but one gets used to it, and it does not shade the eyes and face. These are the two gravest objections to it, but for comfort, softness, and protection to the head and neck, I do not think it can be surpassed.

After crossing the sand, we again entered some thin scrubby acacia jungle, with here and there a moist swampy nullah, with rank green patair jungle growing in the cool dank shade. Here we disturbed a colony of pigs, but the four mahouts being Mahommedans I did not fire. As we went along, one of my men called my attention to some footprints near a small lagoon. On inspection we found they were rhinoceros tracks, evidently of old date. These animals are often seen in this part of the country, but are more numerous farther north, in the great morung forest jungle.

A very noticeable feature in these jungles was the immense quantity of bleached ghastly skeletons of cattle. This year had been a most disastrous one for cattle. Enormous numbers had been swept off by disease, and in many villages bordering on the morung the herds had been well-nigh exterminated. Little attention is paid to breeding. In some districts, such as the Mooteeharree and Mudhobunnee division, fine cart-bullocks are bred, carefully handled and tended, and fetch high prices. In Kurruchpore, beyond the Ganges in Bhaugulpore district, cattle of a small breed, hardy, active, staunch, and strong, are bred in great numbers, and are held in great estimation for agricultural requirements; but in these Koosee jungles the bulls are often ill-bred weedy brutes, and the cows being much in excess of a fair proportion of bulls, a deal of in-breeding takes place; unmatured young bulls roam about with the herd, and the result is a crowd of cattle that succumb to the first ailment, so that the land is littered with their bones.

The bullock being indispensable to the Indian cultivator, bull calves are prized, taken care of, well nurtured, and well fed. The cow calves are pretty much left to take care of themselves; they are thin, miserable, half-starved brutes, and the short-sighted ryot seems altogether to forget that it is on these miserable withered specimens that he must depend for his supply of plough and cart-bullocks. The matter is most shamefully neglected. Government occasionally through its officers, experimental farms, etc., tries to get good sire stock for both horses and cattle, but as long as the dams are bad—mere weeds, without blood, bone, muscle, or stamina, the produce must be bad. As a pretty well established and general rule, the ryots look after their bullocks,—they recognise their value, and appreciate their utility, but the cows fare badly, and from all I have myself seen, and from the concurrent testimony of many observant friends in the rural districts, I should say that the breed has become much deteriorated.

Old planters constantly tell you, that such cattle as they used to get are not now procurable for love or money. Within the last twenty years prices have more than doubled, because the demand for good plough-bullocks has been more urgent, as a consequence of increased cultivation, and the supply is not equal to the demand. Attention to the matter is imperative, and planters would be wise in their own interests to devote a little time and trouble to disseminating sound ideas about the selection of breeding stock, and the principles of rearing and raising stock among their ryots and dependants. Every factory should be able to breed its own cattle, and supply its own requirements for plough and cart-bullocks. It would be cheaper in the end; and it would undoubtedly be a blessing to the country to raise the standard of cattle used in agricultural work.

To return from this digression. We plodded on and on, weary, hot, and thirsty, expecting every moment to see the ghat and my waiting horse. But the country here is so wild, the river takes such erratic courses during the annual floods, and the district is so secluded and so seldom visited by Europeans or factory servants, that my syce had evidently lost his way. After we had crossed innumerable streams, and laboriously traversed mile upon mile of burning sand, we gave up the attempt to find the ghat, and made for Nathpore.

Nathpore was formerly a considerable town, not far from the Nepaul border, a flourishing grain mart and emporium for the fibres, gums, spices, timbers, and other productions of a wide frontier. There was a busy and crowded bazaar, long streets of shops and houses, and hundreds of boats lying in the stream beside the numerous ghats, taking in and discharging their cargoes. It may give a faint idea of the destructive force of an Indian stream like the Koosee when it is in full flood, to say that this once flourishing town is now but a handful of miserable huts. Miles of rich lands, once clothed with luxuriant crops of rice, indigo, and waving grain, are now barren reaches of burning sand. The bleached skeletons of mango, jackfruit, and other trees, stretch out their leafless and lifeless branches, to remind the spectator of the time when their foliage rustled in the breeze, when their lusty limbs bore rich clusters of luscious fruit, and when the din of the bazaar resounded beneath their welcome shade. A fine old lady still lived in a two-storied brick building, with quaint little darkened rooms, and a narrow verandah running all round the building. She was long past the allotted threescore years and ten, with a keen yet mildly beaming eye, and a wealth of beautiful hair as white as driven snow, neatly gathered back from her shapely forehead. She was the last remaining link connecting the present with the past glories of Nathpore. Her husband had been a planter and Zemindar. Where his vats had stood laden with rich indigo, the engulphing sand now reflected the rays of the torrid sun from its burning whiteness. She shewed me a picture of the town as it appeared to her when she had been brought there many a long and weary year ago, ere yet her step had lost its lightness, and when she was in the bloom of her bridal life. There was a fine broad boulevard, shadowed by splendid trees, on which she and her husband had driven in their carriage of an evening, through crowds of prosperous and contented traders and cultivators. The hungry river had swept all this away. Subsisting on a few precarious rents of some little plots of ground that it had spared, all that remained of a once princely estate, this good old lady lived her lonely life cheerful and contented, never murmuring or repining. The river had not spared even the graves of her departed dear ones. Since I left that part of the country I hear that she has been called away to join those who had gone before her.

I arrived at her house late in the afternoon. I had

never been at Nathpore before, although the place was well known to me by reputation. What a wreck it presented as our elephants marched through. Ruined, dismantled, crumbling temples; masses of masonry half submerged in the swift-running, treacherous, undermining stream; huge trees lying prostrate, twisted and jammed together where the angry flood had hurled them; bare unsightly poles and piles, sticking from the water at every angle, reminding us of the granaries and godowns that were wont to be filled with the agricultural wealth of the districts for miles around; hard metalled roads cut abruptly off, and bridges with only half an arch, standing lonely and ruined half way in the muddy current that swept noiselessly past the deserted city. It was a scene of utter waste and desolation.

The lady I mentioned made me very welcome, and I was struck by her unaffected cheerfulness and gentleness. She was a gentlewoman indeed, and though reduced in circumstances, surrounded by misfortunes, and daily and hourly reminded by the scattered wreck around her of her former wealth and position, she bore all with exemplary fortitude, and to the full extent of her scanty means she relieved the sorrows and ailments of the natives. They all loved and respected, and I could not help admiring and honouring her.

She pointed out to me, far away on the south-east horizon, the place where the river ran in its shallow channel when she first came to Nathpore. During her experience it had cut into and overspread more than twenty miles of country, turning fertile fields into arid wastes of sand; sweeping away factories, farms, and villages; and changing the whole face of the country from a fruitful landscape into a wilderness of sand and swamp.

My horse came up in the evening, and I rode over to Inamputtee, leaving my kindly hostess in her solitude.

CHAPTER XXV.

Exciting jungle scene.—The camp.—All quiet.—Advent of the cowherds.—A tiger close by.—Proceed to the spot.—Encounter between tigress and buffaloes.—Strange behaviour of the elephant.—Discovery and capture of four cubs.—Joyful return to camp.—Death of the tigress.—Night encounter with a leopard.—The haunts of the tiger and our shooting grounds.

ONE of the most exciting and deeply interesting scenes I ever witnessed in the jungles, was on the occasion I have referred to in a former chapter, when speaking of the number of young given by the tigress at a birth. It was in the month of March, at the village of Ryseree, in Bhaugulpore. I had been encamped in the midst of twenty-four beautiful tanks, the history and construction of which were lost in the mists of tradition. The villagers had a story that these tanks were the work of a mighty giant, Bheema, with whose aid and that of his brethren they had been excavated in a single night.

At all events, they were now covered with a wild tangle of water lilies and aquatic plants; well stocked with magnificent fish, and an occasional scaly monster of a saurian. They were the haunt of vast quantities of widgeon, teal, whistlers, mallard, ducks, snipe, curlew, blue fowl, and the usual varied *habituès* of an exceptionally good Indian lake. In the vicinity hares were numerous, and in the thick jungle bordering the tanks in places, and consisting mostly of nurkool and wild rose, hog-deer and wild pig were abundant. The dried-up bed of an old arm of the Koosee was quite close to my camp, and abounded in sandpiper, and golden, grey, goggle-eyed, and stilted plover, besides other game.

It was indeed a favourite camping spot, and the village was inhabited by a hardy, independent set of Gwallas, Koormees, and agriculturists, with whom I was a prime favourite.

I was sitting in my tent, going over some village accounts with the village putwarrie, and my gomasta. A possé of villagers were grouped under the grateful shade of a gnarled old mango tree, whose contorted limbs bore evidence to the violence of many a *tufan*, or tempest, which it had weathered. The usual confused clamour of tongues was rising from this group, and the subject of debate was the eternal 'pice.' Behind the bank, and in rear of the tent, the cook and his mate were disembowelling a hapless *moorghee*, a fowl, whose decapitation had just been effected with a huge jagged old cavalry sword, of which my cook was not a little proud ; and on the strength of which he adopted fierce military airs, and gave an extra turn to his well-oiled moustache when he went abroad for a holiday.

Farther to the rear a line of horses were picketed, including my man-eating demon the white Cabool stallion, my gentle country-bred mare Motee—the pearl —and my handsome little pony mare, formerly my hockey or polo steed, a present from a gallant sportsman and rare good fellow, as good a judge of a horse, or a criminal, as ever sat on a bench.

Behind the horses, each manacled by weighty chains, with his ponderous trunk and ragged-looking tail swaying too and fro with a never-ceasing motion, stood a line of ten elephants. Their huge leathery ears flapped lazily, and ever and anon one or other would seize a mighty branch, and belabour his corrugated sides to free himself of the detested and troublesome flies. The elephants were placidly munching their *chana* (bait, or food), and occasionally giving each other a dry bath in the shape of a shower of sand. There was a monotonous clank of chains, and an occasional deep abdominal rumble like distant thunder. All over the camp there was a confused subdued medley of sound. A hum from the argumentative villagers, a lazy flop in the tank as a raho rose to the surface, an occasional outburst from the ducks, an angry clamour from the water-hens and blue-fowl. My dogs were lying round me blinking and winking, and making an occasional futile snap at an imaginary fly or flea. It was a drowsy and peaceful scene. I was nearly dropping off to sleep, from the heat and the monotonous drone of the putwarrie, who was intoning nasally some formidable document about fishery rights and privileges.

Suddenly there was a hush. Every sound seemed to stop simultaneously as if by pre-arranged concert. Then three men were seen rushing madly along the elevated ridge surrounding one of the tanks. I recognised one of my peons, and with him two cowherds. Their head-dresses were all disarranged, and their parted lips, heaving chests, and eyes blazing with excitement, shewed that they were brimful of some unusual message.

Now arose such a bustle in the camp as no description could adequately pourtray. The elephants trumpeted and piped; the *syces*, or grooms, came rushing up with eager queries; the villagers bustled about like so many ants aroused by the approach of a hostile foe ; my pack of terriers yelped out in chorus ; the pony neighed ; the Cabool stallion plunged about ; my servants came rushing from the shelter of the tent verandah with disordered dress ; the ducks rose in a quacking crowd, and circled round and round the tent ; and the cry arose of ' Bagh ! Bagh ! Khodamund ! Arree Bap re Bap ! Ram Ram, Seeta Ram !'

Breathless with running, the men now tumbled up, hurriedly salaamed, and then each with gasps and choking stops, and pell-mell volubility, and amid a running fire of cries, queries, and interjections from the mob, began to unfold their tale. There was an infuriated tigress at the other side of the nullah, or dry watercourse, she had attacked a herd of buffaloes, and it was believed that she had cubs.

Already Debnarain Singh was getting his own pad elephant caparisoned, and my bearer was diving under my camp bed for my gun and cartridges. Knowing the little elephant to be a fast walker, and fairly staunch, I got on her back, and accompanied by the gomasta and mahout we set out, followed by the peon and herdsmen to shew us the way.

I expected two friends, officers from Calcutta, that very day, and wished not to kill the tigress but to keep her for our combined shooting next day. We had not proceeded far when, on the other side of the nullah, we saw dense clouds of dust rising, and heard a confused, rushing, trampling sound, mingled with the clashing of horns, and the snorting of a herd of angry buffaloes.

It was the wildest sight I have ever seen in connection with animal life. The buffaloes were drawn together in the form of a crescent ; their eyes glared fiercely, and as they advanced in a series of short runs, stamping with their hoofs, and angrily lashing their tails, their horns would come together with a clanging, clattering crash, and they would paw the sand, snort and toss their heads, and behave in the most extraordinary manner.

The cause of all this commotion was not far to seek. Directly in front, retreating slowly, with stealthy, prowling, crawling steps, and an occasional short, quick leap or bound to one side or the other, was a magnificent tigress, looking the very personification of baffled fury. Ever and anon she crouched down to the earth, tore up the sand with her claws, lashed her tail from side to side, and with lips retracted, long moustaches quivering with wrath, and hateful eyes scintillating with rage and fury, she seemed to meditate an attack on the angry buffaloes. The serried array of clashing horns, and the ponderous bulk of the herd, seemed however to daunt the snarling vixen; at their next rush she would bound back a few paces, crouch down, growl, and be forced to move back again, by the short, blundering rush of the crowd.

All the calves and old cows were in the rear of the herd, and it was not a little comical to witness their ungainly attitudes. They would stretch their clumsy necks, and shake their heads, as if they did not rightly understand what was going on. Finding that if they stopped too long to indulge their curiosity, there was a danger of their getting separated from the fighting members of the herd, they would make a stupid, headlong, lumbering lurch forward, and jostle each other, in their blundering panic.

It was a grand sight. The tigress was the embodiment of lithe and savage beauty, but her features expressed the wildest baffled rage. I could have shot the striped vixen over and over again, but I wished to keep her for my friends, and I was thrilled with the excitement of such a novel scene.

Suddenly our elephant trumpeted, and shied quickly to one side, from something lying on the ground. Curling up its trunk it began backing and piping at a prodigious rate.

'Hullo! what's the matter now?' said I to Debnarain.

'God only knows,' said he.

'A young tiger!' 'Bagh ka butcha!' screams our mahout, and regardless of the elephant or of our cries to stop, he scuttled down the pad rope like a monkey down a backstay, and clutching a young dead tiger cub, threw it up to Debnarain; it was about the size of a small poodle, and had evidently been trampled by the pursuing herd of buffaloes.

'There may be others,' said the gomasta; and peering into every bush, we went slowly on.

The elephant now shewed decided symptoms of dislike and a reluctance to approach a particular dense clump of grass.

A sounding whack on the head, however, made her quicken her steps, and thrusting the long stalks aside, she discovered for us three blinking little cubs, brothers of the defunct, and doubtless part of the same litter. Their eyes were scarcely open, and they lay huddled together like three enormous striped kittens, and spat at us and bristled their little moustaches much as an angry cat would do. All the four were males.

It was not long ere I had them carefully wrapped in the mahout's blanket. Overjoyed at our good fortune, we left the excited buffaloes still executing their singular war-dance, and the angry tigress, robbed of her whelps, consuming her soul in baffled fury.

We heard her roaring through the night, close to camp, and on my friends' arrival, we beat her up next morning, and she fell pierced by three bullets, after a fierce and determined charge. We came upon her across the nullah, and her mind was evidently made up to fight. Nearly all the villagers had turned out with the line of elephants. Before we had time to order them away, she came down upon the line, roaring furiously, and bounding over the long grass,—a most magnificent sight.

My first bullet took her full in the chest, and before she could make good her charge, a ball each from Pat and Captain G. settled her career. She was beautifully striped, and rather large for a tigress, measuring nine feet three inches.

It was now a question with me, how to rear the three interesting orphans; we thought a slut from some of the villages would prove the best wet nurse, and tried accordingly to get one, but could not. In the meantime an unhappy goat was pounced on and the three young tigers took to her teats as if 'to the manner born.' The poor Nanny screamed tremendously at first sight of them, but she soon got accustomed to them, and when they grew a little bigger, she would often playfully butt at them with her horns.

The little brutes throve wonderfully, and soon developed such an appetite that I had to get no less than six goats to satisfy their constant thirst. I kept the cubs for over two months, and I shall not soon forget the excitement I caused, when my boat stopped at Sahribgunge, and my goats, tiger cubs, and attendants, formed a procession from the ghat or landing-place, to the railway station.

Soldiers, guards, engineers, travellers, and crowds of

natives surrounded me, and at every station the guard's van, with my novel menagerie, was the centre of attraction. I sold the cubs to Jamrach's agent in Calcutta for a very satisfactory price. Two of them were very powerful, finely marked, handsome animals; the third had always been sickly, had frequent convulsions, and died a few days after I sold it. I was afterwards told that the milk diet was a mistake, and that I should have fed them on raw meat. However, I was very well satisfied on the whole with the result of my adventure.

I had another in the same part of the country, which at the time was a pretty good test of the state of my nerves.

I was camped out at the village of Purindaha, on the edge of a gloomy sal forest, which was reported to contain numerous leopards. The villagers were a mixed lot of low-caste Hindoos, and Nepaulese settlers. They had been fighting with the factory, and would not pay up their rents, and I was trying, with every probability of success, to make an amicable arrangement with them. At all events, I had so far won them round, that they were willing to talk to me. They came to the tent and listened quietly, and except on the subject of rent, we got on in the most friendly manner.

It was the middle of April. The heat was intense. The whole atmosphere had that coppery look which denotes extreme heat, and the air was loaded with fine yellow dust, which the daily west wind bore on its fever laden wings, to disturb the lungs and tempers of all good Christians. The *kanats*, or canvas walls of the tent, had all been taken down for coolness, and my camp bed lay in one corner, open all round to the outside air, but only sheltered from the dew. It had been a busy day. I had been going over accounts, and talking to the villagers till I was really hoarse. After a light dinner I lay down on my bed, but it was too close and hot to sleep. By and bye the various sounds died out. The tom-toming ceased in the village. My servants suspended their low muttered gossip round the cook's fire, wrapped themselves in their white cloths, and dropped into slumber. 'Toby,' 'Nettle,' 'Whisky,' 'Pincher,' and my other terriers, resembled so many curled-up hairy balls, and were in the land of dreams. Occasionally an owl would give a melancholy hoot from the forest, or a screech owl would raise a momentary and damnable din. At intervals, the tinkle of a cow-bell sounded faintly in the distance. I tossed restlessly, thinking of various things, till I must have dropped off into an uneasy fitful sleep. I know not how long I had been dozing, but of a sudden I felt myself wide awake, though with my eyes yet firmly closed.

I was conscious of some terrible unknown impending danger. I had experienced the same feeling before on waking from a nightmare, but I knew that the danger now was real. I felt a shrinking horror, a terrible and nameless fear, and for the life of me I could not move hand or foot. I was lying on my side, and could distinctly hear the thumping of my heart. A cold sweat broke out behind my ears and over my neck and chest. I could analyse my every feeling, and I knew there was some PRESENCE in the tent, and that I was in instant and imminent peril. Suddenly in the distance a pariah dog gave a prolonged melancholy howl. As if this had broken the spell which had hitherto bound me, I opened my eyes, and within ten inches of my face, there was a handsome leopardess gazing steadily at me. Our eyes met, and how long we confronted each other I know not. It must have been some minutes. Her eyes contracted and expanded, the pupil elongated and then opened out into a round lustrous globe. I could see the lithe tail oscillating at its extreme tip, with a gentle waving motion, like that of a cat when hunting birds in the garden. I seemed to possess no will. I believe I was under a species of fascination, but we continued our steady stare at each other.

Just then, there was a movement by some of the horses. The leopard slowly turned her head, and I grasped the revolver which lay under my pillow. The beautiful spotted monster turned her head for an instant, and shewed her teeth, and then with one bound went through the open side of the tent. I fired two shots, which were answered with a roar. The din that followed would have frightened the devil. It was a beautiful clear night, with a moon at the full, and everything shewed as plainly as at noonday. The servants uttered exclamations of terror. The terriers went into an agony of yelps and barks. The horses snorted, and tried to get loose, and my chowkeydar, who had been asleep on his watch, thinking a band of dacoits were on us, began laying round him with his staff, shouting, *Chor, chor! lagga, lagga, lagga!* that is, 'thief, thief! lay on, lay on, lay on!'

The leopard was hit, and evidently in a terrible temper. She halted not thirty paces from the tent, beside a jhamun tree, and seemed undecided whether to go on or return and wreak her vengeance on me. That moment decided her fate. I snatched down my Express rifle, which was hanging in two loops above my bed, and shot her right through the heart.

I never understood how she could have made her way past dogs, servants, horses, and watchman, right into the tent, without raising some alarm. It must have been more from curiosity than any hostile design. I know that my nerves were very rudely shaken, but I became the hero of the Purindaha villagers. I believe that my night adventure with the leopardess did more to bring them round to a settlement than all my eloquence and figures.

The river Koosee, on the banks of which, and in the long grass plains adjacent, most of the incidents I have recorded took place, takes its rise at the base of Mount Everest, and, after draining nearly the whole of Eastern Nepaul, emerges by a deep gorge from the hills at the north-west corner of Purneah. The stream runs with extreme velocity. It is known as a snow stream. The water is always cold, and generally of a milky colour, containing much fine white sand. No sooner does it leave its rocky bed than it tears through the flat country by numerous channels. It is subject to very sudden rises. A premonitory warning of these is generally given. The water becomes of a turbid, almost blood-like colour. Sometimes I have seen the river rise over thirty feet in twenty-four hours. The melting of the snow often makes a raging torrent, level from bank to bank, where only a few hours before a horse could have forded the stream without wetting the girths of the saddle.

In 1876 the largest channel was a swift broad stream called the Dhaus. The river is very capricious, seldom flowing for any length of time in one channel. This is owing in great measure to the amount of silt it carries with it from the hills, in its impetuous progress to the plains.

In these dry watercourses, among the sand ridges, beside the humid marshy hollows, and among the thick strips of grass jungle, tigers are always to be found. They are much less numerous now however than formerly. As a rule, there is no shelter in these water-worn, flood-ravaged tracts and sultry jungles. Occasionally a few straggling plantain trees, a clump of sickly-looking bamboos, a cluster of tall shadowless palms, marks the site of a deserted village. All else is waving grass, withered and dry. The villages, inhabited mostly by a few cowherds, boatmen, and rice-farmers are scattered at wide intervals. In the shooting season, and when the hot winds are blowing, the only shadow on the plain is that cast by the dense volumes of lurid smoke, rising in blinding clouds from the jungle fires.

According to the season, animal life fluctuates strangely. During the rains, when the river is in full flood, and much of the country submerged, most of the animals migrate to the North, buffaloes and wild pig alone keeping possession of the higher ridges in the neighbourhood of their usual haunts.

The contrasts presented on these plains at different seasons of the year are most remarkable. In March and April they are parched up, brown, and dead; great black patches showing the track of a destroying fire, the fine brown ash from the burnt grass penetrating the eyes and nostrils, and sweeping along in eddying and blinding clouds. They then look the very picture of an untenable waste, a sea of desolation, whose limits blend in the extreme distance with the shimmering coppery horizon. In the rainy season these arid-looking wastes are covered with tall-plumed, reed-like, waving grass, varying from two to ten feet in height, stretching in an unbroken sweep as far as the eye can reach, except where an abrupt line shews that the swift river has its treacherous course. After the rains, progress through the jungle is dangerous. Quicksands and beds of tenacious mud impede one at every step. The rich vegetation springs up green and vigorous, with a rapidity only to be seen in the Tropics. But what a glorious hunting ground! What a preserve for Nimrod! Deer forest, or heathered moor, can never compete with the old Koosee Derahs for abundance of game and thrilling excitement in sport. My genial, happy, loyal comrades too—while memory lasts the recollection of your joyous, frank, warm-hearted comradeship shall never fade.

CHAPTER XXVI.

Remarks on guns.— How to cure skins.— Different recipes.— Conclusion.

My remarks on guns shall be brief. The true sportsman has many facilities for acquiring the best information on a choice of weapons. For large game perhaps nothing can equal the Express rifle. My own trusty weapon was a ·500 bore, very plain, with a pistol grip, point blank up to 180 yards, made by Murcott of the Haymarket, from whom I have bought over twenty guns, every one of which turned out a splendid weapon.

My next favourite was a No. 12 breachloader, very light, but strong and carefully finished. It had a side snap action with rebounding locks, and was the quickest gun to fire and reload I ever possessed. I bought it from the same maker, although it was manufactured by W. W. Greener.

Avoid a cheap gun as you would avoid a cheap Jew pedlar. A good name is above riches so far as a gun is concerned, and when you have a good gun take as much care of it as you would of a good wife. They are both equally rare. An expensive gun is not necessarily a good one, but a cheap gun is very seldom trustworthy. Have a portable, handy black leather case. Keep your gun always clean, bright, and free from rust. After every day's shooting see that the barrels and locks are carefully cleaned and oiled. Nothing is better for this purpose than rangoon oil.

For preserving horns, a little scraping and varnishing

are all that is required. While in camp it is a good plan to rub them with deer, or pig, or tiger fat, as it keeps them from cracking.

To clean a tiger's or other skull. If there be a nest of ants near the camp, place the skull in their immediate vicinity. Some recommend putting in water till the particles of flesh rot, or till the skull is cleared by the fishes. A strong solution of caustic water may be used if you wish to get the bones cleaned very quickly. Some put the skulls in quicklime, but it has a tendency to make the bones splinter, and it is difficult to keep the teeth from getting loose and dropping out. The best but slowest plan is to fix them in mechanically by wire or white lead. A good preservative is to wash or paint them with a very strong solution of fine lime and water.

To cure skins. I know no better recipe than the one adopted by my trainers in the art of *shibar*, the brothers S. I cannot do better than give a description of the process in the words of George himself.

'Skin the animal in the usual way. Cut from the corner of the mouth, down the throat, and along the belly. A white stripe or border generally runs along the belly. This should be left as nearly as possible equal on both sides. Carefully cut the fleshy parts off the lips and balls of the toes and feet. Clean away every particle of fatty or fleshy matter that may still adhere to the skin. Peg it out on the ground with the hair side undermost. When thoroughly scraped clean of all extraneous matter on the inner surface, get a bucket or tub of buttermilk, which is called by the natives *dahye* or *mutha*. It is a favourite article of diet with them, cheap and plentiful. Dip the skin in this, and keep it well and entirely submerged by placing some heavy weight on it. It should be submerged fully three inches in the tub of buttermilk.

'After two days in the milk bath, take it out and peg it as before. Now take a smooth oval rubbing-board about twelve inches long, five round, and about an inch thick in the middle, and scrub the skin heartily with this instrument. On its lower surface it should be cuts in grooves, semicircular in shape, half an inch wide, and one inch apart. During scrubbing use plenty of pure water to remove filth. In about half an hour the pinkish-white colour will disappear, and the skin will appear white, with a blackish tinge underneath. This is the true hide.

'Again submerge in the buttermilk bath for twenty-four hours, and get a man to tread on it in every possible way, folding it and unfolding it, till all has been thoroughly worked.

'Take it out again, peg out and scrub it as before, after which wash the whole hide well in clear water. Never mind if the skin looks rotten, it is really not so.

'When washed put it into a tub, in which you have first placed a mixture consisting of half an ounce of alum to each gallon of water. Soak the skin in this mixture for about six hours, taking it up occasionally to drain a little. This is sufficient to cure your skin and clean it.'

The tanning remains to be done.

'Get four pounds of babool, tamarind, or dry oak bark. (The babool is a kind of acacia, and is easily procurable, as the tamarind also is). Boil the bark in two gallons of water till it is reduced to one half the quantity. Add to this nine gallons of fresh water, and in this solution souse the skin for two, or three, or four days.

'The hairs having been set by the soaking in alum, the skin will tan more quickly, and if the tan is occasionally rubbed into the pores of the skin it will be an improvement. You can tell when the tanning is complete by the colour the skin assumes. When this satisfies the eye, take it out and drain on a rod. When nearly dry it should be curried with olive oil or clarified butter if required for wear, but if only for floor covering or carriage rug, the English curriers' common 'dubbin,' sold by shopkeepers, is best. This operation, which must be done on the inner side only, is simple.

'Another simple recipe, and one which answers well, is this. Mix together of the best English soap, four ounces; arsenic, two and a half grains; camphor, two ounces; alum, half an ounce; saltpetre, half an ounce. Boil the whole, and keep stirring, in a half-pint of distilled water, over a very slow fire, for from ten to fifteen minutes. Apply when cool with a sponge. A little sweet oil may be rubbed on the skins after they are dry.

'Another good method is to apply arsenical soap, which may be made as follows: powdered arsenic, two pounds; camphor, five ounces; white soap, sliced thin, two pounds; salt of tartar, twelve drams; chalk, or powdered fine lime, four ounces; add a small quantity of water first to the soap, put over a gentle fire, and keep stirring. When melted, add the lime and tartar, and thoroughly mix; next add the arsenic, keeping up a constant motion, and lastly the camphor. The camphor should first be reduced to a powder by means of a little spirits of wine, and should be added to the mess after it has been taken off the fire.

'This preparation must be kept in a well-stoppered

CONCLUSION.

jar, or properly closed pot. When ready, the soap should be of the consistency of Devonshire cream. To use, add water till it becomes of the consistency of clear rich soup.'

I have now finished my book. It has been pleasant to me to write down these recollections. Ever since I began my task, death has been busy, and the ranks of my friends have been sadly thinned. Failing health has driven me from my old shooting grounds, and in sunny Australia I have been trying to recruit the energies enervated by the burning climate of India. That my dear old planter friends may have as kindly recollections of 'the Maori' as he has of them, is what I ardently hope; that I may yet get back to share in the sports, pastimes, joys, and social delights of Mofussil life in India, is what I chiefly desire. If this volume meets the approbation of the public, I may be tempted to draw further on a well-stocked memory, and gossip afresh on Indian life, Indian experiences, and Indian sport. Meantime, courteous reader, farewell.

BEDFORD STREET, STRAND, LONDON, W.C.
October 1878.

MACMILLAN & CO.'S CATALOGUE of Works in the Departments of History, Biography, Travels, Critical and Literary Essays, Politics, Political and Social Economy, Law, etc.; and Works connected with Language.

HISTORY, BIOGRAPHY, TRAVELS, &c.

Albemarle.—FIFTY YEARS OF MY LIFE. By GEORGE THOMAS, Earl of Albemarle. With Steel Portrait of the first Earl of Albemarle, engraved by JEENS. Third and Cheaper Edition. Crown 8vo. 7s. 6d.

"*The book is one of the most amusing of its class. . . . These reminiscences have the charm and flavour of personal experience, and they bring us into direct contact with the persons they describe.*"—EDINBURGH REVIEW.

Anderson.—MANDALAY TO MOMIEN; a Narrative of the Two Expeditions to Western China, of 1868 and 1875, under Colonel E. B. Sladen and Colonel Horace Browne. By Dr. ANDERSON, F.R.S.E., Medical and Scientific Officer to the Expeditions. With numerous Maps and Illustrations. 8vo. 21s.

"*A handsome, well-timed, entertaining, and instructive volume.*"—ACADEMY.

"*A pleasant, useful, carefully-written, and important work.*"—ATHENÆUM.

Appleton.—Works by T. G. APPLETON:—
A NILE JOURNAL. Illustrated by EUGENE BENSON. Crown 8vo. 6s.
SYRIAN SUNSHINE. Crown 8vo. 6s.

Arnold.—ESSAYS IN CRITICISM. By MATTHEW ARNOLD. New Edition, Revised and Enlarged. Crown 8vo. 9s.

Atkinson.—AN ART TOUR TO NORTHERN CAPITALS OF EUROPE, including Descriptions of the Towns, the Museums, and other Art Treasures of Copenhagen, Christiania, Stockholm,

Abo, Helsingfors, Wiborg, St. Petersburg, Moscow, and Kief. By J. BEAVINGTON ATKINSON. 8vo. 12s.

"*Although the main purpose of the book is strictly kept in view, and we never forget for long that we are travelling with a student and connoisseur, Mr. Atkinson gives variety to his narrative by glimpses of scenery and brief allusions to history and manners which are always welcome when they occur, and are never wordy or overdone. We have seldom met with a book in which what is principal and what is accessory have been kept in better proportion to each other.*"—SATURDAY REVIEW.

Awdry.—THE STORY OF A FELLOW SOLDIER. By FRANCES AWDRY. With Six Illustrations. Second Edition. Extra fcap. 8vo. 3s. 6d.

"*This is a life of that brave, single-minded, and untiring Christian Soldier, Bishop Patteson, written for the young. It is simply and pleasantly written, and presents a lively picture of the labours, hardships, troubles, and pleasures of earnest Missionary work among the Polynesian Islands.*"—STANDARD.

Baker (Sir Samuel W.)—Works by Sir SAMUEL BAKER, Pacha, M.A., F.R.G.S. :—

ISMAILIA : A Narrative of the Expedition to Central Africa for the Suppression of the Slave Trade, organised by Ismail, Khedive of Egypt. With Portraits, Maps, and fifty full-page Illustrations by ZWECKER and DURAND. New and Cheaper Edition. Crown 8vo. 6s.

"*A book which will be read with very great interest.*"—TIMES. "*Well written and full of remarkable adventures.*"—PALL MALL GAZETTE. "*Adds another thrilling chapter to the history of African adventure.*"—DAILY NEWS. "*Reads more like a romance .... incomparably more entertaining than books of African travel usually are.*"—MORNING POST.

THE ALBERT N'YANZA Great Basin of the Nile, and Exploration of the Nile Sources. Fifth Edition. Maps and Illustrations. Crown 8vo. 6s.

"*Charmingly written;*" says the SPECTATOR, "*full, as might be expected, of incident, and free from that wearisome reiteration of useless facts which is the drawback to almost all books of African travel.*"

THE NILE TRIBUTARIES OF ABYSSINIA, and the Sword Hunters of the Hamran Arabs. With Maps and Illustrations. Sixth Edition. Crown 8vo. 6s.

HISTORY, BIOGRAPHY, TRAVELS, ETC.

The TIMES *says*: *"It adds much to our information respecting Egyptian Abyssinia and the different races that spread over it. It contains, moreover, some notable instances of English daring and enterprising skill; it abounds in animated tales of exploits dear to the heart of the British sportsman; and it will attract even the least studious reader, as the author tells a story well, and can describe nature with uncommon power."*

Bancroft.—THE HISTORY OF THE UNITED STATES OF AMERICA, FROM THE DISCOVERY OF THE CONTINENT. By GEORGE BANCROFT. New and thoroughly Revised Edition. Six Vols. Crown 8vo. 54s.

Barker (Lady).—Works by LADY BARKER :—

A YEAR'S HOUSEKEEPING IN SOUTH AFRICA. With Illustrations. Crown 8vo. 9s.

" We have to thank Lady Barker for a very amusing book, over which we have spent many a delightful hour, and of which we will not take leave without alluding to the ineffably droll illustrations which add so very much to the enjoyment of her clear and sparkling descriptions."—MORNING POST.

Beesly.—STORIES FROM THE HISTORY OF ROME. By Mrs. BEESLY. Extra fcap. 8vo. 2s. 6d.

Blackburne.—BIOGRAPHY OF THE RIGHT HON. FRANCIS BLACKBURNE, Late Lord Chancellor of Ireland. Chiefly in connexion with his Public and Political Career. By his Son, EDWARD BLACKBURNE, Q.C. With Portrait Engraved by JEENS. 8vo. 12s.

Blanford (W. T.)—GEOLOGY AND ZOOLOGY OF ABYSSINIA. By W. T. BLANFORD. 8vo. 21s.

Brimley.—ESSAYS BY THE LATE GEORGE BRIMLEY, M.A. Edited by the Rev. W. G. CLARK, M.A. With Portrait. Cheaper Edition. Fcap. 8vo. 2s. 6d.

Brontë.—CHARLOTTE BRONTË. A Monograph. By T. WEMYSS REID. With Illustrations. Second Edition. Crown 8vo. 6s.

Mr. Reid's little volume, which is based largely on letters, hitherto unpublished, from Charlotte Brontë to her school-fellow and life-long friend, Miss Ellen Nussey, is meant to be a companion, and not a rival, to Mrs. Gaskell's well-known "Life." To speak of the advantage of making biography autobiographical by the liberal use of correspondence has she was by nature (as Mr. Reid puts it) "*a happy and high-spirited girl, and that even to the very last she had the faculty of overcoming her sorrows by means of that steadfast courage which was her most precious possession, and to which she was indebted for her successive victories over trials and disappointments of no ordinary character."*

The book is illustrated by a Portrait of the Rev. Patrick Brontë, several Views of Haworth and its neighbourhood, and a facsimile of one of the most characteristic of Charlotte's letters.

Brooke.—THE RAJA OF SARAWAK : an Account of Sir James Brooke, K.C.B., LL.D.. Given chiefly through Letters or Journals. By GERTRUDE L. JACOB. With Portrait and Maps. Two Vols. 8vo. 25s.

"*They who read Miss Jacob's book—and all should read it: all who are under the delusion that in our time there is no scope for heroism, and no place for romantic adventure, and no place for enterprise and ambition—will see how incident is crowded upon incident, and struggle upon struggle, till in the very abundance of materials that come to her hand the authoress can scarcely stop to give sufficient distinctness to her wonderful narrative.*"—ACADEMY.

Brooke.—RECOLLECTIONS OF THE IRISH CHURCH. By RICHARD S. BROOKE, D.D., late Rector of Wyton, Hunts. Crown 8vo. 4s. 6d.

Bryce.—Works by JAMES BRYCE, D.C.L., Regius Professor of Civil Law, Oxford :—

THE HOLY ROMAN EMPIRE. Sixth Edition, Revised and Enlarged. Crown 8vo. 7s. 6d.

"*It exactly supplies a want : it affords a key to much which men read of in their books as isolated facts, but of which they have hitherto had no connected exposition set before them.*"—SATURDAY REVIEW.

TRANSCAUCASIA AND ARARAT: being Notes of a Vacation Tour in the Autumn of 1876. With an Illustration and Map. Third Edition. Crown 8vo. 9s.

"*Mr. Bryce has written a lively and at the same time an instructive description of the tour he made last year in and about the Caucasus. When so well-informed a jurist travels into regions seldom visited, and even walks up a mountain so rarely scaled as Ararat, he is justified in thinking that the impressions he brings home are worthy of being communicated to the world at large, especially when a terrible war is casting a lurid glow over the countries he has lately surveyed.*"—ATHENÆUM.

Burgoyne. — POLITICAL AND MILITARY EPISODES DURING THE FIRST HALF OF THE REIGN OF GEORGE III. Derived from the Life and Correspondence of the Right Hon. J. Burgoyne, Lieut.-General in his Majesty's Army, and M.P. for Preston. By E. B. DE FONBLANQUE. With Portrait, Heliotype Plate, and Maps. 8vo. 16s.

Burke.—EDMUND BURKE, a Historical Study. By JOHN MORLEY, B.A., Oxon. Crown 8vo. 7s. 6d.

"*The style is terse and incisive, and brilliant with epigram and point. Its sustained power of reasoning, its wide sweep of observation and reflection, its elevated ethical and social tone, stamp it as a work of high excellence.*"—SATURDAY REVIEW.

Burrows.—WORTHIES OF ALL SOULS: Four Centuries of English History. Illustrated from the College Archives. By MONTAGU BURROWS, Chichele Professor of Modern History at Oxford, Fellow of All Souls. 8vo. 14s.

"*A most amusing as well as a most instructive book.*—GUARDIAN.

Campbell.—LOG-LETTERS FROM THE "CHALLENGER." By LORD GEORGE CAMPBELL. With Map. Fifth and cheaper Edition. Crown 8vo. 6s.

"*A delightful book, which we heartily commend to the general reader.*" —SATURDAY REVIEW.

"*We do not hesitate to say that anything so fresh, so picturesque, so generally delightful, as these log-letters has not appeared among books of travel for a long time.*"—EXAMINER.

"*A more lively and amusing record of travel we have not had the fortune to read for some time. The whole book is pervaded by a spirit of life, animation, and fun.*"—STANDARD.

Campbell.—MY CIRCULAR NOTES: Extracts from Journals; Letters sent Home; Geological and other Notes, written while Travelling Westwards round the World, from July 6th, 1874, to July 6th, 1875. By J. F. CAMPBELL, Author of "Frost and Fire." 2 vols. Crown 8vo. 25s.

"*We have read numbers of books of travel, but we can call to mind few that have given us more genuine pleasure than this. A more agreeable style of narrative than his it is hardly possible to conceive. We seem to be accompanying him in his trip round the world, so life-like is his description of the countries he visited.*"—LAND AND WATER.

Campbell.—TURKS AND GREEKS. Notes of a recent Excursion. By the Hon. DUDLEY CAMPBELL, M.A. With Coloured Map. Crown 8vo. 3s. 6d.

Carstares.—WILLIAM CARSTARES: a Character and Career of the Revolutionary Epoch (1649—1715). By ROBERT STORY, Minister of Rosneath. 8vo. 12s.

Chatterton : A BIOGRAPHICAL STUDY. By DANIEL WILSON, LL.D., Professor of History and English Literature in University College, Toronto. Crown 8vo. 6s. 6d.

The EXAMINER *thinks this "the most complete and the purest biography of the poet which has yet appeared."*

Chatterton : A STORY OF THE YEAR 1770. By Professor MASSON, LL.D. Crown 8vo. 5s.

Combe.—THE LIFE OF GEORGE COMBE, Author of "The Constitution of Man." By CHARLES GIBBON. With Three Portraits engraved by JEENS. Two Vols. 8vo. 32s.

"A graphic and interesting account of the long life and indefatigable labours of a very remarkable man."—SCOTSMAN.

Cooper.—ATHENÆ CANTABRIGIENSES. By CHARLES HENRY COOPER, F.S.A., and THOMPSON COOPER, F.S.A. Vol. I. 8vo., 1500—85, 18s.; Vol. II., 1586—1609, 18s.

Correggio.—ANTONIO ALLEGRI DA CORREGGIO. From the German of Dr. JULIUS MEYER, Director of the Royal Gallery, Berlin. Edited, with an Introduction, by Mrs. HEATON. Containing Twenty Woodbury-type Illustrations. Royal 8vo. Cloth elegant. 31s. 6d.

" The best and most readable biography of the master at present to be found in the English language."—ACADEMY. *" By its pictures alone the book forms a worthy tribute to the painter's genius."*—PALL MALL GAZETTE.

Cox (G. V.)—RECOLLECTIONS OF OXFORD. By G. V. Cox, M.A., New College, late Esquire Bedel and Coroner in the University of Oxford. *Cheaper Edition.* Crown 8vo. 6s.

" An amusing farrago of anecdote, and will pleasantly recall in many a country parsonage the memory of youthful days."—TIMES.

" Daily News."—THE DAILY NEWS' CORRESPONDENCE of the War between Germany and France, 1870—1. Edited with Notes and Comments. New Edition. Complete in One Volume. With Maps and Plans. Crown 8vo. 6s.

THE DAILY NEWS' CORRESPONDENCE of the War between Russia and Turkey, to the fall of Kars. Including the letters of Mr. Archibald Forbes, Mr. J. E. McGahan, and other Special Correspondents in Europe and Asia. Second Edition, enlarged. Crown 8vo. 10s. 6d.

FROM THE FALL OF KARS TO THE CONCLUSION OF PEACE. Crown 8vo. 10s. 6d.

HISTORY, BIOGRAPHY, TRAVELS, ETC.

Davidson.—THE LIFE OF A SCOTTISH PROBATIONER; being a Memoir of Thomas Davidson, with his Poems and Letters. By JAMES BROWN, Minister of St. James's Street Church, Paisley. Second Edition, revised and enlarged, with Portrait. Crown 8vo. 7s. 6d.

Deas.—THE RIVER CLYDE. An Historical Description of the Rise and Progress of the Harbour of Glasgow, and of the Improvement of the River from Glasgow to Port Glasgow. By J. DEAS, M. Inst. C.E. 8vo. 10s. 6d.

Denison.—A HISTORY OF CAVALRY FROM THE EARLIEST TIMES. With Lessons for the Future. By Lieut.-Col. GEORGE DENISON, Commanding the Governor-General's Body Guard, Canada, Author of "Modern Cavalry." With Maps and Plans. 8vo. 18s.

Dilke.—GREATER BRITAIN. A Record of Travel in English-speaking Countries during 1866-7. (America, Australia, India.) By Sir CHARLES WENTWORTH DILKE, M.P. Sixth Edition. Crown 8vo. 6s.

"*Many of the subjects discussed in these pages,*" *says the* DAILY NEWS, "*are of the widest interest, and such as no man who cares for the future of his race and of the world can afford to treat with indifference.*"

Doyle.—HISTORY OF AMERICA. By J. A. DOYLE. With Maps. 18mo. 4s. 6d.

"*Mr. Doyle's style is clear and simple, his facts are accurately stated, and his book is meritoriously free from prejudice on questions where partisanship runs high amongst us.*"—SATURDAY REVIEW.

Drummond of Hawthornden: THE STORY OF HIS LIFE AND WRITINGS. By PROFESSOR MASSON. With Portrait and Vignette engraved by C. H. JEENS. Crown 8vo. 10s. 6d.

"*Around his hero, Professor Masson groups national and individual episodes and sketches of character, which are of the greatest interest, and which add to the value of a biographical work which we warmly recommend to the lovers of thoroughly healthy books.*"—NOTES AND QUERIES.

Duff.—NOTES OF AN INDIAN JOURNEY. By M. E. GRANT-DUFF, M.P., late Under Secretary of State for India. With Map. 8vo. 10s. 6d.

"*These notes are full of pleasant remarks and illustrations, borrowed from every kind of source.*"—SATURDAY REVIEW.

Eadie.—LIFE OF JOHN EADIE, D.D., LL.D. By JAMES BROWN, D.D., Author of "The Life of a Scottish Probationer." With Portrait. Second Edition. Crown 8vo. 7s. 6d.

"*An ably written and characteristic biography.*"—TIMES.

Elliott.—LIFE OF HENRY VENN ELLIOTT, of Brighton. By JOSIAH BATEMAN, M.A., Author of "Life of Daniel Wilson, Bishop of Calcutta," &c. With Portrait, engraved by JEENS. Extra fcap. 8vo. Third and Cheaper Edition, with Appendix. 6s.

Elze.—ESSAYS ON SHAKESPEARE. By Dr. KARL ELZE. Translated with the Author's sanction by L. DORA SCHMITZ. 8vo. 12s.

"*A more desirable contribution to criticism has not recently been made.*"—ATHENÆUM.

English Men of Letters. Edited by JOHN MORLEY. A Series of Short Books to tell people what is best worth knowing as to the Life, Character, and Works of some of the great English Writers. In crown 8vo. Price 2s. 6d. each.

I. DR. JOHNSON. By LESLIE STEPHEN.

"*The new series opens well with Mr. Leslie Stephen's sketch of Dr. Johnson. It could hardly have been done better; and it will convey to the readers for whom it is intended a juster estimate of Johnson than either of the two essays of Lord Macaulay.*"—PALL MALL GAZETTE.

II. SIR WALTER SCOTT. By R. H. HUTTON.

"*The tone of the volume is excellent throughout.*"—ATHENÆUM.

"*We could not wish for a more suggestive introduction to Scott and his poems and novels.*"—EXAMINER.

III. GIBBON. By J. C. MORISON.

"*As a clear, thoughtful, and attractive record of the life and works of the greatest among the world's historians, it deserves the highest praise.*"—EXAMINER.

SHELLEY. By J. A. SYMONDS. [*In the press.*

HUME. By Professor HUXLEY. [*In the press.*

GOLDSMITH. By WILLIAM BLACK. [*In the press.*

Others in preparation.

Eton College, History of. By H. C. MAXWELL LYTE, M.A. With numerous Illustrations by Professor DELAMOTTE, Coloured Plates, and a Steel Portrait of the Founder, engraved by C. H. JEENS. New and cheaper Issue, with Corrections. Medium 8vo. Cloth elegant. 21s.

"*Hitherto no account of the College, with all its associations, has appeared which can compare either in completeness or in interest with this. . . . It is indeed a book worthy of the ancient renown of King Henry's College.*"—DAILY NEWS.

"*We are at length presented with a work on England's greatest public school, worthy of the subject of which it treats. . . . A really valuable and authentic history of Eton College.*"—GUARDIAN.

HISTORY, BIOGRAPHY, TRAVELS, ETC.

European History, Narrated in a Series of Historical Selections from the best Authorities. Edited and arranged by E. M. SEWELL and C. M. YONGE. First Series, crown 8vo. 6s.; Second Series, 1088–1228, crown 8vo. 6s. Third Edition.

"*We know of scarcely anything,*" says the GUARDIAN, "*of this volume, which is so likely to raise to a higher level the average standard of English education.*"

Faraday.—MICHAEL FARADAY. By J. H. GLADSTONE, Ph.D., F.R.S. Second Edition, with Portrait engraved by JEENS from a photograph by J. WATKINS. Crown 8vo. 4s. 6d. PORTRAIT. Artist's Proof. 5s.

CONTENTS:—*I. The Story of his Life. II. Study of his Character. III. Fruits of his Experience. IV. His Method of Writing. V. The Value of his Discoveries.*—*Supplementary Portraits. Appendices:*—*List of Honorary Fellowships, etc.*

Forbes.—LIFE AND LETTERS OF JAMES DAVID FORBES, F.R.S., late Principal of the United College in the University of St. Andrews. By J. C. SHAIRP, LL.D., Principal of the United College in the University of St. Andrews; P. G. TAIT, M.A., Professor of Natural Philosophy in the University of Edinburgh; and A. ADAMS-REILLY, F.R.G.S. 8vo. with Portraits, Map, and Illustrations, 16s.

"*Not only a biography that all should read, but a scientific treatise, without which the shelves of no physicist's library can be deemed complete.*"—STANDARD.

Freeman.—Works by EDWARD A. FREEMAN, D.C.L., LL.D.:—
HISTORICAL ESSAYS. Third Edition. 8vo. 10s. 6d.

CONTENTS:—*I.* "*The Mythical and Romantic Elements in Early English History;*" *II.* "*The Continuity of English History;*" *III.* "*The Relations between the Crowns of England and Scotland;*" *IV.* "*St. Thomas of Canterbury and his Biographers;*" *V.* "*The Reign of Edward the Third;*" *VI.* "*The Holy Roman Empire;*" *VII.* "*The Franks and the Gauls;*" *VIII.* "*The Early Sieges of Paris;*" *IX.* "*Frederick the First, King of Italy;*" *X.* "*The Emperor Frederick the Second;*" *XI.* "*Charles the Bold;*" *XII.* "*Presidential Government.*"

A SECOND SERIES OF HISTORICAL ESSAYS. 8vo. 10s. 6d.

The principal Essays are:—"*Ancient Greece and Mediæval Italy:*" "*Mr. Gladstone's Homer and the Homeric Ages:*" "*The Historians of Athens:*" "*The Athenian Democracy:*" "*Alexander the Great:*" "*Greece during the Macedonian Period:*" "*Mommsen's History of Rome:*" "*Lucius Cornelius Sulla:*" "*The Flavian Cæsars.*"

COMPARATIVE POLITICS.—Lectures at the Royal Institution. To which is added the "Unity of History," the Rede Lecture at Cambridge, 1872. 8vo. 14s.

Freeman—*continued.*

THE HISTORY AND CONQUESTS OF THE SARACENS. Six Lectures. Third Edition, with New Preface. Crown 8vo. 3s. 6d.

"*Mr. Freeman opportunely reprints his erudite and valuable lectures.*"—DAILY TELEGRAPH.

HISTORICAL AND ARCHITECTURAL SKETCHES: chiefly Italian. With Illustrations by the Author. Crown 8vo. 10s. 6d.

"*Mr. Freeman may here be said to give us a series of 'notes on the spot' in illustration of the intimate relations of History and Architecture, and this is done in so masterly a manner—there is so much freshness, so much knowledge so admirably condensed, that we are almost tempted to say that we prefer these sketches to his more elaborate studies.*"—NONCONFORMIST.

HISTORY OF FEDERAL GOVERNMENT, from the Foundation of the Achaian League to the Disruption of the United States. Vol. I. General Introduction. History of the Greek Federations. 8vo. 21s.

OLD ENGLISH HISTORY. With *Five Coloured Maps.* Fourth Edition. Extra fcap. 8vo., half-bound. 6s.

"*The book indeed is full of instruction and interest to students of all ages, and he must be a well-informed man indeed who will not rise from its perusal with clearer and more accurate ideas of a too much neglected portion of English history.*"—SPECTATOR.

HISTORY OF THE CATHEDRAL CHURCH OF WELLS, as illustrating the History of the Cathedral Churches of the Old Foundation. Crown 8vo. 3s. 6d.

"*The history assumes in Mr. Freeman's hands a significance, and, we may add, a practical value as suggestive of what a cathedral ought to be, which make it well worthy of mention.*"—SPECTATOR.

THE GROWTH OF THE ENGLISH CONSTITUTION FROM THE EARLIEST TIMES. Crown 8vo. 5s. Third Edition, revised.

GENERAL SKETCH OF EUROPEAN HISTORY. Being Vol. I. of a Historical Course for Schools edited by E. A. FREEMAN. New Edition, enlarged with Maps, Chronological Table, Index, &c. 18mo. 3s. 6d.

"*It supplies the great want of a good foundation for historical teaching. The scheme is an excellent one, and this instalment has been accepted in a way that promises much for the volumes that are yet to appear.*"—EDUCATIONAL TIMES.

THE OTTOMAN POWER IN EUROPE: its Nature, its Growth, and its Decline. With Three Coloured Maps. Crown 8vo. 7s. 6d.

HISTORY, BIOGRAPHY, TRAVELS, ETC.

Galileo.—THE PRIVATE LIFE OF GALILEO. Compiled principally from his Correspondence and that of his eldest daughter, Sister Maria Celeste, Nun in the Franciscan Convent of S. Matthew in Arcetri. With Portrait. Crown 8vo. 7s. 6d.

Geddes.—THE PROBLEM OF THE HOMERIC POEMS. By W. D. GEDDES, LL.D., Professor of Greek in the University of Aberdeen. 8vo. 14s.

Gladstone—Works by the Right Hon. W. E. GLADSTONE, M.P. :—

JUVENTUS MUNDI. The Gods and Men of the Heroic Age. Crown 8vo. cloth. With Map. 10s. 6d. Second Edition.

"*Seldom,*" says the ATHENÆUM, "*out of the great poems themselves, have these Divinities looked so majestic and respectable. To read these brilliant details is like standing on the Olympian threshold and gazing at the ineffable brightness within.*"

HOMERIC SYNCHRONISM. An inquiry into the Time and Place of Homer. Crown 8vo. 6s.

"*It is impossible not to admire the immense range of thought and inquiry which the author has displayed.*"—BRITISH QUARTERLY REVIEW.

Goethe and Mendelssohn (1821—1831). Translated from the German of Dr. KARL MENDELSSOHN, Son of the Composer, by M. E. VON GLEHN. From the Private Diaries and Home Letters of Mendelssohn, with Poems and Letters of Goethe never before printed. Also with two New and Original Portraits, Facsimiles, and Appendix of Twenty Letters hitherto unpublished. Crown 8vo. 5s. Second Edition, enlarged.

"*. . . Every page is full of interest, not merely to the musician, but to the general reader. The book is a very charming one, on a topic of deep and lasting interest.*"—STANDARD.

Goldsmid.—TELEGRAPH AND TRAVEL. A Narrative of the Formation and Development of Telegraphic Communication between England and India, under the orders of Her Majesty's Government, with incidental Notices of the Countries traversed by the Lines. By Colonel Sir FREDERIC GOLDSMID, C.B., K.C.S.I., late Director of the Government Indo-European Telegraph. With numerous Illustrations and Maps. 8vo. 21s.

"*The merit of the work is a total absence of exaggeration, which does not, however, preclude a vividness and vigour of style not always characteristic of similar narratives.*"—STANDARD.

Gordon.—LAST LETTERS FROM EGYPT, to which are added Letters from the Cape. By LADY DUFF GORDON. With a Memoir by her Daughter, Mrs. Ross, and Portrait engraved by JEENS. Second Edition. Crown 8vo. 9s.

"*The intending tourist who wishes to acquaint himself with the country he is about to visit, stands embarrassed amidst the riches presented for his choice, and in the end probably rests contented with the sober usefulness of Murray. He will not, however, if he is well advised, grudge a place in his portmanteau to this book.*"—TIMES.

Gray.—CHINA. A History of the Laws, Manners, and Customs of the People. By the VENERABLE JOHN HENRY GRAY. LL.D., Archdeacon of Hong Kong, formerly H.B.M. Consular Chaplain at Canton. Edited by W. Gow Gregor. With 150 Full-page Illustrations, being Facsimiles of Drawings by a Chinese Artist. 2 Vols. Demy 8vo. 32s.

"*Its pages contain the most truthful and vivid picture of Chinese life which has ever been published.*"—ATHENÆUM.

"*The only elaborate and valuable book we have had for many years treating generally of the people of the Celestial Empire.*"—ACADEMY.

Green.—Works by JOHN RICHARD GREEN :—

HISTORY OF THE ENGLISH PEOPLE. Vol. I.—Early England—Foreign Kings—The Charter—The Parliament. With 8 Coloured Maps. 8vo. 16s. Vol. II.—The Monarchy, 1461—1540; the Restoration, 1540—1603. 8vo. 16s.

[*To be completed in 5 Vols.*

"*Mr. Green has done a work which probably no one but himself could have done. He has read and assimilated the results of all the labours of students during the last half century in the field of English history, and has given them a fresh meaning by his own independent study. He has fused together by the force of sympathetic imagination all that he has so collected, and has given us a vivid and forcible sketch of the march of English history. His book, both in its aims and its accomplishments, rises far beyond any of a similar kind, and it will give the colouring to the popular view to English history for some time to come.*"—EXAMINER.

A SHORT HISTORY OF THE ENGLISH PEOPLE. With Coloured Maps, Genealogical Tables, and Chronological Annals. Crown 8vo. 8s. 6d. Fifty-fifth Thousand.

"*To say that Mr. Green's book is better than those which have preceded it, would be to convey a very inadequate impression of its merits. It stands alone as the one general history of the country, for the sake of which all others, if young and old are wise, will be speedily and surely set aside.*"

STRAY STUDIES FROM ENGLAND AND ITALY. Crown 8vo. 8s. 6d. Containing : Lambeth and the Archbishops—The Florence of Dante—Venice and Rome—Early History of Oxford—The District Visitor—Capri—Hotels in the Clouds—Sketches in Sunshine, &c.

"*One and all of the papers are eminently readable.*"—ATHENÆUM.

HISTORY, BIOGRAPHY, TRAVELS, ETC.

Hamerton.—Works by P. G. HAMERTON:—

THE INTELLECTUAL LIFE. With a Portrait of Leonardo da Vinci, etched by LEOPOLD FLAMENG. Second Edition. Crown 10s. 6d. 8vo.

"*We have read the whole book with great pleasure, and we can recommend it strongly to all who can appreciate grave reflections on a very important subject, excellently illustrated from the resources of a mind stored with much reading and much keen observation of real life.*"—SATURDAY REVIEW.

THOUGHTS ABOUT ART. New Edition, revised, with an Introduction. Crown 8vo. 8s. 6d.

"*A manual of sound and thorough criticism on art.*"—STANDARD.
"*The book is full of thought, and worthy of attentive consideration.*"—DAILY NEWS.

Hill.—WHAT WE SAW IN AUSTRALIA. By ROSAMOND and FLORENCE HILL. Crown 8vo. 10s. 6d.

"*May be recommended as an interesting and truthful picture of the condition of those lands which are so distant and yet so much like home.*"—SATURDAY REVIEW.

Hodgson.—MEMOIR OF REV. FRANCIS HODGSON, B.D., Scholar, Poet, and Divine. By his Son, the Rev. JAMES T. HODGSON, M.A. With Portrait engraved by JEENS. Crown 8vo. [*Immediately.*

Hole.—A GENEALOGICAL STEMMA OF THE KINGS OF ENGLAND AND FRANCE. By the Rev. C. HOLE, M.A., Trinity College, Cambridge. On Sheet, 1s.

A BRIEF BIOGRAPHICAL DICTIONARY. Compiled and Arranged by the Rev. CHARLES HOLE, M.A. Second Edition. 18mo. 4s. 6d.

Hooker and Ball.—MAROCCO: Journal of a Tour in. By Sir JOSEPH D. HOOKER, K.C.S.I., C.B., P.R.S., &c., and JOHN BALL, F.R.S. With Illustrations and Map. 8vo. [*Immediately.*

Hozier (H. M.)—Works by CAPTAIN HENRY M. HOZIER, late Assistant Military Secretary to Lord Napier of Magdala:—

THE SEVEN WEEKS' WAR; Its Antecedents and Incidents. *New and Cheaper Edition.* With New Preface, Maps, and Plans. Crown 8vo. 6s.

"*All that Mr. Hozier saw of the great events of the war—and he saw a large share of them—he describes in clear and vivid language.*"—SATURDAY REVIEW.

Hozier (H. M.)—*continued.*
THE INVASIONS OF ENGLAND : a History of the Past, with Lessons for the Future. Two Vols. 8vo. 28s.
The PALL MALL GAZETTE says :—"*As to all invasions executed, or deliberately projected but not carried out, from the landing of Julius Cæsar to the raising of the Boulogne camp, Captain Hozier furnishes copious and most interesting particulars.*"

Hübner.—A RAMBLE ROUND THE WORLD IN 1871. By M. LE BARON HÜBNER, formerly Ambassador and Minister. Translated by LADY HERBERT. New and Cheaper Edition. With numerous Illustrations. Crown 8vo. 6s.
"*It is difficult to do ample justice to this pleasant narrative of travel . . . . it does not contain a single dull paragraph.*"—MORNING POST.

Hughes.—Works by THOMAS HUGHES, Q.C., Author of "Tom Brown's School Days."
MEMOIR OF A BROTHER. With Portrait of GEORGE HUGHES, after WATTS. Engraved by JEENS. Crown 8vo. 5s. Sixth Edition.
"*The boy who can read this book without deriving from it some additional impulse towards honourable, manly, and independent conduct, has no good stuff in him.*"—DAILY NEWS.
ALFRED THE GREAT. New Edition. Crown 8vo. 6s.

Hunt.—HISTORY OF ITALY. By the Rev. W. HUNT, M.A. Being the Fourth Volume of the Historical Course for Schools. Edited by EDWARD A. FREEMAN, D.C.L. 18mo. 3s.
"*Mr. Hunt gives us a most compact but very readable little book, containing in small compass a very complete outline of a complicated and perplexing subject. It is a book which may be safely recommended to others besides schoolboys.*"—JOHN BULL.

Irving.—THE ANNALS OF OUR TIME. A Diurnal of Events, Social and Political, Home and Foreign, from the Accession of Queen Victoria to the Peace of Versailles. By JOSEPH IRVING. *Fourth Edition.* 8vo. half-bound. 16s.
ANNALS OF OUR TIME. Supplement. From Feb. 28, 1871, to March 19, 1874. 8vo. 4s. 6d.
"*We have before us a trusty and ready guide to the events of the past thirty years, available equally for the statesman, the politician, the public writer, and the general reader.*"—TIMES.

James.—Works by HENRY JAMES, Jun. FRENCH POETS AND NOVELISTS. Crown 8vo. 8s. 6d.
CONTENTS :—*Alfred de Musset ; Théophile Gautier ; Baudelaire ; Honoré de Balzac ; George Sand ; The Two Ampères ; Turgenieff, &c.*
THE EUROPEANS. A Novel. Two Vols. Crown 8vo. 21s.

Johnson's Lives of the Poets.—The Six Chief Lives—Milton, Dryden, Swift, Addison, Pope, Gray. With Macaulay's "Life of Johnson." Edited, with Preface, by MATTHEW ARNOLD. Crown 8vo. 6s.

Killen.—ECCLESIASTICAL HISTORY OF IRELAND, from the Earliest Date to the Present Time. By W. D. KILLEN, D.D., President of Assembly's College, Belfast, and Professor of Ecclesiastical History. Two Vols. 8vo. 25s.
"*Those who have the leisure will do well to read these two volumes. They are full of interest, and are the result of great research. . . . We have no hesitation in recommending the work to all who wish to improve their acquaintance with Irish history.*"—SPECTATOR.

Kingsley (Charles).—Works by the Rev. CHARLES KINGSLEY, M.A., Rector of Eversley and Canon of Westminster. (For other Works by the same Author, *see* THEOLOGICAL and BELLES LETTRES Catalogues.)
ON THE ANCIEN RÉGIME as it existed on the Continent before the FRENCH REVOLUTION. Three Lectures delivered at the Royal Institution. Crown 8vo. 6s.
AT LAST: A CHRISTMAS in the WEST INDIES. With nearly Fifty Illustrations. Fifth Edition. Crown 8vo. 6s.
Mr. Kingsley's dream of forty years was at last fulfilled, when he started on a Christmas expedition to the West Indies, for the purpose of becoming personally acquainted with the scenes which he has so vividly described in "Westward Ho!" These two volumes are the journal of his voyage. Records of natural history, sketches of tropical landscape, chapters on education, views of society, all find their place. "We can only say that Mr. Kingsley's account of a 'Christmas in the West Indies' is in every way worthy to be classed among his happiest productions."—STANDARD.
THE ROMAN AND THE TEUTON. A Series of Lectures delivered before the University of Cambridge. New and Cheaper Edition, with Preface by Professor MAX MULLER. Crown 8vo. 6s.
PLAYS AND PURITANS, and other Historical Essays. With Portrait of Sir WALTER RALEIGH. Second Edition. Crown 8vo. 5s.
In addition to the Essay mentioned in the title, this volume contains other two—one on "Sir Walter Raleigh and his Time," and one on Froude's "History of England."

Kingsley (Henry).—TALES OF OLD TRAVEL. Re-narrated by HENRY KINGSLEY, F.R.G.S. With *Eight Illustrations* by HUARD. Fifth Edition. Crown 8vo. 5s.
"*We know no better book for those who want knowledge or seek to refresh it. As for the 'sensational,' most novels are tame compared with these narratives.*"—ATHENÆUM.

Lang.—CYPRUS: Its History, its Present Resources and Future Prospects. By R. HAMILTON LANG, late H.M. Consul for the Island of Cyprus. With Two Illustrations and Four Maps. 8vo. 14s.

Laocoon.—Translated from the Text of Lessing, with Preface and Notes by the Right Hon. SIR ROBERT J. PHILLIMORE, D.C.L. With Photographs. 8vo. 12s.

Leonardo da Vinci and his Works.—Consisting of a Life of Leonardo Da Vinci, by MRS. CHARLES W. HEATON, Author of "Albrecht Dürer of Nürnberg," &c., an Essay on his Scientific and Literary Works by CHARLES CHRISTOPHER BLACK, M.A., and an account of his more important Paintings and Drawings. Illustrated with Permanent Photographs. Royal 8vo. cloth, extra gilt. 31s. 6d.

"*A beautiful volume, both without and within. Messrs. Macmillan are conspicuous among publishers for the choice binding and printing of their books, and this is got up in their best style. . . . No English publication that we know of has so thoroughly and attractively collected together all that is known of Leonardo.*"—TIMES.

Liechtenstein.—HOLLAND HOUSE. By Princess MARIE LIECHTENSTEIN. With Five Steel Engravings by C. H. JEENS, after Paintings by WATTS and other celebrated Artists, and numerous Illustrations drawn by Professor P. H. DELAMOTTE, and engraved on Wood by J. D. COOPER, W. PALMER, and JEWITT & Co. Third and Cheaper Edition. Medium 8vo. cloth elegant. 16s.

Also, an Edition containing, in addition to the above, about 40 Illustrations by the Woodbury-type process, and India Proofs of the Steel Engravings. Two vols. medium 4to. half morocco elegant. 4l. 4s.

"*When every strictly just exception shall have been taken, she may be conscientiously congratulated by the most scrupulous critic on the production of a useful, agreeable, beautifully-illustrated, and attractive book.*"—TIMES. "*It would take up more room than we can spare to enumerate all the interesting suggestions and notes which are to be found in these volumes. . . . . The woodcuts are admirable, and some of the autographs are very interesting.*"—PALL MALL GAZETTE.

Lloyd.—THE AGE OF PERICLES. A History of the Arts and Politics of Greece from the Persian to the Peloponnesian War. By W. WATKISS LLOYD. Two Vols. 8vo. 21s.

"*No such account of Greek art of the best period has yet been brought together in an English work. . . . . Mr. Lloyd has produced a book of unusual excellence and interest.*"—PALL MALL GAZETTE.

Macarthur.—HISTORY OF SCOTLAND, By MARGARET MACARTHUR. Being the Third Volume of the Historical Course for Schools, Edited by EDWARD A. FREEMAN, D.C.L. Second Edition. 18mo. 2s.

"*It is an excellent summary, unimpeachable as to facts, and putting them in the clearest and most impartial light attainable.*"—GUARDIAN.
"*No previous History of Scotland of the same bulk is anything like so trustworthy, or deserves to be so extensively used as a text-book.*"—GLOBE.

Macmillan (Rev. Hugh).—For other Works by same Author, see THEOLOGICAL and SCIENTIFIC CATALOGUES.

HOLIDAYS ON HIGH LANDS; or, Rambles and Incidents in search of Alpine Plants. Second Edition, revised and enlarged. Globe 8vo. cloth. 6s.

"*Botanical knowledge is blended with a love of nature, a pious enthusiasm, and a rich felicity of diction not to be met with in any works of kindred character, if we except those of Hugh Miller.*"—TELEGRAPH. "*Mr. Macmillan's glowing pictures of Scandinavian scenery.*"—SATURDAY REVIEW.

Macready.—MACREADY'S REMINISCENCES AND SELECTIONS FROM HIS DIARIES AND LETTERS. Edited by Sir F. POLLOCK, Bart., one of his Executors. With Four Portraits engraved by JEENS. New and Cheaper Edition. Crown 8vo. 7s. 6d.

"*As a careful and for the most part just estimate of the stage during a very brilliant period, the attraction of these volumes can scarcely be surpassed. . . . Readers who have no special interest in theatrical matters, but enjoy miscellaneous gossip, will be allured from page to page, attracted by familiar names and by observations upon popular actors and authors.*"—SPECTATOR.

Mahaffy.—Works by the Rev. J. P. MAHAFFY, M.A., Fellow of Trinity College, Dublin :—

SOCIAL LIFE IN GREECE FROM HOMER TO MENANDER. Third Edition, revised and enlarged, with a new chapter on Greek Art. Crown 8vo. 9s.

"*It should be in the hands of all who desire thoroughly to understand and to enjoy Greek literature, and to get an intelligent idea of the old Greek life, political, social, and religious.*"—GUARDIAN.

RAMBLES AND STUDIES IN GREECE. With Illustrations. Crown 8vo. 10s. 6d. New and enlarged Edition, with Map and Illustrations

"*A singularly instructive and agreeable volume.*"—ATHENÆUM.

"Maori."—SPORT AND WORK ON THE NEPAUL FRONTIER; or, Twelve Years' Sporting Reminiscences of an Indigo Planter. By "MAORI." With Map and Illustrations. 8vo.
[*Immediately.*

Margary.—THE JOURNEY OF AUGUSTUS RAYMOND MARGARY FROM SHANGHAE TO BHAMO AND BACK TO MANWYNE. From his Journals and Letters, with a brief

Biographical Preface, a concluding chapter by Sir RUTHERFORD ALCOCK, K.C.B., and a Steel Portrait engraved by JEENS, and Map. 8vo. 10s. 6d.

"*There is a manliness, a cheerful spirit, an inherent vigour which was never overcome by sickness or debility, a tact which conquered the prejudices of a strange and suspicious population, a quiet self-reliance, always combined with deep religious feeling, unalloyed by either priggishness, cant, or superstition, that ought to commend this volume to readers sitting quietly at home who feel any pride in the high estimation accorded to men of their race at Yarkand or at Khiva, in the heart of Africa, or on the shores of Lake Seri-kul.*"—SATURDAY REVIEW.

Martin.—THE HISTORY OF LLOYD'S, AND OF MARINE INSURANCE IN GREAT BRITAIN. With an Appendix containing Statistics relating to Marine Insurance. By FREDERICK MARTIN, Author of "The Statesman's Year Book." 8vo. 14s.

"*We have in the editor of the 'Statesman's Year Book' an industrious and conscientious guide, and we can certify that in his 'History of Lloyd's' he has produced a work of more than passing interest.*"—TIMES.

Martineau.—BIOGRAPHICAL SKETCHES, 1852—1875. By HARRIET MARTINEAU. With Additional Sketches, and Autobiographical Sketch. Fifth Edition. Crown 8vo. 6s.

"*Miss Martineau's large literary powers and her fine intellectual training make these little sketches more instructive, and constitute them more genuinely works of art, than many more ambitious and diffuse biographies.*"—FORTNIGHTLY REVIEW.

Masson (David).—For other Works by same Author, *see* PHILOSOPHICAL and BELLES LETTRES CATALOGUES.

CHATTERTON: A Story of the Year 1770. By DAVID MASSON, LL.D., Professor of Rhetoric and English Literature in the University of Edinburgh. Crown 8vo. 5s.

"*One of this popular writer's best essays on the English poets.*"—STANDARD.

THE THREE DEVILS: Luther's, Goethe's, and Milton's; and other Essays. Crown 8vo. 5s.

WORDSWORTH, SHELLEY, AND KEATS; and other Essays. Crown 8vo. 5s.

Maurice.—THE FRIENDSHIP OF BOOKS; AND OTHER LECTURES. By the REV. F. D. MAURICE. Edited with Preface, by THOMAS HUGHES, Q.C. Crown 8vo. 10s. 6d.

"*The high, pure, sympathetic, and truly charitable nature of Mr. Maurice is delightfully visible throughout these lectures, which are excellently adapted to spread a love of literature amongst the people.*"—DAILY NEWS.

HISTORY, BIOGRAPHY, TRAVELS, ETC. 19

Mayor (J. E. B.)—WORKS edited by JOHN E. B. MAYOR, M.A., Kennedy Professor of Latin at Cambridge :—
CAMBRIDGE IN THE SEVENTEENTH CENTURY. Part II. Autobiography of Matthew Robinson. Fcap. 8vo. 5s. 6d.
LIFE OF BISHOP BEDELL. By his SON. Fcap. 8vo. 3s. 6d.

Melbourne.—MEMOIRS OF THE RT. HON. WILLIAM, SECOND VISCOUNT MELBOURNE. By W. M. TORRENS, M.P. With Portrait after Sir. T. Lawrence. Second Edition. 2 Vols. 8vo. 32s.

"*As might be expected, he has produced a book which will command and reward attention. It contains a great deal of valuable matter and a great deal of animated, elegant writing.*"—QUARTERLY REVIEW.

Mendelssohn.—LETTERS AND RECOLLECTIONS. By FERDINAND HILLER. Translated by M. E. VON GLEHN. With Portrait from a Drawing by KARL MÜLLER, never before published. Second Edition. Crown 8vo. 7s. 6d.

"*This is a very interesting addition to our knowledge of the great German composer. It reveals him to us under a new light, as the warm-hearted comrade, the musician whose soul was in his work, and the home-loving, domestic man.*"—STANDARD.

Merewether.—BY SEA AND BY LAND. Being a Trip through Egypt, India, Ceylon, Australia, New Zealand, and America—all Round the World. By HENRY ALWORTH MEREWETHER, one of Her Majesty's Counsel. Crown 8vo. 8s. 6d.

Michael Angelo Buonarotti; Sculptor, Painter, Architect. The Story of his Life and Labours. By C. C. BLACK, M.A. Illustrated by 20 Permanent Photographs Royal 8vo. cloth elegant, 31s. 6d.

"*The story of Michael Angelo's life remains interesting whatever be the manner of telling it, and supported as it is by this beautiful series of photographs, the volume must take rank among the most splendid of Christmas books, fitted to serve and to outlive the season.*"—PALL MALL GAZETTE.

Michelet.—A SUMMARY OF MODERN HISTORY. Translated from the French of M. MICHELET, and continued to the present time by M. C. M. SIMPSON. Globe 8vo. 4s. 6d.

"*We are glad to see one of the ablest and most useful summaries of European history put into the hands of English readers. The translation is excellent.*"—STANDARD.

Milton.—LIFE OF JOHN MILTON. Narrated in connection with the Political, Ecclesiastical, and Literary History of his Time. By DAVID MASSON, M.A., LL.D., Professor of Rhetoric and English Literature in the University of Edinburgh. With Portraits. Vol. I. 18s. Vol. II., 1638—1643. 8vo. 16s. Vol. III. 1643—1649. 8vo. 18s. Vols. IV. and V. 1649—1660. 32s.

This work is not only a Biography, but also a continuous Political, Ecclesiastical, and Literary History of England through Milton's whole time.

Mitford (A. B.)—TALES OF OLD JAPAN. By A. B. MITFORD, Second Secretary to the British Legation in Japan. With upwards of 30 Illustrations, drawn and cut on Wood by Japanese Artists. New and Cheaper Edition. Crown 8vo. 6s.

"*These very original volumes will always be interesting as memorials of a most exceptional society, while regarded simply as tales, they are sparkling, sensational, and dramatic, and the originality of their idea and the quaintness of their language give them a most captivating piquancy. The illustrations are extremely interesting, and for the curious in such matters have a special and particular value.*"—PALL MALL GAZETTE.

Monteiro.—ANGOLA AND THE RIVER CONGO. By JOACHIM MONTEIRO. With numerous Illustrations from Sketches taken on the spot, and a Map. Two Vols. crown 8vo. 21s.

"*Gives the first detailed account of a part of tropical Africa which is little known to Englishmen. . . . The remarks on the geography and zoology of the country and the manners and customs of the various races inhabiting it, are extremely curious and interesting.*"—SATURDAY REVIEW. "*Full of valuable information and much picturesque description.*" PALL MALL GAZETTE.

Morison.—THE LIFE AND TIMES OF SAINT BERNARD, Abbot of Clairvaux. By JAMES COTTER MORISON, M.A. New Edition. Crown 8vo. 6s.

The PALL MALL GAZETTE *calls this* "*A delightful and instructive volume, and one of the best products of the modern historic spirit.*"

Murray.—ROUND ABOUT FRANCE. By E. C. GRENVILLE MURRAY. Crown 8vo. 7s. 6d.

"*These short essays are a perfect mine of information as to the present condition and future prospects of political parties in France. . . . It is at once extremely interesting and exceptionally instructive on a subject on which few English people are well informed.*"—SCOTSMAN.

Napoleon.—THE HISTORY OF NAPOLEON I. By P. LANFREY. A Translation with the sanction of the Author. Vols. I. II. and III. 8vo. price 12s. each.

The PALL MALL GAZETTE *says it is* "*one of the most striking pieces of historical composition of which France has to boast,*" *and the* SATURDAY REVIEW *calls it* "*an excellent translation of a work on every ground deserving to be translated. It is unquestionably and immeasurably the best that has been produced. It is in fact the only work to which we can turn for an accurate and trustworthy narrative of that extraordinary career. . . . The book is the best and indeed the only trustworthy history of Napoleon which has been written.*"

Nash.—OREGON; There and Back in 1877. By WALLIS NASH. With Map and Illustrations. Crown 8vo. 7s. 6d.

"*This unpretentious little volume is a bright and very clever record of a journey which the author made to Oregon . . . which will tell any one who reads it a very great deal worth knowing about Oregon. . . . Altogether, he has written an interesting and amusing book.*"—SPECTATOR.

Nichol.—TABLES OF EUROPEAN LITERATURE AND HISTORY, A.D. 200—1876. By J. NICHOL, LL.D., Professor of English Language and Literature, Glasgow. 4to. 6s. 6d.

TABLES OF ANCIENT LITERATURE AND HISTORY, B.C. 1500—A.D. 200. By the same Author. 4to. 4s. 6d.

Oliphant (Mrs.).—THE MAKERS OF FLORENCE: Dante Giotto, Savonarola, and their City. By Mrs. OLIPHANT. With numerous Illustrations from drawings by Professor DELAMOTTE, and portrait of Savonarola, engraved by JEENS. Second Edition. Medium 8vo. Cloth extra. 21s.

"*Mrs. Oliphant has made a beautiful addition to the mass of literature already piled round the records of the Tuscan capital.*"—TIMES

"*We are grateful to Mrs. Oliphant for her eloquent and beautiful sketches of Dante, Fra Angelico, and Savonarola. They are picturesque, full of life, and rich in detail, and they are charmingly illustrated by the art of the engraver.*"—SPECTATOR.

Oliphant.—THE DUKE AND THE SCHOLAR; and other Essays. By T. L. KINGTON OLIPHANT. 8vo. 7s. 6d.

"*This volume contains one of the most beautiful biographical essays we have seen since Macaulay's days.*"—STANDARD.

Otte.—SCANDINAVIAN HISTORY. By E. C. OTTE. With Maps. Extra fcap. 8vo. 6s.

"*We have peculiar pleasure in recommending this intelligent résumé of Northern history as a book essential to every Englishman who interests himself in Scandinavia.*"—SPECTATOR.

Owens College Essays and Addresses.—By PROFESSORS AND LECTURERS OF OWENS COLLEGE, MANCHESTER. Published in Commemoration of the Opening of the New College Buildings, October 7th, 1873. 8vo. 14s.

Palgrave (R. F. D.)—THE HOUSE OF COMMONS; Illustrations of its History and Practice. By REGINALD F. D. PALGRAVE, Clerk Assistant of the House of Commons. New and Revised Edition. Crown 8vo. 2s. 6d.

Palgrave (Sir F.)—HISTORY OF NORMANDY AND OF ENGLAND. By Sir FRANCIS PALGRAVE, Deputy Keeper of Her Majesty's Public Records. Completing the History to the Death of William Rufus. Vols. I.—IV. 21s. each.

Palgrave (W. G.)—A NARRATIVE OF A YEAR'S JOURNEY THROUGH CENTRAL AND EASTERN ARABIA, 1862-3. By WILLIAM GIFFORD PALGRAVE, late of the Eighth Regiment Bombay N. I. Sixth Edition. With Maps, Plans, and Portrait of Author, engraved on steel by Jeens. Crown 8vo. 6s.

"*He has not only written one of the best books on the Arabs and one of the best books on Arabia, but he has done so in a manner that must command the respect no less than the admiration of his fellow-countrymen.*"—FORTNIGHTLY REVIEW.

ESSAYS ON EASTERN QUESTIONS. By W. GIFFORD PALGRAVE. 8vo. 10s. 6d.

"*These essays are full of anecdote and interest. The book is decidedly a valuable addition to the stock of literature on which men must base their opinion of the difficult social and political problems suggested by the designs of Russia, the capacity of Mahometans for sovereignty, and the good government and retention of India.*"—SATURDAY REVIEW.

DUTCH GUIANA. With Maps and Plans. 8vo. 9s.

"*His pages are nearly exhaustive as far as facts and statistics go, while they are lightened by graphic social sketches as well as sparkling descriptions of scenery.*"—SATURDAY REVIEW.

Patteson.—LIFE AND LETTERS OF JOHN COLERIDGE PATTESON, D.D., Missionary Bishop of the Melanesian Islands. By CHARLOTTE M. YONGE, Author of "The Heir of Redclyffe." With Portraits after RICHMOND and from Photograph, engraved by JEENS. With Map. Fifth Edition. Two Vols. Crown 8vo. 12s.

"*Miss Yonge's work is in one respect a model biography. It is made up almost entirely of Patteson's own letters. Aware that he had left his home once and for all, his correspondence took the form of a diary, and as we read on we come to know the man, and to love him almost as if we had seen him.*"—ATHENÆUM. "*Such a life, with its grand lessons of unselfishness, is a blessing and an honour to the age in which it is lived; the biography cannot be studied without pleasure and profit, and indeed we should think little of the man who did not rise from the study of it better and wiser. Neither the Church nor the nation which produces such sons need ever despair of its future.*"—SATURDAY REVIEW.

Pauli.—PICTURES OF OLD ENGLAND. By Dr. REINHOLD PAULI. Translated, with the approval of the Author, by E. C. OTTÉ. Cheaper Edition. Crown 8vo. 6s.

Payne.—A HISTORY OF EUROPEAN COLONIES. By E. J. PAYNE, M.A. With Maps. 18mo. 4s. 6d.

The TIMES *says:*—"*We have seldom met with a historian capable of forming a more comprehensive, far-seeing, and unprejudiced estimate of events and peoples, and we can commend this little work as one certain to prove of the highest interest to all thoughtful readers.*"

Persia.—EASTERN PERSIA. An Account of the Journeys of the Persian Boundary Commission, 1870-1-2.—Vol. I. The Geography, with Narratives by Majors ST. JOHN, LOVETT, and EUAN SMITH, and an Introduction by Major-General Sir FREDERIC GOLDSMID, C.B., K.C.S.I., British Commissioner and Arbitrator. With Maps and Illustrations.—Vol. II. The Zoology and Geology. By W. T. BLANFORD, A.R.S.M., F.R.S. With Coloured Illustrations. Two Vols. 8vo. 42s.

"*The volumes largely increase our store of information about countries with which Englishmen ought to be familiar. . . . They throw into the shade all that hitherto has appeared in our tongue respecting the local features of Persia, its scenery, its resources, even its social condition. They contain also abundant evidence of English endurance, daring, and spirit.*"—TIMES.

Prichard.—THE ADMINISTRATION OF INDIA. From 1859 to 1868. The First Ten Years of Administration under the Crown. By I. T. PRICHARD, Barrister-at-Law. Two Vols. Demy 8vo. With Map. 21s.

Raphael.—RAPHAEL OF URBINO AND HIS FATHER GIOVANNI SANTI. By J. D. PASSAVANT, formerly Director of the Museum at Frankfort. With Twenty Permanent Photographs. Royal 8vo. Handsomely bound. 31s. 6d.

The SATURDAY REVIEW *says of them,* "*We have seen not a few elegant specimens of Mr. Woodbury's new process, but we have seen none that equal these.*"

Reynolds.—SIR JOSHUA REYNOLDS AS A PORTRAIT PAINTER. AN ESSAY. By J. CHURTON COLLINS, B.A. Balliol College, Oxford. Illustrated by a Series of Portraits of distinguished Beauties of the Court of George III.; reproduced in Autotype from Proof Impressions of the celebrated Engravings, by VALENTINE GREEN, THOMAS WATSON, F. R. SMITH, E. FISHER, and others. Folio half-morocco. £5 5s.

Rogers (James E. Thorold).—HISTORICAL GLEANINGS: A Series of Sketches. Montague, Walpole, Adam Smith, Cobbett. By Prof. ROGERS. Crown 8vo. 4s. 6d. Second Series. Wiklif, Laud, Wilkes, and Horne Tooke. Crown 8vo. 6s.

24 MACMILLAN'S CATALOGUE OF WORKS IN

Routledge.—CHAPTERS IN THE HISTORY OF POPULAR PROGRESS IN ENGLAND, chiefly in Relation to the Freedom of the Press and Trial by Jury, 1660—1820. With application to later years. By J. ROUTLEDGE. 8vo. 16s.
"*The volume abounds in facts and information, almost always useful and often curious.*"—TIMES.

Rumford.—COUNT RUMFORD'S COMPLETE WORKS, with Memoir, and Notices of his Daughter. By GEORGE ELLIS. Five Vols. 8vo. 4l. 14s. 6d.

Seeley (Professor).—LECTURES AND ESSAYS. By J. R. SEELEY, M.A. Professor of Modern History in the University of Cambridge. 8vo. 10s. 6d.
CONTENTS:—*Roman Imperialism:* 1. The Great Roman Revolution; 2. The Proximate Cause of the Fall of the Roman Empire; The Later Empire.—*Milton's Political Opinions*—*Milton's Poetry*—*Elementary Principles in Art*—*Liberal Education in Universities*—*English in Schools*—*The Church as a Teacher of Morality*—*The Teaching of Politics: an Inaugural Lecture delivered at Cambridge.*

Shelburne.—LIFE OF WILLIAM, EARL OF SHELBURNE, AFTERWARDS FIRST MARQUIS OF LANSDOWNE. With Extracts from his Papers and Correspondence. By Lord EDMOND FITZMAURICE. In Three Vols. 8vo. Vol. I. 1737—1766, 12s.; Vol. II. 1766—1776, 12s.; Vol. III. 1776—1805. 16s.
"*Lord Edmond Fitzmaurice has succeeded in placing before us a wealth of new matter, which, while casting valuable and much-needed light on several obscure passages in the political history of a hundred years ago, has enabled us for the first time to form a clear and consistent idea of his ancestor.*"—SPECTATOR.

Sime.—HISTORY OF GERMANY. By JAMES SIME, M.A. 18mo. 3s. Being Vol. V. of the Historical Course for Schools, Edited by EDWARD A. FREEMAN, D.C.L.
"*This is a remarkably clear and impressive History of Germany. Its great events are wisely kept as central figures, and the smaller events are carefully kept not only subordinate and subservient, but most skilfully woven into the texture of the historical tapestry presented to the eye.*"—STANDARD.

Squier.—PERU: INCIDENTS OF TRAVEL AND EXPLORATION IN THE LAND OF THE INCAS. By E. G. SQUIER, M.A., F.S.A., late U.S. Commissioner to Peru. With 300 Illustrations. Second Edition. 8vo. 21s.
The TIMES *says:*—"*No more solid and trustworthy contribution had been made to an accurate knowledge of what are among the most wonderful ruins in the world. . . . The work is really what its title implies.*

HISTORY, BIOGRAPHY, TRAVELS, ETC. 25

While of the greatest importance as a contribution to Peruvian archæology, it is also a thoroughly entertaining and instructive narrative of travel. . . . . Not the least important feature must be considered the numerous well executed illustrations."

Strangford.—EGYPTIAN SHRINES AND SYRIAN SEPULCHRES, including a Visit to Palmyra. By EMILY A. BEAUFORT (Viscountess Strangford), Author of "The Eastern Shores of the Adriatic." New Edition. Crown 8vo. 7s. 6d.

Tait.—AN ANALYSIS OF ENGLISH HISTORY, based upon Green's "Short History of the English People." By C. W. A. TAIT, M.A., Assistant Master, Clifton College. Crown 8vo. 3s. 6d.

Thomas.—THE LIFE OF JOHN THOMAS, Surgeon of the "Earl of Oxford" East Indiaman, and First Baptist Missionary to Bengal. By C. B. LEWIS, Baptist Missionary. 8vo. 10s. 6d.

Thompson.—HISTORY OF ENGLAND. By EDITH THOMPSON. Being Vol. II. of the Historical Course for Schools, Edited by EDWARD A. FREEMAN, D.C.L. New Edition, revised and enlarged, with Maps. 18mo. 2s. 6d.

"Freedom from prejudice, simplicity of style, and accuracy of statement, are the characteristics of this volume. It is a trustworthy text-book, and likely to be generally serviceable in schools."—PALL MALL GAZETTE.
"In its great accuracy and correctness of detail it stands far ahead of the general run of school manuals. Its arrangement, too, is clear, and its style simple and straightforward."—SATURDAY REVIEW.

Todhunter.—THE CONFLICT OF STUDIES; AND OTHER ESSAYS ON SUBJECTS CONNECTED WITH EDUCATION. By ISAAC TODHUNTER, M.A., F.R.S., late Fellow and Principal Mathematical Lecturer of St. John's College, Cambridge. 8vo. 10s. 6d.

CONTENTS:—*I. The Conflict of Studies. II. Competitive Examinations. III. Private Study of Mathematics. IV. Academical Reform. V. Elementary Geometry. VI. The Mathematical Tripos.*

Trench (Archbishop).—For other Works by the same Author, see THEOLOGICAL and BELLES LETTRES CATALOGUES, and page 30 of this Catalogue.

GUSTAVUS ADOLPHUS IN GERMANY, and other Lectures on the Thirty Years' War. Second Edition, revised and enlarged. Fcap. 8vo. 4s.

PLUTARCH, HIS LIFE, HIS LIVES, AND HIS MORALS. Five Lectures. Second Edition, enlarged. Fcap. 8vo. 3s. 6d.

LECTURES ON MEDIEVAL CHURCH HISTORY. Being the substance of Lectures delivered in Queen's College, London. 8vo. 12s.

Trench (Maria).—THE LIFE OF ST. TERESA. By MARIA TRENCH. With Portrait engraved by JEENS. Crown 8vo. cloth extra. 8s. 6d.

"*A book of rare interest.*"—JOHN BULL.

Trench (Mrs. R.)—REMAINS OF THE LATE MRS. RICHARD TRENCH. Being Selections from her Journals, Letters, and other Papers. Edited by ARCHBISHOP TRENCH. New and Cheaper Issue, with Portrait. 8vo. 6s.

Trollope.—A HISTORY OF THE COMMONWEALTH OF FLORENCE FROM THE EARLIEST INDEPENDENCE OF THE COMMUNE TO THE FALL OF THE REPUBLIC IN 1831. By T. ADOLPHUS TROLLOPE. 4 Vols. 8vo. Half morocco. 21s.

Uppingham by the Sea.—A NARRATIVE OF THE YEAR AT BORTH. By J. H. S. Crown 8vo. 3s. 6d.

Wallace.—THE MALAY ARCHIPELAGO: the Land of the Orang Utan and the Bird of Paradise. By ALFRED RUSSEL WALLACE. A Narrative of Travel with Studies of Man and Nature. With Maps and numerous Illustrations. Fifth Edition. Crown 8vo. 7s. 6d.

"*The result is a vivid picture of tropical life, which may be read with unflagging interest, and a sufficient account of his scientific conclusions to stimulate our appetite without wearying us by detail. In short, we may safely say that we have never read a more agreeable book of its kind.*"—SATURDAY REVIEW.

Ward.—A HISTORY OF ENGLISH DRAMATIC LITERATURE TO THE DEATH OF QUEEN ANNE. By A. W. WARD, M.A., Professor of History and English Literature in Owens College, Manchester. Two Vols. 8vo. 32s.

"*As full of interest as of information. To students of aramatic literature invaluable, and may be equally recommended to readers for mere pastime.*"—PALL MALL GAZETTE.

Ward (J.)—EXPERIENCES OF A DIPLOMATIST. Being recollections of Germany founded on Diaries kept during the years 1840—1870. By JOHN WARD, C.B., late H.M. Minister-Resident to the Hanse Towns. 8vo. 10s. 6d.

Wedgwood.—JOHN WESLEY AND THE EVANGELICAL REACTION of the Eighteenth Century. By JULIA WEDGWOOD. Crown 8vo. 8s. 6d.

"*In style and intellectual power, in breadth of view and clearness of insight, Miss Wedgwood's book far surpasses all rivals.*"—ATHENÆUM.

Whewell.—WILLIAM WHEWELL, D.D., late Master of Trinity College, Cambridge. An Account of his Writings, with Selections from his Literary and Scientific Correspondence. By I. TODHUNTER, M.A., F.R.S. Two Vols. 8vo. 25s.

White.—THE NATURAL HISTORY AND ANTIQUITIES OF SELBORNE. By GILBERT WHITE. Edited, with Memoir and Notes, by FRANK BUCKLAND, A Chapter on Antiquities by LORD SELBORNE, Map, &c., and numerous Illustrations by P. H. DELAMOTTE. Royal 8vo. Cloth, extra gilt. Cheaper Issue. 21s.

Also a Large Paper Edition, containing, in addition to the above, upwards of Thirty Woodburytype Illustrations from Drawings by Prof. DELAMOTTE. Two Vols. 4to. Half morocco, elegant. 4l. 4s.

"*Mr. Delamotte's charming illustrations are a worthy decoration of so dainty a book. They bring Selborne before us, and really help us to understand why White's love for his native place never grew cold.*"—TIMES.

Wilson.—A MEMOIR OF GEORGE WILSON, M.D., F.R.S.E., Regius Professor of Technology in the University of Edinburgh. By his SISTER. New Edition. Crown 8vo. 6s.

"*An exquisite and touching portrait of a rare and beautiful spirit.*"—GUARDIAN.

Wilson (Daniel, LL.D.)—Works by DANIEL WILSON, LL.D., Professor of History and English Literature in University College, Toronto :—

PREHISTORIC ANNALS OF SCOTLAND. New Edition, with numerous Illustrations. Two Vols. demy 8vo. 36s.

"*One of the most interesting, learned, and elegant works we have seen for a long time.*"—WESTMINSTER REVIEW.

PREHISTORIC MAN : Researches into the Origin of Civilization in the Old and New World. New Edition, revised and enlarged throughout, with numerous Illustrations and two Coloured Plates. Two Vols. 8vo. 36s.

"*A valuable work pleasantly written and well worthy of attention both by students and general readers.*"—ACADEMY.

CHATTERTON : A Biographical Study. By DANIEL WILSON, LL.D., Professor of History and English Literature in University College, Toronto. Crown 8vo. 6s. 6d.

Wyatt (Sir M. Digby).—FINE ART : a Sketch of its History, Theory, Practice, and application to Industry. A Course of Lectures delivered before the University of Cambridge. By Sir M. DIGBY WYATT, M.A. Slade Professor of Fine Art. Cheaper Issue. 8vo. 5s.

"*An excellent handbook for the student of art.*"—GRAPHIC. "*The book abounds in valuable matter, and will therefore be read with pleasure and profit by lovers of art.*"—DAILY NEWS.

Yonge (Charlotte M.)—Works by CHARLOTTE M. YONGE, Author of "The Heir of Redclyffe," &c. &c. :—

A PARALLEL HISTORY OF FRANCE AND ENGLAND: consisting of Outlines and Dates. Oblong 4to. 3s. 6d.

CAMEOS FROM ENGLISH HISTORY. From Rollo to Edward II. Extra fcap. 8vo. Third Edition. 5s.

A SECOND SERIES, THE WARS IN FRANCE. Extra fcap. 8vo. Third Edition. 5s.

A THIRD SERIES, THE WARS OF THE ROSES. Extra fcap. 8vo. 5s.

"*Instead of dry details,*" says the NONCONFORMIST, "*we have living pictures, faithful, vivid, and striking.*"

Young (Julian Charles, M.A.)—A MEMOIR OF CHARLES MAYNE YOUNG, Tragedian, with Extracts from his Son's Journal. By JULIAN CHARLES YOUNG, M.A. Rector of Ilmington. With Portraits and Sketches. New and Cheaper Edition, Crown 8vo. 7s. 6d.

"*In this budget of anecdotes, fables, and gossip, old and new, relative to Scott, Moore, Chalmers, Coleridge, Wordsworth, Croker, Mathews, the third and fourth Georges, Bowles, Beckford, Lockhart, Wellington, Peel, Louis Napoleon, D'Orsay, Dickens, Thackeray, Louis Blanc, Gibson, Constable, and Stanfield, etc. etc., the reader must be hard indeed to please who cannot find entertainment.*"—PALL MALL GAZETTE.

POLITICS, POLITICAL AND SOCIAL ECONOMY, LAW, AND KINDRED SUBJECTS.

Anglo Saxon Law.—ESSAYS IN. Contents: Law Courts—Land and Family Laws and Legal Procedure generally. With Select cases. Medium 8vo. 18s.

Ball.—THE STUDENT'S GUIDE TO THE BAR. By WALTER W. BALL, M.A., of the Inner Temple, Barrister-at-Law. Crown 8vo. 2s. 6d.

"*The student will here find a clear statement of the several steps by which the degree of barrister is obtained, and also useful advice about the advantages of a prolonged course of 'reading in Chambers.'*"—ACADEMY.

Bernard.—FOUR LECTURES ON SUBJECTS CONNECTED WITH DIPLOMACY. By MONTAGUE BERNARD, M.A., Chichele Professor of International Law and Diplomacy, Oxford. 8vo. 9s.

"*Singularly interesting lectures, so able, clear, and attractive.*"—SPECTATOR.

Bright (John, M.P.)—SPEECHES ON QUESTIONS OF PUBLIC POLICY. By the Right Hon. JOHN BRIGHT, M.P. Edited by Professor THOROLD ROGERS. Author's Popular Edition. Globe 8vo. 3s. 6d.

"*Mr. Bright's speeches will always deserve to be studied, as an apprenticeship to popular and parliamentary oratory; they will form materials for the history of our time, and many brilliant passages, perhaps some entire speeches, will really become a part of the living literature of England.*"—DAILY NEWS.

LIBRARY EDITION. Two Vols. 8vo. With Portrait. 25s.

Bucknill.—HABITUAL DRUNKENNESS AND INSANE DRUNKARDS. By J. C. BUCKNILL, M.D., F.R.S., late Lord Chancellor's Visitor of Lunatics. Crown 8vo. 2s. 6d.

Cairnes.—Works by J. E. CAIRNES, M.A., Emeritus Professor of Political Economy in University College, London.

ESSAYS IN POLITICAL ECONOMY, THEORETICAL and APPLIED. By J. E. CAIRNES, M.A., Professor of Political Economy in University College, London. 8vo. 10s. 6d.

"*The production of one of the ablest of living economists.*"—ATHENÆUM.

Cairnes.—*continued.*
POLITICAL ESSAYS. 8vo. 10s. 6d.
 The SATURDAY REVIEW *says:*—"*We recently expressed our high admiration of the former volume; and the present one is no less remarkable for the qualities of clear statement, sound logic, and candid treatment of opponents which were conspicuous in its predecessor. . . . We may safely say that none of Mr. Mill's many disciples is a worthier representative of the best qualities of their master than Professor Cairnes.*"

SOME LEADING PRINCIPLES OF POLITICAL ECONOMY NEWLY EXPOUNDED. 8vo. 14s.
 CONTENTS:—*Part I. Value. Part II. Labour and Capital. Part III. International Trade.*
 "*A work which is perhaps the most valuable contribution to the science made since the publication, a quarter of a century since, of Mr. Mill's 'Principles of Political Economy.'*"—DAILY NEWS.

THE CHARACTER AND LOGICAL METHOD OF POLITICAL ECONOMY. New Edition, enlarged. 8vo. 7s. 6d.
 "*These lectures are admirably fitted to correct the slipshod generalizations which pass current as the science of Political Economy.*"—TIMES.

Clarke.—EARLY ROMAN LAW. THE REGAL PERIOD. By E. C. CLARKE, M.A., of Lincoln's Inn, Barrister-at-Law, Lecturer in Law and Regius Professor of Civil Law at Cambridge. Crown 8vo. 5s.
 "*Mr. Clarke has brought together a great mass of valuable matter in an accessible form.*"—SATURDAY REVIEW.

Cobden (Richard).—SPEECHES ON QUESTIONS OF PUBLIC POLICY. By RICHARD COBDEN. Edited by the Right Hon. John Bright, M.P., and J. E. Thorold Rogers. Popular Edition. 8vo. 3s. 6d.

Fawcett.—Works by HENRY FAWCETT, M.A., M.P., Fellow of Trinity Hall, and Professor of Political Economy in the University of Cambridge:—
THE ECONOMIC POSITION OF THE BRITISH LABOURER. Extra fcap. 8vo. 5s.
MANUAL OF POLITICAL ECONOMY. Fifth Edition, with New Chapters on the Depreciation of Silver, etc. Crown 8vo. 12s.
 The DAILY NEWS *says:* "*It forms one of the best introductions to the principles of the science, and to its practical applications in the problems of modern, and especially of English, government and society.*"
PAUPERISM: ITS CAUSES AND REMEDIES. Crown 8vo. 5s. 6d.
 The ATHENÆUM *calls the work* "*a repertory of interesting and well digested information.*"

Fawcett.—*continued.*

SPEECHES ON SOME CURRENT POLITICAL QUESTIONS. 8vo. 10s. 6d.

"*They will help to educate, not perhaps, parties, but the educators of parties.*"—DAILY NEWS.

ESSAYS ON POLITICAL AND SOCIAL SUBJECTS. By PROFESSOR FAWCETT, M.P., and MILLICENT GARRETT FAWCETT. 8vo. 10s. 6d.

"*They will all repay the perusal of the thinking reader.*"—DAILY NEWS.

FREE TRADE AND PROTECTION: an Inquiry into the Causes which have retarded the general adoption of Free Trade since its introduction into England. 8vo. 7s. 6d.

"*No greater service can be rendered to the cause of Free Trade than a clear explanation of the principles on which Free Trade rests. Professor Fawcett has done this in the volume before us with all his habitual clearness of thought and expression.*"—ECONOMIST.

Fawcett (Mrs.)—Works by MILLICENT GARRETT FAWCETT.

POLITICAL ECONOMY FOR BEGINNERS. WITH QUESTIONS. New Edition. 18mo. 2s. 6d.

The DAILY NEWS *calls it* "*clear, compact, and comprehensive;*" *and the* SPECTATOR *says,* "*Mrs. Fawcett's treatise is perfectly suited to its purpose.*"

TALES IN POLITICAL ECONOMY. Crown 8vo. 3s.

"*The idea is a good one, and it is quite wonderful what a mass of economic teaching the author manages to compress into a small space...The true doctrines of International Trade, Currency, and the ratio between Production and Population, are set before us and illustrated in a masterly manner.*"—ATHENÆUM.

Freeman (E. A.), M.A., D.C.L.—COMPARATIVE POLITICS. Lectures at the Royal Institution, to which is added "The Unity of History," being the Rede Lecture delivered at Cambridge in 1872. 8vo. 14s.

"*We find in Mr. Freeman's new volume the same sound, careful, comprehensive qualities which have long ago raised him to so high a place amongst historical writers. For historical discipline, then, as well as historical information, Mr. Freeman's book is full of value.*"—PALL MALL GAZETTE.

Goschen.—REPORTS AND SPEECHES ON LOCAL TAXATION. By GEORGE J. GOSCHEN, M.P. Royal 8vo. 5s.

"*The volume contains a vast mass of information of the highest value.*"—ATHENÆUM.

Guide to the Unprotected, in Every Day Matters Relating to Property and Income. By a BANKER'S DAUGHTER. Fourth Edition, Revised. Extra fcap. 8vo. 3s. 6d.

"*Many an unprotected female will bless the head which planned and the hand which compiled this admirable little manual. . . . This book was very much wanted, and it could not have been better done.*"—MORNING STAR.

Hamilton.—MONEY AND VALUE: an Inquiry into the Means and Ends of Economic Production, with an Appendix on the Depreciation of Silver and Indian Currency. By ROWLAND HAMILTON. 8vo. 12s.

"*The subject is here dealt with in a luminous style, and by presenting it from a new point of view in connection with the nature and functions of money, a genuine service has been rendered to commercial science.*"—BRITISH QUARTERLY REVIEW.

Harwood.—DISESTABLISHMENT: a Defence of the Principle of a National Church. By GEORGE HARWOOD, M.A. 8vo. 12s.

Hill.—Works by OCTAVIA HILL :—

HOMES OF THE LONDON POOR. Extra fcap. 8vo. 3s. 6d.
"*She is clear, practical, and definite.*"—GLOBE.

OUR COMMON LAND; and other Short Essays. Extra fcap. 8vo. 3s. 6d.

CONTENTS:—*Our Common Land. District Visiting. A More Excellent Way of Charity. A Word on Good Citizenship. Open Spaces. Effectual Charity. The Future of our Commons.*

Historicus.—LETTERS ON SOME QUESTIONS OF INTERNATIONAL LAW. Reprinted from the *Times*, with considerable Additions. 8vo. 7s. 6d. Also, ADDITIONAL LETTERS. 8vo. 2s. 6d.

Holland.—THE TREATY RELATIONS OF RUSSIA AND TURKEY FROM 1774 TO 1853. A Lecture delivered at Oxford, April 1877. By T. E. HOLLAND, D.C.L., Professor of International Law and Diplomacy, Oxford. Crown 8vo. 2s.

Hughes (Thos.)—THE OLD CHURCH: WHAT SHALL WE DO WITH IT? By THOMAS HUGHES, Q.C. Crown 8vo. 6s.

Jevons.—Works by W. STANLEY JEVONS, M.A., Professor of Political Economy in University College, London. (For other Works by the same Author, *see* EDUCATIONAL and PHILOSOPHICAL CATALOGUES.)

Jevons.—*continued.*

THE COAL QUESTION: An Inquiry Concerning the Progress of the Nation, and the Probable Exhaustion of our Coal Mines. Second Edition, revised. 8vo. 10s. 6d.

THE THEORY OF POLITICAL ECONOMY. 8vo. 9s.

"*Professor Jevons has done invaluable service by courageously claiming political economy to be strictly a branch of Applied Mathematics.*"—WESTMINSTER REVIEW.

PRIMER OF POLITICAL ECONOMY. 18mo. 1s.

Laveleye.— PRIMITIVE PROPERTY. By EMILE DE LAVELEYE. Translated by G. R. L. MARRIOTT, LL.B., with an Introduction by T. E. CLIFFE LESLIE, LL.B. 8vo. 12s.

"*It is almost impossible to over-estimate the value of the well-digested knowledge which it contains; it is one of the most learned books that have been contributed to the historical department of the literature of economic science.*"—ATHENÆUM.

Leading Cases done into English. By an APPRENTICE OF LINCOLN'S INN. Third Edition. Crown 8vo. 2s. 6d.

"*Here is a rare treat for the lovers of quaint conceits, who in reading this charming little book will find enjoyment in the varied metre and graphic language in which the several tales are told, no less than in the accurate and pithy rendering of some of our most familiar 'Leading Cases.'*"—SATURDAY REVIEW.

Macdonell.—THE LAND QUESTION, WITH SPECIAL REFERENCE TO ENGLAND AND SCOTLAND. By JOHN MACDONELL, Barrister-at-Law. 8vo. 10s. 6d.

Martin.—THE STATESMAN'S YEAR-BOOK: A Statistical and Historical Annual of the States of the Civilized World, for the year 1878. By FREDERICK MARTIN. Fifteenth Annual Publication. Revised after Official Returns. Crown 8vo. 10s. 6d.

The Statesman's Year-Book is the only work in the English language which furnishes a clear and concise account of the actual condition of all the States of Europe, the civilized countries of America, Asia, and Africa, and the British Colonies and Dependencies in all parts of the world. The new issue of the work has been revised and corrected, on the basis of official reports received direct from the heads of the leading Governments of the world, in reply to letters sent to them by the Editor. Through the valuable assistance thus given, it has been possible to collect an amount of information, political, statistical, and commercial, of the latest date, and of unimpeachable trustworthiness, such as no publication of the same kind has ever been able to furnish. "*As indispensable as Bradshaw.*"—TIMES.

Monahan.—THE METHOD OF LAW: an Essay on the Statement and Arrangement of the Legal Standard of Conduct. By J. H. MONAHAN, Q.C. Crown 8vo. 6s.

"*Will be found valuable by careful law students who have felt the importance of gaining clear ideas regarding the relations between the parts of the complex organism they have to study.*"—BRITISH QUARTERLY REVIEW.

Paterson.—THE LIBERTY OF THE SUBJECT AND THE LAWS OF ENGLAND RELATING TO THE SECURITY OF THE PERSON. Commentaries on. By JAMES PATERSON, M.A., Barrister at Law, sometime Commissioner for English and Irish Fisheries, etc. Two Vols Crown 8vo. 21s.

"*Two or three hours' dipping into these volumes, not to say reading them through, will give legislators and stump orators a knowledge of the liberty of a citizen of their country, in its principles, its fulness, and its modification, such as they probably in nine cases out of ten never had before.*"—SCOTSMAN.

Phillimore.—PRIVATE LAW AMONG THE ROMANS, from the Pandects. By JOHN GEORGE PHILLIMORE, Q.C. 8vo. 16s.

Rogers.—COBDEN AND POLITICAL OPINION. By J. E. THOROLD ROGERS. 8vo. 10s. 6d.

"*Will be found most useful by politicians of every school, as it forms a sort of handbook to Cobden's teaching.*"—ATHENÆUM.

Stephen (C. E.)—THE SERVICE OF THE POOR; Being an Inquiry into the Reasons for and against the Establishment of Religious Sisterhoods for Charitable Purposes. By CAROLINE EMILIA STEPHEN. Crown 8vo. 6s. 6d.

"*The ablest advocate of a better line of work in this direction that we have ever seen.*"—EXAMINER.

Stephen.—Works by Sir JAMES F. STEPHEN, K.C.S.I., Q.C.
A DIGEST OF THE LAW OF EVIDENCE. Third Edition with New Preface. Crown 8vo. 6s.
A DIGEST OF THE CRIMINAL LAW. (Crimes and Punishments.) 8vo. 16s.

"*We feel sure that any person of ordinary intelligence who had never looked into a law-book in his life might, by a few days' careful study of this volume, obtain a more accurate understanding of the criminal law, a more perfect conception of its different bearings a more thorough and intelligent insight into its snares and pitfalls, than an ordinary practitioner can boast of after years of study of the ordinary text-books and practical experience of the Courts unassisted by any competent guide.*"—SATURDAY REVIEW.

Stubbs.—VILLAGE POLITICS. Addresses and Sermons on the Labour Question. By C. W. STUBBS, M.A., Vicar of Granborough, Bucks. Extra fcap. 8vo. 3s. 6d.

Thornton.—Works by W. T. THORNTON, C.B., Secretary for Public Works in the India Office :—

ON LABOUR : Its Wrongful Claims and Rightful Dues ; Its Actual Present and Possible Future. Second Edition, revised, 8vo. 14s.

A PLEA FOR PEASANT PROPRIETORS : With the Outlines of a Plan for their Establishment in Ireland. New Edition, revised. Crown 8vo. 7s. 6d.

INDIAN PUBLIC WORKS AND COGNATE INDIAN TOPICS. With Map of Indian Railways. Crown 8vo. 8s. 6d.

Walker.—Works by F. A. WALKER, M.A., Ph.D., Professor of Political Economy and History, Yale College :—

THE WAGES QUESTION. A Treatise on Wages and the Wages Class. 8vo. 14s.

MONEY. 8vo. 16s.

"*It is painstaking, laborious, and states the question in a clear and very intelligible form. . . . The volume possesses a great value as a sort of encyclopædia of knowledge on the subject.*"—ECONOMIST.

Work about the Five Dials. With an Introductory Note by THOMAS CARLYLE. Crown 8vo. 6s.

"*A book which abounds with wise and practical suggestions.*"—PALL MALL GAZETTE.

WORKS CONNECTED WITH THE SCIENCE OR THE HISTORY OF LANGUAGE.

Abbott.—A SHAKESPERIAN GRAMMAR : An Attempt to illustrate some of the Differences between Elizabethan and Modern English. By the Rev. E. A. ABBOTT, D.D., Head Master of the City of London School. New and Enlarged Edition. Extra fcap. 8vo. 6s.

"*Valuable not only as an aid to the critical study of Shakespeare, but as tending to familiarize the reader with Elizabethan English in general.*"—ATHENÆUM.

Besant.—STUDIES IN EARLY FRENCH POETRY. WALTER BESANT, M.A. Crown 8vo. 8s. 6d.

Breymann.—A FRENCH GRAMMAR BASED ON PHILOLOGICAL PRINCIPLES. By HERMANN BREYMANN, Ph.D., Professor of Philology in the University of Munich, late Lecturer on French Language and Literature at Owens College, Manchester. Extra fcap. 8vo. 4s. 6d.

"*We dismiss the work with every feeling of satisfaction. It cannot fail to be taken into use by all schools which endeavour to make the study of French a means towards the higher culture.*"—EDUCATIONAL TIMES.

Ellis.—PRACTICAL HINTS ON THE QUANTITATIVE PRONUNCIATION OF LATIN, FOR THE USE OF CLASSICAL TEACHERS AND LINGUISTS. By A. J. ELLIS, B.A., F.R.S., &c. Extra fcap. 8vo. 4s. 6d.

Fleay.—A SHAKESPEARE MANUAL. By the Rev. F. G. FLEAY, M.A., Head Master of Skipton Grammar School. Extra fcap. 8vo. 4s. 6d.

Goodwin.—SYNTAX OF THE GREEK MOODS AND TENSES. By W. W. GOODWIN, Professor of Greek Literature in Harvard University. New Edition. Crown 8vo. 6s. 6d.

Hadley.—ESSAYS PHILOLOGICAL AND CRITICAL. Selected from the Papers of JAMES HADLEY, LL.D., Professor of Greek in Yale College, &c. 8vo. 16s.

Hales.—LONGER ENGLISH POEMS. With Notes, Philological and Explanatory, and an Introduction on the Teaching of English. Chiefly for use in Schools. Edited by J. W. HALES, M.A., Professor of English Literature at King's College, London, &c. &c. Fifth Edition. Extra fcap. 8vo. 4s. 6d.

Helfenstein (James).—A COMPARATIVE GRAMMAR OF THE TEUTONIC LANGUAGES: Being at the same time a Historical Grammar of the English Language, and comprising Gothic, Anglo-Saxon, Early English, Modern English, Icelandic (Old Norse), Danish, Swedish, Old High German, Middle High German, Modern German, Old Saxon, Old Frisian, and Dutch. By JAMES HELFENSTEIN, Ph.D. 8vo. 18s.

Masson (Gustave).—A COMPENDIOUS DICTIONARY OF THE FRENCH LANGUAGE (French-English and English-French). Followed by a List of the Principal Diverging Derivations, and preceded by Chronological and Historical Tables. By GUSTAVE MASSON, Assistant-Master and Librarian, Harrow School. Fourth Edition. Crown 8vo. Half-bound. 6s.

"*A book which any student, whatever may be the degree of his advancement in the language, would do well to have on the table close at hand while he is reading.*"—SATURDAY REVIEW.

Mayor.—A BIBLIOGRAPHICAL CLUE TO LATIN LITE-RATURE. Edited after Dr. E. HUBNER. With large Additions by JOHN E. B. MAYOR, M.A., Professor of Latin in the University of Cambridge. Crown 8vo. 6s. 6d.

"*An extremely useful volume that should be in the hands of all scholars.*—ATHENÆUM.

Morris.—Works by the Rev. RICHARD MORRIS, LL.D., Member of the Council of the Philol. Soc., Lecturer on English Language and Literature in King's College School, Editor of "Specimens of Early English," etc., etc. :—

HISTORICAL OUTLINES OF ENGLISH ACCIDENCE, comprising Chapters on the History and Development of the Language, and on Word-formation. Sixth Edition. Fcap. 8vo. 6s.

ELEMENTARY LESSONS IN HISTORICAL ENGLISH GRAMMAR, containing Accidence and Word-formation. Third Edition. 18mo. 2s. 6d.

Oliphant.—THE OLD AND MIDDLE ENGLISH. By T. L. KINGTON OLIPHANT, M.A., of Balliol College, Oxford. A New Edition, revised and greatly enlarged, of "The Sources of Standard English. Extra fcap. 8vo. 9s.

"*Mr. Oliphant's book is, to our mind, one of the ablest and most scholarly contributions to our standard English we have seen for many years.*"—SCHOOL BOARD CHRONICLE. "*The book comes nearer to a history of the English language than anything we have seen since such a history could be written, without confusion and contradictions.*"—SATURDAY REVIEW.

Peile (John, M.A.)—AN INTRODUCTION TO GREEK AND LATIN ETYMOLOGY. By JOHN PEILE, M.A., Fellow and Tutor of Christ's College, Cambridge. Third and revised Edition. Crown 8vo. 10s. 6d.

"*The book may be accepted as a very valuable contribution to the science of language.*"—SATURDAY REVIEW.

Philology.—THE JOURNAL OF SACRED AND CLASSICAL PHILOLOGY. Four Vols. 8vo. 12s. 6d. each.

THE JOURNAL OF PHILOLOGY. New Series. Edited by W. G. CLARK, M.A., JOHN E. B. MAYOR, M.A., and W. ALDIS WRIGHT, M.A. 4s. 6d. (Half-yearly.)

Roby (H. J.)—A GRAMMAR OF THE LATIN LANGUAGE, FROM PLAUTUS TO SUETONIUS. By HENRY JOHN ROBY, M.A., late Fellow of St. John's College, Cambridge. In Two Parts. Second Edition. Part I. containing :—Book I. Sounds. Book II. Inflexions. Book III. Word Formation. Appendices. Crown 8vo. 8s. 6d. Part II.—Syntax, Prepositions, &c. Crown 8vo. 10s. 6d.

"The book is marked by the clear and practical insight of a master in his art. It is a book which would do honour to any country."—ATHENÆUM. *"Brings before the student in a methodical form the best results of modern philology bearing on the Latin language."*—SCOTSMAN.

Taylor.—Works by the Rev. ISAAC TAYLOR, M.A.:—

ETRUSCAN RESEARCHES. With Woodcuts. 8vo. 14s.

The TIMES *says:*—" *The learning and industry displayed in this volume deserve the most cordial recognition. The ultimate verdict of science we shall not attempt to anticipate; but we can safely say this, that it is a learned book which the unlearned can enjoy, and that in the descriptions of the tomb-builders, as well as in the marvellous coincidences and unexpected analogies brought together by the author, readers of every grade may take delight as well as philosophers and scholars.*"

WORDS AND PLACES; or, Etymological Illustrations of History, Ethnology, and Geography. By the Rev. ISAAC TAYLOR. Third Edition, revised and compressed. With Maps. Globe 8vo. 6s.

Trench.—Works by R. CHENEVIX TRENCH, D.D., Archbishop of Dublin. (For other Works by the same Author, *see* THEOLOGICAL CATALOGUE.)

SYNONYMS OF THE NEW TESTAMENT. Eighth Edition, enlarged. 8vo. cloth. 12s.

"He is," the ATHENÆUM *says, "a guide in this department of knowledge to whom his readers may entrust themselves with confidence."*

ON THE STUDY OF WORDS. Lectures Addressed (originally) to the Pupils at the Diocesan Training School, Winchester. Seventeenth Edition, enlarged. Fcap. 8vo. 5s.

ENGLISH PAST AND PRESENT. Tenth Edition, revised and improved. Fcap. 8vo. 5s.

A SELECT GLOSSARY OF ENGLISH WORDS USED FORMERLY IN SENSES DIFFERENT FROM THEIR PRESENT. Fourth Edition, enlarged. Fcap. 8vo. 4s.

Whitney.—A COMPENDIOUS GERMAN GRAMMAR. By W. D. WHITNEY, Professor of Sanskrit and Instructor in Modern Languages in Yale College. Crown 8vo. 6s.

"*After careful examination we are inclined to pronounce it the best grammar of modern language we have ever seen.*"—SCOTSMAN.

Whitney and Edgren.—A COMPENDIOUS GERMAN AND ENGLISH DICTIONARY, with Notation of Correspondences and Brief Etymologies. By Professor W. D. WHITNEY, assisted by A. H. EDGREN. Crown 8vo. 7s. 6d.

The GERMAN-ENGLISH Part may be had separately. Price 5s.

Yonge.—HISTORY OF CHRISTIAN NAMES. By CHARLOTTE M. YONGE, Author of "The Heir of Redclyffe." Cheaper Edition. Two Vols. Crown 8vo. 12s.

www.ingramcontent.com/pod-product-compliance
Lightning Source LLC
Chambersburg PA
CBHW030541300426
44111CB00009B/822